A Literary Guide
TO THE
EASTERN CAPE

A Literary Guide
TO THE
EASTERN CAPE

Places
and the Voices of Writers

Jeanette Eve

with drawings
and photographs by Basil Mills

DOUBLE
STOREY
a juta company

For my husband, Desmond
our children, Robin, Beatrice and Catherine
and our grandchildren, Malcolm, Andrew, Maryanne and Sarah

First published 2003 by Double Storey Books,
a Juta company, Mercury Crescent, Wetton,
Cape Town

copyright: 2003 Jeanette Eve (text); Basil Mills (drawings & photos)

ISBN 1-919930-15-9

Editing by Helen Laurenson
Design and page layout by Sarah-Anne Raynham
Cover design by Toby Newsome
Map by Sue Abraham
Repro by Virtual Colour, Cape Town
Printing and binding by ABC Press, Epping, Cape Town

Contents

Author's preface

A large team has assisted in the making of this book. I am indebted to members of the Council of the National English Literary Museum for adopting my proposals as an 'approved project' of the Museum, and for support through more than ten years. I am especially grateful to Professors Laurence Wright, Paul Walters and Malvern van Wyk Smith for constant interest, and to the late Professor Guy Butler, mentor, friend and champion encourager. The Director, Malcolm Hacksley, has never wavered in sanctioning access to NELM's treasury of material, and sponsoring travel, photography and other expenses. The faith and interest in the project shown by Deputy Director, Jeremy Fogg, has spurred me on. Secretary Chante Norton has cheerfully provided help. The library staff, under Debbie Landman, has been unstinting in its assistance with database searches and queries. I thank Lynne Grant for help with the bibliography and Crystal Warren for all she has done; Ann Torlesse for helping with archive material, especially author photographs; and Jenny Mosdell for providing access to the clippings collection, which passed into her care after I retired from NELM. Every other member of the staff has helped in one way or another and I thank them all. The untimely death last year of Elaine Pearson, NELM's head of research, deprived me of a friend to whom I am deeply grateful for advice and the meticulous editing of drafts.

Basil Mills, NELM's chief technical officer, has been a marvellous, entertaining and informative travel companion on expeditions to explore the Eastern Cape and collect photographs, many of which he has converted into imaginative drawings.

Russell Martin, publishing director of Double Storey Books, has guided an inexperienced first author along many a difficult path, and I value every contact I have had with him. A special relationship has flourished (via e-mail) with Helen Laurenson, who edited the final text in an efficient and friendly way. Sarah-Anne Raynham's design and careful working with the text has been a delight. Thank you, Sue Abraham of the Rhodes Graphics Services Unit, for special help in producing the map of the Eastern Cape without which we might all have gone astray.

I thank all authors or members of their families, as well as people in many parts of the province, who provided information; relations and friends, including the Cathedral community in Grahamstown, for understanding and support; Denise and Geoffrey Louw for being alongside for many years; and Beth Dickerson for friendship and invaluable practical help. Lastly I thank my children, Robin, Beatrice and Catherine, and especially my husband, Desmond, without whose loving encouragement the book would never have been completed.

THE NATIONAL ENGLISH LITERARY MUSEUM (NELM)

The National English Literary Museum is a repository for materials illustrating the development of English literature in South Africa. The Museum's collections of books, journals and newspapers; manuscripts and the personal papers and memorabilia of authors; publishers' records; photographs; press cuttings; sound and video recordings; and historic printing equipment constitute a unique cultural and archival resource assembled and maintained for the benefit of the people of South Africa. Visitors, visiting researchers, and written or telephonic queries are welcome.

The Museum is currently housed in the historic Priest's House at 87 Beaufort Street, Grahamstown. Two satellite galleries opened in 1987: the *Eastern Star* Press Museum in Grahamstown, and the Olive Schreiner House in Cradock. The Museum publishes a biannual newsletter, *NELM News*, to which free subscription is available on request.

All enquiries should be addressed to:
The Director
National English Literary Museum
Private Bag 1019
GRAHAMSTOWN
6140

Tel: 046 622 7042
Fax: 046 622 2582
E-mail: m.hacksley@ru.ac.za

An invitation

*T*his is a book of journeys – journeys that focus on the literature of place. All travelling is within the borders of the Eastern Cape – one of the nine provinces of South Africa – and, at the same time, it is within the realm of literature – literature that encompasses the personal or imaginative responses of writers to the myriad little worlds contained within this extensive province. You are invited to join this tour, literally or imaginatively.

The journeys begin in the south-west corner of the Eastern Cape, where the Bloukrans River forms the border with the Western Cape. They continue north-eastwards towards the Mtamvuna River, which forms the border with KwaZulu-Natal. Some routes follow parts of the Eastern Cape's long coastline; others climb through mountain ranges or cross open plains; some meander among hills or through nature reserves; others explore urban areas. Places are seen as they are today or as they may have been in the past: as they are in reality or as literary interpretations. The emphasis is on the response of writers to the outer world, but their interactions with place may also involve explorations of the political, the philosophic, the spiritual and the artistic, as well as the personal.

Many writers will be encountered along the way, some will be met in passing, others may become friends. Each journey focuses on literature associated with a specific part of the country, and a selection of poems and quotations from short stories, novels, travel writing, autobiographies, myths and legends has been chosen to reflect some of the varied landscapes and townscapes of the Eastern Cape. A map assists in getting from place to place and drawings complement the written word with visual images, while author portraits accompany information about writers.

If it is not possible to undertake every journey or to follow them in the book's given sequence, choose a region or a writer; then set out from an armchair or by road to explore the Eastern Cape through the eyes of word artists, who range from traditional poets and storytellers who lived in the days before the written word came to southern Africa, and 18th century travellers from Europe who first recorded its topography in books, to contemporary poets, dramatists and writers of personal or imaginative prose. The focus is on English writings, but translations from other languages such as Xhosa and Afrikaans will occasionally be encountered.

Place and literature can be mutually illuminating. Read a poem in the environment in which it was conceived, and both poem and place take on new significance. Recognise in the landscape something encountered on the page of a novel or recognise something on the page visible in the town or city, and experience each in a new way. Whether place makes you want to read the literature or the literature makes you want to visit the place, give yourself to both, explore the ideas they evoke, add a dash of your own imagination and enjoy the riches of the Eastern Cape and its literary heritage.

1 PASSAGEWAYS

AND PASSING WRITERS

THE GARDEN ROUTE

THE LANGKLOOF

AND THE GAMTOOS VALLEY

THE MAIN DESTINATION after crossing the Bloukrans River – the border with the Western Cape – into the Eastern Cape is Port Elizabeth, which is now part of the Nelson Mandela Metropole. There are two possible approaches – the Garden Route along the coast and the Langkloof through the mountains. We shall follow both, lingering along the way with poets who have visited the coastal resorts of Storms River Mouth and St Francis Bay, and accompanying travellers from different eras who have recorded their experiences of the Langkloof and of the Gamtoos Valley in prose and verse. Both routes are fitting gateways to a province that holds many surprises in the diversity of its landscape and of its imaginative literature.

STORMS RIVER MOUTH

At Storms River Mouth, against a backdrop of mountain slopes and indigenous forest, the wooden bungalows of the Tsitsikamma National Park holiday resort overlook a rocky coastline and a wild sea. Here the poet C J Driver sat one winter's day watching the waves, and out of the experience created the poem 'Storms River: Chaos Theory'. It contemplates both the here and now of this place and the infinite world beyond it. 'Poets', the French philosopher Gaston Bachelard says, 'will help us to discover within ourselves such joy in looking that sometimes, in the presence of a perfectly familiar object, we experience an extension of our intimate space.' This is particularly true of the first poem on our literary journey, which invites us to look anew at the familiar object of breaking waves, while the poem itself and the place it celebrates link the outer world of scenic splendour and the inner world of thoughts and aspirations: the poet's and our own 'intimate space'.

C J Driver
Ruth Miller

C J DRIVER
Storms River:
Chaos Theory

I watch the winter waves all day
To guess the place they'll start to gather up
And lift, and lift so slowly to the cusp
Which hangs a moment as it breaks
In sudden downward curve of lighter green
Before the backward spray of spume
Which tags the wave
Appends a rainbow briefly to its edge.

Though gravity has not yet trapped
The further stars in ordered evidence
(For light allows I may not see them now
  Where curves the fleeting universe)
This random music in my head includes
  The rainbow, cusp and spray,
    The light and stars,
The wave's return, the certain night to come.

from In the Water-Margins

C J (Jonty) Driver's poem comes from his collection *In the Water-Margins* the second half of which deals mainly with places re-encountered during a 1992 visit to South Africa, the country of his birth, from which he had been exiled for many years. Driver was born in 1939 in Cape Town, and has lived outside South Africa since 1964, but his roots are in the Eastern Cape. During the later years of the Second World War, while his father was a prisoner of war, the family stayed with his grandfather who was rector of St Peter's Anglican Church in Cradock. After returning from the war, his father became chaplain at St Andrew's College in Grahamstown, and there Jonty remained to complete his schooling. He now returns to South Africa regularly to visit family and travel to places familiar and new which seem to speak to his mind and spirit, but that privilege was for many years denied him. While a student at the University of Cape Town he became president of the National Union of South African Students (NUSAS) and came to know people who were involved in the African Resistance Movement (ARM), one of the more radical anti-apartheid organisations. He denies having been involved in their activities but, on suspicion that he was involved, Driver was detained in 1964 under the 90-day detention Act and kept in solitary confinement. No charges were ever brought against him and he was released after 30 days and allowed to proceed to Oxford University. While he was there, his South African passport was withdrawn and he was banned from returning to South Africa. After Oxford, Driver taught in schools in England and, for a while, in Hong Kong. He has recently retired from the position of Master of Wellington College in Berkshire. As C J Driver, he has published novels, a biography, and several volumes of poetry. Forced separation from loved places makes him see them afresh, and many of his poems are tinged with the poignancy of loss and exile, as we shall see when we encounter his works on other journeys through the province.

From the Storms River Mouth resort a boardwalk leading to a suspension bridge passes through part of the Tsitsikamma forest along the steep banks of the Storms River. Between branches and tangles of monkey rope there are glimpses of the churning tidal waters washing in and out of the river's mouth and, at the end of the trail, a slight detour leads to a mysterious wave-cut Strandloper cave.

There are other similar caves along the Tsitsikamma coast, but it seems probable that this is the one Ruth Miller refers to in 'After the Caves (Tzitzikama)'. A board display near the entrance to the cave tells the story of the archaeological investigation of this site, and a section across a midden just inside the cave's mouth reveals something of the story of its occupation, the kind of artefacts made by its inhabitants and some interesting facts about their diet. It takes a poet, however, to capture the atmosphere of this dark, cold place and to explore some of the thoughts and feelings about it which may linger in the memory.

RUTH MILLER
After the Caves (Tzitzikama)

Now there is nothing to say
About the caves.
Distance has made them cold.
They float, like a cloak in the wind
An old man's cloak. They have lost their existence
In a tired fable,
In an old
Repeated story, too often told.

In a smooth corner of the furthest caves
An arrowhead
Inert a million sullen years
Feels cold to the touch. But do the dead
Feel cold in the grave?
Do disused hearths feel lonely with
blank embers?
We are too skilled, too wise
To blow them alive with nothing but our breath.

Yet we remember
The caves, though there is nothing to be told
About them, but that they were cold as death;
And we left them cold.

from Ruth Miller: Poems, Prose, Plays

RUTH MILLER was born in Uitenhage in 1919, but left the Eastern Cape as a small child to live in the northern part of the then Transvaal. There she stayed until her marriage to Wolfe Miller in 1940, when she moved to Johannesburg, where she worked for a while as a secretary and, later, as a teacher. She had two children. The death of her son in his teens, anxiety about her daughter, the failure of her marriage and consequent separation from Wolfe and, finally, a long and painful battle with cancer, cast dark shadows over the later part of her life. She died in 1959. There had always been an elegiac note in her poetry, which she had begun publishing in the 1940s, yet there was a delight in the visible world of landscape, creatures, plants and sea. These outward things were drawn into her poetry, and out of them were drawn, often with deep compassion, hints about life and its puzzles. Miller was a reticent person and there is a hiddenness in her poems which makes it impossible (and probably irrelevant) to extricate the personal from the more general awareness of suffering, but the personal response to objects in the world around her is obvious, whether it be to a tree or a leaf, a pebble or a shell, a spider or a beetle; to views from a moving train, to a seascape or a cave. We shall encounter Ruth Miller and more of her beautifully crafted poems conceived on holidays spent in the Eastern Cape when we reach Port Elizabeth.

The name Tsitsikamma is derived from the Khoe language and means 'place of abundant water', with the onomatopoeic overtone of 'the sound of rain or running water'. Certainly the sound of water, gurgling along streambeds, splashing down waterfalls or crashing on the rocky coastline is as memorable as the visual riches of this region. Its poetry, too, may echo in the mind, rather like the 'random music in my head' of Driver's poem or the cold silence of Miller's remembered caves.

ST FRANCIS BAY

Alan James

The twin resorts of Cape St Francis and St Francis Bay are situated at the western end of a bay that stretches from Seal Point (the site of the Cape St Francis lighthouse) to Seaview on the outskirts of Port Elizabeth. Alan James is poet of this locale, where he has spent many family holidays. Scattered through his published works is a gallery of ten poems about the area.

In 1575 the Portuguese explorer Manuel Perestrelo named the bay after St Francis, the patron saint of sailors. Some believe that it is the same bay christened *Golfo dos Pastores* (gulf of the shepherds) by Bartolomeu Dias on a map drawn up shortly after his historic rounding of the Cape in 1488. Alan James's 'St Francis Bay' offers a serene picture in which images of air, earth and water, colour, light and movement merge into one another. Dias's name seems to the poet appropriate, although the traditional elements of the pastoral – shepherds, lambs and meadows – are absent, except perhaps in the imagination. Through the slow even movement of the verse, through imagery and the sound of words, James conveys a feeling of calm and a deep delight in the wholeness of the scene. He has submerged himself in it and absorbed its atmosphere. The poem invites us to do the same.

ALAN JAMES
St Francis Bay

Entireness of whose, its
consecration: so blue,
most often: and brightness
of evidences: the
light bare over it: how
its cooling lies without
cold discontent and as
grace answers to grace: yes
the supply of it, so
thus exposed, laid before
and mouthed here, opened that
there may be in bathos
where hardly movement but
simply a slow drift to
left then to right, where green
foliage folding in its
slowness – that there may be
drawn down blue oxygen
into continuous
voiding, reforming, the
cycling, what waits, starts or
gives start, stops or is stopped
(depending in part on
your point of view), where the
colours lose compressed or
dissipated or not
meant, where heaviness and
where silence recover.

That's how it is. Or so
I am led to believe.
Which is enough. And which
on the Martellus map
(1489) made
shortly after Dias
had returned, was inscribed:
Golfo de Pastori:
so composed together,
and so onefolded, so
nice lapped, modest in waves,
so purposed to serve, to
yield, so given over,
so scrupulous really,
so indeed pastoral
although now herdsmen and
shepherds are not much in
evidence and there are
no meadows enamelled,
'pretty lambs with bleating ...
a shepherd's boy piping
as though he should never
be old ... ', although there is
that as well if you want
it. So begotten and
so conciliated.

from Producing the Landscape

ALAN JAMES
Cape St Francis:
At the End of Summer

And yet again. Its discovering
that goes on and on,
repeatedly lest disaster. 'Towering with
so sublime a boldness above
the bosom of the ocean.'
(Which is actually a description
of some other lighthouse: but
why not apply it here?)
And above its apron of
rock warped, folded, fissured, corroded:
where on sunny days trippers
and residents will be seen
scrambling or fishing or gazing
perhaps towards Australia or randomly.
Here where there is 'clash
and clangour' and fury, and
at times 'the agitation of
tempests' and 'billows' that rage
excessively and formidably: but much
of the time it's just noisy
and windy and there is
always the smell of salt
and oxygen and kelp: and
when the wind blows from
the land, the smell of
kapokbos and of buchu whose
volatile oils spill into the
air that is blown. A
place of discovery, and also
of auguries, testimonies of disaster
always at hand and implying

responsibilities: the turning light, squalling birds,
the cast-off, torn-off
bits that your feet brush
against as you pursue your
own way. Oh the summer's
almost ended, season of grace
to close, not to be
extended (why should it?): discovering
not to continue indefinitely though
it might appear otherwise,
cold and withdrawal to follow,
and hardening: and the disaster
(if that's your merit) to
happen utterly at last, surely,
despite all this rock and
bush and noise and the
smells I have spoken about
and the movement of air,
such definite circumstances having no
real consequence in them. That
is the first point. And
here's the second. What then
about those here occupying themselves
as they wish? Shall inertia
be gingered? Or insensitivity touched,
intransigence be charmed, or whatever
wrong confidence overthrown? How shall
they make discovery, receive? For
them, what more's to be
done than is already done?

from Morning near Genadendal

'Cape St Francis: At the End of Summer', which focuses on the lighthouse at the western extremity of St Francis Bay, reminds us that there is also a harsh side to the life of this bay, for it is the setting of many stories of sea disasters and shipwrecks. The recently refurbished circular lighthouse, whose lamp was first lit in 1878, is a site worth visiting – grand in itself and providing excellent views of the ocean and coastline. James's evocation of the lighthouse and its rocky base; smells from sea and land; the sound of squalling birds and noisy wind; and images of windblown vegetation create a powerful impression of the place. Beyond the present scene are hints of disaster in the past and possibly in the future, and a need for an inner change as the summer of the outer world draws to a close. For everyone, James suggests, there must be discovery; there must be change.

ALAN JAMES was born in 1947 in Pretoria, and lived in a number of different centres in South Africa before moving to Perth, Australia, where he pursues a career in the legal profession. Founder of the literary magazine *Upstream*, James has published poetry in anthologies and journals as well as in five collections. Landscape is a major concern. 'It is', he says, 'what we find ourselves in and must cope with.' Dislocated syntax and the spicing of his texts with quotations from other writings sometimes make James's poems difficult to understand, but repeated reading is very rewarding. The flow of history through a place; exile and return along with the problem of belonging; and celebration as well as sadness are frequent themes. The poems are not overtly religious yet are, he says, 'essentially Christian in origin, intention', and they do convey the sense of a world pervaded by a spiritual dimension.

Cape St Francis and its milieu has provided Alan James with many opportunities for leisurely meditation. As he discloses at the end of a poem of farewell to Cape St Francis, written prior to emigration, it is very close to the poet's heart and to his sense of home:

> ... You shall
> be my locus and light,
> and still my keep.

His poems about the Cape St Francis milieu are found in two of James's collections – *Producing the Landscape* (1987) and *Morning near Genadendal* (1992). An appreciation of this beautiful part of the Eastern Cape coastline, with its beaches, rivers and estuaries, nature reserves and rich assortment of shells, fish, birds and indigenous plants, is enhanced by contemplating it through the eyes and mind of the poet, who writes that he 'still hankers back to that area and its vegetation and wind and sun and clean seas'.

THE LANGKLOOF

18th-century travellers

C P Thunberg
A Sparrman
John Barrow
Wm Paterson

About half this roughly 200-km-long inland valley, known from as early as 1789 as the *Langé Kloof*, lies in the Eastern Cape, where it stretches from Misgund in the west to Kareedouw in the east. It is a beautiful area of farmlands, villages and small towns set against the Kouga and Tsitsikamma mountain ranges.

The earliest written responses to the Eastern Cape are recorded in the journals of late-18th-century travellers, most of them private individuals from Europe, a few of them government officials charged with reporting on the outlying districts of the colony and beyond. In the Enlightenment's spirit of inquiry the main concern of private travellers was to describe the topography, the fauna and flora and the peoples of southern Africa to satisfy the curiosity of their contemporaries about this region. The route to the east for most of these travellers lay through the Langkloof. Originally the preserve of the San and the Khoekhoe, this fertile region had attracted some of the first Dutch farmers to leave the more settled areas to the west. Visitors were, therefore, assured of hospitality along the way and could avoid the dense Tsitsikamma forest to the south and the impassable gorges gouged by rivers making their way from the mountains to the sea.

Descriptions of the Eastern Cape were first recorded in writing by Ensign Beutler of the Dutch East India Company (DEIC) who, in 1752, led an officially sponsored expedition as far as the Kei River. Twenty years later, Swedish botanist Dr Carl Peter Thunberg began the first of three expeditions to the region, on two of which he was accompanied by the Scottish gardener William Paterson. Paterson's brief description of his travels, published in 1776, is the first such written account in English. Part of the English edition of Thunberg's journal, first published in 1793, was reproduced in 1986 by the Van Riebeeck Society, making it once again accessible to a general readership. 'In so wild and almost desert a country as this part of Africa may justly be called,' writes Thunberg, 'I have attempted to depict nature as she really is, and as she has exhibited herself to me after an attentive survey.' He sees the country through the eyes of a botanist and is known as the 'Father of Cape Botany' but he did record, albeit somewhat sketchily, many features other than the flora of what appeared a strange new land.

Thunberg was followed by another Swede – the medical doctor Anders Sparrman – but his journal (also reproduced by the Van Riebeeck Society) was first published in 1785, some eight years before that of the botanist. Sparrman

has little to say about the landscape, his chief interest being the animals and the people of the region, which he describes in detail.

William Paterson, a botanical collector from Scotland, made four journeys through the Cape during 1778 and 1779 and recorded his impressions in abrupt diary form, while a Dutchman of Scottish descent, Colonel Robert Gordon, left a much fuller and more erudite account of his lengthy explorations, undertaken as an official of the DEIC and spread over nearly ten years from the mid-1770s to the mid-1780s.

John Barrow's *Travels into the Interior of Southern Africa in the Years 1797 and 1798*, published in 1801, became the most influential of these journals. He was sent by the British authorities at the Cape to gather information about their newly acquired domain. A keen observer, Barrow records in elegant prose his impressions of the geographical features of the country and of the people he encountered, and his two-volume *Travels* is the first major text in English to focus on what was to become the Eastern Cape. It is contemporary with Lady Anne Barnard's accounts of Cape Town and its environs.

William Paterson, who passed through the Langkloof early in 1779, comments: 'The farmers have corn land, gardens and vineyards and in general exceeding good houses.' A year earlier Colonel Robert Gordon notes that 'the peaches [were] beginning to ripen in the Lange Kloof'; and John Barrow, who travelled through the valley twenty years later, remarks, 'Langé Kloof abounds with streams of water and good pasturage. The ground throughout consists of a fine rich soil, and annexed to almost all the habitations are good gardens, fruiteries, and vineyards.'

Hospitality and productive farms are still characteristic of the Langkloof. Today's travellers will find that every season has its attractions in this fruit-growing district, spring being particularly beautiful as the pinks of peach blossom give way, early in October, to orchards of white apple blossom. The views from a car window are dominated for long distances by the giant cone of Formosa Peak, and either side of the highway the sight of Cape fold mountains and patches of natural vegetation are reminders of scenes from early journals. It is worth venturing away from the main highway to admire some of the plants and birds first identified by their authors or to visit some of the farms, villages and beauty spots that are easily missed if one flashes past in a car, in contrast to those who lumbered along in oxwagons.

A contemporary Grahamstown poet, Beth Dickerson, has recorded her experiences of Langkloof travel in two poems: 'Journey through the Langkloof' and 'Flying over the Langkloof'. From the road she observes:

Every dam so glassy still that trees
And reeds and even ducks are double,
And hills stand on their heads.

What I thought were flowers on that bush
Are flirting birds with yellow breasts,
And flocks of birds on wires
Lift and wheel as one.

The hills are topped with cloud
And mist lies in the hollows,
While eagles sit
Like totem heads on poles.

Naturalists Thunberg and Sparrman would recognise the birds mentioned by the poet, but what would they make of the 'wires' and 'poles'? They would be even more puzzled by Dickerson's other view – from an airliner. Her two poems depict the same place from different viewpoints, both moving, but one at '30 000 feet', the other at car window level. Both present memorable impressions of the Langkloof, but neither indicates time to linger and absorb a view or capture it in detail. In our fast-moving world place is often experienced as something passing by. On our literary journeys we shall sometimes pass by, sometimes linger and reflect.

BETH DICKERSON
Flying over the Langkloof

Looking down I see,
On the seaward side of this long valley,
Sharply folded ridges,
Ridge on ridge of mountains
Kneed up from the plain,
Deep olive-green and shadowed black.

And there a master-hand has drawn
In outline on the crest
A pale clear line.
Impossible it seems,
But must be – yes,
A road.

Who would travel such a knife-edge course?
A shiny spot proclaims a dam;
No homestead visible from thirty-thousand feet.
Yet some habitation there must be
Some need to trace the cutting edge of mountain
To span these deep-indented valley-sides,
To reach perhaps a haven
Or a place where things may grow.

And down below,
In twists made tortuous
By ridge on folded ridge,
A river winds.
Out of sight its outcome
In the sea,
But sunlight shows it clear
Mercurial, metallic,
To distinguish it from roads.

How remote this landscape:
Inaccessible it seems –
Not what we know
On swift and easy passages
Along the Garden Route
Or through the Langkloof's placid length.

unpublished

M E H DICKERSON, who publishes poems as Beth Dickerson and stories as Elizabeth Dickerson, has been interested in writing and in drama all her life. She was born in 1928 in Basutoland (now Lesotho) and moved to Stutterheim when she was six years old. Schooling there and in Bloemfontein was punctuated by participation in dramatic presentations and the award of prizes for writing: the first at the age of six – a prize of 2/6 (25c) for a published poem! After reading for a Bachelor of Arts degree at Rhodes University, Dickerson went on to London to study speech and drama and, later, education. Periods as a student were interspersed with teaching positions in South Africa and Rhodesia (now Zimbabwe) and were followed by a teaching spell at a school in England. When, however, Dickerson returned to South Africa on holiday in the mid-1960s, she realised that this was where she belonged.

The challenge of setting up a department of drama at Rhodes University brought Dickerson in 1966 to Grahamstown, where she still lives. Many student productions have benefited from her direction, and stages and screens have been enriched by actors who have passed through her hands. Now retired, she still occasionally devises and directs dramatic presentations for various occasions, including programmes in Grahamstown's cathedral, where the celebration of faith in the context of the arts has become a regular feature of the annual National Arts Festival. She also devotes time to writing: a number of her poems and short stories have been published in magazines and journals, and she has won several prizes for published and unpublished works. Although she does write of other places, many of Dickerson's poems and short stories have been inspired by features of the Eastern Cape, and we shall encounter her works again as we travel eastwards.

THE GAMTOOS VALLEY

Some of the early travellers who approached the east via the Langkloof then passed through the valley of the Gamtoos River on their way towards the sea. Today it is more usual to turn into this valley off the coastal road and, as we enter the Gamtoos Valley, our attention – like that of the Rev. Christian Ignatius Latrobe and his party, who passed through the valley in 1815 – is soon 'engrossed by the ever-changing scenery of this lovely spot'. Everywhere there are attractive views, whether of farmlands, riverbeds, rounded hills covered in indigenous bush, or the mountains of the Groot Winterhoek and the Elandsberg ranges which dominate the horizons to the north. Most spectacular of all is the 1789 m Cockscomb, whose Khoe name – *T'Numkwa* – means mountain in the clouds.

Three quaintly named towns – Hankey, Loerie and Patensie – are located in the Gamtoos Valley. Hankey was established in 1822 as a London Missionary Society settlement for Khoe people. It was named after the society's treasurer. Loerie is named for the Knysna loeries that

Loerie

The Philip tunnel at Hankey

frequent the adjacent forests. The approach to this town passes through hill-sides that in winter are ablaze with aloes, while overhead, from an aerial rope-way, buckets carrying limestone from quarries in the hills to the Loerie railway station are suspended like beads on a giant necklace. The name Patensie is thought to be a corruption of a Khoe word meaning 'resting place for cattle', which is an apt reminder of the pastoral occupation of the Khoekhoe who once lived here. Now, citrus orchards and fields of vegetables and other crops demonstrate the district's agricultural abundance, while Baviaanskloof, a wilderness area north of the valley, confirms Latrobe's view that 'the bountiful Creator has been pleased to clothe this country ... with an astonishing profu-sion of vegetable beauty'.

JEANETTE EVE
Gamtoos Valley Orchestra

Loerie, Hankey, Patensie,
Gamtoos, Kouga
And Baviaanskloof:
Names making music in the mind.

Named for the wily lion,
For a resting place for cattle,
For restless loeries
Scrambling in the branches
Of age-old yellowwoods,
For barking baboons
Deep in a ravine,
For a missionary treasurer
Lending, not money, but his name:
Inspirations for a chorus in the mind.

And there's a backing like percussion
In the names of the flora:
Erica
Acacia
Cycad
Protea
Pelargonia
Euphorbia
Kiepersol
And arum;
Aloe ferox
Blazing on the hillsides;
Crassula coccinea
Sparking in the mountains:
Sounds beating rhythms in the mind.

Ruled out on the valley floor
Orchards of fruit trees
Lush fields of vegetables:
Staves on the page
Of a grand orchestral score.
A backdrop of rolling hills
Lines the valley, either side,
Beyond that mountains
Proclaim their powerful presence:
The Groot Winterhoek
The distant Elandsberg
And, in striking silhouette,
The Cockscomb - *T'Numkwa*
('The mountain in the clouds'):
Wood-wind and brass blowing in the mind.

The Gamtoos and the Loerie,
The Kouga and the Klein,
Roar furiously at flood time,
Moan in anguish during drought,
Now sigh with satisfaction
As their life-giving waters
Flow gently, smoothly,
Along a network of canals,
Pump strongly, rhythmically
Through a thousand irrigation pipes:
A bowing and plucking of strings in the mind.

The Khoekhoe ('Men-of-Men'),
Now vanished from their clan lands,
Britons and Dutch
Who thought to tame the wilds,
Naming the natural,
Composed a symphony.
The notes of their languages
Reverberate
Reverberate:
Harmonies that echo and re-echo in the mind.

2 A METROPOLE AND

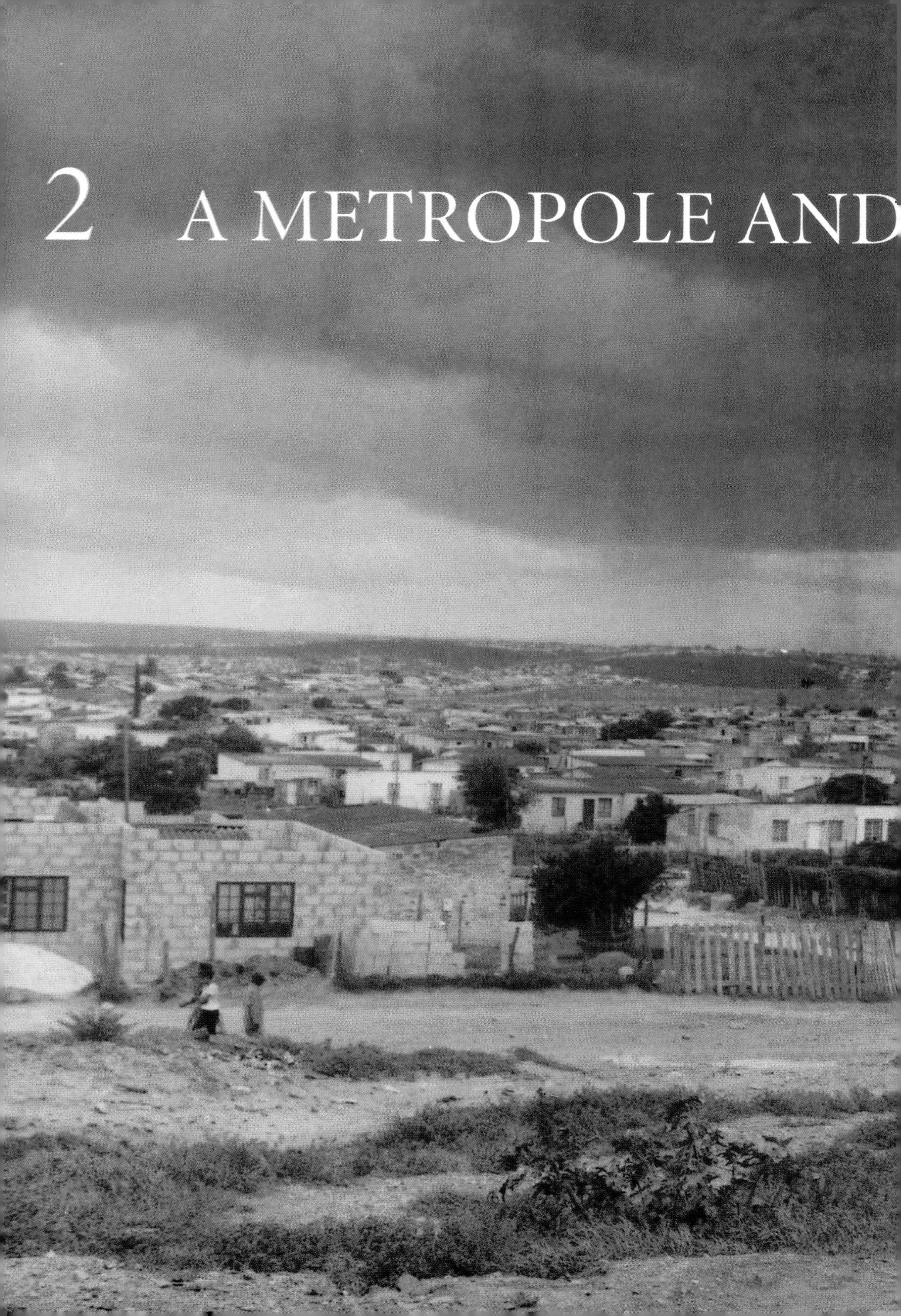

A MEDLEY OF WRITERS

THE NELSON MANDELA METROPOLE

(MAINLY PORT ELIZABETH)

T HE NELSON MANDELA METROPOLE, of which Port
Elizabeth (PE) is the major component, offers a scene of urban diversity
almost as great as the natural diversity of the Eastern Cape's landscapes. It has
also elicited more – and more varied – literary responses than any other part
of the province.

PORT ELIZABETH

Port Elizabeth has a long coastline, part of which is on its southern side and
the rest along the beautiful, wide Algoa Bay. Coastscapes and seascapes are
often depicted in poetry and prose about the metropole. Away from the
immediate coastline Port Elizabeth's topography is unremarkable, and it is the
imprint of history rather than geography that provides its many-sided character. It is a history reflected in place names, in a multicultural population and
in its architecture. All are, in turn, reflected in literature.

The Khoe-San left names such as Kraggakamma and Coega. Portuguese
explorers of the 15th and 16th centuries imprinted on their maps names
which became Cape Recife and Algoa Bay. From the era of the Dutch East
India Company – the 17th and 18th centuries – came the name Baakens for
the river mouth at which a beacon was erected claiming the established landing place for the DEIC, while Dutch farmers moving eastwards provided
names such as Buffelsfontein and Papenkuilsfontein. Fort Frederick was
named by the British, who wished to protect the eastern parts of the Cape
Colony, which was, by the end of the 18th century, in their hands. Until 1820
'Port Elizabeth' did not exist; it was Sir Rufane Donkin, acting governor of the
Cape of Good Hope, who named the embryonic town after his deceased wife.
Xhosa-speaking people added words such as Kwazakhele and Zwide to the
city's symphony of place names. The metropolitan council has been named
Nelson Mandela after the great struggle leader and statesman whose inaug-
uration as South Africa's first black president signalled the end of apartheid.

During the 19th and 20th centuries PE grew from village to town, and town
to city. Some British settlers filtered back to the place of their landing; later,
Afrikaners from the hinterland came to town; Jewish people arrived in the
early years of the 20th century, as well as new immigrants from Britain, Europe
and the East; Chinese immigrants formed a special community; and coloured
people of local descent made Port Elizabeth their home. At different times there

were influxes of Xhosa people, who now form the majority of the population.

The architecture of Port Elizabeth also bears witness to its diversity: Settler homes; churches, synagogues and mosques; grand Victorian and Edwardian houses and public buildings; modern houses, blocks of flats and townhouses; little box-like dwellings and huge factories and warehouses; shantytowns; extensive townships; compact as well as spacious suburbs. Port Elizabeth evidences in its buildings and its urban layout much that is good from the past, but its face also bears many scars. It has been a townscape of conflict, division and poverty as well as of affluence; of industry as well as of ease; and many of these contrasts are considered in its literature of place.

Before journeying round the metropole to view more than fifteen sites to which a medley of writers have responded, we focus on just one creative artist, Athol Fugard, and on the sites associated with his life and works.

ATHOL FUGARD'S PORT ELIZABETH

Port Elizabeth's foremost literary figure is the world-renowned playwright, actor and director Athol Fugard. Paying tribute to Fugard at the 1992 National Arts Festival Winter School, his poet friend, Don Maclennan, said the playwright figuratively carried a piece of Eastern Cape earth with him wherever he went. To take the image further, one could say that that piece of earth is a composite of the soils of the Karoo and those of Port Elizabeth.

In the poem 'For Athol Fugard' by Margaret Gough, a series of impressionistic images suggests Athol Fugard's Port Elizabeth – the place where his 'muse began to sing'. There are also hints in the poem of the portrayal, in Fugard's plays, of ordinary people and the meagre circumstances of their lives. Rundown houses, trellised verandas, wind-twisted trees and the wind itself characterise his city. His characters are thwarted by adverse circumstances like plants which are 'blighted', 'twisted', 'stunted', 'bent awry'. Gough's poem is a succinct expression of the way in which Port Elizabeth and Fugard's plays are intertwined.

How did Fugard come to be what Gough calls 'the attentive recorder / of existences eked out in side streets'?

HAROLD ATHOL LANNIGAN FUGARD was born in 1932 in the Karoo town of Middelburg, where his parents ran a cash-store. When Athol (or Hally as he was then known) was three years old, the family moved to Port Elizabeth, which became the springboard of his life and many of his works. Fugard's mother, born Elizabeth Magdalena Potgieter, was of Afrikaner stock. Her influence and that of her family were strong in his life, but Fugard was

MARGARET GOUGH
For Athol Fugard

You'd see a window flung open
a door ajar
innuendoes of lives
fleeting, unsatisfactory –

and became the attentive recorder
of existences eked out in side streets
houses with stained fronts standing
silent, side by side –
the dull paper mauve of the bougainvillaea
interrupting the diamond
trellis of verandas

It is here, and here only
(you yourself have dubbed it the 'ugly city')
that your muse began to sing, whispering
in a minor key of lives
grotesque and blighted
by love
turned back upon itself
unable to blossom
stifled by the fog
of a limited view

lives petrified
by the gorgons
so early encountered

or twisted
to the awkward symmetry
of saplings, stunted
bent awry by
our salt prevailing winds

from Selected Poems

educated in English and always writes in English. His father, Harold David Lannigan Fugard, was of Anglo-Irish extraction. In his heyday Mr Fugard was a jazz pianist, and his playing was one of the pleasures of young Hally's life, although there was much that was turbulent in their relationship.

There are two aspects to Fugard's Port Elizabeth: places associated with his life and places used as settings in his plays. Both take us to many sites in PE.

PE AND FUGARD'S LIFE

Fugard's autobiographical work *Cousins*, published in 1994, is almost as much an exploration of Port Elizabeth as of the early life of its author and the influences on his work of people and places. Among those influences were the family's homes in Port Elizabeth. First the Fugards lived in 'quiet and very respectable Clevedon Road'; then came the Jubilee Hotel at the top of Constitution Hill managed by Mr and Mrs Fugard – 'far and away the most exciting of the four homes, of my youth'; this was followed by 'the world of small-holdings and scabby little farms' when they moved to 'Devon' out on the Cape Road; while Newton Park, the fourth home, 'was a prototype middle-class white South African world'. Fugard also recounts how he and one of his cousins explored the beachfront and the Main Street area of PE. Fugard was thus exposed to a variety of experiences of the city, particularly of what he called its 'little worlds'.

> All my life, and I don't really know why, it has been those humble and desperate little worlds that have fired my imagination; I have studied them and tried to imagine my way into their secret life as eagerly and passionately as others do with palaces and mansions of the mighty.

At the same time he was encountering so-called 'ordinary' people, although he says:

> that is not the adjective I would use to describe the lives I studied on the pavements of Main Street and in the dark little rooms of the Jubilee, and which gave me my understanding of words like courage and hope and despair'.

Other sites were also important. For 30 years his mother ran the St George's Park Tearoom – 'my mom's pride and joy' and one of the places that influenced Fugard's work, as did the general dealer's store out on the Buffelsfontein Road in Salisbury Park run, for a while, by his mother's sister and her husband.

I write, read or even just think the names 'Buffelsfontein Road' or 'Salisbury Park' and I smell

STGEORGES SWIMMING BATH

a heavy fragrance compounded of paraffin and chew-tobacco, ground coffee and blue soap, all stirred into the clammy sweetness from sacks of moist brown sugar; I close my eyes and I see again a dimly lit world of shadows and muted, deferential voices as soft as the moths fluttering around an old Coleman lamp that is hissing away on a wooden counter. Every Sunday night, in the house behind the store, he and his cousin Johnnie entertained the family with their 'musical stories'. Fugard believes that these evenings and the shared storytelling with his father at the piano in the Jubilee Hotel were the first formative experiences in the development of his career as a playwright.

Fugard attended Marist Brothers College and the Port Elizabeth Technical College, but much of his early education came from observing people, places and events in and around Port Elizabeth and from avid reading in the Port Elizabeth Public Library on Market Square. That library, with its terracotta façade, is one of PE's most noteworthy buildings – a splendid example of Victorian Gothic architecture. Inside, among its beautifully designed halls, galleries and alcoves, there is a quiet atmosphere of busy inquiry in which one can imagine the eager young boy exploring the world of books. 'I prowled those galleries', he writes, 'with their beautiful wrought iron railings, looking down with disdain on the common folk grubbing around for cheap thrillers and love stories on the ground floor'.

In 1950 Fugard left Port Elizabeth to study at the University of Cape Town but, in spite of doing well, he left just before his finals to hike with his friend, the poet Perseus Adams, through Africa. Then, for nearly a year, he sailed the world on a tramp steamer.

In 1954 Fugard returned to South Africa. He met and married, in 1956, the Cape Town actress Sheila Meiring, and his interest in drama was rekindled; together they established a theatre workshop in Cape Town known as the Circle Players. Sheila Fugard was also to become an artist with words, as poet and novelist. She spent many years in Port Elizabeth, yet it does not feature as prominently in her writings as other regions of the Eastern Cape, where we shall meet her and her work.

The Fugards moved to Johannesburg, where Athol came into contact with many of the personalities and problems of the city's black population. Sophiatown provided setting and situation for two of his early plays: *No-Good Friday* and *Nongogo*. It was *The Blood Knot*, with its Port Elizabeth setting, however, which put him on the map as a contemporary playwright.

After a brief spell in London, the Fugards returned to Port Elizabeth in 1960 and, during the next decade, four major plays emerged from Fugard's fertile imagination, three of them set in Port Elizabeth.

PE IN FUGARD'S PLAYS

Korsten and 'The Blood Knot'

The Blood Knot is set in Korsten, which Fugard describes in the introduction to *Three Port Elizabeth Plays*.

> Korsten: The Berry's Corner bus, then up the road past the big motor-assembly and rubber factories. Turn right down a dirt road – badly pot-holed, full of stones, donkeys wandering loose, Chinese and Indian grocery shops – down this road until you come to the lake. Dumping ground for waste products from the factories. Terrible smell. On the far side, like a scab, Korsten location. A collection of shanties, pondoks, lean-to's. No streets, names, or numbers. A world where anything goes.

In this setting he places the brothers Zach and Morris, struggling with the problem of being judged by their colour – one is 'whiter' than the other – and with the awful conditions of shanty life in Korsten.

Today Korsten is a mixture of commercial, industrial and residential buildings, dominated by Livingstone Hospital. Empty plots bear witness to earlier uprootings of residents, but its fortunes are rising. There are well-kept houses and Korsten's lakes have largely been drained and cleansed of industrial waste.

Remnants, however, of the shanty areas described in Fugard's play, and patches of water in a large neighbouring depression – still frequented by Morris's 'white birds' – are reminders of scenes in *The Blood Knot*.

> MORRIS: ... In between my cleaning and making the room ready when you're at work, I look at the lake. Even when I can't smell it I just come here to the window and look. It's a remarkable sheet of water. Have you noticed it never changes colour? On blue days or grey days it stays the same dirty brown. And so calm, hey, Zach! Like a face without feeling. But the mystery of my life, man, is the birds. Why, they come and settle here and fly around so white and beautiful on the water and never get dirty from it too!
>
> MORRIS: Yes. It's the mystery of my life, that lake. I mean ... It smells dead, doesn't it? If ever there was a piece of water that looks dead and done for, that's what I'm looking at now. And yet, who knows? Who really knows what's at the bottom?

Morris's musings about the lake and its birds suggest that however dreadful the suffering and confusion of a situation, beauty and sensitivity may be discerned, and that perhaps there is an underlying purpose or a true identity – for himself and for others like him. The human spirit remains indomitable.

The Swartkops mudflats and 'Boesman and Lena'

Boesman and Lena is set in an even bleaker world than that of Korsten – the Swartkops mudflats.

> LENA: Mud! Swartkops!
> 'Here' Boesman! What's here? This ... (*the mud between her fingers*) ... and tomorrow. And that will be like this! Vrot! This piece of world is rotten. Put down your foot and you're in it up to your knee.
>
> LENA: So I followed you. Didn't even know where until I felt the mud between my toes. Then I knew. Swartkops again! Digging for bait. Mudprawns and worms in an old jam tin. A few live ones on top, the dead ones at the bottom.
> 'Three bob, my baas. Just dug them out!' Lieg your soul into hell for enough to live.
> How we going to dig? We haven't even got a spade.

Lena's desperate efforts to identify where she is and to remember where she has come from are also frantically attempts to identify herself and to make some sense of her life. The play resonates with a litany of names: Redhouse – Swartkops – Veeplaas – Korsten – Missionvale – Kleinskool – Bethelsdorp. All are real places on the periphery of Port Elizabeth. All are familiar to Boesman and Lena, yet none of them is home. The Swartkops mudflats is the most desolate of all and certainly not a place where they can put down roots. All that is certain is that it is here and now.

Sometimes on the Swartkops mudflats one sees the figures of prawn diggers reminiscent of Lena. They are dwarfed by the old power station with its huge chimneys, which dominate the skyline across the river.

Port Elizabeth Central, the Baakens Valley and 'Hello and Goodbye'

In *Hello and Goodbye*, set in Valley Road in the Baakens Valley, white Afrikaans siblings Johnnie and Hester examine the past, which has crippled them both. Johnnie's soliloquies and Hester's account of her journey home from Johannesburg, imagining the scenes of her youth, are brilliant re-creations of the sights, smells and sounds of the central part of PE that Fugard had explored in his own youth. Here, Johnnie imagines Market Square:

And sooner or later it starts to get dark in the square, the sun sets, the last light goes riding away on the backs of the buses, and then it's twilight with a sky stretching all the way down Main Street and beyond who knows where, the ends of the earth ... And all being well I'm in the gloom on Jetty Street corner watching while it gathers, waiting for nothing in particular with the City Hall clock telling the time, some time, dingdong, start to count forget to finish because it's all the same ... the cars get fewer, the newspaper boys stop calling and count their pennies on the pavement while darkness is coming it seems from the sea up Jetty Street ... Bringing peace, the end of the day, my moment, everybody hurrying away from it, leaving it, for me, just me, there in the shadows and no questions asked, for once enough, ME is enough, need nothing, whisper my name without shame ... Until the lights go on ... Suddenly like a small fright, ON, which is my sign to think of going ...

Hester's memories of home are equally sharp:

Those windy days with nothing to do; the dust in the street! Even the colour of things – so clear, man, it could have been yesterday. The way the grass went grey around the laundry drain on the other side, the foam in the river, and inside those Indian women ironing white shirts. And the smell, that special ironing smell – warm and damp – with them talking funny Indian and looking sad. Smells! I could give you smells a mile long

– backyard smells, Sunday smells, and what about the Chinaman shop on the corner! Is he still there? That did it. Don't ask me why – something to do with no pennies for sweets – but that did it.

Deeply serious but never dull, these plays of the '60s are enlivened by bouts of humour and spiced with the flavour of the 'little worlds' of Port Elizabeth and the idiosyncratic speech patterns of their characters.

New Brighton and 'The Coat', 'Sizwe Bansi is Dead' and 'The Island'

It was also in the '60s that Fugard's involvement began with the Serpent Players of PE's black residential area of New Brighton. At first he helped with the production of established plays and then, in collaboration with John Kani and Winston Ntshona, began to develop plays which brought to his work a new dimension and new settings. The player introducing *The Coat*, specially devised for a white audience in Port Elizabeth, explains:

New Brighton. I often wonder what that name means to outsiders, like you. I am using the word in its purely descriptive sense – we live inside and you live outside. That world where your servants go at the end of the day, that ugly scab of pondokkies and squalor that spoils the approach to Port Elizabeth. If you are interested in knowing something about it we might be able to help you, because we accepted the chance to come here tonight so that we could tell you about a coat, a man's coat, which came back to New Brighton in a stranger's shopping bag.

The hilarious but profoundly sad *Sizwe Bansi is Dead* is set in the township studio of a photographer – 'a strong-room of dreams ... Walk into the houses of New Brighton and on the walls you'll find hanging the story of the people the writers of big books forget about.' Although *The Island* is set on Robben Island, the prisoners come from and often refer to New Brighton, a facet of PE into which these plays took audiences from many parts of the world. Kani and Ntshona not only made major contributions to the development of these plays, they also went on to win international acclaim for their acting, and Kani has subsequently become an independent playwright.

Walmer Township, Skoenmakerskop and 'Marigolds in August'

Film became a focus of Fugard's interest for a while. *Boesman and Lena*, with its Swartkops setting, was filmed with Yvonne Bryceland and Athol Fugard himself in the two-person cast. *Marigolds in August* opens in Walmer township and the main action is set at Skoenmakerskop on the southern coastline of PE, where the Fugards had made their home. According to its film directions, Daan walks from his 'humble corrugated-iron shack in Walmer location' along a 'rutted and stony township street' out into the country along a 'deserted tarred road' to the 'obviously affluent little village of Skoenmakers-kop'. *Marigolds* was filmed in this milieu.

Algoa Park and 'A Lesson from Aloes'

After a brief departure from regional settings, Port Elizabeth featured again when *A Lesson from Aloes*, set in Algoa Park, was first performed in 1978, and *Master Harold and the Boys* in 1982. In the introduction to *A Lesson from Aloes*, Fugard explains the aloe metaphor of the play: 'Aloes are distinguished above all else for their inordinate capacity for survival in the harsh-est of possible environments. In writing this play I have at one level tried to examine and question the possibility and nature of survival in a country for which "drought," with its harsh and relentless resonances, is a very apt metaphor.' The play is set in a small house in Algoa Park whose garden is cluttered with a collection of aloes in containers and whose characters – 'little people' from the white community – struggle for survival, their lives 'bent awry' by apartheid society.

St George's Park and 'Master Harold and the Boys'

Master Harold is set in St George's Park Tearoom. Today the tearoom, painted in psychedelic colours, bears little resemblance to the art deco build-ing of Mrs Fugard's day. A little imagination, however, may place Hally, Sam and Willie inside it, as the stage directions state, on 'a wet and windy Port Elizabeth afternoon', to play out the drama of their circumstances and rela-tionships.

Fugard's later plays explore new pastures, including the Karoo, so we shall meet him again in Chapter Six.

Athol Fugard prefers to be known as a regional rather than a political playwright and his region is, pre-eminently, Port Elizabeth. Many of the Fugard sites in PE will be revisited as we wend our way around the

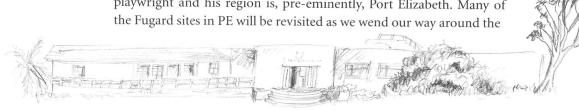

coast and into its urban terrain in the company of other writers, conscious that in many parts of the metropole the spirit of this great playwright lingers.

Our tour of Port Elizabeth takes us along its sparsely populated southern coastline from Maitland River Mouth to Cape Recife, where we round the cape to explore the very different Algoa Bay coastline all the way to Bluewater Bay beyond the Swartkops estuary. Along the way we shall venture into the heart of PE to view various sites, visit North End and then survey the historically coloured and black residential areas beyond that. Our itinerary includes fourteen different parts of PE, all of them portrayed in imaginative writings of one kind and another, and some twenty writers will be our guides.

MAITLAND RIVER MOUTH

Maitland River Mouth is a secluded place of leisure where, between giant *N Roy Clifton* sand dunes and a bushy hillside, the rather insignificant Maitland River is lost in a lagoon before gradually seeping underground towards the sea. Beyond the lagoon is a broad beach, with a white fringe of rollers, a scattering of rocks, and a coming-and-going of seabirds.

The poem 'At Maitland River Mouth' by N Roy Clifton poses some interesting philosophical questions through its interlacing of images of this site and ideas that come to the poet as he contemplates it. Maitland River Mouth is a place where one may well feel insignificant, like the figures in the poem, against the backdrop of the dunes that dominate the scene and in the 'hazy chaos' of drifting sand particles.

N ROY CLIFTON
At Maitland River Mouth
Port Elizabeth, 1977

My knees and arms bedded in cool sand,
My back tremulous in a sea wind,
I watch the grains flit landward,
Forming the wavering edges, neat-cut and lined by shadow,
That ripple the dunes like a fossil pond,
Some in length less than a span, others many spans,
The start and end of each clear and sharp,
Their multitudes creasing the sandy hills,
Farther and farther and finer, without count.

Beyond a near clear knoll of grey
Light softens all solid things
Into a hazy chaos,
And lines of electric scintillations
Creep through its dense glow,
In which I can but fancy
The hills and headlands known at other times.

Those are men,
Tiny splinters in the mist,
Knobbed like desert bones,
Floating apart and then together,
Seeming void of will or purpose,
As if the shining tide they floated in
Wholly determined them.

Here my eye is held in bright fascination,
Where colour, shape, and size are not articulate,
Motion is all but stopped,
Identity emulsified in light;
And ocean's constant wash sinks
Into a white silence.

Shall I, rising from a brief abandoned body,
See in some after-glow like this
Men distanced, like memories, to a proper puniness,
Whose arduous wrestles of decision
Are shrunk to the floating to and fro of specks
Which merely plot the enigmatic shifts of drift and wind
In some never-ceasing system.

from Moments in a Journey

N ROY CLIFTON was not a South African; he writes from the perspective of a sojourner, but one who has so immersed himself in the local milieu that his responses to it carry the validity of someone rooted here. Clifton was born in 1908 in England. Most of his life was spent in Canada but, during the 1970s, after he retired from a teaching post there, he and his wife paid a number of extended visits to their daughter, who was then living near Port Elizabeth. Clifton's poem about Maitland River Mouth was first published in *New Coin* in 1978, but it also appears, along with thirteen other poems about Port Elizabeth, in his collection *Moments in a Journey*, which he calls 'my life in brief'. It was published in 1983, the year before his death. Other moments in the journey of his life, and recalled as poems, occurred in Auckland, New Zealand, and Ontario, Canada, where he made his mark in education, theatre, film and conservation. Clifton is almost unknown in South Africa, but the Eastern Cape can be proud to have a literary connection with this erudite man who was fascinated with words and with the visual.

SARDINIA BAY AND THE SACRAMENTO TRAIL

The reserve of which Sardinia Bay forms a part stretches 2 km out to sea, and on the coastal side includes a bathing beach tucked between dunes and an extension of the rocky outcrops of Skoenmakerskop. In the hills adjacent to the coast, cultivated areas and nature harmonise in the form of a patchwork of smallholdings. The dark, glossy foliage and contorted shapes of milkwood trees embellish the area's blend of rock, sand, fynbos, coastal vegetation, garden and paddock. Birds abound and small wildlife such as tortoises, duiker, vervet monkeys and hares live in the bush. Sometimes, however, the landscape is marred by the effects of runaway bush fires fanned by berg winds. These are all characteristics that are given literary life in Marguerite Poland's youth novel *The Bush Shrike*.

Marguerite Poland

Ruth Miller

Cathal Lagan

Marguerite Poland, novelist and children's author, grew up on a smallholding at Lovemore Park, between Sardinia Bay and Skoenmakerskop. She counts herself fortunate to have spent her formative years in such a place.

> It wasn't very beautiful or particularly wild, but it was surrounded by thick coastal vegetation in which lived the smaller, less appreciated animals of the bush – snakes, monkeys, bushbuck, duikers and porcupines. For me it was – and is – endlessly beautiful, and what I write is often a celebration of a childhood spent there.[1]

The Bush Shrike is just such a celebration, as well as being an exciting story for adolescents, touching on a number of adult prejudices and questionable moral attitudes. It tells a story of loss and disillusionment, but there is much to delight the reader, especially in the absorbing interest in the bush and its creatures that binds the two main characters despite their different backgrounds:

> And as I stood in the shade, ankle-deep in dune-sand, I saw a movement in a tree, like a leaf turning. Then the bush shrike called, for that is what it was. A bush shrike, calling so close, so loudly, challenging me from its branch, with its thick, dark bill. I stood immobile, clutching my book with damp hands. I seemed to wait forever as the bush shrike watched me, leaning down.
>
> It flew to a smaller, denser tree nearby. I strained to see where it had gone in the twilight of the leaves. The bird was silent and then suddenly it reappeared and flew off. I heard it call further away. I put down the book and clambered up the tree where it had perched, the thorny bark tearing my jeans.
>
> I found the nest. It was not easy to reach. I moved clumsily, hurrying, for I did not want the bird to return and find me. Three eggs lay in the cup of rootlets and twigs, buff-coloured and freckled with pale reddish spots, like the rust marks on fallen leaves. I gazed at them, trying to absorb their size and the pattern of their marking, so I could tell Josh.

Many other features of this locale are woven into the narrative as, for instance, the effects of a bush fire:

> It was a burnt-out landscape. Skeletal trees, forged grotesquely in the grip of fire, stood against the fall of earth. The ground was wet with ash and runnels of sludge. It was a naked landscape, stripped of life. Only the rocks and the limestone banks remained the same.
>
> I walked along the edge of the wild trees. Tattered leaves, singed and beaded with resin, hung where angry flames had leapt at the bush. A spider's web, newly-made, dangled across my path, bridging the green of a thicket and the charred twigs of a fallen tree.

MARGUERITE POLAND, born in Johannesburg in 1950, and resident in KwaZulu-Natal for most of her adult life, is deeply attached to the Eastern Cape where she grew up and was educated, and her fiction evokes its landscapes with haunting intensity. Poland achieved literary fame in South Africa initially through her award-winning children's stories, many of which have Eastern Cape settings. She believes that children need to know about the wildlife, flora and legends of their own country, and her stories for them are usually based on African folklore and pose an African view of nature. She is well qualified to do this as Poland has studied social anthropology and African languages and folklore and, in 1997, was awarded a doctorate for a study of the naming of Nguni cattle based on their colour patterns. There is nothing, however, that is coldly academic about her writings – they are full of life and a delight to readers of all ages. As well as her children's and youth stories, Poland has published three adult novels, all set in the Eastern Cape. We shall meet her again.

Between Sardinia Bay and Skoenmakerskop, the Sacramento Trail passes Cannon Bay, off which one of the most beautiful Portuguese ships of the day, the *Santissimo Sacramento*, was wrecked in 1647. The wreck and its aftermath represent a story of courage and hardship: it is recalled in Cathal Lagan's poem '"The Sacramento Way": Christmas 1996', part 1 of which is reproduced here. A total of 72 survivors of the wreck set off to walk to Mozambique; only nine arrived there, of whom only four lived to sail back to Goa. A cannon lying in a rock pool close to the bay was discovered by Colonel Robert Gordon in 1678, but it was another 300 years before the site was positively identified as that of the wreck of the *Sacramento* and, in 1977, a salvage team removed more than 40 cannon from the seabed close to the adjacent shore. These had been carried as both equipment and cargo, some as a gift for the king of Portugal. Today one of them stands at the beginning of the trail in Skoenmakerskop, pointing to the site of the wreck. The cast of another – one of the largest and most ornate of the Bocarro cannon from the *Sacramento* – is on display in the Port Elizabeth Museum.

'*Lectio*' is the first part of Lagan's four-part poem, '"The Sacramento Way": Christmas 1996', which takes as its form a monastic method of meditation which begins with *lectio*, the reading of a text for its immediate sense. The text for Lagan is a place – the Sacramento Trail – and this section of the poem sets the scene (that is, gives the immediate sense) for a pilgrimage in which the material and the spiritual, the present and the past, are intertwined. In describing the site of the wreck of the *Sacramento*, Lagan quotes from a tourist

CATHAL LAGAN
'The Sacramento Way': Christmas, 1996

i. Lectio

They saunter at ease, Holy Landers,
on this Christmas Eve,
along the 'Sacramento Way',
stopping nostalgically beyond Cannon Bay,
at the old shelling-crushing mill
that ghosts a rusting graphic
of its form for the passing visitor.
The tourists' handout boasts
'the vegetated dunes' where stunted milkwood integrates, and fynbos
flourishes against 'the stand of rooikrans
and Port Jackson willow'.
'Freshwater seepages abound';
ironic note for those diced up
upon these spines of rock in 1647,
when the galleon 'Sacramento'
on her maiden voyage from Goa,
caught in great shocks of broken sea,
and broaching to, was ripped
from stern to stern on Peter's feast,
unholding her heavy cargo of land cannon,
iron and ornamented bronze, great
Bocarro guns from the foundry at Macao,
birthday gift for John the Fourth of Portugal.
Feyo's diary notes: 'In the afternoon of June 29th,
they fought in vain to stand out to sea'
against the current's pull, and then began
the two hour drift to land,
'in spite of rudder and management
of sail ... the bows ever turning
towards the shore'. The Fathers' prayers,
and Blessings of the waves were all in vain.
Nothing could turn them from the face of fate.
Thrown then against harsh shins and jaws of rock,
and rolled ashore on shale and sand, seventy-two survivors
camped, living on wreckage for eleven days
before the coastal trek to Delagoa Bay.

from New Contrast (25), Sept. 1997

pamphlet about the trail and from a diary contemporary with the event, as well as adding his own touches of narrative and description. In other sections (*'Meditatio'* and *'Oratio'*) the poet delves more deeply into some of the strange stories which the diarist Feyo records about the survivors' trek to Mozambique. The poem's concluding section (*'Contemplatio'*), set at Cannon Bay, takes the meditation beyond words into the silence of contemplation.

THE REV. CHARLES LAGAN, who has lived in the Eastern Cape since 1962, was born in 1937 in Northern Ireland and uses the Gaelic form of his name – Cathal Lagan – for his published poetry. Rural Ireland and various Eastern Cape locations are the primary landscapes of his heart and are recreated with care and sensitivity in many of the lyrical and meditative poems he has written.

From 1956 to 1960 Lagan was in the merchant navy and his Sacramento poem indicates an acquaintance with the lore of seafarers. The nautical meaning of baptism, for instance, is a sunken wreck, an idea with which the poet plays. It is significant that nautical and religious imagery are combined here, for ministry as a priest, initially in the Roman Catholic and more recently in the Anglican tradition, has been the pivotal occupation of Lagan's life. He has also worked as an academic in the English department at Fort Hare University. These religious and academic pursuits, along with close attention to details of the environment, particularly what he calls the 'honest landscape' of the Eastern Cape, produce poems that are philosophically challenging as well as pleasing in the pictures they conjure up.

Now resident in King William's Town, Lagan has lived in a number of other Eastern Cape places: South End and Swartkops in Port Elizabeth, Cradock and Alice. Literary journals as well as a number of slim volumes published by the Echo poets of Fort Hare include poems by Cathal Lagan and, together with poems by friends and colleagues Brian Walter, Norman Morrissey and Basil Somhlahlo, some have formed the text of the Caversham Press poetry and print projects undertaken with the artist Hillary Graham. Among these are poems about other parts of Port Elizabeth, and about Alice. The varied landscapes of Lagan's heart, both here and in Ireland, are recreated with care and sensitivity in the lyrical and meditative poems collected in *Sandbird* (1999).

Ruth Miller was inspired, on one of her Eastern Cape holidays, to write the enigmatic poem 'Sardinia Bay'. One feels that she must have sat all day contemplating the rocky outcrops to the west of the bay. Miller's craft is consummate and each word is aptly chosen and positioned to create a visual picture of what she sees, yet she does not give away the secret of her poem: what is the wisdom of the rocks that are perceived as crouching animals watching the fine spray of breaking waves?

RUTH MILLER
Sardinia Bay

The rocks are wiser than they know,
Gnarled with age, they find this generation
Particularly granular, with pebbly hearts;
Sand sifting in the wind's cold caves.

They sit with their paws folded, round-rumped,
Sharp-spined, compressed with the weight
Of heaviness within them. All day long
They watch the sea – animal most unlike:
Movement to their static strength,
Change to their stability,
Light, colour, airiness; and the graven face.

The rocks permit the cat to play.
But oh! they are watchful.
They remember being scratched and clawed,
They recall their shabby, snubbed relations –
The endless sandy shores.

The spray falls slower than its rise,
Gracefully, like a dancer.
Thundering, each ninth wave
Supplies the answer.
Learning, unlearning lessons,
The rocks recite together
With their dumb tongues, paean,
With their dead mouths, a prayer:
The spray falls slower than its rise.
Carefully, the rocks look wise.

from Ruth Miller: Poems, Prose, Plays

CAPE RECIFE

Hugh Finn's poem 'Wooden Figurehead' was inspired by an artefact in the *Hugh Finn*
Port Elizabeth Museum, but its setting is Cape Recife. There, in a swirl of sand
dunes, stands an impressive 24-metre-high octagonal lighthouse completed in
1851. More than twenty shipwrecks have occurred off this turning point into
Algoa Bay and Finn's poem reflects on the chance discovery of a ship's figurehead at this site. The poem may be based on fact or on an imagined event trig-
gered in the poet's imagination by seeing a figurehead in the museum and
informed by his acquaintance with the stories of
wrecks and with Cape Recife. Coldness and a sense of
doom and death pervade Finn's compassionate evocation of a present scene and a past shipwreck, of
which there have been so many around PE's coast.

HUGH FINN
Wooden Figurehead
Museum, Port Elizabeth

Trawled laboriously up, off Cape Recife,
The dim submarine cloud of the net dragged
Heavily, shimmering with promise. The fishing-boat
Leaned to the flickering silver weight, looked
Down through the green lens of the swell's passing
With the eyes of men whose arms felt that pull
As the brandy-bottle-heavy weight of a bonus
Nagging their Friday pockets. Once aboard,
The cascading pyramid of fish parted to show
The iron-black irony of its burden:
Cumbrous among limp dog-fish and soles valueless
Mashed beneath it lay the figurehead.
Too long ago for their death to seem quite real
Men had drowned with it, shrunk into bones'
Pallor among the dark ribs of the ship.
Touching that carved face, one could look with its eyes
Upward through years of luminous green oblivion
Until now, with a ship's shadow poised
Above, and the muscular cursing of sailors round one,
And the sun and the long-lost sough of the waves and wind;
And colder than the wind on the wet timber
One might see death in one's own face looking down.

from The Sunbathers

HUGH FINN was born in 1925 in Port Elizabeth and died in 1995 in Harare, Zimbabwe, where he had spent more than 40 years. One of the absorbing interests of his early life was the sea. His family had a house at Amsterdamhoek, used initially for holidays and, later, as a permanent home. Even after moving to what was then Rhodesia, there were holiday visits to this attractive spot on the banks of the Swartkops River to see family and to enjoy the ambience of river and sea and other favourite parts of Port Elizabeth, such as Cape Recife. From these experiences emerged poems such as 'Wooden Figurehead' and 'The Sun-bathers: Amsterdam Hoek'.

Hugh Finn's other link with the Eastern Cape was Rhodes University, where he studied chemistry and geology. In what was then Rhodesia, to which he moved in 1950, his professional life focused on teaching chemistry, his personal life on family and poetry. Hugh and Betty Finn (the poet D E Borrell) did much to promote the literary arts in that country, encouraging the reading and the writing of poetry, and making friends among writers of all races. More than 300 of Finn's own poems were published, some in journals, including scientific ones, and some in his collection, *The Sunbathers* (1977).

Of his poetry, Hugh Finn wrote:

> My own ideal has always been to write a poem like a piece of quartz rounded by the sea; with a natural, inescapable perfection of form, with the surface texture that one longs to touch, and the immutable inner strength of a crystal, and a memory of the sea still clinging to it. Have I achieved this? Has any poet yet?[2]

Some of Finn's Port Elizabeth poems come close to this ideal as well as having, in a more literal sense, the memory of the sea of his early home clinging to them.

THE BEACHFRONT

Dennis Brutus
Ruth Miller

Two short poems from writers we meet elsewhere evoke Port Elizabeth's long beachfront, which stretches from Summerstrand near the Cape Recife end of Algoa Bay to the harbour about halfway along its margin. Pollock, Hobie, Shark Rock Pier, the Boardwalk Casino, Happy Valley, Humewood, Bayworld, King's: what different images these names conjure up from the litany in Athol Fugard's *Boesman and Lena*: Redhouse, Swartkops, Veeplaas, Korsten, Missionvale, Bethelsdorp, Kleinskool!

The beachfront is the sunny, sophisticated side of Port Elizabeth, where residents and year-round holiday makers enjoy beach life and watersports, restaurants and entertainment, shopping and gambling. But for poets and those with a more thoughtful outlook on life it is a place where natural rather than artificial attractions catch their attention.

Those who enjoy walking on the beach and observing the shells, bits of sea-weed, flotsam and jetsam thrown up by the tides, will recognise the shellfish whose actions are so vividly described in Ruth Miller's poem 'The Scribe'. Despite human intrusions, these creatures are still busy inscribing their 'singing hieroglyphs' on the sand of PE's beaches and entrapping us, as they did the poet, in their mysterious world.

RUTH MILLER
The Scribe

The wet sands bear the signature of tides
Which tides erase, as though their document
Were only for the ears and not the eyes.

But once, upon an open beach intent
I found a pale ribbed shell poised to discover
In lurching slime, the ecstasy of space.

It moved in slow gyrations, turned and doubled
Upon its tracks, moved east, then plunged to west,
Heaving, awkward and directionless.

Beneath its bony cusp it slowly cast
A flight of singing hieroglyphs, that travelled
in ever wider lariats and arcs.

Obdurate, who must believe in signs
I stood breathstill, until the sliding shell
Entrapped me in its maculate design.

from Ruth Miller: Poems, Prose, Plays

In 'Tomorrow' the beautiful image of waves unrolling bales of 'foamlace / on the wetsilk sands' juxtaposed with images of forbidden signs, barbed wire and barricades is typical of the poet Dennis Brutus, who saw beauty but fought during the years of racial separation against the barricades that hindered people from sharing in it. King's Beach – wide and sandy with safe bathing – is so called because the British Royal Family bathed there during their visit to South Africa in 1947. The tomorrow of Brutus's poem has become today and, as he predicts, the 'Forbidden' signs have gone.

DENNIS BRUTUS
Tomorrow

King's Beach, Port Elizabeth

The waves will unroll
their bales of foamlace
on the wetsilk sands
over the stumps of the
'*Forbidden*' signs:
the barbed wire and
barricades
will be gone.

from Still the Sirens

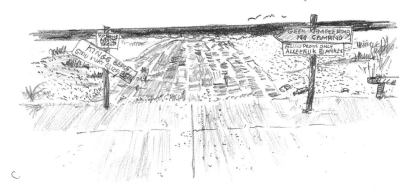

THE HARBOUR

Yvonne Burgess
Ruth Miller

The locomotive slid to a screeching halt near the Customs sheds and released steam with a roar. Scholtz grimaced sourly towards the town, at the Campanile and the rows of dull roofs rising tier upon tier, hugging the hills up into the thin blanket of smoke.

Over the harbour basin the gulls wheeled and then chattered, alarmed, as the *John Dock* suddenly sounded its siren with a noise shrill enough to drown out the grinding of the locomotive as it started off towards Scholtz again.

This noisy, busy little scene is from one of Yvonne Burgess's short stories – 'And Out of the City' – which, like her novels, presents a vibrant sense of Port Elizabeth. Here the movements and sounds of the locomotive, the siren of the well-known tug the *John Dock*, the wheeling and chattering of gulls, are set against the apparently quiet, unmoving background of the town with its 'dull roofs' and 'thin blanket of smoke'. Burgess is a major Port Elizabeth writer: she will be introduced a little later in our tour.

In Ruth Miller's poem 'Dredger', noise and activity are set not against the dullness of the town, but against the quietness of the circling gulls that do not chatter, as in Burgess's description, but drift silently and 'fold / The very shape of quietness on the water'. Miller is doing far more than describing PE's harbour: the scene figures her own state of mind.

The dredgers of Miller's poem and the shunting trains of Burgess's story, the gigantic cranes that dominate the scene, and the 52-metre-high Campanile built in 1923 to commemorate the landing of the 1820 British Settlers close to this site, will be associated with the harbour for many decades; but a new deep-water harbour with modern facilities at the mouth of the Coega River about 10 km away is likely to change the character of Algoa Bay as much as the older harbour did more than 100 years ago.

RUTH MILLER
Dredger

Oblivious to the massive clangour
Of chain and winch
Lifting, drifting, the quiet gulls
Feel the seabed move a sullen inch.

Docks are never peaceful, but the gulls
Seem not to care.
Through the white glare
The whiter birds returning, fold
The very shape of silence on the water.

But I can find no birdpeace, nor succeed
In marking on my busy dragging wheel
Anything but broken shell
And choking weed.

from Ruth Miller: Poems, Prose, Plays

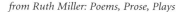

SOUTH END

André Lemmer
Brian Walter
Dennis Brutus
Arthur Nortje
Cathal Lagan
Jean Edmunds

On a steep hill overlooking Port Elizabeth's harbour and the wide sweep of Algoa Bay, there are two suburbs, one superimposed on the other. One is the old South End, razed to the ground in the 1970s, its inhabitants removed to more than half-a-dozen parts of Port Elizabeth. The other is an assemblage of affluent townhouses and complexes built over its ruins. Images of the old South End exist, for the most part, only in photographs, the memories of its people, and in literary recreations.

From the earliest days of settlement along the Algoa Bay coast, people lived in what initially was known as 'the place over the river'. The district came to include a broad spectrum of cultural groupings, representing different races, ethnicities, faiths and denominations, who lived harmoniously side by side. Sometimes it takes an imaginative writer rather than a historian to capture the sense of place of an urban landscape that no longer exists, and in André Lemmer's 'Song for South End' people, sights, smells, tastes and incidents from the past of South End are recalled with appealing clarity.

ANDRÉ LEMMER
Song for South End

Sing a song of South End
A pocket full of pain ...

The mosques still stay
Like twin accusations,
Their balconied minarets now mute.
Two prayerless pink turrets
Tower over crowds of
White townhouses and
B M W parking bays.

Now in the last sunset
Filling the hollow harbour
And fresh-painting the old mosques
Proud-pink above the guilty huddle,
I let the ghosts wander:

There is Mrs Williams' house
Where starched and bibbed
We sat for Sunday lunch,
And drank condensed-milk in our tea.
I remember the sacred bleeding heart,
The art-deco mirrors and the family
Photographs frozen on the walls.
And there's the boy whose bicycle
Brought the ginger smell
Of still-warm Boston Bread.

O, the smells of South End:
Curry-reek at Nackerdien the tailor's
Scent-smell on Sheik Abdul Marak
Orchard odours at Imperial Fruiterers
Sick-sweet Kabeljou tang
And the salt harbour smells:
There where the silver-sequined fish
Lay in the fly buzz
On the cement steps of the
Electric sub-station,
At the very foot of Walmer Road:
Long before the Fly-overs and Express-ways
The Bull-dozers and Group-areas.

Look, there's the little shop
Which sold the lead
We'd won from the fisherman-robbing rocks
At Willows and Noordhoek and Malay Pool:
We smelted the old sea-crusted sinkers,
Skimmed off the scum and sold
The pure-shining metal lumps
To the old Indian in the Tackle shop.

On Guy Fawkes nights
We pranced in the choking rubber
Stink of burning tyres;
The big-bangs banging
And innocent rockets necklacing
The black night.

Flanagan the sailor went away,
Bull-dozers came and shoved
His Malay love and her bitter brown brood
All the way to Bethelsdorp.

Sing a song of South End
Pockets full of pain ...

in Where the Rainbow Ends

ANDRÉ LEMMER describes himself as 'an Eastern Caper born and bred' who spent most of his childhood living in 'the lower avenues of Walmer – just up the road from South End'. He is best known in PE for his participation in amateur dramatic presentations and his contributions, in the field of education, to the appreciation of the writings of others. He writes occasional poems and has published a historical novel for young adults, *Pathfinders* (1996), which is about Dias's encounter with the Eastern Cape.

South End's many places of worship bore testimony to its religious diversity. The earliest, the Anglican Church of St Peter, was founded in 1871. A hundred years later it had to be deconsecrated after being vandalised following removals and demolitions under the Group Areas Act. The empty frames of perpendicular windows, skeletal walls of pale sandstone and a network of foundations have survived as affecting reminders of what must have been a beautiful church. It stood high above PE's old cemetery, its huge cross a beacon to sailors. Brian Walter's 'Old Holy Places' describes a visit to St Peter's ruins. Nothing could more poignantly express the inhumanity of what was done to South End than the image of the cracked font lying in the grass.

Church buildings of other denominations suffered similar fates, and most have left even fainter traces of their existence. Under Islamic law, mosques cannot be demolished and two mosques remain as striking landmarks in this locality, standing, as Lemmer says, 'like twin accusations'.

BRIAN WALTER
Old Holy Places

'The cared-for character
of the old, stone churches',
your mother said,
'is what I regret most.

'They tore them down and, instead,
gave us such ugly buildings
to worship in: to marry, to bury,
and take the Host.'

And up in St Peter's ruins
we found the very font
where you were christened
– cracked sheer across:

and spirit spilt from your face.
Grasping for a human faith
you asked, 'Could people want
to ruin this place?'

in Mendi

In 1970 more than 6 000 'non-whites' were removed from South End. Schools, sports and recreational facilities, shops and businesses, many of which had existed for decades, were swept away. In 'For Them Burness Street is a Familiar Entity', Dennis Brutus, who taught at St Thomas Aquinas School in South End, focuses on a particular street in a place for which he grieves and whose memory he wishes to preserve. In the minds of those who had lived there, time and space are compacted and the street 'lies whole, like a snake'. It is a place and a time that have gone, but through the poem it lives in the reader's mind.

For them, all South End is the familiar map
of their existence, all their growth and lives
though for me it is mere knowledge, mere report:
yet even I can sorrow, knowing their loss
their uprooting from their homely paradise
and all their yearnings and their sense of loss.

from Stubborn Hope

Another poet who recalls South End, where he worked as a priest, is Cathal Lagan. In a sequence of four poems published in *Mendi* (1994) Lagan imagines the soul of old South End contemplating the past. This poignant reverie is the third of the poems – 'The Soul Dances at the Baakens Valley':

> The soul, dwelling on the dismembered years,
> Looks across the Baakens Valley
> And turns in angry toyi-toyi
> For the unremembered
> Whose lives, considered of no account
> In official eyes, were uprooted,
> And they without consolation
> Wandered in their own land.
> Torn from sun and moon
> And their birth's star-rise
> They have been turned and crushed
> In the millstone labyrinth.

What of South End today? Jean Edmunds, in the poem 'South End', paints a harsh picture of what, for many, seems a pleasant suburb, well situated with magnificent views of the bay.

JEAN EDMUNDS
South End

> Town houses,
> Vying to be ugly, uglier, ugliest,
> Disfigure the skyline.
>
> Across the road, the newly-planted trees
> Flutter and shiver,
> Their roots in the grave of a house.
>
> Lines and angles ruled in the grass
> Define the past,
> As giant patterns on a desert floor,
> As crop circles,
> Show the geometry of other lives.
>
> Cars sweep up and down,
> Up and down the hill,

Past the crumbling stone steps
That lead to nothing
And the pavements –
Cracked and broken gingerbread.

The townhouses,
Invaders,
With battlements,
Alarms and guard dogs,
Look down from on high
At the temple –
An oasis –
Thoughtful in the valley.

unpublished

DENNIS BRUTUS, author of 'For Them Burness Street', spent most of the first 30 years of his life in Port Elizabeth. Born in 1924 in Salisbury, Southern Rhodesia (now Harare, Zimbabwe) of South African parents of colour, he was taken as a baby to Port Elizabeth, where the family settled and he grew up. Despite a late start, Brutus made good progress at school and won a scholarship to Fort Hare University where he graduated in 1947 with a distinction in English.

Thereafter St Thomas Aquinas School in South End and Paterson High in Gelvandale, where he had been a pupil, benefited for more than a decade from Brutus's teaching skills. He had begun writing poetry while still at school, and continued during his university and teaching years. At the same time, a concern for the victims of social inequality and political injustice was developing, and during the 1950s he became a political activist, concentrating mainly on efforts to have South Africa excluded from international sport.

In the 1960s Brutus's political activities led to his dismissal from teaching, house arrests, bannings, arrests, escapes, re-arrests, hospitalisation and a spell on Robben Island. Eventually – in 1965 – he was allowed to leave South Africa on an exit permit. During nearly 30 years of exile his interest in politics, English literature and the writing of poetry did not wane, nor did he forget South Africa. As soon as it was possible he visited the country, and now, from his base in the United States, he returns regularly to lecture, hold public readings and conduct workshops. Ever an activist, Brutus's latest cause is anti-globalisation.

Brutus has published a substantial number of poems. Four volumes, in particular, reflect his South African experience: *Sirens, Knuckles, Boots* (1962); *Letters to Martha* (1965); *Stubborn Hope* (1979); and *Still the Sirens* (1993).

Several different parts of Port Elizabeth are reflected in Brutus's poems, as we shall see, but another significant Port Elizabeth poet, Arthur Nortje, who is associated with Brutus, does not pinpoint specific sites in PE in his poems. Many of them are, however, imbued with a sense of the city as he experienced it.

ARTHUR NORTJE spent some of his youth in the same part of Port Elizabeth as Dennis Brutus – North End – and was one of his pupils at Paterson High in Gelvandale. He also taught for a short period at St Thomas Aquinas School in South End. Brutus encouraged the younger man's writing career and has done much to champion Nortje's work since his death.

When Arthur Nortje died in 1970, a few days before his 28th birthday, he was alone in rooms in Oxford, far from what he called the 'knife-slashed landscapes' of the Eastern Cape. Most of Nortje's poems were published posthumously, in a collection called *Dead Roots* (1973), and in the same year in a special edition of *New Coin*, entitled *Lonely Against the Light*. In 2000 his collected poems – over 400 of them – were published as *Anatomy of Dark*. They reveal a highly skilled poet and a deeply introspective, tortured being exploring the inner self in the context of an overwhelming sense of injustice and alienation and responding in an unusual way to the landscapes of his homeland.

Arthur Nortje was born in 1942 in Oudtshoorn of racially mixed parentage. At Paterson High, where he proved himself a brilliant student and excellent sportsman, poetry became a passion: he wrote his own and, out of school hours, studied the poetry of others. Nortje attended the University College of the Western Cape and Jesus College, Oxford, on scholarships, his periods of study separated by his two-year teaching stint at South End. The successful completion of his studies at Oxford led to teaching posts in Canada but, in 1970, he returned to study further. By the end of the year he was dead.

Landscape in Nortje's poetry is intertwined with the political situation in South Africa. In several poems he implies that enjoyment of the beauty of the local landscape seduces one away from the real issues of life.

> Yes, there is beauty: you make
> the understandable mistake.
> But the sun doesn't shine for the sun's sake.[3]

The loveliness of his homeland is fatal as it has 'seduced the laager masters to disown us'.[4] Yet he feels the suffering of exile deeply and, as the poem 'In Exile' shows, it may be felt in images of that very loveliness as he remembers 'that southern / blue sky and wind-beautiful / day, creating paradise'. He can portray the attractions of nature with delicacy as in 'Transition', written just before his departure from Port Elizabeth.

Aqua-clear, the bracing sky,
and morning breathes cucumber cool,
invests the leaves with gentle airs.
My final spring grows beautiful.

More often, however, Nortje's view of PE is harsh and bitter:

Air-swept slopes of straining weed
plunge dimly to the dung-dry rocks,
shore cowers under the bilious sky.
The oil-scummed green sea heaves and slides
below my view from concrete heights
in struggle with the lurching wind.
Chopping into the curve the white surge
sprawls among boats in frothing nipples.[5]

Nortje is always bitterly conscious of the disadvantages of his skin colour: 'wrong pigment has no scope', 'because my crust is dark and hard', or 'I skulk in a backseat, darker than white'. He never forgot his past or his people's anguish. He could not live within the landscape of his birthplace, polluted as it was by injustices, and he tried to create an alternative through poetry. In the end, living outside South Africa was equally impossible.

The poem 'Reflections' is not specifically about South End but, rather, a kind of watercolour painting of neighbouring parts of PE: its skies and sea, its hill of houses; its city buildings and landmarks such as the Campanile and Market Square; but the serenity of the picture is disturbed and the reflections broken, so that one is left with the rather repulsive image of black bacteria and a feeling of disappointment.

ARTHUR NORTJE
Reflections

Fogged morning, clockwork city
of sewers and towers, smoke and sirens.
Sad weather
engenders sombre reflections, reflects
in campanile bell that conveys the hours.

I am not infinite
shuffling my feet over cobbled
public square where pigeons open
those flitting ranks that close behind me.

Skies change from opalescent
to their usual inscrutable blue,
then the shimmering turquoise water
lies under the hill of houses
despite the death of statesmen.
Or the lifting veil reveals
familiar buildings of glass and concrete,
no face or word or happy miracle.

Images shape but so often
wind stirs to ruffle the water,
grey ripples lip the sand, spume clings.
Gradually I let
slip my disappointment.
Wherever flotsam relaxes
black bacteria renew the action.

from Anatomy of Dark

BAAKENS RIVER MOUTH AND VALLEY

*Reginald
Griffiths*

Brian Walter

One of the idiosyncrasies of PE's topography is the deep gorge of the
Baakens River that winds through the city, sometimes necessitating round-
about routes to get from one part of it to another. The name Baakens comes
from the beacon planted by Ensign Beutler at the river mouth, where there
was one of the freshwater lagoons that gave Algoa Bay its name.

Reginald Griffiths's novel *Children of Pride* (1959) brings the Algoa Bay of the
mid-19th century to life in scenes of wind and waves, shipwrecks and stormy
weather, the excitement of whaling, and the growth of the commercial and
residential parts of PE. Its early chapters are set at the mouth of the Baakens.

> The cottage, where I lived with Sebastian Seagrave, stood at the edge of
> a tidal lagoon that formed the mouth of the Baakens River. So close to
> the water were we that, at spring tides, the suds and the drift of the ocean
> were often thrust beneath the flooring by the waves that lapped at the
> foundation piles.
>
> My earliest life was contained by this world of sand and sea and tide
> and dune. Beyond the doorway of the cottage the sands, shaped by the
> ebb and flow of every tide, held upon their flat, wind-wrinkled surfaces
> the pageant of the small life that made my childhood magical. Here
> walked the hermit crabs in borrowed shells, here were realms of wrack
> and weed, of sharks' eggs and the bones of cuttle-fish. Jelly-fish subsided

stricken on the sands and quaked beneath the hungry suctions of the battle snails. My bare feet popped the purple air-sacs of the Portuguese men-of-war. From the debris of the sea and strand, I took my play-things, or wrought my small designs upon the malleable surface of the sands with the daylong busy intensity of a solitary child.

The Baakens lagoon has now been filled in, the river itself diverted into conduits, large stretches of its banks reclaimed for building and its mouth disfigured by Port Elizabeth's harbour, into which the river trickles unobtrusively. Griffiths, however, helps us to see it with the mind's eye and to make connections with other experiences of a beach's 'pageant of small life'.

The adjacent section of the Baakens Valley has also undergone change. Valley Road, Upper Valley Road and Brickmakers Kloof traverse the valley floor through a district of factories and workshops devoid of aesthetic appeal, but Settlers Park compensates, in part, for the natural beauty which has been lost to these developments. It is situated in a nature reserve set up in 1932 in a large area of the Baakens Valley to re-establish the area's original flora and fauna. Here, in the heart of suburban PE, are opportunities to enjoy a blend of the cultivated and the natural and to find links with the bush of earlier times as imagined by Griffiths in *Children of Pride*.

When we hunted or foraged in the bush Sebastian showed me another world. A world of myriad and incredibly beautiful life. He would bend down an overhanging branch to show me a minute nest of woven web that held a clutch of tiny eggs. Daily he would take me to watch the patient hatching of the eggs and the growth and feeding of the tiny fledglings. He found baby bush-buck in their forms for me and young hares and new-born mice, pink, squeaking blindly, hanging from the bending stems of rank grass. Through him I became aware of the drama of life and death that was being enacted perpetually about me. I understood the continuous cycle of all living things, the copulation, birth, death, the end in the beginning and the beginning in the end.

REGINALD GRIFFITHS was born in Bulawayo in 1912 and received his schooling there as well as at Grey High in Port Elizabeth, before attending the London Polytechnic. After serving in the Second World War, Griffiths set up as a professional photographer in Grahamstown and the photographer's eye for composition and detail is certainly evident in his writings. He published four novels, a collection of poems and a number of poems and short stories in anthologies, as well as a history of Grahamstown's First City Regiment. Griffiths died in 1999. A comment he makes in *Contemporary Poets of the English Language* is particularly relevant to *Children of Pride*.

Influenced by perpetual play of light, our spacious sea-shore, variety of peoples, particularly the African, and the infinite variety of bird and animal species, I am trying to convey something of the atmosphere of a beautiful land disrupted by man-made tensions.[6]

As Griffiths, in *Children of Pride*, recreates this locale, so Brian Walter, in the poem 'Direction', imagines the past of the Baakens. It is one of more than 30 poems that make up his collection *Baakens* (2000), which is devoted to explorations of the river through all its twists and turns and personal and historical associations. Although the poet would like, imaginatively, to drift up and down the course of the Baakens contemplating its significance, he must travel towards the beacon at its mouth 'where salt seas and fresh / waters merge their telling ebb and flow'. *Baakens* is in itself an important literary journey, delightful in its evocations and thought-provoking in what it reveals about being part of the divided yet potentially reconciling landscape of Port Elizabeth.

BRIAN WALTER
Direction

You seem so much more
inspired than I when, sluggish,
I drift into the thin stream of
the river's rough mythology.

Once, they say, passing ships,
sailing the spice route, watered
at its mouth. And – God save
them – some old souls made up

a beacon on the wind-blown
beach to mark the watercourse
that opened fresh into the roll
of salt breakers. And so the bay

of the lagoon, da Lagoa,
became mapped in the minds
of thirsty sea-farers. Meantime,
the Dutch word 'Baakens'

crept up the waters, hanging
mistily over the new English
town that now struck camp.
The story waded thus slow

upstream, till you cut right back
to the beginning: 'But *there*
is the focus, where your beacon
draws all words back to its source.'

But I seek out some other way,
countering that this is your idea,
which your words may better show:
that I don't wish to plot direction,

would prefer, like the mists, to drift
that way or this, upstream and
down, wending with an eel's twists.
But there it is. Your thoughts

have led me where I would not go.
You have set your mark and challenge
at the mouth, where salt seas and fresh
waters merge their telling ebb and flow.

from Baakens

BRIAN WALTER grew up in Port Elizabeth, where he was born in 1956 in
the milieu of white suburbia. He was educated at Herbert Hurd Primary
School, Grey High and the University of Port Elizabeth. After a brief spell as a
journalist, Walter returned to university to read for Honours in English before
taking up a teaching post at Chapman Senior School in Gelvandale, later moving to Fort Hare University to lecture in the English department. 'My teaching
positions at Chapman and at Fort Hare', he says, 'have both been formative:
befriending people classified differently to oneself was not always an option in
segregated PE, but both institutions have helped me to become a fuller
Eastern Caper, and more South African.' His wife, Cheryl Pillay, was born and
brought up in South End, which has focused an interest in that part of PE
across the divide of the Baakens.

Brian Walter's poems have been published in journals, in several slim anthologies produced with Fort Hare colleagues, and in two collections: *Tracks* (1999), for which he won the Ingrid Jonker Prize, and *Baakens* (2000). Walter's poetry is visual in its effect and one of his concerns is the combination of art and poetry. He has worked with other poets and with artists on several projects in which visual and literary arts enhance each other.

In his poems divisions are emphasised and Walter sees around him a landscape of conflict, yet the oneness of humankind and a close identification with the environment underlie the poet's world. These are qualities that are apparent not only in Walter's poems about the Baakens Valley and South End, but also in others we shall encounter – about the Swartkops mudflats in PE and about Nieu-Bethesda and Alice.

Central

Lyn Harrison

As commercial Port Elizabeth developed, Market Square became a vibrant meeting place for farmers, sailors and local people, where goods from far and near were traded along with news and opinions. It was close to the old landing places, and at market time a bell would ring, signalling that there were opportunities to buy and sell. Then it would be jam-packed with oxwagons and horsedrawn carts spilling over with wares.

The liveliness of buying and selling in the open air which characterised early Market Square has now shifted to Govan Mbeki Avenue, originally Main Street, which leads off it. Street traders from the environs of Port Elizabeth and from all over Africa and beyond vend their wares along its pavements – a scene vividly captured in Lyn Harrison's poem 'Main Street, Port Elizabeth, 1993'.

Lyn Harrison
Main Street, Port Elizabeth, 1993

the streets are coming alive!
in slanted shadow
slanted sun
between highrise and lowlife
there are vital signs
on street corners
peels in the gutter
a rumbustious splurge of colour
on silica sidewalks
the fruits of a nation

lie in neat little piles
fat mammas everywhere
sitting so nicely
jingle jangle of change
two rand now not one rand
and goods pass from
hand to hand

the streets are coming alive!
gone the aseptic nothing
gone the conformity of
business suits and polished shoes
here's life as it is lived on the pavements
here's a Mr. Potato and
a Mr. Boerewors Roll
and a Hot Dog Stand with
sauces of your choice
appetite is in the air
here's a coat flapping its arms
a skirt plying its trade
in the street – the tout
shouts bargains of the day
dangling enticements
at the door to Aladdin's Cave

Saudi Supermarket nudges
staid Standard Bank
the spicy smell-feast
of its wares rivalling
the smoking sausages
in the Something Good trolley
'Clothing for Africa'
(the store that gives the hawker more)
blazons its guts on the wall
jackets, jerseys, teeshirts and tackies
– the Happy Hawker Home
(and all that jive)
Yes man! the streets are coming alive!

from Poems from the Bay, 1986–1997

LYN HARRISON knows the centre of Port Elizabeth well, having worked in Main Street (Govan Mbeki Avenue) for 30 years. She is a member of the Eastern Province Writers' Club and has been awarded a number of their prizes, as well as having stories, articles and poems published in magazines and newspapers. 'Main Street' comes from an unpublished collection called *Poems from the Bay*, for which PE has provided much of the inspiration.

Of another member of the Eastern Province Writers' Club – Margaret Gough – Lyn Harrison writes:

> A wordspinner, her decipherable style
> delicately unravels mysteries,
> frugally she drapes her web of thought,
> her notions, on a page and simply
> in unlaboured elegance the essence of
> the underlying truth is deftly caught.

The poem 'For Athol Fugard' by Margaret Gough, which introduced the tour of Athol Fugard's Port Elizabeth at the beginning of this chapter, is a good example of how 'an underlying truth is deftly caught' in the web of Gough's poetry. People and objects, minor items of news and small creatures are catalysts for poems that are miniatures rather than landscapes. As we shall see at later stages of our tour, Gough's poems often convey a particular and sharply focused sense of the world in which the poet lives.

MARGARET GOUGH has master's degrees in both psychology and English, and has worked as a psychologist in Cape Town and on the staff of the English department at Rhodes University in Grahamstown. Since the 1980s she has lived in Port Elizabeth, where she was born and spent the first nine years of her life. A number of Gough's poems have been published in *New Coin*, and in 1999 about 50 lyrical verses were collected in a privately published volume called, simply, *Selected Poems*. It is a fitting record of a particularly sensitive response to some of the underlying issues that affect the lives of people – ordinary and famous – who live in the Eastern Cape.

An interest in people and their surroundings, partnered with a choice of vigorous, contemporary words and images, helps this versatile, part-time writer to convey a colourful picture of what is now the metropole and to probe some of its enigmas.

THE HILL

Rising steeply above Port Elizabeth's central business district is what is known as the Hill. Three features of this historic part of Port Elizabeth to have inspired literary responses are Fort Frederick, the Donkin Reserve, and the cultural history museum at Number Seven Castle Hill.

Hugh Finn
N Roy Clifton
Yvonne Burgess
William Selwyn

Fort Frederick stands on a high promontory overlooking the Baakens Valley. Completed in 1800, its siting gave the fort a commanding view of the landing beaches below and it has remained to this day solid-looking and impressive, but the cannons protruding from its oddly angled stone walls have never been fired in anger. The fort has an interesting literary association, for it is believed that Shakespeare's *Hamlet* was performed within its ramparts by members of the military garrison. In 1999, 200 years after work on Fort Frederick was commenced, the play was performed again in this apt setting.

HUGH FINN
Fort Frederick: From the Sea

Stumbling up from the longboat with the other
Troops, the weeks of nausea sour in the mouth,
My grandfather must have seen with some relief
Above the dunes' uncertainty and the tousled
Irregular hills the Fort's assured rampart:
Neat, precise, Europe's order ruled
Across the untidy squabbles of Africa.
Its barrack-windows, perhaps, glittered like grains
Of salt as the sunlight whipped between the gusts,
And an order could grow, it was clear, from the squared stones
As a crystal compels solutions, imposes pattern.
Look up, now, to that past strength of the Fort.
The slap of the wet south-easter's at my back,
As the windows signal sunset down to me
Here, where shadow lengthens towards night.

from The Sunbathers

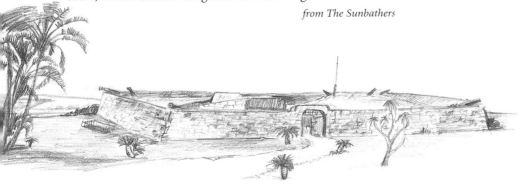

In Hugh Finn's 'Fort Frederick: From the Sea', grandfather and grandson observe identical features of the fort, but their responses are not the same. In the colonial past the fort has seemed like a symbol of European orderliness imposed on the supposedly disorderly continent of Africa. To the grandson the fort represents a 'past strength'; and the same barrack windows which for his grandfather had glittered like grains of salt now, in the sunset, seem to signal the uncertainty of approaching night. The idea may be ambivalent but the poem is well formed, like the crystal which Finn, the chemistry teacher, uses as one of his images.

About halfway between Fort Frederick and the Donkin Reserve runs the steep road known as Castle Hill. Number Seven, originally Parsonage House and one of the oldest houses still standing in Port Elizabeth, has been converted into a welcoming and homely museum that is furnished to portray an aspect of PE settler life as it could have been between the years 1840 and 1870.

In the long poem 'Thoughts at Number Seven Castle Hill', N Roy Clifton paints a picture of the settlers' arrival as he imagines the scene below Castle Hill. Each precious object brought with them and now preserved in the museum is preserved in the poem as a delicate pen sketch. Place and poem take us on journeys into the past.

N Roy Clifton
From Thoughts at Number Seven Castle Hill
Port Elizabeth, 1978

Astounding the pallid autumn sandhills
Below the moat, the palisade,
The twelve-foot ramparts of stone,
An adventure gathered, of ships and crews,
Of bullock waggons and their drivers,
And a thousand men, women and children in tents;
Infants and wives chaired ashore by soldiers,
Men and boys wading waist-high through frothing breakers
From boats warped in until they grounded.
Lighters brought supplies,
Chests and baskets
Holding things chosen with difficult care
As those whose loss would most be felt
In the pattern of their day,
To comfort them in botched-up mud huts,

From which they must for some time go
To clear, to plough, to sow, on working days,
Half a world away
From roads and houses known up to then for all their years,
From friends and parents they knew they had left forever.
. . .

Some are named in white stone on church walls,
Some are under long heaps of rocks,
Who they were all but smoothed from their headstones,
Their lives erased, as all must sometime be,
Except for their things
(Part of the outwardness in which they dressed,
Little metonymies of them):
Large Bible beside the bed,
Solander box, Bible-big,
Pewter candlesticks,
Table-top desk with quill and pot,
Copper kettle, sad iron,
Tea caddie square with country scenes,
Butter pats,
Pin cushion printed with verses of comfort.
. . .

In this house
Whose things are sturdy,
Its thick stone wall snug on a rocky terrace,
Its plain shape quietly white in the sun,
Their ambience lingers.

from Moments in a Journey

A good place to sit and absorb something of the spirit of Port Elizabeth and its contrasting aspects is on a bench on the Donkin Reserve, a few blocks from Castle Hill. In the novel *Anna and the Colonel*, Yvonne Burgess describes the scene through the eyes of Anna.

Whenever I felt like a breath of fresh air, when the wind was not blowing too hard and the Colonel felt fairly well (once or twice a month we both felt fairly well at the same time) we would take a stroll down the street to the Hill.

We'd try to go early in the morning, usually, before the wind and the vagrants took over, when the sea was still calm and bright, rippling with sunlight like shot taffeta, before the wind freshened and it would turn grey and choppy, crested with white foam, except in the calmer waters of the harbour.

Both arms of the Bay would be visible then, beyond the harbour wall on the right, below the cranes which stood at intersecting angles, to the sandbanks which stretched like a creamy ribbon into the grey-blue sea, and on the left, the stark ugliness of the industrial area, softened somewhat in the early morning by the clouds of smog like a filmy chiffon curtain.

We'd sit on our favourite bench under the tall date palm, to meditate and philosophise (I tended to meditate while the Colonel philosophised) and if the wind became too strong we'd shelter behind the stone monument and look out at the changing sea, banded with grey as clouds obscured the sun, the breakers growing bigger and bigger, their crest changing to off-white.

The 'stone monument' behind which Anna and the Colonel shelter on windy days is a pyramid erected in 1820 to commemorate Elizabeth Donkin. This slim stone pyramid, a solid well-proportioned keeper's dwelling and a tall slender lighthouse make a striking picture on the edge of the grassy, palm-dotted tract of land which was proclaimed an open space in perpetuity by Acting Governor Donkin shortly after supervising the landing of British settlers in 1820. Two plaques are embedded on the pyramid. One bears the inscription: 'To the memory of one of the most perfect of human beings who has given her name to the town below'; the other carries a brief account of Elizabeth's birth in England and death in India. The lighthouse was built in 1861 and, although its lamp is no longer lit, it still serves as a beacon to ships, while the keeper's house serves as the home of Port Elizabeth Tourism.

William Selwyn, in a poem too long to quote here, sees these three buildings – the pyramid, the lighthouse and the keeper's lodge – which are such a prominent landmark on the Hill, as a moral lesson about heavenly consolation. Seeing the material world as a reflection of the spiritual is one of his ways of responding to place. Selwyn's 'The Port Elizabeth Pyramid' concludes:

When gloomy night her sable mantle spreads,
And storm-winds fill the seaman's heart with fear,
The lighthouse pours its placid ray, and sheds
A soft effulgence on this tribute dear.
The keeper's cottage, nestling low between
The lighthouse and the sombre monument,

Shares the mild radiance that o'erspreads a scene
Whose light appears with mystic shadows blent.

What sober thought may Faith's clear eye perceive
With Fancy's pictures fair to interweave?
Light from above reveals the rocks and shoals
Whose earth-born flashes shipwreck storm-toss'd souls.
Light from above illumes the smiling home;
Light from above irradiates the tomb;
Light from above with sympathetic glow
O'ergilds the memories of our deepest woe.

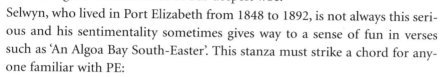

Selwyn, who lived in Port Elizabeth from 1848 to 1892, is not always this serious and his sentimentality sometimes gives way to a sense of fun in verses
such as 'An Algoa Bay South-Easter'. This stanza must strike a chord for anyone familiar with PE:

His chill blast bears tic douloureux,
    The toothache and the mumps,
Rheumatic pains, and all the crew
    Of ills that gender dumps.
Your collar droops, your hat is grimy,
    Your eyes are bleared, your nose is rimy,
Life's loosened harp-strings jar untimely,
    Your hopes are leaden lumps.[7]

After a literary silence of nearly twenty years, 1997 saw a welcome return to
writing of YVONNE BURGESS who, through her novels and short stories,
draws the Port Elizabeth scene vividly and sensitively. The less affluent areas
are her domain: North End, Holland Park, the townships, the Hill. Her characters are apparently unimportant people, often weighed down by the problems of their dreary existences in circumstances not of their own making.

Yvonne Burgess was born in Pretoria in 1936. Her family moved to Port
Elizabeth when she was five years old and, apart from a seven-year sojourn in
Nelspruit (1974 to 1981), she has lived there ever since. Schooling was in PE
and tertiary education at Rhodes University in Grahamstown. A bachelor's
degree in fine art and English, followed by a teaching diploma, led to a very
brief teaching career before Burgess found her real forte: writing. As a freelance journalist, she wrote book reviews and informative articles on art for the
Eastern Province Herald while developing her skills as a writer of fiction.

During the 1970s almost a dozen of her short stories appeared in journals and anthologies, and three novels were published: *A Life to Live* (1973), *The Strike* (1975) and *Say a Little Mantra for Me* (1979), all set in Port Elizabeth. Burgess's life was gravely affected by a personal crisis, but a religious experience in 1974 changed that and brought peace and healing. It also turned her away, for many years, from the writing of fiction.

Anna and the Colonel (1997) marks Burgess's literary revival. It is a mixture of humour and pathos, charting the experiences of two disparate characters in a halfway house (near the Donkin Reserve) between a psychiatric hospital and the outside world. It is a novel that justifies, in both religious and literary terms, this PE writer's return to her craft.

St George's Park

Jean Edmunds

St George's Park is best known as the scene of many an exciting cricket or rugby test; indeed, it can boast of having staged the first test match in South Africa in each of those sports as well as the first international bowls competition in South Africa. The cricket ground and other sports facilities are set in an extensive park, inaugurated in 1861. The park also incorporates a botanical garden with a beautiful Victorian conservatory, a playground, a swimming pool and a tearoom – the tearoom made famous in literature by Athol Fugard.

Also within the park is the outdoor Manville Theatre, where every year a Shakespearian play is staged. Jean Edmunds's poem 'Shakespeare in the Park' was written in anticipation of the 1999 production of *The Tempest*: an appropriate play for a region which has experienced storms of great magnitude and witnessed many a wreck. The poem is a reminder that even here, far from Prospero's magic island, place may be transformed into something 'rich and strange' through the enchantment of poetry and of drama.

JEAN EDMUNDS
Shakespeare in the Park

This corner of a small provincial park,
In a bourgeois town at the bottom of Africa,
Is far, far away from the Forest of Arden and
Many a mile from a wood near Athens ...

It's damp tonight.
The plastic chairs are cold and wet with dew.
I sit, huddled in blankets, while
Reluctant school children,
Unhappy castaways on the coast of culture,
Grumble around me.

Palm trees and shrubs
Loom in the half-light,
And the night is full of noises.
Birds swirl, shrieking, above the grass stage
And – 'Testing, testing!' –
The sound system twitters and burps and falters.

But soon, out of the darkness,
Will come shipwrecked mariners,
A marooned magician, his daughter,
A king's son, a sprite, a monster ...
And a story rich and strange ...

Four hundred years –
And the fabric of this vision
Not quite such an insubstantial pageant
As the author thought,
Bewitches still.

Now, thunder and sudden surf rage!
Cheerly, good hearts!
The actors enter ... and the play begins.

unpublished

JEAN EDMUNDS was born in England but has lived in Port Elizabeth since her early teens. The combination of businesswoman; lover of music, movies and books; mother and grandmother; thinker, dreamer and observer has proved a good recipe for imaginative writing. She writes book reviews and articles for newspapers and magazines. An active member of the Eastern Province Writers' Club and other writers' circles, Edmunds has won many awards within and beyond these organisations for her perceptive and well-crafted poems and short stories. Poems such as 'Shakespeare in the Park' and 'South End' arise from experiences of PE and some of its underlying concerns.

North End

Yvonne Burgess
Dennis Brutus

Yvonne Burgess is the writer most closely connected with North End, and her early novels and short stories frequently invoke this conglomeration of commercial, industrial and residential locales. Burgess has a gift for noticing details that bring a scene alive, and the settings of her fiction are carefully described, often as if on a tour. In this extract from her short story 'If You Swallow You're Dead' we are taken along the route of a funeral procession to the North End cemetery.

> Seven days after Mr Labuschagne's visit the hearse, adorned with four wreaths and followed by two cars, wound its way slowly past the Mercedes Benz showroom.
>
> At Berry's Corner, where the traffic is always heavy, it went through against the red light, and on, past the neat grass verges of the factories, past the General Dealer's, Gents' Tailors and Star of the East Fruit, painted in dry, scratchy, childish strokes on boards nailed to the communal dirty-brown verandas, past the shanties huddled incongruously under the bright new Gold Dollar sign, and on to the cemetery where the prickly pears and headstones are a uniform sooty-grey from the smoke of the shunting trains, where the khaki-coloured trees lean crookedly, their naked boles turned like camels' backs to the wind, where a bedraggled brown donkey, having wandered in through a hole in the fence, was snuffling at the sour scrub for food.

There Alida Slabbert was, as the dominee put it, 'laid to rest'.

In North End dreariness contrasts with brightly painted shop signs and façades; streets are crowded with vehicles battling for a chance to move on to their destinations; and pedestrians are constantly on the move, except when queuing for the minibuses which ply their trade in every direction. The wind still sweeps over the cemetery where, in Burgess's story, Alida is buried far from the Karoo farm where she had hoped to lie with her own people 'on the koppie behind the windbreak'.

In the novel *A Life to Live,* Burgess shows us a North End suburb as Nel tramps through it looking for accommodation:

> With her bag knocking against her knee, Nel walked on. The area, she saw, must once have been a select one for the houses were all large, many of them double-storeyed. They must have belonged to big, wealthy families but now, almost without exception, they had been turned into 'boarding-houses'. Too big for the new owners – who had in any case to make ends meet by letting rooms, which in turn lowered the tone of the neighbourhood – they had fallen into disrepair; their balconies sagged and they needed not only repainting, but plastering as well. They had become hives, warrens, swarming with children, dogs, fleas and flies.
>
> From the board tacked onto its front door Nel saw that the most derelict of all the big houses was called Hall's Annex. Its walls were crumbling alarmingly; its broken window panes were stuffed with newspaper or blacked-out with strips of cardboard. It did not look, Nel decided, too expensive.

Here and there in the North End suburb of Sydenham are old double-storeys converted into the kind of boarding-houses described here, although not all of them are as run down as 'Hall's Annex'. Another suburb, Holland Park, is, today, very much as Burgess describes it in 'And Out of the City', although Cadbury has built a new factory which overshadows the old silo.

> Scholtz lived in Holland Park, in the north of the town, beyond the fruit-canning factory and Cadbury-Fry's tall white silo, where the little houses were squashed up against each other, all alike, with unpainted rough-cast plaster walls and corrugated iron roofs, each on a tiny plot of greyish earth, hemmed in by a dusty myrtle hedge.
>
> On the verge in front of the house, Scholtz kept his 1937 Chevrolet and the bits and pieces of a variety of other old cars which he used for 'spares'. At the back Trixie Scholtz grew a few sticks of rhubarb, some broad-beans and three or four tomato plants. She had also ten scraggy, multicoloured bastard fowls, known as 'kaffir hoenders'. Those 'spares' which Scholtz had considered useless for his immediate purposes, she had used. 'Toiings', their battle-scarred mongrel, slept under the rusting bonnet of an Austin 7, and the fowl 'hok' had been made with two ancient Pontiac mudguards, tied together with netting-wire and string.

Three other writers from Port Elizabeth spent some of their early years in parallel streets in Sydenham: Agnes Sam in Edgar Lane, Arthur Nortje in Short Street and Dennis Brutus in Shell Street. These streets are close to the railway line in an area where most houses have been converted into small business premises and all is hustle and bustle and clutter. Broken glass and bits of discarded junk along the railway line are reminiscent of Brutus's poem 'It was a Sherded World I Entered', which images the fractured lives of many inhabitants of the poet's home town and becomes his 'vision of the world':

> It was a sherded world I entered:
> of broken bottles, rusty tins and split rooftiles:
> the littered earth was full of menace
> with jagged edges waiting the naked feet:
> holes, trenches, ditches were scattered traps
> and the broken land in wasteplots our playing field:
> this was the world through which I learnt the world
> and this the image for my vision of the world.[8]

GELVANDALE AND BETHELSDORP

Dennis Brutus
H Lichtenstein
C I Latrobe
Thomas Pringle

The Jameson Road of Dennis Brutus's poem 'Jameson Road, Gelvandale' leads up a hill to Paterson High, the school where its author was both pupil and teacher, and Arthur Nortje pupil. The poem is similar in thought to Morris's observation of the Korsten lake and the white birds in Athol Fugard's *The Blood Knot*. In spite of the harshness and ugliness which characterise life in what Brutus calls, in a sub-heading to the poem, 'a township ghetto', there are redeeming moments of beauty:

> Suddenly, those asphalt streets
> rain-washed and sun-silvered
> imaged for me the essence of the world:
>
> *there was this harshness, this ugliness*
> *which remained at the bottom a constant*
> *but there were also those instants*
> *of unearned, unexpected beauty*
> *that momentarily redeemed the world.*[9]

Gelvandale does not really deserve the designation 'ghetto', although it was developed in the late 1940s to provide housing for coloured families. There are, in parts, the 'harshness' and 'ugliness' Brutus perceives, but also much in Gelvandale that is attractive. It is situated at the foot and on the slopes of a long line of hills, and it is possible that Brutus's poem 'Daylight', like 'Jameson Road', had its genesis here, for Gelvandale's situation provides views across the saltpans of Bethelsdorp and the sprawling townships of New Brighton to the Swartkops estuary and the distant sea, places towards which our literary journey is leading us.

> The sunlight comes slowly from the hills
> slowly the sunlight drives away the dark
> the grey around the townships
> is softly touched by the light
> slowly the daylight comes.
>
> The day will come
> The light will come
> Peace and joy will come
> Will come at last.[10]

Bethelsdorp, established in 1803 as a London Missionary Society station for the Khoekhoe, is not far from Gelvandale. It was famous – to some, infamous – as a mission and is described in the journals of several early 19th- century visitors who came to this region before the growth of Port Elizabeth. Their perceptions of the place are not without bias.

Henry Lichtenstein, who visited Bethelsdorp in 1803, is very disparaging about the settlement.

> It is scarcely possible to describe the wretched situation in which this establishment appeared to us ... On a wide plain, without a tree, almost without water fit to drink, are scattered forty or fifty little huts in the form of hemispheres, but so low that a man cannot stand upright in them. In the midst is a small clay-hut thatched with straw, which goes by the name of a church, and close by, some smaller huts of the same materials for the missionaries. All are so wretchedly built, and are kept with so little care and attention, that they have a perfectly ruinous appearance.[11]

The Rev. C I Latrobe, visiting in 1816, was equally disparaging about Bethelsdorp's 'external situation'.

> We had been willing to believe, that the very unfavourable accounts, given by travellers of Bethelsdorp, were greatly exaggerated, if not altogether false ... But I am sorry to say, that as to its external situation, nothing can be more miserable and discouraging. Men, therefore, who judge only from outward appearance, are apt to draw inferences to the prejudice of its inhabitants ... Not a tree is to be seen, excepting two or three ragged speckbooms, standing before Mr. Read's house, and scarcely a blade of grass. The hills, enclosing the small kloof near the village, are completely barren, and their outlines tame and uninteresting.[12]

Thomas Pringle rode out to Bethelsdorp within days of his arrival in Algoa Bay with the 1820 Settlers. His romantic expectation of a pastoral scene such as he has left behind in Scotland is deflated by the totally foreign character of the place.

> I came in sight of the village just as the sun was setting. The shadows of the barren hills which rise above it to the westward were falling quietly over the plain. The smoke of the fires just lighted to cook the evening meal of the home-coming herdsmen, was curling calmly in the serene evening air. The bleating of flocks returning to the fold, the lowing of the kine to meet their young, and other pleasant rural sounds, recalling to my recollection all the pastoral associations of a Scottish glen, gave a very agreeable effect to my first view of this missionary village. When I entered the place, however, all associations connected with the rural scenery of Europe were at once dispelled. The groups of woolly-haired, swarthy-complexioned natives, many of them still dressed in the old sheep-skin mantle or *kaross*; the swarms of naked or half-naked children; the wigwam hovels of mud or reeds; the queer-shaped, low thatched church, erected by old Vanderkemp; the long-legged, large-horned cattle; the broad-tailed African sheep, with hair instead of wool; the strange words of the evening salutation (*goeden avond* – 'good evening'), courteously given, as I passed, by old and young; the uncouth clucking sounds of the Hottentot language, spoken by some of them to each other; these, and a hundred other traits of wild and foreign character, made me feel that I was indeed far from the glens of Cheviot, or the pastoral groups of a Scottish hamlet – that I was at length in the Land of the Hottentot.[13]

On a later visit (1825), Pringle did concede that he was 'most agreeably surprised by the amazing improvement which had taken place in the condition of the inhabitants since my former visit' and, as Latrobe warns, it is not always advisable to judge by outward appearances.

Nearby saltpans have proved an economic asset, but poor soil, low rainfall and exposure to wind make Bethelsdorp unsuited to agriculture and the population prone to poverty. Bethelsdorp is, as the travellers recount, situated on a rather barren plateau, but the site has its attractions. Van der Kemp's Kloof, adjacent to the village, offers a pleasant picnic area and hiking trail through indigenous vegetation. The most attractive features of the village are its oldest relic – the mission bell erected in 1815 as well as a long row of almshouses built in 1822 that gives a quaint, old-worldly impression, and the tiny stone cottage behind the church used from early times by visitors and said once to have been occupied by David Livingstone. It needs a Brutus or a Fugard to see the beauty behind the barrenness observed by early travellers.

NEW BRIGHTON

Athol Fugard first put New Brighton on the literary map in the 1960s through the plays he developed with John Kani and Winston Ntshona, which showed outsiders important aspects of township life. For insiders New Brighton is part of the fabric of their lives, its texture often communicated through the stories, poems, drama, music, craft and art that flourish in this part of Port Elizabeth. We shall view it mainly through the eyes of three contemporary writers: Jimmy Matyu, Mzi Mahola and Mxolisi Nyezwa.

Mzi Mahola
Jimmy Matyu
Mxolisi Nyezwa

Established in 1903, New Brighton was the first official municipal black residential area in Port Elizabeth. Since then others have grown from and around it. The oldest part of New Brighton is Red Location, settled before 1910 and now a very poor area. In 1938 McNamee Village was laid out as a model township with well-built houses and good services. Its life is recalled in Jimmy Matyu's book, *Shadows of the Past: Memories of Jabavu Road, New Brighton* (1996). He and his family were moved there from Korsten in the late 1930s.

> On arrival in New Brighton, the resettled Africans were verbally promised, or so it is said, that after fifteen to twenty years the houses would be allocated to them permanently, rent-free. They were told, so the story goes, that by the end of that period, they would have paid in full for the cost of the houses.
>
> But today, and governments have changed, those people who arrived in the late 1930s are still paying rent or what is termed as service charges,

which keep on increasing. The houses are an eyesore, unlike in the past when just before Christmas the Municipality would come around, paint the houses and repair damages to make them look bright for the festive season. And the trees are no longer there.

The second official black township in Port Elizabeth, Kwazakhele, was established in 1956 to accommodate further removals from Korsten. Elundini and Zwide are other offshoots of New Brighton, as well as Kwamagxabi, an elite area. Soweto by the Sea, a shantytown, features in Matyu's story 'Pay-day Murder'.

> Litha Felemntwini was struggling to put on his tattered trousers in the backyard shack rented by his mother in the run-down settlement outside Port Elizabeth, nicknamed Soweto by the Sea. As he peered out of the broken windowpane, he noticed these signs. 'Shit,' he swore as he caught a whiff of the stench coming from the garbage which had collected behind the shack that had been his home for the full eighteen years of his life. He looked older though, with a frightening scar running across his left cheek.

> . . .
>
> Then Felemntwini stepped out of the shack and, taking slow strides, walked towards the bus terminus. It was a hive of activity as hawkers sold everything from pieces of tree bark for muti, to fruit, braaied meat, cooked 'smiley' (goat jaw) and offal, displayed on bare wooden tables, with the flies getting a first taste before the prospective buyers.[14]

The character of Soweto by the Sea has changed in recent years but an idea of conditions in such a place may be gained from more recent informal settlements, such as 'Chris Hani' and 'Cyril Ramaphosa', erected on the site of a refuse dump on the outskirts of New Brighton.

JAMES (JIMMY) TYHILEKILE MATYU was born in Korsten in 1936. Three years later his family was resettled in McNamee Village. Schooling, for Matyu, fostered a love of the English language and a passion for reading. Coupled with a gift for writing which found expression in poems, stories and profiles published in his school magazine, and in letters to the press, these interests led to a career in journalism. Today Matyu is a senior member of the staff of the *Eastern Province Herald* (now *The Herald*), amalgamated at the end of the year 2000 with the *Evening Post*, on which he had worked for over 20 years. He still lives in the New Brighton area, in Kwamagxabi. The manner of this courteous gentleman – affectionately known as Sir James – conceals a tough determination, which has taken him far.

Matyu's early career as a journalist included associations with publications such as the *Golden City Post, Drum, World, Weekend World* and the Xhosa paper *Imvo Zabantsundu*, all of which targeted black readers and fostered black writing, and over his years with the *Evening Post* and now *The Herald* he has covered many topics of interest to black readers. Today, Matyu says, he likes to write for what he calls a mixed audience.

During the years of resistance to apartheid Matyu was often the only reporter covering political activities in PE's townships. In 1976 – the year of student protests – he was the BBC's correspondent in New Brighton. Many of his assignments fulfilled his desire to fight apartheid with the pen and, as he does this, his pen often creates a strong sense of the place and the community from which he springs.

Matyu regards as highlights of his career the inclusion of his short story 'Pay-day Murder' in the anthology *Crossing Over: New Writing for a New South Africa*, and the publication of his memoir, *Shadows of the Past: Memories of Jabavu Road, New Brighton*, in 1995 and 1996 respectively. In both the fictional and the autobiographical work, New Brighton is brought to life: its neighbourliness; its colourful characters; its joys and sorrows; its frustrations and its violence.

Mzi Mahola lives in Zwide, where he owns and runs a spaza shop – attached to his home – where customers gather to buy bread and sugar, fresh fruit and soft drinks, sweets, coffee, tea and other daily requirements. Few of them know that their shopkeeper was once the South African amateur bantamweight champion and that behind his smiling face and sparkling eyes there is a man of deep thought who has expressed many of his concerns about the past, the present and the future of his people and his country through deceptively simple verse, which has been published in two collections: *Strange Things* (1994) and *When Rains Come* (2000).

Born in 1949 in Durban where his father – from the Eastern Cape – was in government service, Mzikayise (or Winston, as his parents called him) was sent to live with his paternal grandmother at Lushington in the Amatola basin between Alice and Hogsback. When he was twelve years old his parents were transferred to Port Elizabeth and he went to live with them in New Brighton. Apart from intervals at school and college – Lovedale and Healdtown – near his old haunts, an interrupted spell at Fort Hare University and a period in Lesotho for Umkhonto weSizwe training, Mahola has remained in PE. He worked for a while as an education officer at the Port Elizabeth Museum, where he was active in educating children about the need to protect wildlife, often teaching them through the telling of traditional stories.

Wishing to continue his interrupted education, Mahola enrolled in 1997 at Vista University's Port Elizabeth campus and, in 1999, completed a BA Honours degree with a special focus on the poetry of Tatamkhulu Afrika. Now he is back running 'Siyacamile', his spaza shop, with the help of his family. Despite long hours, he finds time to participate in a writers' group, to attend workshops and to encourage young people to develop writing skills. One of his painful memories is the confiscation, by the apartheid security police, of all his early poetry, of which he had no copy. It silenced him as a writer for nearly eleven years. Now his pen is always busy.

Mahola is a man of the city, which he knows intimately and where he has lived for 40 years, yet his roots are rural: it is the topography of his childhood home in the vicinity of Hogsback that is most clearly evoked in his poetry, as we shall see later. The poet regrets the loss of a traditional way of life and the wisdom it offers and would like to see tradition restored but knows that, in many respects, it is irretrievable because of Western influences and the effects of years of oppression.

> The nation is silent now
> There's nothing more to say.
> With bowed heads
> Let us lament our shame,
> Fly flags at half-mast.
> We've bartered our manhood,
> Our pride,
> For values of the West.
> Paralysed our dreams.[15]

As here, most of Mahola's city poems deal more with people and ideas than with place but they need to be read in the context of New Brighton. Short poems, on the other hand, such as 'Dying in the Sun', 'He Came down the Street' and 'The Same Procession' provide glimpses of life in township streets and reveal something of the compassion for suffering individuals and the tenderness towards family, friends and ordinary people that offsets the anger and sorrow Mahola's poetry often conveys.

MZI MAHOLA
Dying in the Sun

A man bends in a murky trench
And searches through the rotten rubbish.
He picks and shakes a floppy orange,
Peels and stealthily swallows a portion,
Throws down the rest.
Then loiters up the road:
A luckless prostitute.

Next his gaze beams
On a rubbish bin
Nailed to a pole,
But after a few ruffles
Zigzags down the road
Out of sight
Except from my life.

I, who can see
The bony grip of hunger
Forcing him into a ditch
To grovel in filth,
To learn the habits
Of neglected scum,
And lose himself with this lot:
The defeated bastards
Who also braved the fire-spitting beast
And now strain under sprained backs
And broken shoulders.

from When Rains Come

MZI MAHOLA
He Came down the Street

He came down the street
In one hand
Holding a live chicken
By its wings,
In the other
A packet of onions
And potatoes.

from When Rains Come

MZI MAHOLA
The Same Procession

He looked up the street
And saw a procession.

Scratching his beard
He went inside the house
For a camera.

When he came out
And focused on the target,
Through the eye of the camera
He saw the same procession.

from When Rains Come

The streets of New Brighton are the focus of much of its life and they often feature in its literature – from Mzi Mahola's descriptions of people and events in its streets to Nyezwa's references to them as places of pain and Matyu's lively evocation of a bus terminus in 'Pay-day Murder'. Shops such as the photo studio in Fugard's play *Sizwe Bansi is Dead*, beauty salons, shebeens and spaza shops as well as sophisticated commercial centres alongside informal trading areas indicate enterprise and industry. On the darker side, there is a tsotsi subculture (to which Felemntwini in 'Pay-day Murder' belongs) which is often involved in violence and crime and, despite the vibrancy of some aspects of township life, there is evidence of a great pool of suffering such as the poet Mxolisi Nyezwa describes.

MXOLISI NYEZWA
I cannot think of all the pains

i cannot think of all the pains in men's breasts
without the urge to sleep, or to lie down, i cannot think
without seeing God's face in the child's smile,
or in the lonely cry in the night and in the sea.

i cannot think of all the pains that have come
and gone, pains in men's waists
and in men's shoes –
i cannot have relief proper, wearing a neat tie.

i run around in circles, like sprinkling water,
i can't have true relief, swearing out loud
and counting out the pains in my breast,
and in my pants.

i cannot think of all the pains and the years wasted,
all the craze of lonely men in village rooms,
and all the bodies that lie out cold, in avoided streets –
i can't run out old, like a joyful child

and watch a sky pregnant with pain, or with turbulent rain,
i cannot think of the soil without lying down,
i cannot think of tears, lonely geographies
and the third world, without the urge to cry or to sit down.

from song trials

Poems by Nyezwa had been appearing in journals and anthologies for some years, but the publication in 2000 of his collection, *song trials*, brought a new poetic voice firmly into our literature.

MXOLISI NYEZWA was born in New Brighton in 1967 and still lives there. He edits *Kotaz*, a quarterly township arts publication devoted to contemporary South African writing, and is involved in organisations and informal groups which encourage the arts. Of poetry, Nyezwa writes:

> We don't read and write poetry to protect particular views about the world. The world of literature is a vast sea that all of [us] have to swim in to cleanse us of our sins. The world still welcomes the artist's creativity, which it has correctly identified as one of the few constant factors in our ever-changing times.[16]

At the same time, Nyezwa regards poetry as an important channel for expressing not only the spirit of an individual, but also that of a time and place and people. 'Poetry', he writes, 'works against society to uncover truths and hear for the first time the voice of God.'[17] He believes that readers need to familiarise themselves with a writer's circumstances and traditions – 'for it is only from these that true artists derive their creative insight'[18] – and he feels a sense of failure that poets have not always spoken out about the sufferings of their circumstances: 'we had words in us that we never said'.[19] A sense of the suffering of his people certainly permeates Nyezwa's own poetry and is inextricably bound up with the circumstances of New Brighton and places like it.

In *song trials* specific places are mentioned only occasionally: Motherwell ('a weary township in PE / where logic has been doomed'); Zwide ('today in the streets of Zwide / i make it clear to the words of my pain'); New Brighton ('i once sat in a street in New Brighton / and watched the mulberry leaves sway in the wind'). They are points of reference not portrayed in any detail, yet overall Nyezwa's poems create an awareness of the milieu of PE's townships. At the same time, place is connected to everything else. There is a gathering of the exterior world into the self – 'the fruits of the universe in my hands' – and the self is incorporated into that world physically and emotionally:

> and i feel the full terror of sunlight in my eyes
> i feel the implacable destiny of pain
> lying like sand-roses on a floor ...[20]

There is beauty in the midst of suffering; there is sadness and anger; there is a despondency which stops just short of despair and, for all its philosophical depth, Nyezwa's is a poetry of the heart:

and it is plain, it is our heart that touches
tenderly the melodies from the moon and from the stars.[21]

Poetry, he suggests, can be healing. It is also humbling. In a review of an oral
poetry exhibition and performance festival, Nyezwa writes:

> I believe poetry above everything else should teach us to be humble.
> Humble in the sense that we are ushered into the unpretentious lives of
> others and we begin to be aware of the various things that connect them
> to earth, in their intensity.[22]

The works of Matyu, Mahola and Nyezwa usher readers 'into the unpreten-
tious lives of others' and into the environment in which they live. Entering
into the world of PE townships, whether through literature or physically, is
indeed – particularly for outsiders – a humbling experience.

THE SWARTKOPS ESTUARY AND BLUEWATER BAY

The poet Hugh Finn has chosen Amsterdamhoek as the setting for his
poem 'The Sun-Bathers'; fiction writer Agnes Sam has chosen Bluewater Bay
beach for the setting of her story 'Nana and Devi'; and playwright Athol
Fugard, the bleak mudflats of the Swartkops estuary for his play *Boesman and
Lena*. Brian Walter favours the broad Swartkops scene for a series of nine
reflective poems entitled 'Swartkops', and Thomas Baines composes a picture
from a vantage point above the river. These writers, representing different
experiences and views of life, have selected features from within the same
range of the Port Elizabeth landscape and used them for artistic purposes.
Through them they also explore, in quite different contexts, their sense of
identity and of belonging.

Hugh Finn
Athol Fugard
Brian Walter
Agnes Sam
Thomas Baines

Picturesque Amsterdamhoek – a row of houses along a narrow road at the
base of the steep east bank of the Swartkops estuary – suggests a place of affluence and leisure. Here recreational boating, birding and fishing are popular
and, although there are permanent residents, Amsterdamhoek has a holiday
atmosphere. Hugh Finn wrote 'The Sun-Bathers' about a 1950s holiday visit
to the home of his childhood and youth. In a poem that is full of colour, light
and movement, he evokes the more beautiful aspects of this locale. The careful drawing of the six cormorants bathing, like the poet, in the sun completes
the picture of ease and contentment and provides the missing sense of home
the poet is seeking.

HUGH FINN
The Sun-Bathers
Amsterdam Hoek, Cape Province

Blue, impossibly-blue above me,
The sky of my home,
As I drifted past the sand-bank in the river in my boat,
Sun-bathing;
Steel-blue-hot for the fire of the sun behind it,
And that sky lensing the sun
To the burning-glass brilliance of an African sea-summer;
And all around me, as always,
The miles of reeds on the black, sulphurous mud-banks,
Now green, now gold, as the light south-easter smoothed them,
With the blue alchemy of summer
To turn them to aquamarine in the silken distance;
And, with its delicate salt lapping and lulling of ripples,
The same slow, warm river between the green;
And beyond the hill with its aromatic sea-bushes
And one lonely grey-green aloe exclaiming the sky-line,
The gentle remembered roar of the Indian Ocean,
Its mile-long brilliance of breakers sun-white on the beach,
Its green holiday-thunder the same as ever ...
Home was nearly home for me, nearly, nearly,
As I basked in the welcoming sun ...
Yet a touch was missing, some colour of memory ...

And then in the midst of the splendour,
Not twenty yards away as I drifted by,
With drops from the shipped oars
Ticking my way through time and that sun-bright water,
There, I say,
Sedate on the brown sand-bank as if they owned it,
Six black cormorants,
Sun-bathing too ...

There they dozed, sun-blissful,
Lean black bodies iridescent with that watered-silk oily gleam
Of fish-fed feathers;

Each clumsy, black-webbed foot
Loaded into the sand
By the crop's crammed apotheosis
Of mullet;
Each long dark drowsy head
Loaded down to the shoulders
By a silver weight of dreams –
Glazing the dim, dyspeptic sun-lulled eyes –
Dreams of the luscious silvery darting
Of still more
Fish ...

And as I watched them, smiling,
And they, blissful, regarded me –
All of us linked in a brotherhood of basking sunlight
Like flies immortal in the same vast airy amber –
The fluid memories crystallized
Into home –
In those six black strokes of the bright remembering brush
On the waiting world
A whole sea-enchanted childhood blossomed again.

from The Sunbathers

On the other side of the Swartkops River, directly opposite Amsterdamhoek, are the extensive mudflats where, as we have seen, Fugard places Boesman and Lena digging – as many do to this day – for mudprawns to sell as bait to fishermen. Lena's is a much more desperate search for a sense of home.

A series of nine poems by Brian Walter under the general title 'Swartkops' was published in the March 1998 edition of *New Contrast* and incorporated in Walter's 1999 collection, *Tracks*. Only the first poem in the sequence is reproduced here, but ideally they should be read as a group. Each poem reflects on the sights, sounds and smells of a scene from the past and events associated with it, and together they present a broad canvas encompassing the whole Swartkops estuary. Interwoven with the poet's memories of fishing, birdwatching or picnicking with his family are images of mudflats and flood plains, sedgefields and islets. There are birds, particularly gulls; there are mudprawns and grunters; and there are distant views of the Swartkoppen in one direction and St Croix Island in the other, with Port Elizabeth laid out along the margins of the Bay, demonstrating all the divisions of its society. And within the Swartkops scene itself, contrasting with the natural, is the industrial: the power station and pipeline, the old steel-girded bridge and the railroad. Boesman and Lena are remembered, as well as the murdered Matthew Goniwe and his friends. The poet seeks identity for himself and his society in 'iBhayi's nether world'.

BRIAN WALTER
Swartkops
i. Looking back on a Walk with my Father

With care I chose companion and route, and
we walked from the rod club across the flats,
past the sewage works, to where the flood plains
lay hurt by pipe-line and pumping station,

for beneath the mud of iBhayi's nether world,
of Swartkops, New Brighton and Salt Lake,
my verse crawls in its own dark shell,
wafts in the smell of saltwind and riverweed
and shrieks in the cry of wader and gull.

These are the sedged flood flats of Fugard
and Lena. Once, when I came here to watch birds,
some woman waded fifty yards, shin deep,
to sell me prawns for bait: 'Ek vang'ie vis'ie,'
I said, then watched as, with muddy skirt held
with her free hand to a woman-dark shank,
she waded slowly to where, on the far bank,
she had left a silent companion to wait.

There was that in me that went with her,
and looked back to see a birdwatcher stand
like a fool, binoculars in hand. These salt
flats can fix those frail shapes of humanity
we hold most dear: the salt-flesh of heart,
an underfoot of mud, breath-lapped waters
that in their tides wash everything apart.

So I stood, empty on the sedge-field,
my prying eye-piece blank in hand,
with a vision of a woman ferrying my soul
from me, wading to the dead land
of her windswept Saturday afternoon.

Now, let me confess that I wanted to walk
here again to fish out that muse of a woman.
Of course, there's always some catch. I found
no living verse on this pilgrimage. But her old
memory shone like a barbel, river dark,
as we walked from the rod club across the mud
to the pipe-lines, and then looked back
over the flats, out beyond the power station,
to where men mine their barren salt works.

from Tracks

Just beyond Amsterdamhoek is the suburb of Bluewater Bay, which appears rather bleak to passersby. It is almost devoid of trees, and most properties are enclosed by concrete or brick walls, but it has its attractions, particularly its undulating beach and views across the waters of Algoa Bay. Before 'whites only' regulations were imposed, Agnes Sam had often visited this beach, on which she sets her story 'Nana and Devi'.

Devi was now grey haired, but the water at Blue Waters Bay was still that brilliant, inky blue; the sun still scintillated off its surface the way it, and they, had danced about when they were girls, from one end of the beach to where the eye could barely see, on sand that still had that buff coloured, dry look. The sand dunes still surreptitiously changed shape before her eyes, forming restful, pleasing contours. Nothing changed, only she. Everything intact as she left it, but for broken sea shells, even up here on the path around the rondavel. They felt brittle and sharp underfoot. And to ageing eyes trying to avoid them, it was like looking for faded jewels in one's past.

In this idyllic setting, which Nana and Devi had enjoyed as teenagers 'before it had been declared white', the friends meet after a fifteen-year separation. A tragic situation is gradually revealed and Devi learns the truth of her relationship with Nana. Looking for 'faded jewels' in her past, she finds only broken sea shells, 'brittle and sharp underfoot'. The return to Blue Waters Bay is not the homecoming she has visualised; indeed, it had never been home, but a snatched 'picnic' in a world in which migrant women like herself were not allowed to belong and self-identity was difficult.

AGNES SAM was born in Port Elizabeth in 1942 and grew up in a house in Edgar Lane, Sydenham, not far from the family business. After attending a Roman Catholic school in Port Elizabeth, Sam left South Africa to study first at Roma University in Lesotho and then in Zimbabwe. A brief period of teaching in Zambia was followed by twenty years of self-exile in York, England. She returned to the Eastern Cape only in 1993. In spite of this long separation from the place she regards as home, almost all the stories in Agnes Sam's collection, *Jesus is Indian and Other Stories* (1989), have their roots in Port Elizabeth.

Short stories by Sam reveal a lightness of touch and an ability to portray ordinary characters in everyday situations. There is, however, pain, often the pain of living within an alien society or of being misunderstood or excluded while longing for recognition. Sam became conscious of the ways in which the history of Indians in South Africa had been suppressed when she learned that her great-grandfather had come to the country as an indentured labourer on the sugar plantations of Natal; she had never been taught at school about such indentures. This background and the separation of peoples brought about by the policy of apartheid cast their shadows over her work, yet it is sad rather than gloomy or bitter; and the resilience of women living as migrants offers hope for the triumph of bonds of affection over the harsher bonds of a suppressive society.

Above the cliff between Bluewater Bay and Amsterdamhoek stands an unusually shaped Second World War observation post, evidence of the commanding view of Algoa Bay which Thomas Baines – from a point a little further inland – observed on 2 March 1848:

> We crossed the Zwartkops River the next day, and, on reaching the top of the hill on the farther side, the beauty of the prospect, bounded in the distance by the swelling ocean with the waves of Algoa Bay whitening under the effect of a south-easter, the broad river winding beneath me, and the magnificent aloes and wild flowers beside the road, tempted me to stay awhile to sketch it.[23]

The view becomes, on the pages of Baines's journal, a carefully composed picture; he also sketches the scene, which is later reworked on canvas to become one of the highly prized works of art for which Thomas Baines is famous.

THOMAS BAINES was born in 1820 in King's Lynn, Norfolk, where instead of following the family occupation of seafaring, he trained as a decorative artist. In 1842 he sailed for Cape Town and in 1848 moved on to Algoa Bay. Between February 1848 and June 1853 Baines travelled extensively through the Eastern Cape from his headquarters in Grahamstown, first with an expedition travelling northward through the mountains of the Eastern Cape midlands as far as the Orange River and returning via the Karoo, and later on a 'solitary journey', heading east towards East London and just beyond. Between these expeditions were shorter sorties into the interior and, during 1851 and 1852, Baines acted as 'war artist', recording some of the battles that were being fought in the Amatola region. He therefore covered much of the territory of our Eastern Cape tours, and many of the features we shall encounter are recorded with a painterly eye in Baines's *Journal of Residence in Africa, 1842–1853*, reprinted in the 1960s by the Van Riebeeck Society.

Baines left the Eastern Cape in 1853 but, after five years spent in Britain and in Australia, he returned to Africa to explore and paint territory as far north as the Victoria Falls; and some of the experiences of this era are also recorded in journal form. He died in Durban in 1875. His tomb bears the inscription 'He was a man to whom the wilderness brought gladness and the mountains peace.' As a word artist and painter, Thomas Baines has himself brought gladness to generations of lovers of the African scene.

As in his description of the Swartkops scene, the observations Baines records include the general and the particular. Everywhere he travels Baines notices plants and flowers. Aloes are often remarked upon, as are those other icons of the region – euphorbia. In Howieson's Poort, adjacent to what is now the Thomas Baines Nature Reserve near Grahamstown, he observes not only aloes and euphorbia, but also mesembryanthemums, arum lilies, proteas and the 'splendid flowers' of oldenburghia; in the Kat River region there are sparaxis 'bending with their weight their slender reedy stems into a delicate and graceful curve'; and in the Winterberg he is intrigued by the cycads. Fauna as well as flora, San paintings, and the people encountered on his journeys are depicted in words and paint against the landscape to which they belong. It is a landscape Baines interprets as a wild, romantic place, apart from himself.

As we tour the rest of the Eastern Cape we shall not be able to stop and admire every scene recorded by Baines, but it will be worth following his example of observing both the detailed foreground and the distant vista as we encounter further literary interpretations of the province.

3   WILDERNESS

AND CULTIVATION

THE SUNDAYS RIVER VALLEY

ADDO PARK AND THE ZUURBERG

Exploration of an area north of Port Elizabeth and the rest of the Nelson Mandela Metropole takes us around a district associated with Sir Percy FitzPatrick, renowned author of *Jock of the Bushveld*, on a route that includes his farm Amanzi and a meander along the valley of the Sundays River taking in the FitzPatrick Library at Addo and 'The Lookout' where Sir Percy and his family are buried. We then visit the Addo Elephant Park and, after calling in at the old mission station of Enon, cross the Zuurberg (or Suurberg). In the works that accompany us wilderness and wildlife, rural quiet and agricultural development are contemplated by authors who span some 200 years.

FitzPatrick country

SIR PERCY FITZPATRICK'S fame as a writer resides in *Jock of the Bushveld*. Although this South African classic is not set in the Eastern Cape, its author can be claimed for the province as he was born (in 1862) in King William's Town, received some of his schooling at St Aidan's College in Grahamstown, and was associated with the Coega and Sundays River valleys for the last eighteen years of his life. During that time, he made a major contribution to the economy and development of the region through his promotion of the citrus industry and of land settlement in the Sundays River Valley.

Sir Percy FitzPatrick

The farm Amanzi, which was owned by Sir Percy FitzPatrick from 1913 and is still occupied and worked by his descendants, lies on the Coega River in a valley that parallels that of the Sundays. Literary pilgrims to this family home (which may be visited only by arrangement) discover that Sir Percy's spirit permeates farm and homestead and that his family preserves many tales of their charismatic forefather. In a letter to his son Nugent dated 28 October 1913,[1] Fitzpatrick writes:

> The farm itself is a beautiful spot – all the hills around covered with the dense many-coloured scrub & mimosa of the Addo bush – which you must remember of old. The valley was just as densely overgrown a few years ago when a man named Magennis groped his way through the thorns & prickly pears & thought he discovered something that made it worthwhile to pledge all he had & buy 8 000 acres of the most awful tangled bush you ever saw – with only one little spring on it. What he thought he saw was geological peculiarities that indicated subterranean water.

The main house on Amanzi, the Homestead, became the FitzPatricks' home in 1920 and is where Sir Percy died in 1931. It is a gracious house, fronted by a wide veranda with an outlook in which its owner delighted:

> Viewed from the house with the setting sun slanting across the fields, groves, bush & river, one gets a picture which I don't think can be equalled in the Union.[2]

Family portraits and Edward Caldwell's original marginal drawings and paintings for *Jock of the Bushveld* adorn the Homestead's walls. Some of the bronzes of various scenes from the book which were cast to commemorate the centenary of its hero – the dog, Jock – are also reminders that this was the home of the writer of one of South Africa's best-known books.

Lady FitzPatrick suggested the name, *Amanzi* (Zulu and Xhosa for water), because the outstanding feature of the farm was the abundance of underground water. Sir Percy was intrigued from the start by what he called the 'craters', both as sources of water and evidence of Stone Age occupation of the land, and he describes them graphically in his only written responses to this place: his letters and the booklet *Amanzi: A Personal Record of the First Decade.*

> There seemed to be something of a challenge in the place, and it passed through many hands. There was a secret and a fascination in the mysterious 'craters' that appealed to the adventurous. The rugged ironstone throats, choked with treacherous black mud or with blue and yellow clays, whence came the ooze and the hot mineral springs and the faint smell of sulphur, might lead anywhere and mean anything ...
>
> The old history is not written in books or told by word of mouth. It is recorded in the stones, but in a form which cannot certainly be interpreted ...
>
> The material contained in these old craters was a kind of mud. The dried crust crumbled to dust; the layer below that was black mud of a most adhesive nature – almost gluey – which absorbed moisture readily from the lightest of rains and retained it for months. Below that again was pure white sand of extreme fineness and almost as fluid as quicksand. These excavations were not more than 10 to 12 feet in depth, and throughout that mass there was no evidence of any stone or gravel from the adjacent formation. Nevertheless, as soon as the work began, odd stones of a flinty character, quite different from any found either in the

regular formation or loose on the surface of the hill, began to turn up. Some had been untouched, but nearly all had been split or chipped for the purpose of making stone implements ...

The craters have been covered over by irrigation machinery but the springs on Amanzi remain an excellent source of water, and Stone Age implements are still found on the farm. At times the faint smell of sulphur can be detected and water gushing along a furrow near the Homestead from 'The Hill of Waters' leaves a distinctly yellow deposit. Another feature of Amanzi that FitzPatrick describes in his booklet is the 'Castle':

> The most striking feature of 'Balmoral', the name by which the Amanzi Estate was then (1913) known, was the 'Castle'. It was a miniature copy of a portion of Balmoral Castle ... But in truth, this 'castle' was a very small and a rather ludicrous single-storey affair of mud-bricks and plaster. The Gothic doors and windows and the courtyard, the towers, turrets and embattlements were but bare suggestions. The building was nowhere more than 20 feet high; the rooms were small and hopelessly unsuited for use.

A use has been found for what remains of this edifice: it is now Amanzi's farm office. Near it hangs the bell from the Pretoria prison in which FitzPatrick was incarcerated after the Jameson Raid: a reminder of the political side of his personality, and of an era in South Africa's history recorded in one of his many non-fiction works: *The Transvaal from Within* (1899).

On the outskirts of the small town of Addo, about 30 km from Amanzi, stands the FitzPatrick Library, where a plaque announces that it was 'built in 1959 in honoured memory of Sir Percy FitzPatrick, KCMG, who devoted much of his life and substance to the development of the Sundays River Valley.' It was just before the First World War that FitzPatrick bought Amanzi and invested in a scheme to develop the nearby Sundays River Valley. From then on his promotion of land settlement for English immigrants, and of the citrus industry and irrigation schemes which would help them to flourish, absorbed the interest of a man who never did anything by halves.

The road to Kirkwood – the valley's main centre – passes a turn-off about 10 km from Addo, where a short footpath leads to the Lookout, from which one may view part of the valley of the Sundays River. The widespread pattern of lucerne and vegetable fields, citrus orchards and irrigation canals that meets the eye is evidence of a thriving agricultural industry,

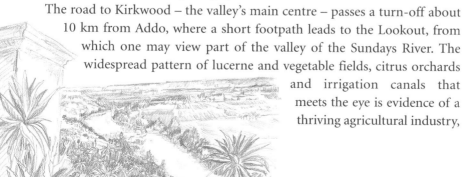

to which Sir Percy made an important contribution. The site of the Lookout was purchased by FitzPatrick in 1915 and on it he built a structure of 'the stone of the country', which he surrounded with aloes and other indigenous plants. There the famous author, politician and agricultural developer is buried beside his wife and near his sons Oliver and Alan, while a plaque commemorates his eldest son, Nugent.

ADDO ELEPHANT PARK

Bruce Hewett
Beth Dickerson
William Selwyn

The literature of the Eastern Cape – from early myths to contemporary poems – often features the wildlife once found here, as travellers record in their journals, in great abundance. Gradually, with the increase of settled agriculture, and the popularity of hunting for gain and for sport, animal numbers were drastically diminished, and several species wiped out. Today the preservation and sometimes reintroduction of game in parks large and small are becoming a major feature of the province. One such reserve is the Addo Elephant Park, which has an interesting history and has evoked some thought-provoking poems.

Some threatened creatures of the region managed to survive by retreating into the least accessible parts of bush and forest, among them the elephants of the Addo district. Determined efforts were made to exterminate them because they were seen as a threat to agriculture and to human life but, in 1931, with only eleven elephant remaining, a national park for their protection was declared – the Addo Elephant Park – and now the herd has grown to well over 300. New territory has been incorporated into Addo and progress is being made to link it up with the Zuurberg section of the park and the Woody Cape Reserve on the coast. Eventually a park stretching from the fringes of the Karoo to the sea will become one of the world's most biologically diverse reserves for fauna and flora.

The Addo Park abounds with the favourite food of elephants – the spekboom – and provides them with ample opportunity to wander at will, safe from their former enemies, who are now their protectors. Usually in family groups, they may be found browsing; trundling through the bush; protecting themselves against parasites in orgies of dust-throwing; or, at waterholes, wallowing in mud, showering themselves and drinking in their inimitable way. Sometimes they vanish mysteriously into Addo's dense entanglement of thorn and thicket, creeper and succulent or emerge equally mysteriously from the mist. To a poet they may be larger in their implications than themselves.

Bruce Hewett
Elephants in the Addo Mist

Amidst great gusts of mist
that absorb the details
of smaller game
the massive Truth appears.
We behold elephants
on the threshold
of unapproachable worlds
of consciousness.
Elephants
whose thick skinned presence
confirms all possibility
of improbable miracles.
They trumpet their verities
against our disbelief.
They disappear
from our astonished gaze
and wonder spreads the word
across the veld.

from Song with Silent Music

Elephants are not the only attraction of the park, which is inhabited by dozens of other species of bird, insect and beast including the black rhinoceros. FitzPatrick records that the last bull rhinoceros to be killed in the Eastern Cape was shot in 1858 on what became Amanzi.

An endangered species of flightless dungbeetle, *Circellium bacchus*, has one of its last strongholds in the Addo Park. It is protected because of its important ecological function in the recycling of the earth's nutrients. Because the dung which these beetles form into brood-balls or food-balls and carry off into the bush, is often found on the roads, their existence is threatened by vehicles. Drivers are, therefore, requested to avoid riding over mounds of dung. Hence,

one of the world's most unusual traffic signs is encountered in the park – a warning sign depicting a dung beetle! Watching these busy little creatures at work is a fascinating pastime. They have inspired more than one poet and also have an intriguing literary association with Sir Percy FitzPatrick. Early editions of *Jock of the Bushveld* are collectors' pieces because one of Caldwell's marginal drawings pictures a beetle pushing its ball of dung with its front feet. Later editions were corrected, for it is far more usual for the back feet to be used.

BETH DICKERSON
Dungbeetle

Ambition has defeated you:
not content with rolling dung
to golf-ball size – provender enough
for your small progeny –
you made instead a ball
to fill our human hands.

Now you strive, an insect Sisyphus,
to roll it up the slope.
But when you reach the crest,
repeatedly the balance tips
and down it rolls again,
sometimes oversetting you.
You flail to right yourself;
then once more set your hindlegs to the task.

It seems beyond your strength.

Yet, for all I know,
when we are on our way,
no longer here to see,
persistence may well win the day.

I hope it may be so –
a fitting tribute for your kind
here where the signboards say:
DUNGBEETLES HAVE RIGHT OF WAY!

ENON AND THE ZUURBERG

Thomas Pringle came to the Cape as leader of the Scottish party of British settlers of 1820, which was allocated land in the valley of the Baviaans River near present-day Bedford. More details about his life and his literary links with the Eastern Cape will be provided when we journey through that region.

Thomas Pringle
C I Latrobe

Soon after Pringle arrived he began travelling round the country, familiarising himself with the people and the landscapes of the colony and, in 1821, he undertook an expedition through the Zuurberg to visit the Moravian mission station of Enon. Pringle records in his *Narrative of a Residence in South Africa* (1834), which was republished in 1970 as *Thomas Pringle in South Africa* – the edition quoted here – that he had brought with him from England, and forwarded to the missionaries at Enon, 'some packages of books, and a letter of introduction from the Rev. Mr Latrobe, the superintendent of their society's missions, who is favourably known to the public as the author of a volume of Travels in this colony'. Both Latrobe's *Journal of a Visit to South Africa in 1815 and 1816* and his own *Narrative* show how deeply these two writers were impressed by the site of the mission chosen in 1816 by Latrobe.

THE REV. CHRISTIAN IGNATIUS LATROBE was born in England in 1758 and he died in 1836. His father was English, of Huguenot descent; his mother American, of part English, part German descent. They belonged to a Christian sect of German origin: the Moravians, or, as they were called in Britain, the United Brethren and, in accordance with Moravian practice, Christian was educated in Germany. In 1815 the Brethren sent Latrobe out to inspect their two established mission stations near Cape Town and to seek a site for a new one nearer to the colony's frontier.

Frank R Bradlow, in his introduction to the 1969 facsimile edition of Latrobe's *Journal of a Visit to South Africa*, writes:

> From the moment Latrobe set foot in Cape Town on the 24th December 1815 he recorded in his *Journal* with meticulous care, objective comment, and tolerant kindness, his detailed observations of the people he met, the places he visited, and the nature of the country, as well as 'the wonders of God's creation spread around him'.

Latrobe certainly took a keen interest in his surroundings, particularly in the geology of the countryside through which he travelled, and his marked gift for descriptive writing as well as for drawing makes his illustrated narrative one of the best of its kind. Perhaps his admiration for the scenery influenced his choice of Enon for the new station:

But much as we were pleased, and almost enchanted, with the beauty of the glen, Brother Schmitt at first objected to its narrow width, which indeed, on entering, appeared little more than a few hundred yards, till we had penetrated about a quarter of an English mile into it, when it spread considerably, the hills receding on both sides. To the left, they are high, and full of kloofs, containing large timber. A range of lower eminences lies at their foot; having, as we were informed, plenty of good pasturage upon them. To the right, the hills are lower, but more interesting in their appearance. Their tops are covered with bushes, the lower region steep, and, in many places, supported, as it were, by rocks of a deep red colour. These rocks are concrete masses of pebbles and clay, strongly impregnated with iron. The colour of some of them approaches even to pink or lake, with white or yellow veins. At every turn, the outline of the hills varies, presenting some picturesque scenery.[3]

Pringle was equally enthusiastic about the locale:

The whole length of the vale [of the White River] may be altogether, probably, about ten or twelve miles, from the spot where the little river abruptly emerges from the recesses of the mountains to where it joins the Sundays River. The scenery of the upper part of the dell is very picturesque. Accompanying the course of the stream, as it meanders through the meadows, you have, on the right, lofty hills covered with woods of evergreens, and broken by *kloofs*, or subsidiary dells, filled with large forest-timber. On the left the hills are lower, but also covered with copsewood, and in many places diversified by rocks and cliffs of deep red and other lively colours. The valley, winding among those woody heights, spreads out occasionally to a considerable breadth; and then again the converging hills appear to close it in entirely with huge masses of rock and forest. At every turn the outline of the hills varies, presenting new points of picturesque scenery.[4]

He was also impressed by the settlement for Khoekhoe converts as he observed it three years after its inception:

The appearance of the whole place was neat, orderly and demure. There was no hurried bustle, no noisy activity, even in the missionary workshops, though industry plied there its regular and cheerful task; but a sort of pleasing pastoral quiet seemed to reign throughout the settlement, and brood over the secluded valley.[5]

Some of the same sense of order and tranquillity that Pringle describes has persisted in Enon despite the many difficulties with which it has had to contend since its establishment in 1818. The original *pastorie*, workshops and double row of little houses along the village's main street have survived, although in a somewhat dilapidated state, and the general view of the station, nestling at the foot of the Zuurberg in a wide plain on the banks of the Witte River, must be very much as it was in the 19th century. The church, dedicated in 1821, standing red-roofed and whitewashed in neatly kept gardens, is the oldest church building in the Eastern Cape still used for services. Inside, walls and ceilings and almost all furnishings are, in accordance with Moravian tradition, white, symbolising unity. There is a beautiful simplicity and sense of worship and care about Enon in spite of the obvious poverty of this remote spot, where there is little to sustain an adequate economy.

To reach Enon from the Baviaans River settlement Pringle had to cross the Zuurberg, where the scenery 'far surpassed anything of the kind I had either witnessed elsewhere, or formed a conception of from the description of others'. The chapter on the Zuurberg expedition in the *Narrative* is adorned with several passages that, like this, resemble grandiose landscape paintings.

> On the left, a billowy chaos of naked mountains, rocks, precipices, and yawning abysses, that looked as if hurled together by some prodigious convulsion of nature, appalled and bewildered the imagination. It seemed as if this congeries of gigantic crags, or rather the eternal hills themselves, had been tumultuously uptorn and heaved together, in some pre-adamite conflict of angelic hosts, with all the veins and strata of their deep foundations disrupted, bent and twisted in the struggle into a thousand fantastic shapes; while, over the lower declivities and deep-sunk dells, a dark impenetrable forest spread its shaggy skirts, and added to the whole a character of still more wild and savage sublimity.
>
> This was the fore-ground of a vast but sombre landscape. Before us, and on either hand, extended, far as the eye could reach, the immense forest-jungle which stretches from the Zuurberg even to the sea-coast at the mouth of the Bushmans River. Through the bosom of this jungle we could distinctly trace the winding course of the Sundays River, like the path of some mythological dragon, – not from the course of its waters, but from the hue of the light-green willow trees (*Salix babylonica*) which

grow along its margins. Beyond, far to the south, appeared the Indian Ocean and the shores of Algoa Bay. To the right and west, rose the Rietberg mountains and the fantastic peaks of the Winterhoek. Nearer us, but hidden among the lower hills, and surrounded by dense forests, lay the Moravian settlement of Enon, which we were in search of.[6]

The Zuurberg range, which stretches for about 45 km between the Sundays and Bushmans rivers, separates the coastal plain from the Karoo. A regular wagon route was opened up more than twenty years after Pringle passed that way when, between 1848 and 1858, the Zuurberg Pass was constructed. For many years it was an important gateway between Port Elizabeth and the interior, dotted with outspans and staging posts. The Zuurberg Inn, at the summit of the pass, remains as a popular country hotel with views similar to those observed by Pringle. Ann's Villa, at the western end of the pass, has recently been restored. In its heyday it offered accommodation, and outbuildings included a blacksmith's shop and wagon maker's yard where damaged wagons could be repaired, while oxen recuperated on nearby grazing after the tortuous journey over the pass. Present-day travellers find the journey along an untarred steeply winding road equally tortuous but, like Pringle, find it an impressive experience.

The region is characterised by successive mountain ridges and deep kloofs, and by some of the most varied vegetation of the province. With the current reintroduction of game it may soon resemble 'the exuberance of animal life' at the Cape in which Pringle was intensely interested. He devotes a whole chapter of the *Narrative* to detailing the characteristics of every creature – from elephants to ants – that he encountered or heard of during his six years in South Africa, and to anecdotes about them. In the account of his Zuurberg expedition Pringle notices that the mountains 'were still frequented by several species of beautiful wild animals, which in former years had been more numerous – such as the quagga, the zebra, the hartebeest, reebok, steenbok, klipspringer, oribi etc. The rocky ravines also were inhabited by multitudes of baboons, and by the *dassie* or coney.' He also describes – with the accuracy of a scientist and the grace of an artist – its bird life and flora. Knowledgeable but seldom dry, romantic but always practical, Pringle presents the region as a place of wonder where he is reminded of Psalm 104, which concludes: 'O Lord, how manifold are thy works! In wisdom hast thou made them all: the earth is full of thy riches.'

4

A CITY

OF WRITERS

GRAHAMSTOWN

Grahamstown has several nicknames including City of Saints, Festival City and Settler City. It could also be called City of Writers, for a wide range of word artists have responded creatively to its appearance and life. The circle of hills that embraces the valley in which Grahamstown lies and the history that has imprinted on that valley a unique South African city have claimed the attention of many, while some have noticed that urban Grahamstown presents two faces – one expressing hardship, the other comfort – and have reflected this dichotomy in their writings. As we notice these themes during our journeys through and around the city, we shall meet some twenty writers representing both sojourners and residents.

Hills of the hinterland

From whichever direction one approaches Grahamstown, there are hills to be crossed – hills which hide the valley in which it is situated from sight until one is almost upon it, so that the city suddenly appears as if by magic. Departing from Grahamstown by rail or on any of the five major roads radiating from the city, one climbs out of its valley towards other hills that present varied landscapes: valley bushveld, ploughed fields and grassy pastures, ruled lines of pineapple plants, rocky krantzes, the occasional blaze of aloes. Two poems celebrate these hills of Grahamstown's hinterland.

Beth Dickerson
Lynne Bryer

Beth Dickerson, in 'Kenton Road', travelling in the dusk towards Grahamstown, experiences rest for the heart and a profound sense of belonging. In 'Love of Hills' Lynne Bryer, driving away from Grahamstown in the early morning, recognises that this landscape is 'the country of the heart'.

LYNNE BRYER
Love of Hills

Driving from Grahamstown
in the early morning
through hills that are less geography
than familiar shapes, welling deeply
out of myself like members of my own
family, figures not truly separate since relation
gives them unconditional shelter in the self –

I see a field of earth lying lilac in the light,
and on its curve a man with a tractor,
ploughing,
so that a small, far spurt of purple dust
hangs as a cloud.
Then such a rush of love and longing
fills me – joy, shards of regret,
an ancient, fierce belonging – that my breast
begins to burst, unable to contain
the pure reflection rising:
hill, field, cloud of dust,
the whole blest, well beloved
country of the heart.

from A Time in the Country

BETH DICKERSON
Kenton Road

Flaming gold
The sun slips down;
Trees and cattle
Sharp against last light
Lose their colour;

The far blue mountain line
Draws close
Darkens into black;
The air grows chill;

Silver grasses edge the road
That winds and dips
On these high ridges;

Along the verge
Dark figures
Wander homeward.

Profoundly now
My heart knows rest.

The space,
The air,
The darkening hour
Are part in some deep
Sense of who I am,
Where I belong.

unpublished

Throughout the life of L Y N N E B R Y E R a love of books was intertwined with love of family, of home-making, of South African history and literature and of what she called 'the country of the heart'. Her interest in books was expressed in many ways: reading, reviewing, writing, publishing, and promoting that very interest. Born Lynne Coetzee in Port Elizabeth in 1946 and schooled there, she had her first short story published in a British magazine when she was seventeen years old. While at Rhodes University, where she obtained a BA degree and later went on to a master's degree in English, she edited *Forum*, a university literary magazine, and had poems published in *New Coin*.

Reviewing was the focus of Bryer's literary interests during the 1970s, mainly for the *Eastern Province Herald*, and briefly for the *Times Educational Supplement* on which her husband worked for about three years in London. Back in South Africa, where she became the mother of two children, Lynne Bryer won the English Academy's Thomas Pringle Award for criticism. This was for reviews published in the *E P Herald* in 1977.

A move to Cape Town led Bryer into the world of publishing, where she worked intermittently for different publishers, but when she started her own independent publishing house, Chameleon Press, her love of books and working with them came into its own. At the same time, Bryer's love of writing was being expressed in the publication of poems and short stories in various literary magazines. In 1991 she was joint winner, with John Eppel, of the Vita–Arthur Nortje Poetry Award for works published in *New Contrast*.

In 1991 a collection of poems, *A Time in the Country*, came out in tandem with Fiona Zerbst's *Parting Shots*. Reviewing *A Time in the Country* in the *Weekly Mail* in January 1992, Rod Mackenzie writes:

> Lynne Bryer's poetry is a uniquely intimate experience. The relation between author, poem and reader is a contract: the contract Bryer creates compels a very personal response from the reader. Her poetry leaves

me with a warm sense of a kind of poetic motherliness. The poems often enfold their subjects, nourishing them in the melodious conversation that is Bryer's style.

The subjects Bryer's poems enfold are often scenes and experiences from her life, including that part of it spent in the Eastern Cape. She died of cancer in 1994, at the age of 47, leaving behind a collection of poems that was published in 1999 as *The Cancer Years*. In 'Vindication', the last poem of the volume, 'the country of the heart' takes on a new significance:

> And here I am, still
> kneeling by a flower,
> steeped
> in eternity –
> home.

GRAHAMSTOWN STREETS

Dan Wylie
Workshop poems

Grahamstown is a good place to explore on foot, and to get one's bearings High Street is the place to start. It runs through the city from Rhodes University and the Drostdy Arch at its western end, past the Cathedral of St Michael and St George in its very centre, to the brown stone railway station at its eastern end. There are other fascinating streets along which to ramble, absorbing the atmosphere of the city, enjoying changing vistas of hills and of buildings of different styles, and encountering the conglomeration of people who make up Grahamstown's population. Tree-lined and paved, barren and rutted, her roads offer variety and interest. They have not escaped the notice of poets.

In 'The Road Out' we accompany Dan Wylie along some of Grahamstown's highways and byways, noticing important landmarks and incidental sights as anyone might when taking a walk, but in which the poet finds reverberations that speak of the life of the town and of the individual.

DAN WYLIE
The Road Out

On Hill Street
    I saw a blackened Corsair, its hood
    snarling back from a fire.
I touched its radiator's rictus,
    without pity.
I stumbled along the march of parking meters
    that never missed a step.
At the closed book of the library doors
    I saw the hat of a beggar; but the hat
    was on his head; only the mouth begged.
And only the fist in my pocket replied.

At Cross Street
    I saw the spearheads of a fence
    bristle their category.
I saw a heavy chain padlocked around
    a staunch but impure deed.
In the funeral parlour's polished plaque
    I found reflected only the skull
    of a metal world.
Behind a gate I heard a terrier
    shaggy with the fury of a titan.
I walked on, unmoved.

On Market Street
    a church's spire repelled its pigeons.
Houses struggled to commune,
    their windows heavy-lidded
    with one another's shame.
I saw jungle-gyms of broken colour
    cage a tangled orphanage of cries.
I observed a vowelling dove endow
    a wire with a parallel meaning.
But I was outside the dove,
    and outside the wire.

Climbing Hope Street,
    gravity growled at tendon and bone.
Loud in a nest in the heart of a lily
    two robin chicks gaped vermilion appeal.
Roots wrestled under fragrant tar; cracks
    thrived, amorous with ants.
My jaw ached with avarice for touch.
From the crown of the rise solemnity
    dropped away
    like a kestrel.

And now along Hillsview
    jacarandas jettison their mauve crisis.
At an open gate, a golden retriever
    entrusts his greeting to the flourishing air.
Ruby-and-malachite sunbirds minister
    to futures of hibiscus and rose.
Against all expectations, the moon
    is extracted from earth's leathery purse.

I cross the highway.
    The cutting accepts the traffic
    in the wound of its limestone smile.
Eucalypts' ambling shadows release
    their mortality into the sea.
Crickets and grasses click electric
    among my cells; sudden colour
    riots in my bougainvillaea blood.
A homebound jogger glows and waves:
    raising my hand in answer,
    I conduct the sky.

from The Road Out

To encounter, in Grahamstown, the nuggety figure of the poet Dan Wylie, dressed in shorts and T-shirt, boots and bush hat with knapsack slung behind him, is to recognise a determined traveller. There is also much in his poetry to suggest journeys – tough journeys during which the writer is intensely aware of the outer world, which is often described in strong terms and potently linked to the inner world of thought and emotion. Even technically, there is a

suggestion in his poetry of a grappling with language similar to the struggle
he must have experienced, as hiker or climber, to place hand or foot in just the
right position. Wylie has also travelled literally – in Europe, East Africa, the
United States and the United Kingdom – but it is his two homes in Africa that
have most profoundly influenced him and his poetry: the Eastern Highlands
of Zimbabwe and South Africa's Eastern Cape.

DAN WYLIE was born in Bulawayo in 1959 and grew up in the mountainous Vumba region near Mutare, where he went to school. Like many young
white men of his generation he was conscripted into the then Rhodesian Army
and did two years' national service, an experience powerfully translated into
fiction in the novel *Dead Leaves* (2002). In the restless aftermath he travelled
abroad for a period before attending Rhodes University to read English.
Further wanderings preceded an interval of teaching in a bush school in
Zimbabwe and two years of living as a hermit. The spell of English literature
or of Grahamstown, or perhaps both, drew him back to the Eastern Cape,
where he now works in the Rhodes University English department.

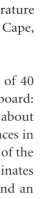

Wylie's first collection, *Migrant*, came out in 1994 in a limited edition of 40
copies printed on recycled paper and hand-bound with corrugated cardboard:
an indication, like his dress, of something unusual and down-to-earth about
its author. Poems in this collection focus mainly on experiences and places in
the United Kingdom and Zimbabwe. *The Road Out* (1996) repeats some of the
earlier poems and adds new ones; now it is the Eastern Cape that dominates
the scene. The volume won, for Wylie, the 1998 Ingrid Jonker Prize and an
Honourable Mention among the Noma Awards of 1997. Academically and as
a writer, Wylie has become a significant voice in the literature of southern
Africa, and his research into attitudes to nature in that literature is an indication of his interest in the interaction between place and the writer, in the
Eastern Cape and elsewhere.

   Wylie's own poems show a strong sense of place and time, partly revealed
through the very way in which he uses language. There can be a rather disconcerting shift between the material and the abstract or between self and the
objects with which he shares the spaces of his life: 'I feel leafless', 'I pace from
one extreme of the white-walled / imagination to the other', 'kicking and kicking the unruly / windfalls of recalcitrant thought'. Through poetry Wylie
explores landscapes of the Eastern Cape and of the soul as he seeks to find 'the
gate out of the garden' or to conquer his heart's cage:

   Obsessed with truth, my heart
   Wrestles to conquer its cage.[1]

Other Grahamstown 'street poems' come from residents of the poorer parts of town, where streets – many named only after letters of the alphabet – are often untarred, littered, badly drained and disorderly, yet busy and alive. Snippets from poems written by men and women eager to express themselves in a language not their own have an appealing immediacy. Some come from courses organised by the 1820 Foundation for teachers and published as *The Way We See It*, others from *Umqgala*, published by Chumani/GPP Writers Group.

WRITING GROUPS
Street poems

We call it 'M' street
I don't know the reason
It may be simple
Because it's the main street.
...
Khwela-khwelas are a
Part of the scene.
Running around at speeds
Which make me wonder.

from 'My Street' by Alicia Nombeko Hermanus

Raglan road, a road with no ending,
The road that always invites people,
Invites cars, donkeys, cats and dogs
And even small creatures.
...
How beautiful you are in the evening,
With bright lights like pretty flowers,
That invite bees in summer,
Everybody admires you, Raglan road.

from 'Raglan Road' by R N Mdlele

It is a narrow street
It is a dirty street
Where mud huts stand
With boys and girls peeping out
With dogs running up and down.
...
There is a beautiful church
Up in Hope street
Where old and young gather to pray
every Sunday.
Fathers and mothers come up the street with
Bibles and hymns all.

from 'Hope Street' by Stephen

Right at the back of Tantyi Location
There is a street called 'X'
A dusty, stony, pitholed street
Very muddy on rainy days.
...
Sympathetic scene during week ends
As occupants of this street watch funerals
Ministers say, 'Dust to dust'
What can they do? X street is
Next to Grahamstown graveyard.

from 'X Street' by Nomandla

In good 'n bad times
you kept us and
we were born.
You herded us
the sheep and goats
in one kraal
we learned to crawl
in your soft manure
for grazing wasn't really a matter.
On our grazing we learned to
choose the trees and bush
we could feed on.
In you we could
communicate in one natural language
despite our different languages.

In Joza we were without water
I tried to get water from our tears
from Matyala.
I got a misty view
of you Albany Road
I will always remember you
I will teach my children
that your manure was
warm and had comfort
Albany Road my nest
my kraal
Albany Road my home
I will love you
I will visit you
when I remember.

from 'Albany Road' by Zim Mnotoza

It is a great pleasure
A great joy without measure,
To lived in this street,
A happy and lovely street.
...
You put out homes on your breast as babies,
You give them different numbers and different colours
Everyone of them is proud of having you as a mother,
Everyone of them is proud of sitting on your tarred road.

from 'Mahlasela Street' by Thobeka Maselana

HISTORY, PLACE AND LITERATURE

To understand how Grahamstown came to be the kind of place that Dan Wylie describes in 'The Road Out' and that the people of the townships describe in their verse, it is helpful to look back over its history, focusing on some of the different ways this place has been perceived by imaginative writers.

Beginnings

The history of Grahamstown as a colonial settlement begins in 1811. Colonel John Graham and Ensign Andries Stockenström, commissioned to find a suitable site for a permanent military settlement in the district, had been toiling for some days in the vicinity, examining various possible locales, when they found relief from the heat under a mimosa tree on the deserted land of the Dutch farmer Lucas Meyer, where the only sign of human habitation was a burnt-out farmhouse. On either side of the eminence on which the tree grew were converging streams: a ready water supply! Colonel Graham made his decision, and work began on establishing barracks, officers' quarters and a parade ground. Governor Cradock ratified the decision in 1812 and named the place Graham's Town.

Lucas Meyer's abandoned farmhouse may have been the only sign of human settlement when Graham arrived, but neither Dutch farmers nor British soldiers were the first to inhabit the valley. The mimosa tree grew near the site of today's cathedral, and tradition maintains that the cathedral stands on what was once the Great Place of the Xhosa chief Ndlambe. Xhosa pastoralists had occupied large tracts of the Zuurveld, until their ruthless expulsion by British forces under the command of Colonel Graham to lands beyond the Great Fish River.

Harold Sampson's 'Grahamstown', written with hindsight a little over a century later, reminds us that human associations with this locality go back further. The poem suggests the freshness of a past in which nature is supreme and occupation of the land by hunter-gathering people temporary. Now, the poet reflects, nature is spoilt, and for what purpose? 'Profit and poverty' – characteristics of what were to become Grahamstown's contrasting faces.

Harold Sampson
Thomas Pringle

HAROLD FEHRSEN SAMPSON was born in Grahamstown in 1890. Educated there, he became a Rhodes Scholar in 1910 and studied law at Trinity College, Oxford. After serving in the First World War he was called to the Bar in London and then in South Africa. He returned to his birthplace and joined the staff of Rhodes University, where he became professor of law. Apart from legal and political writing he published a book of literary criticism and, between 1915 and 1937, three collections of poetry. His *Selected Poems* was published in 1972. We shall encounter poems by Sampson about Bushmans River Mouth, Kasouga and the Wild Coast which suggest a delight in holidays spent away from the pressures of his working life, but there is often, as in his poem about Grahamstown, a serious, even sombre note in his writings, and sometimes a satirical one. He died in 1973.

HAROLD FEHRSEN SAMPSON
Grahamstown

The clouds had nests in this hollow valley
    among wet stones and insignificant flowers.
    The sun, a silent Bushman hunter,
    moving upon the mountains of the morning
    from rock to rock, unstrung a shaft
    into the late dews of the valley:
    like swans on the air upsliding
    one after one, the clouds smoothly
    (unseen but of the standing hunter)
    lifted and passed from their discovered hills
    on tides of transience –

That was before
    the white man came with his whited walls
    his drains and quarrels and corroding hands,
    before the heathery stream became an effluent
    and streets trod down the singing earth
    to make profit and poverty –
    before the great spike of the church
    uttered its exclamation!

from Selected Poems of Harold Fehrsen Sampson

A rare eye-witness account of the appearance of embryonic Graham's Town comes from the entry, for 21 April 1813, in John Campbell's *Travels in South Africa*. 'The situation is pleasant,' he writes, 'and enjoys sufficient water all the year ... Some of the officers have already good gardens, though the town has not existed a year.' It sounds peaceful enough, but six years later came near-disaster for its white inhabitants and real disaster for its black attackers.

Today Grahamstown is part of the municipality of Makana, named for the prophet, Makana, nicknamed Nxele ('left-handed'), who, in 1819, led an attack on the town. Thousands of warriors in battle array poured over the hills to the east of the town, intending to destroy the military garrison and drive away the British, who had deprived them of their land and homes. In spite of vastly superior numbers the battle went badly for them and they had to retreat, leaving behind hundreds of dead and dying men. Makana was exiled to Robben Island. Less than a decade after the battle Thomas Pringle wrote 'Makanna's Gathering', in which he assumes the persona of the warrior prophet and expresses the aspirations of the Xhosa. Near the base of Makana's hill on a site known as Egazini ('place of blood'), a monument has been built to commemorate all those involved in the battle. It is dedicated to reconciliation.

THOMAS PRINGLE
Makanna's Gathering

Wake! Amakósa, wake!
  And arm yourselves for war.
As coming winds the forest shake,
  I hear a sound from far:
It is not thunder in the sky,
  Nor lion's roar upon the hill,
But the voice of HIM who sits on high,
  And bids me speak his will!

He bids me call you forth,
  Bold sons of Káhabee,
To sweep the White Men from the earth,
  And drive them to the sea:
The sea, which heaved them up at first,
  For Amakósa's curse and bane,
Howls for the progeny she nurst,
  To swallow them again.

  ...

Then come, ye Chieftain's bold,
  With war-plumes waving high;
Come, every warrior young and old,
  With club and assagai.
Remember how the spoiler's host
  Did through our land like locusts range!
Your herds, your wives, your comrades lost –
  Remember – and revenge!

....

Wake! Amakósa, wake!
  And muster for the war:
The wizard-wolves from Keisi's brake,
  The vultures from afar,
Are gathering at UHLANGA's call,
  And follow fast our westward way –
For well they know, ere evening-fall,
  They shall have glorious prey!

1820 to 1850: frontier town

Margaret Gough
H H Dugmore
Harriet Ward
F C Slater

The Battle of Grahamstown accelerated the plan of the governor of the Cape Colony, Lord Charles Somerset, to settle British immigrants on farms in what was known at the time as the Zuurveld – later as the district of Albany – in order to form a buffer against the Xhosa. In 1820 approximately 4 000 men, women and children – largely unaware of the role they were intended to play – arrived in Algoa Bay and moved into the interior, where they changed the history of the Eastern Cape in countless ways and gave an important impetus to its literature. The writings of transient explorers gave way, increasingly, to those for whom the Eastern Cape became, initially, a second home and eventually a motherland.

After several years of struggling to farm under severe difficulties, many of these settlers moved into Grahamstown. Margaret Gough's poem 'In the Settlers' Museum' reminds us of some of the personal treasures these newcomers brought to Grahamstown. Today this museum, renamed the History Museum, commemorates not only the British settlers but all sectors of the community of the Eastern Cape. The message remains the same: remember the past through the preservation of small personal artefacts.

MARGARET GOUGH
In the Settlers' Musuem

Cups that have felt the touch
of fingers, long decayed
whose rims were touched by lips
turned white by news of raid

For those in quiet despair
lift cups and drink their tea –
strive to hide their grief from those
in deeper misery

School books with poems of wrath
and messages of Hell –
The little reader sighed and stitched
and shaped her sampler well

A doll with yellow hair
and eyes that stare ahead
oblivious of loving hands
that clutched it and are dead

Grandfather clock that chimed
in passage paced by those
who struggled with capricious crops
and planted yet a rose

A dress worn by a bride
evokes a day that's past
saddens now in retrospect –
only the dress could last

They're gone and we are here
enjoined to contemplate
their little tender vestiges
of spoon and cup and plate

A hundred years from now
dear child, you'll be away
Pray God some soul may catch a gleam
of what we love today.

from Selected Poems

The cultural influence of the 1820 Settlers was imprinted on the appearance of Grahamstown as domestic and public buildings with an English flavour began to fill the valley: cottages with their frontages on the street, churches, canteens and shops. Grahamstown became a civil and commercial rather than a military settlement, as Thomas Baines's lively description of New Street in 1848 suggests:

> Passing the Cape Corps barracks and several very pretty suburban villas on our left and the main barracks and drostdy on our right, we entered the town by New Street which seemed, by far, more prolific of canteens and negotie winkels, or retail stores, than of private dwellings. Whipsticks of bamboo fifteen feet or more in length, ropes of hide from the ox, the buffalo, or eland, and other wagon gear, cheap guns, tiger skins, pumpkins, beads, brass rings, camp kettles, and pots of tin or iron, were displayed at every door.[2]

During the post-settler period Grahamstown became the second largest town in the Cape, and a commercial and cultural centre of note. But all was not peace and prosperity. Though never itself attacked, Grahamstown suffered upheaval and distress during the frontier wars of 1834–35, 1846–47 and 1850–53 when refugees came to town and many of its menfolk were called upon to defend the eastern parts of the colony against the Xhosa, who were attempting its repossession. In his *Reminiscences of an Albany Settler* (1871), Henry Hare Dugmore describes the scene in Grahamstown during the first of these wars:

> The aspect of Graham's Town, when made the central refuge, was such as it has never, in the same degree, presented since. Every tenement of every class was thronged with families of white, brown, or black, who had pressed in from every side for protection. The portions of the flocks and herds that had been saved from the Kaffers, crowded the vacant spaces in yards and gardens at nights, and covered the slopes of the hills around the town by day, exhausting very speedily the pasturage of the neighbourhood. Sad confusion and paralyzing depression prevailed at first, and strange scenes, combining the pathetic and the ludicrous in about equal proportions, were presented, especially when St. George's Church, the present Cathedral, was occupied at night as the place of greatest safety by the women and children.

Harriet Ward, the wife of an officer stationed on the frontier, describes even more vividly the Grahamstown scene during the second of these wars:

> Behold us, then, preparing for our pilgrimage across the open, un-

defended square of the Drostdy ground! ... The young ladies of the party, my own girl among them, collected what they considered most valuable, their books, work-boxes, trinkets, a guitar, a doll in a polka dress, a monkey, and their dogs; and the wife of one in command at Fort Peddie thrust money, jewels, and papers into a box, which she carried under her arm. Ere we were ready for the *trek*, the servants appeared with *their* 'valuables', the hoards and savings of many years. Oh, the confusion of tongues on that night, as we passed through the Square! Exclamations in Dutch, Irish, Fingo, broad Scotch, and provincial English, assailed us on all sides; children cried and laughed alternately, women screamed, Hottentots danced, and sang, and swore, the oxen attached to the waggons which had accompanied the 90th, uttered frightful roars, and muskets were going off in all quarters of the town.[3]

After the 1834–35 conflict numbers of the Dutch compatriots of these British settlers decided to leave the Cape Colony to seek new pastures beyond the reach of what they considered the injustices of British rule. Piet Retief – one of the leaders of this so-called Great Trek – had played a fairly important role in early Grahamstown as wagon maker and property owner, and as building contractor for a number of military installations. The poem by Francis Carey Slater 'Retief's Farewell to Albany', although written more than a century after Retief's departure, paints a picture of the hills and valleys in the neighbourhood of Grahamstown and of the 'frontier town' of this period, as he imagines Retief to have experienced them. It provides a vivid literary reconstruction of early Grahamstown and conveys that sense of affection and nostalgia many people with Grahamstown connections have experienced.

FRANCIS CAREY SLATER
From Retief's Farewell to Albany

'You dales and downs of Albany,
On your curved slopes, like scattered sheep,
Grey rocks and lichened boulders lie
Half-hidden in the grass and sleep,
Sun-washed, serene, in breathless ease.
In your deep kloofs are ancient trees,
Grey yellow-woods, whose creaking breath
Is spent in droning songs of death –
Dim and unending threnodies.

Oft in such grove a kaffir-boom
Flaunts gaily many a flame-like plume,
And perforates the woodland-gloom,
As veld-fires slash the fur of night
Making it bleed with angry light.
Green dales and downs of Albany,
Sadly, to you I bid, Good-bye.

'Good-bye to you, fair frontier-town,
Whose white-walled houses, churches brown,
Glow from a cup-like vale rimmed round
By gentle hills. In you I found
Friendship and love. At first success
Came with full hands to bless:
Drought-like misfortune followed fast
Blighting the blooms too bright to last;
So now, once more, though weary age
Brings its dull load, I must engage
In other ventures, start again
Far from these pleasant haunts of men.
And so, farewell, proud frontier-town;
Farewell again to dale and down.

from The Trek

1850 to 1900: new features

Isobel Dixon
Olive Schreiner
Marianne North

Between 1850 and 1900 the appearance of Grahamstown changed dramatically. Many fine buildings were constructed, including the neo-Gothic cathedral, its 54 m spire, completed in 1879, being the highest structure in South Africa at the time. The railway cut its way through what was now a city, providing passengers with new vistas of Grahamstown. T Sheffield, approaching by train in 1884, describes some of the changes he observes: 'we wonder if the lovely panorama of villas and gardens, of houses and stores, of churches and spires, half-hidden in forests of trees, spread out to view in the valley below, is really the old, old place we left forty years ago!'[4] What Sheffield does not notice here are changes occurring on the eastern hills. The few areas set aside for peoples other than the white settlers soon grew too small and had to be expanded. The black and coloured populations grew rapidly and there was overcrowding, poverty and sometimes squalor. The Group Areas Act had not yet come into being but the two faces of Grahamstown became clearly delineated well before 1950. Unlike the black areas of many other South African towns they are visible to all, for the townships are not tucked away out of sight of the affluent.

Even the vegetation around Grahamstown – Sheffield notices 'forests of trees' – changed as indigenous plants gave way to exotic pines and other species thought to be more decorative and useful. Today attempts are being made to rid Grahamstown of these very trees in order to conserve water, and the city's surrounding hills are emerging in their original garb of grass and bush. Isobel Dixon's 'Aliens' contemplates the situation as it is today. Is there, indeed, anything in Grahamstown 'not hybrid, grafted, spliced'?

ISOBEL DIXON
Aliens

They're burning the pines
around Grahamstown, I'm told.
Working For Water wiping out
the foreign moisture stealers, greedy roots.
I should be glad, for I love Africa.
Am African, want only to be whole,
indigenous. So why do I feel sad
to think the Settler City now is ringed
by charcoaled hills?

The easy comfort of horizons
ranged with Christmas trees,
not gawky cycads – clumsy,
strange, half-palms?
The tug of European ancestries
and seeds they tended once
to make them feel at home
in all this scrubby space,
hot ochre earth and aloe flames?

Nothing's more meaningful than thirst
and how one makes dry, tired soil
sprout green and plentiful and true.
We'll wait and watch the new life
nudging through, and puzzling
how to answer, '*Who was first?*'
know that there's nothing here
not hybrid, grafted, spliced.

from Weather Eye

The Cape Colony's first botanical garden, laid out in 1853 at the foot of the hill on which the 1820 Settler Monument now stands, has interesting literary associations. A scene in Olive Schreiner's *The Story of an African Farm* (1883) conveys something of the graciousness of one of Grahamstown's most beautiful Victorian landmarks:

> One day I went to the Botanic Gardens. It was a half-holiday, and the band was to play. I stood in the long raised avenue and looked down. There were many flowers, and ladies and children were walking about beautifully dressed. At last the music began. I had not heard such music before. At first it was slow and even, like the everyday life, when we walk through it without thought or feeling; then it grew faster, then it paused, hesitated, then it was quite still for an instant, and then it burst out. Lyndall, they made heaven right when they made it all music. It takes you up and carries you away, away till you have the things you longed for; you are up close to them. You have got out into a large, free, open place. I could not see anything while it was playing; I stood with my head against my tree; but when it was done, I saw that there were ladies sitting close to me on a wooden bench, and the stranger who had talked to me that day in the karroo was sitting between them.

Another remarkable woman of her time, MARIANNE NORTH (1830–1890), visited this same garden in the early 1880s on one of her global excursions to paint indigenous flowering plants, as she put it, 'in their homes'. We read of her impressions of Grahamstown and its botanical garden in *A Vision of Eden* (1980), an abridged version of *Recollections of a Happy Life* (1893), based on North's letters and journals:

> The hills became very bare as we descended to Grahamstown, which is built in a perfect hole; but it was pretty inside, with many nice people in comfortable houses with lovely gardens. Its Botanical Garden was particularly well kept, full of interesting plants, the wild hillside and rocks coming down into it at the back.

This was one of many such gardens North visited throughout the world, but the only one in which the artist was photographed at work. Her diminutive figure, in heavy Victorian garb, seated before easel and canvas and dwarfed, but not overwhelmed, by huge cacti and tree aloes, tells its own story of artistic dedication.

North's often solitary travels included nearly twenty countries spanning four of the world's continents. Nothing seems to have daunted her, and the vicissitudes of her journeys to remote places are recorded with matter-of-fact good humour. She was met with hospitality and help wherever she went and in Grahamstown Dr Guybon Atherstone, who was largely responsible for establishing the botanical garden, provided her with a venue for her work:

> Dr. A. [Atherstone] had asked me to stay in his house on my return, but all his rooms were so darkened with vegetation that I despaired of finding one I could see to paint in. At last I was taken across a sort of drawbridge to an attic or wide verandah, dark with a solid mass of creepers, bougainvillaea, banksia-roses, etc. It was full of old boxes of rubbish, and some crazy steps led into another attic with a small room at either end, one of them given up entirely to a colony of bees, which had built in a corner and resisted intruders; the other belonged to a son, who was on the opposite side of the colony. There I settled myself, digging out a hole in the bougainvilleas, which let in a blaze of rosy light through their flowery wreaths. It took me some time to make the opening sufficiently large to get natural-coloured light enough to paint by. One side of the room was separated from the verandah by broken green-house-sashes, one of them off its hinges. The roof itself was all of a slant, books, hats, pipes, and various treasures of men in delightful disorder, but it was deliciously quiet and out of the way. I bolted myself in at night, and shared the whole storey with the bees and an occasional rat, bird, or lizard, and through my hole in the bougainvillea, I looked on wonderful groups of aloes of many species, and other rare things collected by the Doctor in his long African life.

The blend of exotic and indigenous plants that North describes in Atherstone's garden is still characteristic of Grahamstown suburbia; but 'Bots', as it is affectionately known, retains little of its former splendour.

The Eastern Cape is fortunate to have been graced by Marianne North's presence, and paintings of flora that she observed in the Port Elizabeth area, Grahamstown, the Kowie and Port St John's are among the more than 800 paintings housed in the Marianne North Gallery in Kew Gardens. Each is more than a botanical record, although plants are always accurately identified. Landscape is often combined with close-up views of flowering plants, and birds, beasts or butterflies are sometimes artistically combined with plant material. Her written impressions of the Eastern Cape, recorded in her published recollections, show the same passionate response to the visual.

1900 to 1950: looking back

Marguerite
Poland

Kathleen
van der Riet

The most vivid picture in fiction of the Grahamstown of the early 20th century comes nearly a century later from the pen of Marguerite Poland whose historical novel *Iron Love*, published in 1999, is set principally in the Grahamstown of 1913. Personal pictures of the Grahamstown of this period come from Kathleen van der Riet's memoir, *Morning in the Heart*, published in 2000.

The focus of Poland's *Iron Love* is St Andrews' College, one of a number of schools – state and private – that help make Grahamstown a major educational centre. Neither town nor school is named in the novel yet many recognisable features of both are depicted in an environment which enfolds the story of a class of boys, a number of whom die during the First World War.

One of the devices Poland uses to create a sense of place – and uses with great skill and delicacy – is the photograph. It becomes a way of seeing the past from the present – both the present of the novel and the reader's present. Here Herbert, as an adult, is looking at a photograph of his old dormitory stuck into the album of his schoolfriend Charlie Fraser:

The sixth bed was Charlie Fraser's.

In the picture, the light from the window just above fell across the head and then dipped, slanting to the floor. It was the last picture in the album, stuck in the bottom right-hand port. The end of school.

For Herbert, that empty room, that sunlit bed, the reflection of the summer morning drifting on the ceiling, were more telling somehow than the picture of the new Memorial chapel, the grey stone edifice of the House, the Clock Tower, even the great iron-bolted door where the sports teams posed for photos. And the sixth bed, lit by the window, was the vantage from which Charlie Fraser used to prop himself against the sill and look out, quite detached. Once Herbert said, 'What are you looking at, Fraser?' but he'd made no reply. Herbert had climbed on Charlie's bed and gazed out himself one day, to see what it was that interested him so much. There was nothing. Only the playing fields and the roofs of the classrooms and the Drill Hall and the little *sloot* at the bottom of the footer field. It was only later that he guessed that Charlie must have been tracing the road leading north-east, up past the stone pines which crowned the lost hill.

From that crest the valleys fall away on either side, the vegetation changes, it is wild and inhospitable: aloes, euphorbias, kiepersols, prickly pear. The dense green enamelled leaves catch the sun, glinting sharply and way, way off the Amatolas rise up out of that green-blue distance. For Charlie Fraser that was home. Herbert hadn't thought about it then, hav-

ing his own homesickness to contend with. In after years he knew – Charles Fraser had been homesick like the rest of them. But he'd never said.

The tree-crowned hill of this passage is a link between school and the world beyond – the world of home – and eventually the further world of the war in which the boys become involved. The haunting image of the stone pines against the eastern skyline – still a dominant feature of Grahamstown – runs through the novel gathering associations and memories as the story unfolds. Many other features of Grahamstown, as well as of the school, are recreated with equal clarity. A sequel to the publication of *Iron Love* has been the installation in St Andrew's College chapel of a memorial window honouring a previously unsung hero, Charles Winston Fraser, the young person on whom the Charlie of Poland's *Iron Love* is based. Thus have place and literature, fact and fiction interacted.

Poland's affection for St Andrew's, with which she has many associations, is manifest. She has recently moved from KwaZulu-Natal to settle in Grahamstown near the college. It is a long-desired return to a part of the country that has inspired so much of her work.

Complementing Poland's imagined pictures of Grahamstown in the early years of the 20th century are Kathleen van der Riet's memories of a childhood and youth spent there, published as *Morning in the Heart*. Here is one of her little pictures of Grahamstown and of one of its many churches – St Patrick's:

> Grandma and I used to walk happily through our lovely little town with its quaint houses and beautiful churches. At certain times of the year, especially during Lent, we walked down early every morning to mass at St Patrick's – before Freddie Tasmer had run up and down the long ladder putting out the gas lamps. Sometimes, through grey branches of an overhanging tree we'd see the moon like a little boat with tipped-up ends in a dark blue sky. As it grew lighter, hadedas clattered above, breaking the silence with raucous calls and clapping of big wings as overhead in cool, clear air they flew in flocks from the red-tinged east. On other mornings, mist hung in branches and shrouded hills, brightening the beauty around us; against dark green leaves, woodbine and roses shone silver with dew. Warmly wrapped, we'd arrive at the crenellated, brown stone church, squat, protective and fortress-like, its deeply carved crosses looking like gunslits, and I'd think of Notre Mère striding there, sword in hand, and of mattresses against the windows to absorb the shock of bullets or assegais.

Gaslight, moonlight, sunrise and mist create an ethereal quality, while the church is solid and reassuring, despite the hints of a violent past in the allusions to bullets and assegais. Some of the other views of Grahamstown in *Morning in the Heart* highlight the mixture of the indigenous and the exotic which is of the essence of Grahamstown: roses and mimosa; the birdsong of canaries in an aviary 'in unison with wild birds all around'; aandblom and wistaria.

KATHLEEN VAN DER RIET was born Kathleen McNamee in Grahamstown in 1907, and *Morning in the Heart*, published in 2000 – the year she died – records nearly a century of her impressions of the Eastern Cape. The sufferings of war, illness and bereavement are not ignored, but it is the light of a joyful enthusiasm that dominates the book, which is full of lively anecdote and illuminated by pen portraits of ordinary people and sketches of city and town, farm and seaside, that help us to see and enjoy the author's surroundings. Her book includes descriptions not only of Grahamstown but also of New Brighton in Port Elizabeth, where her father was superintendent of the township and the family lived; of the Alexandria district, where she and her husband farmed; of Alexandria itself, where they bought and restored a number of old houses and cottages of historical interest; and of Bushmans River, where she finally settled.

While her own work brings a sparkle to Eastern Cape literature, Kathleen van der Riet made a contribution to it in another way. She loved books and, during a period working as an antique dealer, found a number of pieces of Africana, including a rare copy of *Under the Yellowwoods* by Robert Michael Bruce. She had it reproduced in a limited facsimile edition – a gem of Eastern Cape literature we shall enjoy when we journey to Salem and the farm Belton.

1950 onwards: light and dark

Don Maclennan
Chris Mann
Guy Butler
Marion Baxter
Robert Berold

The outlines of Grahamstown's encircling hills gained some eye-catching additions during the second half of the 20th century, such as the substantial white buildings of an Afrikaans school; the dominating 1820 Settlers Monument; new Rhodes University buildings, overlooking the core campus. Residential areas covered hillslopes in every direction. Within the sprawling valley legal and commercial establishments, museums, schools and institutions expanded and new ones were set up. Despite all the apparent progress, this era was, for many, a time of turmoil and suffering, and there was a deepening of the divide between that part of the city occupying the eastern hillslopes, known as Rini, and predominantly white Grahamstown across the valley.

Against this background of light and darkness there was a burgeoning of literary activity as Grahamstown became a hub of literary and linguistic studies, producing an interesting array of writers. It is, today, the home of the National English Literary Museum (NELM), the Institute for the Study of English in Africa (ISEA) and the South African Dictionary Unit. It is also home to a university which, through its School of Languages and departments of English, linguistics and drama, promotes the knowledge of language and literature, both international and local, and inspires an enthusiasm for the art of the word that reaches into many corners of South Africa and beyond. Through the Grahamstown Foundation, housed in the 1820 Settlers Monument, Grahamstown has also become the 'Festival City of Africa' and many aspects of the festivals it promotes encourage the production and love of our literature.

The responses of writers to this period of light and darkness are as varied as the topography of the city. Here we touch on recreations and poetic musings regarding just a few aspects of post-1950 Grahamstown: Rhodes University; the 1820 Settlers Monument; museums; and the effects of apartheid.

Rhodes University College began life in 1904 and, within a few decades, its cream and terracotta buildings grouped behind the Drostdy Arch at the top of High Street became one of the major features of Grahamstown. In 1951 Rhodes became an independent university, and development continued. In the 1970s the buildings, gardens and chapel of the Grahamstown Training College were incorporated into the Rhodes campus. A new hall and residences extended the campus up the hills to the west. Narrow, tree-lined streets, bricked quadrangles, lawns, paths and gardens link these distinct sections of the university to form a pleasing whole.

Don Maclennan captures a sense of the Rhodes University campus in his poem 'Prospect'. The prospect of the Library quadrangle – a 1980s development – observed by the poet on a quiet spring noonday from the balcony of his study is presented to the reader. An inner prospect that is both personal and pertinent to much literary endeavour emerges as he muses over past and future:

DON MACLENNAN
Prospect

Viewed from my top-floor balcony,
bridge of a docked ship,
the red-tiled quad is empty,
washed with sun
and lunchtime quiet.
Solitary students cross the square,
ducking the budding trees
as though the space and light
were hazardous.
They walk quickly
through the glare.
Pigeons' lazy bubbling
fills the vacant hour.
Everything succumbs to noon:
north-west above the hospital
floats a thin, oxidised moon.

Behind me in my room,
the fading blue calligraphy
of lectures half-forgotten
filed and foldered in the cabinet
keeps pointless order.
There is no place to store
the fragments that I prize –
not even my head is the right size.
But out here on the balcony
I repossess
the privilege of silence,
imagining what was possible,
and everything that might be.
I have outlived my intellect –
washed up on a vacant beach,
watching, listening
on the emptied day.

Warm wind flutters
the pages of my book,
stirring memory:
a dish of figs, black coffee,
and a brilliant canvas
of cadmium yellow,
black and aquamarine;
below a whitewashed wall
the sea is licking stones.
Here, when I speak,
the sun stands still,
wills me to complete,
gives me my fill.
Here I am not obsolete:
a word may sing like a knife,
and yet imagination
heals the wounds of life.

from Letters

I cannot tell you of the universe
that talks to me
like an inner spring –
a sunrise that I helped achieve itself,
a sea that darkens and darkens
into Homer's wine.

There is much that is characteristic of Don Maclennan in this poem from his
1997 collection *Solstice*: the struggle to express in words the inexpressible; the
spare lines, simple vocabulary and conversational tone, which create an apparently simple poem that cannot be 'explained'; a consciousness of the outer
world; and a resonant literary allusion. He is a poet immersed in the worlds of
the mind, of the senses and of literature.

DON MACLENNAN was born in London in 1929, and came to South Africa
in 1938. He attended school and university in Johannesburg before doing a
degree in philosophy at Edinburgh University. After some years of teaching in
the United States he returned to South Africa with his wife, Shirley, and eventually settled with her and their children in Grahamstown. Here, for more
than thirty years, he spread before the students of the English department at
Rhodes University the joys and mysteries of literature, particularly African lit-

erature. Now that he is retired, reading, writing and resting – he says – fill his time. New collections of poetry come thick and fast.

Maclennan has written scholarly articles, reviews and works of criticism; ten collections of poetry have been published, each slim in size but substantial in content; there have been a number of short stories and plays; he says that he has burned all but one of his novels.

In 1997, shortly after the award of both the Sanlam and Thomas Pringle prizes for poetry, an interview with Maclennan, conducted by Denise Rack Louw, was published in the *Daily Dispatch* of 12 July. In it he says, 'I love the physical world. That's the bass note for me – it's what makes sense for me, and what I find comforting.' It is a love exemplified in his writings. Simple phenomena from the physical world are transformed into poetry through unexpected metaphors: ants vanishing and emerging from the wrinkled anus of a ripe fig; lunar shadows measuring the swept yard; a rainbird and his bottle bubbling down the scale. Remembered images may be literal: a dish of figs, black coffee, fresh flowers, golden candles. Remembered smells are specific: clean sheets, cut grass, museums and cigars, my father's pipe, my mother's skin. Sounds are clearly heard: the drum-cracking crunch of a railway truck; the absurd squeaking of hornbills; mealie stalks rattling in the wind. In almost every poem the time of day, the season, the weather are specified or implied. In the same interview Maclennan confesses to a preference for 'rocks, mountains and gorges – and much of the Karoo'; but spacious landscapes are not evident in his work. Most poems are closely focused and fit into small frames but, within them, the world of the senses is linked, sometimes quite tentatively, to larger thoughts about self, others, the obscurities of life. Maclennan's poems reveal a deep love for the here and now of life and the world of nature, along with a seemingly reluctant rejection of the beyond, but they never stop asking questions.

A significant number of South African writers have been students or, like Don Maclennan, academics at Rhodes University. Pre-eminent among them is Guy Butler, whose 80th birthday in 1998, two years before his death, is celebrated in the poem 'Grahamstown Sage' by Chris Mann, another poet closely associated with the university and the town.

CHRIS MANN
Grahamstown Sage
To Guy Butler on his eightieth birthday

What man is this, who eight decades since birth,
his pulse-beat weak and fluttering through old age,
still treads with cautious zest his patch of earth
and does not deign to grieve his health – or rage?

Unsettled most by those who settle least
the Africa that droughts and feeds his soul,
he shakespeared students in his thorny east,
and linked the native writer to the metropole.

The institutes he built on Grahamstown's clay
were visioned first inside his poet's heart.
His creativity's a gullied sea whose spray
is pressed into the pages of his art.

Their theme's the secret of the joy he gives:
he loves the place and people where he lives.

from Heartlands

CHRISTOPHER MICHAEL ZITHULELE MANN was born in Port Elizabeth in 1948. At the age of seven he was taken away from the Eastern Cape, not to return as a resident for over twenty years. Schooling was in Cape Town and university education began in Johannesburg. At the University of the Witwatersrand, Mann studied English and philosophy before going on a Rhodes Scholarship to Oxford, where he won the Newdigate Prize for Poetry. African Studies at London University confirmed his attachment to the land of his birth and his profound interest in its peoples. After returning to Africa in 1975 he taught at a rural school in Swaziland, where he became fluent in Zulu, and there he was given the sobriquet Zithulele – 'he who is quiet'.

The Eastern Cape became home again between 1977 and 1980, when Mann held a post in the English department at Rhodes University. During that time *First Poems* was published and he edited *A New Book of South African Verse in English* with Guy Butler.

Development projects with the Valley Trust in Natal then claimed Mann's attention and he did not return to the Eastern Cape until 1995, this time to work for the Grahamstown Foundation. He has settled in the city and is now a research associate with the Institute for the Study of English in Africa. Mann is involved in the organisation of Wordfest – component of the National Festival of the Arts that concentrates on the literary arts – and with freelance development projects, several of them associated with the introduction of poetry to new audiences.

Chris Mann regards poetry as a vocation, and the making of poems is, for him, a constant process. Seven collections of his poems have been published, and the latest – *Heartlands* – is described as 'felt encounters with places that resonate in our memories'. It complements a previous collection – *South Africans* (1996) – that focuses on people. Other subjects range from meditations on science and religion to lyrics about potatoes and onions. He likes to link poetry to other media – music, video, painting, slides, dance – and has sometimes performed his poetry or presented it visually as in *The Horn of Plenty* (1997), a series of handwritten poems superimposed on paintings by his artist wife, Julia Skeen.

Moving away from the Eastern Cape to KwaZulu-Natal and then back again has helped Mann to notice how different landscapes affect the psyche of a people. He says that in the Eastern Cape, where the soil is thin, things grow more slowly and vegetation as well as population is more sparse, there is a 'stark clarity about issues'. It is also a factor that affects the region's literature.

In 'Grahamstown Sage', Chris Mann writes of Guy Butler: 'The institutes he built on Grahamstown's clay / were visioned first inside his poet's heart.' One of the institutes associated with Butler, although he was not alone in 'visioning' and building it, is the 1820 Settler Monument on the prominent hill above the Rhodes University campus, known as either Signal Hill or Gunfire Hill. Officially opened in July 1974, it is a solid, uncompromising building said to resemble a ship but with none of the grace of the fragile sailing ships that brought the British settlers it commemorates to the shores of southern Africa. Floodlit at night, however, it resembles a spaceship – an appropriate image for our age – and many of the activities associated with what Butler insisted should be a 'living monument' carry participants to new shores of experience and vision.

Every year South Africa's National Festival of the Arts erupts from the Monument and spills over into every corner of Grahamstown. Music, the visual arts and drama play major roles and literature is manifested in playscripts, prose and poetry readings, workshops, book launches and fairs, or the award of literary prizes, while Wordfest has become an important adjunct to

the main festival. Much of the inspiration for the establishment and continu-
ation of the National Arts Festival came from Guy Butler.

In August 1994 fire gutted the Monument's auditorium and severely damaged other parts of the building's interior. Within days the Phoenix Fund –
spearheaded by Butler – was set up to raise funds for restoration and improvements. Less than two years later, State President Nelson Mandela rededicated
the rejuvenated monument.

During the worst of the apartheid years many local people felt excluded
from the Monument, an attitude encapsulated in this poem by Johannesburg
poet Sipho Sepamla, 'On Gunfire Hill':

> Up there on Gunfire Hill
> Is anchored a ship
> Moored in a virgin green sea
> Portholes glimmer at night
> By day the massive ship stands forlorn
> Awaiting sailors
> To drop book-bottles and hurry up
> In the twilight of a promise

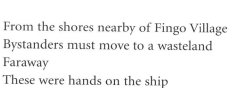

> From the shores nearby of Fingo Village
> Bystanders must move to a wasteland
> Faraway
> These were hands on the ship
> Which might never sail

The hopeful note at the end of Sepamla's poem is becoming a reality. Today,
as well as bringing honour to the 1820 Settlers, the living part of the Monument – the Grahamstown Foundation – incorporates the talents and aspirations of all sections of society into its endeavours:

> Let none say:
> I know only the shadow cast by the ship
> The rides on the ship
> Must be a joy to all
> On Gunfire Hill.[5]

The extract from Guy Butler's 'Signal Hill' speaks of how the Monument has
survived the threat of fire within and a later bush fire that swept round its
exterior: 'a phoenix sings through flame and ash'.

GUY BUTLER
From Signal Hill
After the fires that threatened the 1820 Monument

I am standing in ash alone on Signal Hill.
Still smouldering graffiti of burnt trees
are scrawled upon the huge wall of the sky.
Stripping the hill of its copse the fire has shown
these hand-packed stones, the signallers' old post.

When first I caught my breath at this wide view
it was nothing but a view. I have since written
a history of the refugees from Britain
who were settled between these hills and the sea;
and helped to raise a living monument
whose human roots first sprouted in this view.

A raging interior fire failed to stop
our annual festival, nor will this
succeed. A phoenix sings through flame and ash.

from Guy Butler: Collected Poems

'The Monument' and 'The Festival', as they are known in Grahamstown, are not the only legacies – institutional and literary – left to the city and the country by FREDERICK GUY BUTLER.

His early life in Cradock, where he was born in 1918, and the influences of that Karoo town and its environs on his philosophy and his works, are dealt with in Chapter Six. A student at Rhodes University College from 1936 to 1938, Butler returned to Grahamstown in 1950 after service in the Second World War, studies at Oxford University and a brief teaching spell at the University of the Witwatersrand. These absences provided opportunities to view the Eastern Cape from afar and other places from close quarters, and to extend his lifelong exploration of the meaning of 'belonging'. He came to belong in Grahamstown: for him, a microcosm of multicultural South Africa.

In 1951, one year after his appointment to its staff, Butler became professor and head of the department of English at Rhodes University. Bringing Butler to Rhodes University was like dropping a large stone into a rather calm pond, and the ripple effects are still being felt in Grahamstown. Not only did he provide dynamic leadership in the English department, but he was also instrumental in setting up the departments of speech and drama, linguistics and journalism within the university and, in association with it, the Institute for the Study of English in Africa and the National English Literary Museum. As we have seen, he played a leading role in the conception and development of the 1820 Settlers Monument and the National Arts Festival and he also facilitated the founding of the Shakespeare Society of Southern Africa, which has its headquarters in Grahamstown. In these and other endeavours, English, particularly South African English, is the keynote and the literary arts a major focus. Professor Butler's enthusiasm for the English language and for the literary works of those who have employed it as the medium of their art inspired countless students. While never neglecting the Western literary tradition, he increasingly made students, and the South African public in general, aware of the writings of their own people: he collected South African works in anthologies; he taught South African literature, urging others to do the same; he encouraged writers of all races.

Many buildings in Grahamstown have Butler associations. Together with other, like-minded persons, he strove to preserve and restore a number of the early 19th-century buildings so characteristic of the city. High Corner, home of Guy and Jean Butler for 50 years, where their four children grew up, is at a focal point in the city: the top of High Street, just outside the Drostdy Arch. Beyond that arch is Rhodes University, to which much of the writer's life was devoted and where the theatre he designed is a lively centre of the dramatic arts he loved. Framed in the arch as one looks towards the town is the cathedral where Butler was a regular worshipper. One of the last acts of this man, who was as skilful with his hands as his mind and pen, was to mount a large replica of the Coventry Cathedral cross of nails on two pieces of an old stinkwood banister from his home, to be placed in the lady chapel. It is both an international and a local sign of reconciliation – something he strove for over many years.

Butler's greatest legacy is, however, his writings. He produced works in almost every recognised genre. Six plays were both published and performed; a milestone anthology – *A Book of South African Verse* – was published in 1959 and, with Chris Mann, revised twenty years later; and there were other edited compilations of verse, drama and prose. A foray into historical writing produced the substantial (in size and content) publication *The 1820 Settlers: An Illustrated Commentary* (1974), which Butler edited as well as contributing towards the text. *A Rackety Colt* (1989) tells a lively story for young readers and *Tales of the Old Karoo* (1989) recounts many a good yarn. A collection of his essays and lectures was published, as well as the bizarre story of Olive Schreiner's re-interment on Buffelskop. His last published work was *The Prophetic Nun* (2000), a beautifully illustrated biography of Sister Margaret CR, the artist nun of Grahamstown whose unsigned works Butler tracked down all over South Africa and in Zimbabwe. Three autobiographical works – *Karoo Morning* (1977), *Bursting World* (1983) and *A Local Habitation* (1991) – tell the story of his own life. They are among the best of their kind in South African literature, but probably Butler's best-loved creations are his poems, brought together in 1999 as *Collected Poems*. Many of them are apposite to the theme of 'place' although, strangely, few reflect Grahamstown. The narrative poem *Pilgrimage to Dias Cross* is the subject of a separate section later in this chapter.

In the South African Institute for Aquatic Biodiversity, previously known as the J L B Smith Institute, visitors gaze in wonder at 'old four legs', the coelacanth brought to Grahamstown in the 1950s. Its kind was thought to have been extinct for more than 50 million years. Marion Baxter's poem 'Extinction' is about the later acquisition of a pregnant coelacanth and her eggs. The poem was first published in *New Coin* in 1970 under the title 'Coelacanth' and in 1998 it won the 'Grand Prize' in an anthology called *Under African Skies*. A scientific object observed with a poet's compassionate eye takes on new significance.

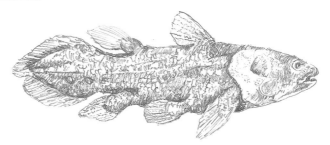

MARION BAXTER
Extinction

She arrived in a large crate at the Institute,
freshly caught, preserved in formalin – a female coelacanth,
very valuable, because found fecund
and reproduction means survival of the species.

There it lay, a great brown beast exposed to the sun,
its dapple-blue sheen of brilliance faded, waiting
to be photographed for science, the fisherman's hook
still hanging from its mouth. Carefully I examined
the fleshy pink tongue and rows of knife-like teeth,
the tooth-like growths on the upper surface of the scales,
the staring, saurian eyes like two dead moons, the armour plating,
deceptive leg-like fins, and curious paddle of the tail –
millions of years had formed this perfect creature
now tagged and measured, destined for dissection,
its precious cargo (eighteen fertilised eggs) aborted.

Moved by some impulse that I couldn't analyse
I placed my hand upon the fish's head. At once
an impulse, like a sharp electric shock leapt up
into my fingers – a force, or deep instinctual power
which emanated from that alien presence, a communication
from the extinct world perhaps, something
I can only call the 'coelacanthness' of its essence.

Behind my spectacles, I wept for her –
worth more in death than she had been in life.

in Under African Skies

Before MARION BAXTER died in 2002 she had lived in Grahamstown for eighteen years during which time she obtained a master's degree in English from the university and worked in turn for four of the city's institutes – the International Library of African Music, the J L B Smith Institute of Ichthyology, the Institute for the Study of English in Africa and the Shakespeare Society of Southern Africa, preparing the works of others for publication. Her own works – short stories and poems – published mainly in journals and magazines, won a number of literary prizes.

Born in England in 1945 and moving from place to place in Africa from the age of eight, she may not, as one of her poems suggests, have felt herself to be *from* Grahamstown, but her writings show that she was certainly *of* it and, in a wider sense, of the Eastern Cape. One of two privately circulated collections of short stories – *Bitter Aloes* – bears the subtitle *Stories from the Eastern Cape* and includes stories set in Hogsback, Nieu-Bethesda, Grahamstown and

Cradock. Baxter brings its landscapes and townscapes to life in prose and verse with clear brushstrokes and a wry sense of irony that sees the beautiful as well as the sordid and the sad.

In Baxter's short story 'Graven Images', a passing salesman of mirrors looks down from hills scarred as they often are by fire, on the two faces of Grahamstown:

> So it was mid-morning by the time he hitched trailer to truck and drove away from the town, up into the burnt-out hills where the aloes still smoked at their finger tips, stopping in a convenient grove of blasted tree trunks, well off the main road. He parked his truck in the concealing shade of an oak tree that had somehow escaped the holocaust. Further back was a small forest of pine trees which had also been spared, though some were badly scorched around the trunks. From this vantage point he could see the town spread out below, contained by the valley, the shadows deep over the settler quarters, the sun glittering on township roofs creeping like snails up the hillside, the roads like slug slime drying in the far distance; and he thought he could almost pinpoint Margie's house with its newly painted roof, even make out the Grand Hotel where Leo Rich was probably writing out the bill for the honeymoon suite at that very moment.[6]

By the 1990s Grahamstown's two faces seemed indelibly etched on her urban landscape. As projects such as the building of the Monument, the extension of the university campus, the development of museums and institutes and of 'whites only' schools and suburbs highlighted the affluent face of Grahamstown, so on the eastern hills poverty, overcrowding and the restrictions of apartheid legislation increasingly emphasised the face of hardship. Many writings of the time reflect this dichotomy, among them 'Dark City' by Robert Berold.

ROBERT BEROLD
Dark City

I
We swept our thoughts.
The afternoon's late light
cut patterns in the walls,

cathedral cutting through
the sky, the brandy-rusted
edges of township,

houses straight and painted white.
Down at the dam the tanned police
have trapped a car in their electric nets.

How will history
gut this town
its letters, timbers, dry graves?

II
Like animals still living
in the surrounding hills
the beggar goes with his instincts
to find his daily bread

the world a permanent prison
where jailers slam doors
where being shut out
is being shut in.

III
A full moon
gathering up the twilight

next to it a narrow cloud
the vapour trail of a military plane.

The moon hung over the town, very close
we looked out over the municipal dam

to the lights of the township opening
people going about the end of their day

the moving car lights and moving human sounds
blotted the town's misery only from far away

The same moon over two parts of the town
whose evening smoke smoothed the houses into hills.

IV
Dark city, houses standing noiselessly,
sun between the mountains, the whole earth
red with carnage. In the open space
inside your heart the bodies lying slaughtered.

Next morning you are calm again, well rested,
but there's last week's newspaper, those
nightmares are all true, people were shot down,
their bodies left to dribble in the dust.

Slow walks as sunset settles on these hills.
A praying mantis left her eggs on the moon.
You shout out to your god to take this darkness out of you –
these splintered darknesses embedded everywhere.

from The Fires of the Dead

ROBERT BEROLD is a well-known literary personality in Grahamstown. Not only is he himself an accomplished poet, but he has done a great deal to promote a culture of poetry reading and to encourage other writers, particularly aspiring poets.

Berold was born in Johannesburg in 1948. He followed an engineering degree from the University of the Witwatersrand with a spell at Cambridge University studying economics and literature. Since returning to South Africa in 1973 he has worked in various community development projects, initially in Soweto and, since 1981 when he moved to the Eastern Cape, in and around Grahamstown, where literary activities have also absorbed much of his time and attention.

From 1989 to 1999 Berold edited one of South Africa's most important poetry journals, *New Coin*, and he has conducted numerous writing and editing workshops and courses. Three collections, *The Door to the River* (1984), *The Fires of the Dead* (1989) and *Rain Across a Paper Field* (1999), as well as a number of poems published in journals and magazines, bear witness to Berold's technical skill and depth of thought and feeling. His poetry reveals a strong sense of place, but landscapes are as much of the mind as of the outer world. There is a constant shift from the one to the other, which is sometimes disconcerting, but careful reading uncovers layers of images which often depend on association rather than on a directly described moment or a specific place. He likes to concentrate on the power of the concrete image rather than on abstract ideas, although personal, social and political concerns clearly motivate much of Berold's work. In an interview with Susan Gardner, conducted in 1984 and published by NELM, he says:

> I've never regarded poetry as confined to literature, I've always regarded it as the written form of a way of seeing the world. From an early age, poetry was for me a way of finding meaning, because it contained the particularity and the sensuality which concepts don't have, it contained music and it contained the movement between the introspective and the outer worlds. I continue to write because it's a way of making meaning for myself. Poetry always seemed to me the closest thing to describing experience without interpretation. What you lose in poetry is the generalization which seems necessary to rational thinking. But what you gain is the power of the image. And the image, the language of the unconscious, is much older than rational thought.[7]

Robert Berold's way of seeing the world illuminates many aspects of the Eastern Cape scene, and complements some of the ways other writers perceive it.

BELLS AND BIRDS

Beauty and ugliness, suffering and comfort, sadness and joy have always existed side by side in Grahamstown, and one of the joyful aspects of the city's life is the birds that frequent her gardens, streambeds and bush-clad hills. Three poets – Don Maclennan, C J Driver and Beth Dickerson – celebrate ways in which the birds of Grahamstown have affected them. It is, indeed, as Maclennan proclaims, a city of birds – and, one may add, of flowers and flowering trees. The churches and schools that abound in every part of it make it also a city of bells.

Don Maclennan
C J Driver
Beth Dickerson

On our journey towards the coast we leave Grahamstown, with the music of its bells, the harsh cry of the hadeda, the bubbling of the rainbird, the incongruous squeak of the crowned hornbill and the sweet song of the sunbird in our ears.

DON MACLENNAN
Grahamstown II

City of bells
and birds:
hornbills squeaking
in the loquat tree
their voices too absurd
for such intrinsic dignity;
a rainbird and his bottle
bubbling down the scale.
City of gentle mediocrity,
your birds and bells
obliterated me.

from Reckonings

C J DRIVER
Grahamstown 2: Aubade

Writing down that raucous early morning cry
    Might make it seem they merely laughed
    When light before the dawn enticed
        Their flight
From Fraser's Valley to the other side
      Of town; and so the chorus goes:
HA – ha a a – ha – ha – a a ha – a ...

And yet of all the sounds I longed to hear
    In years of exile from this place
    (Ten countries and three continents
        So far)
Was what the less-than-sacred ibis called
      At dawn; and so the chorus goes:
HA – ha a a – ha – ha – a a ha – a ...

The hadedah is stretched across the sky
    Of my imagination still;
    I would not want a heaven which had
        Angels
Who did not know a raucous song to greet
      The dawn; and so the chorus goes:
HA – ha a a – ha – ha – a a ha – a ...

from In the Water-Margins

BETH DICKERSON
Sunbird

Early in November
He starts his song.
Who would believe
That so much sound
Could throb
From such a tiny throat?

I saw him singing once:
Perched above the brilliant tubes
Of Tecomaria he loves to sip,
Iridescent in the sun,
The two bright curves of beak
   Apart,
Vibrating with his passion.

But usually
He sings unseen;
Through the weeks of Advent
Fills the garden
With his joyous paean,
Herald of the summer
And the season when we celebrate
His Creator's birth.

unpublished

5

SETTLER COUNTRY

LOWER ALBANY

The area around Grahamstown and the region to the south of the city – bounded on the south by the Indian Ocean and on the west and east respectively by the Sundays and Great Fish Rivers – is now made up of the municipalities of Makana and Ndlambe. It was once known as the Zuurveld and later as the district of Albany. Some have called it 'Settler Country', for it was in this part of the Cape Colony that the majority of the British settlers who arrived in 1820 were located.

When the British settlers arrived, Dutch farmers had already been established here for some 50 years. Various groups of Xhosa – including that under the chieftainship of Ndlambe – had occupied much of the land, once the hunting ground of the San and, in some parts, the pasturage of the Khoekhoe. It was therefore a meeting place of different peoples where frontiers came and went and, in time, varying literary perspectives evolved. The settlers brought with them their language and their literary traditions, which they passed on to others. It is not, therefore, surprising that a great deal of the imaginative literature in English relating to the province – from 1820 to the present time – should come from this relatively small part of the Eastern Cape. We have already sampled some of its riches in Grahamstown. Now we explore other parts of 'Settler Country'.

First we visit the towns of Salem and Bathurst and then we view the countryside through the personal writings of two very different settlers before travelling with the 'historical ghosts' of Guy Butler's *Pilgrimage to Dias Cross* through six sites in Lower Albany. Lastly we share holiday perspectives with a number of poets as we journey along the coast from Woody Cape to Kleinemonde.

Two towns established in 1820 have interesting literary associations. One is Bathurst, on the road between Grahamstown and Port Alfred, the other Salem, on the road between Grahamstown and Kenton-on-Sea. Bathurst began with a vision of making it the administrative centre of the Albany district and it was named for the Colonial Secretary of the time, Lord Bathurst. Salem began with a vision of establishing a place of peace. Its name, meaning peace, was chosen by the Rev. William Shaw.

SALEM

Don Maclennan
William Shaw
Francis Bancroft
Guy Butler
Robert Bruce
Robert Greig
J M Coetzee

Literature associated with Salem far exceeds the size and importance of this straggling little village, but provides a fascinating example of how differently writers may view the same locale and use it for literary purposes.

Don Maclennan's *Rock Paintings at Salem* is a beautiful volume of 34 brief reflections on the dancers depicted in rock paintings in a krantz near Salem, in which the poet's word pictures are complemented by small paintings of his own. The art of the San inspires in him thoughts that range over such subjects as self-discovery, the passage of time, the significance of art, of existence, of death. In poem 3 Maclennan reflects on the transience of the paintings themselves:

> -3-
> It's Sunday:
> a clear winter sky,
> bright sun, cold wind.
> Afternoon heat is trapped
> in this angle of the cliffs.
> The figures in the paintings
> dance in ferric oxide
> on the shelter wall.
> Yet an insistent sadness
> creeps into the afternoon:
> the figures are vanishing
> slowly out of sight;
> weather is eating
> their vibrancy away.

'Art', Maclennan writes in poem 18 of the series, 'lives us into being, / makes us see'. In these poems the poet's word art, his own delicate watercolours, and the visual art of the unknown painters combine to make us see the physical and to perceive the insubstantial that lies behind it.

> -32-
> That which moves
> the human heart
> thrives on being alive
> amidst the deadly
> transience of things.

Then fire the imagination
with dancing figures
on the shelter wall,
flickering outlines
of a tale that none
can prove or disprove
but by living it.

The Rev. William Shaw's letters and diaries, published as *Never a Young Man*, provide a more prosaic view of Salem than do Maclennan's poems. Here he describes his arrival in 1820 at the site assigned to Hezekiah Sephton's party of British settlers on the banks of the Assegaai River. There is much on which to reflect but, dumped in the wilderness and provided with only the barest essentials for survival, he and his wife, like all their compatriots, must fend for themselves.

> It is not easy to describe our feelings at the moment when we arrived. Our Dutch waggon-driver, intimating that we had reached our destination, took out our boxes and placed them on the ground, he bade us 'goeden-dag' or farewell, cracked his long whip, and drove away leaving us to our reflections. My wife sat down on one box and I on another. The beautiful blue sky was above us and the green grass beneath our feet. We looked at each other for a few moments, indulged in some reflections, and exchanged a few sentences: but it was no time for sentiment, hence we were soon engaged in pitching our tent and when that was accomplished we moved into it our trunks, bedding etc. All the other settlers were similarly occupied, and in a short time the valley of the Assagaay Bosch River which was to be the site of our future village presented a lively and picturesque appearance.

William Shaw may have 'no time for sentiment'; the novelist Francis Bancroft has plenty. *The Settler's Eldest Daughter*, published a century later, is at times weighed down by sentiment and sermonising, but it does evoke the early years of the Salem settlement with clarity and skill, particularly when Bancroft is dealing with place itself. Her protagonist, Anne Ashe, arrives in Salem shortly after its establishment.

> On the following morning, walking briskly ahead of the convoy, as she rounded the bend of the long sloping hillside Anne saw before her a wide green valley with precipitous heights to its right, from which rose

the stream that, trickling below through the bosom of the undulating plain, afforded a bounteous supply of pure water to the emigrant camp pitched along its banks.

Behind the camp to the south the valley sloped gently upward in a long incline bare in parts, in others covered by a straggling growth of low thorn bush. The long, flat ridge in which it terminated was topped by two bell tents gleaming white in the dazzling rays of the morning sun. The tents stood out boldly in the midst of a little encampment of round, grass-covered huts, the whole surrounded by a high thorn fence – Anne could only distinguish this latter as a dark object enclosing the little encampment.

'That's your father's place,' Burr, appearing unexpectedly at her elbow, informed her in tones modestly triumphant. 'Quite ship-shape it looks, don't it?'

'Oh . . . yes . . . I suppose so,' Anne catching at words to hide her feelings of dismay, replied politely. Her heart sank low at sight of that feeble attempt at home-making on the solitary hill-top. Never had the African wilds appeared to her so aloof, so uncompromising, so stern, as in this moment when she came face to face with the bare realities of the infant settlement ...

'That long grey building there with the slate roof, right at the foot of that spur of the hill, there – that's Our little Bethel we've built; the first Methodist chapel to be raised to the glory of God in these parts, in the Cape itself, I may say,' Burr said with pride in his tones.

'Oh, a Methodist chapel! For service?' Anne was looking intently, not at the building, but at that long upland rise above it with the bushy foreground and the broken veldt beyond. Down the hillside ran the trampled track cutting through the long grasses between the straggling fringe of the low-growing mimosas, past the spiked branches laden with the cushiony golden balls. A faintly remembered odour filled her senses. Not primroses, yet not unlike. Where had she seen it, known it, felt it all before?

The pseudonym FRANCIS BANCROFT intentionally deceived many readers of her day into thinking Frances Charlotte Slater was a man. Born in 1862 on the family farm Carnarvon Dale on the Bushmans River, near Sidbury, she was the granddaughter of an 1820 Settler and aunt of the writer Francis Carey Slater. After nineteen years as a teacher, Frances Slater trained and worked as a nurse. Exhausted by the rigours of nursing in Francistown during the South

African War, she retreated to the family farm to recover before moving to England, where her literary career commenced with the publication of novels and the writing of reviews and articles for magazines. The outbreak of the First World War in 1914 saw her back in South Africa, living in Port Elizabeth and writing for the *Eastern Province Herald*, all the while keeping up her literary work as novelist and short story writer. It continued after she retired to Carnarvon Dale, where she died in 1947.

In all, Bancroft wrote seventeen novels, a number of short stories and two plays. A romantic novelist, Bancroft reveals serious themes, but ones no longer fashionable. In her own day, particularly in England, she was quite well regarded, perhaps because she had a good visual imagination as well as an ability to unfold a plot in an interesting way, attributes that enabled her to paint scenes in a far-off land which many found intriguing. Her personification of Africa in *The Settler's Eldest Daughter* shows both the attractive and the threatening sides of a land which drew many to its shores and converted them into devotees. Bancroft's is only one of a number of historical novels – among them Anna Howarth's *Sword and Assegaai* (1899) and Vera Buchanan-Gould's *Vast Heritage* (1953) – that deal with similar situations in which a land that is at first strange and threatening becomes home. Settlers become part of the landscape and the landscape part of them.

The Methodist chapel referred to in the passage from *The Settler's Eldest Daughter* is the first of three churches built during Salem's early years. It no longer exists, but the second, built in 1832, and the church of 1850 remain. In front of the 1832 church, and on the brow of the opposite hill, are monuments reminding us of a well-known settler story which underlines the meaning of Salem's name. Richard Gush, a carpenter with Quaker leanings, did not believe in using violence even in defence. When he saw a large party of Xhosa, decked for war and approaching the settlement, he rode out to meet them, unarmed and accompanied only by his son-in-law and a Dutch interpreter. The outcome of his parleying with them was gifts from the settlers of bread, tobacco and some pocket knives, and the departure of the impi, leaving Gush and his fellow settlers unharmed. This was in 1835, during a war which left many farmsteads in ruins, and crops and herds decimated. Guy Butler dramatises this story in *Richard Gush of Salem*, first performed in 1970. Butler says of it, 'I chose the story of Gush because it is an astounding story by any standard; and because it touches issues which still torment and

Richard Gush's home

move us, not merely in Africa, but in Vietnam, Northern Ireland and Israel.' It is as germane today as it was in 1970.

Among the memorials in the 1850 church is a plaque commemorating the deaths in 1877, within hours of each other, of the friends Robert Michael Bruce and William Abercrombie Shaw. Robert Bruce is one of the most intriguing of the Eastern Cape's poets.

Writing in the *Evening Post* of 27 May 1978, Kathleen van der Riet says of the few remaining copies of a slim volume of Bruce's poems published in 1878 that they bear 'the fragile memory of an adopted son of our soil, whose spirit was stirred by the loveliness of the landscape, whose good humour was provoked by the modes and affectations of Settler society and whose sympathy for the customs and life of the colony's tribal inhabitants produced several memorable and evocative poems'. She was instrumental in having *Under the Yellowwoods* reprinted in facsimile to commemorate the centenary of the poet's death, thus ensuring a slightly less 'fragile memory'.

ROBERT MICHAEL BRUCE was born in 1850 and grew up on the farm Belton, near Salem. The family must have come out to South Africa sometime in the 1840s and they set up home at Belton, previously a settler location. Robert ('Bob') attended the neighbouring Salem Academy – a renowned educational institution of its day – and probably received instruction from his father, a former barrister-at-law of Middle Temple in London. His poetry shows evidence of wide reading, particularly in the classics, and a clear familiarity with the poetic forms of his day.

The title *Under the Yellowwoods* suggests a position from which Bruce observed the world around him and wrote of its beauties, its vagaries and some of the legends of local people: legends which had, as their setting, the rivers and forests and grasslands of his part of the Eastern Cape. There are still yellowwoods on Belton, and many of the features of the landscape he describes in the poem 'Belton' may be observed from vantage points on the farm: 'forest, plain and sky'; 'grassy slopes, bushy dells and kloofs'; and, in the distance, the sea. The Bushmans and Ghio rivers feature in a number of Bruce's other lyrical poems that indicate an enjoyment of outdoor activities and the sights of the countryside, including its birds, flowers and insects. At Belton the loeries of his poems still flit among the branches of the yellowwoods, dragonflies still hover over springs and streams, the mimosas and the avondblom still fill the air with their perfume.

B M R (ROBERT MICHAEL BRUCE)
Belton

Oh, for an artist's pen to trace
This wid'ning view in all its grace,
From the loved cot that 'neath me lies,
To the blue sea and brighter skies.
To trace with skilful, loving hand
Hill-top and valley, wave and land,
Shaded by clouds that hurry past
Before the cooling western blast.
And give to forest, plain, and sky
The changing tints that greet the eye,
My cottage home beneath the hill
First would my fond look greet thee still.
Thy white walls sparkling bright, behind
Dark Yellowwoods defy the wind,
Beyond the distant prospect swells
With grassy slopes, and bushy dells
And kloofs, where sounds the wood-dove's tale
And further in yon distant vale
The azure heavens reflected beam
Upon the winding Bushman's stream,
And Buchness' hill which bounds the view,
While round him rolls the ocean blue.

from Under the Yellowwoods

Bruce had a gift with words, an observant eye and acute ear, but must have worked at his verse despite his brother's contention that he wrote 'apparently without study or effort'. Among the 60 poems in *Under the Yellowwoods* are sonnets, lyrics in a variety of verse forms, and some smoothly flowing heroic couplets as well as 'charades' and 'riddles' that show a love of ingenious word-play. The most striking of Bruce's poems are narratives recounting legends or stories heard from workers on the farm, which he retold in classical style but using local imagery, as in this description of Nolai in 'The Snake-Fiend':

Ah! she was lovely as she roamed the field
With all her maiden beauties unconcealed,
Figure as pliant as the bushbuck's fawn,
Eyes bright as dewdrops on the leaves at dawn,

Eyebrows round, arching, like a Bushman's bow,
Lips rippling smiles, like streams when breezes blow,
Plump, rounded arms, down curving to the wrist,
Long taper fingers like the snakes that twist
Thro' the green treetops. Ah! Sekopa's flower,
Twenty fine cows for her were little dower.
But woe is me, the tale I have to tell.

In his use of such stories and images Bruce is a kind of halfway mark between Thomas Pringle, who, writing some 50 years earlier, also used local material, and Francis Carey Slater, who did the same nearly 50 years after Bruce. Professor Butler thought that the story of South African English literature might have been different had this promising poet lived longer and influenced others to adapt their work to local conditions. His potential was never realised because Bruce died in 1878, during the last frontier war, at the age of 27.

Under the Yellowwoods was intended for circulation among family and acquaintances. His brother, who compiled the volume, chose as frontispiece a poem by 'H. M. F.' called 'In Memoriam', in which succeeding stanzas celebrate Robert Bruce as 'poet-soul', 'student-mind', 'hero-heart' and 'friendship's *immortelle*'. In a poem called simply 'Lines', Bruce himself meditates on death and the yearning or 'vague instinct' people have to leave some mark on life. It concludes:

A Stone, a Tow'r, a Lyre, or a Sword,
   Old Time's obliterating march to stay;
Words, thoughts, deeds, griefs, and triumphs to record
   And leave Rememb'rance for a future day.

Although sometimes referred to as a soldier-poet, Bruce leaves the Lyre rather than the Sword as his memorial, as it is for his more famous counterpart, Rupert Brooke.

Almost a century after the time of Robert Bruce, another poet took up residence for a short period near Salem. In Robert Greig's introduction to his collection *In the Provinces* (1991), he attacks Eastern Cape provincialism with some vigour, but the poem 'Revisiting Salem' reveals an affection for Lower Croft, the farm on the outskirts of the village where he and his family had lived in the early '80s. Now, 'eager as tourists', they notice the good – such as the 'vibrant aloes' – and ignore the drawbacks – such as the 'goat-stripped hill'. Salem is a 'notional village which cannot be held / nor quite relinquished, essential as water'. Although Salem never fulfilled the expectations of those who established and built it up, there is something appealing about it. Rewarding experiences for the visitor may be gained from wandering around among Salem's old buildings which overlook a village green where cricket has been played since settler times, or by inspecting the graves in the churchyard against a backdrop brilliant with aloes. Across the river at Lower Croft are the forge and the armoury buildings Greig speaks of in his poem – complete with 'stark-armed pine' and 'bougain-villaea staining the ... wall'. All appears tranquil, in keeping with the name of Salem.

ROBERT GREIG
Revisiting Salem

While we gave birth or parted or cremated parents,
lightning twice struck Lower Croft, once our home,
docking the shrunken gable, till limewashed plaster

snowed the grass. It could be repaired; never was.
Those winter storms which plumped the river
first time in years, erased the nerves

of the stark-armed pine the Settlers sketched
lurching upon The Forge. Whose needles,
clogging gutters, made water taste of resin,

and hard grey shale, the grounds of Xhoi-San,
Xhosa, Gush and Nonquawuse, all held within
till we left for neutral, municipal waters.

Years on, returned in bigger cars, with cameras,
and children leery of cloudy Frieslands,
en route to sharkless beaches, new hotels,

briefly. Discovered a new style of conservation,
changing nothing, breaking nothing down:
just ragged borders replaced by fences for

good neighbours. Our orchard still remained
an idea of holes in the ground, our bougainvillaea
staining the Armoury wall. One new suburban house.

It was we who had changed, now eager as tourists
to applaud the raucous green of meadows,
ignoring charred humus, and vibrant aloes,

but not the goat-stripped hill, and machines
to pick pineapples, no workers to be seen.
Still, blue skies, benign sun were much the same.

I once drove home, seeing bloated smoke rise
where Lower Croft should have been. Imagined
windows awry, cows garrotted and splayed,

my wife dragged through thorn-trees to caves.
Only the annual torching of bush. Nothing changed,
except the black children no longer waved.

I walk to the house where strangers dwell,
see panes in the study missing still.
Someone after us made a wall of cactus:

we tried hydrangeas. Once the valley was famous
for citrus. We also planned a prospect of roses:
our shovels clanged on a roadway for wagons.

I dream of staying, making an offer with money
I do not have, repairing wounded gable and all
that eludes this hallowing recall.

But nothing is left and nothing brought
will remain. We change gears, the road now
is tarred. Going we leave no dust

to curtain the air and slowly drift
like the songs of returning choirs in buses
we used to hear on Sundays descend through

late sunlight into Salem Valley,
this notional village which cannot be held
nor quite relinquished, essential as water.

from In the Provinces

ROBERT GREIG has been both journalist and poet, winning awards in both fields. He was born in Johannesburg in 1948, attended school in what he calls 'the barbarian wilds of Natal', and studied at the University of the Witwatersrand. Witty and provocative criticism of various branches of the arts characterises his writings for a number of Cape Town and Johannesburg newspapers and, as well as poems in journals, Greig has published three collections of poetry: *Twenty-Four by Eighteen* (1967), *Talking Bull* (1975) and *In the Provinces* (1991). During the early 1980s he worked for the Grahamstown Foundation, which is what brought him to Salem. Greig's outsider view adds satirical spice to Eastern Cape literature and a realistic view of the landscape.

A smallholding 'at the end of a winding track some miles outside town' – the town being Salem – is the setting for important scenes in J M Coetzee's contemporary novel *Disgrace*. It is a work that has been widely acclaimed and has earned for its author the 1999 Booker Prize. The novel tells a bleak story, disturbing in its implications, and the Salem it depicts is far from peaceful. Details of setting are scant – 'a wind-pump', a 'sprawling farmhouse painted yellow, with a galvanised-iron roof and a covered stoep', 'a wire fence', 'a mud-walled dam', 'dust and gravel', 'red hills dotted with sparse, bleached grass'. However, like the notes of tenderness that occasionally relieve the grimness of the story, 'clumps of nasturtiums and geraniums' growing near a fence or the 'solid blocks of colour: magenta, carnelian, ash-blue' of the beds of flowers grown for sale, lighten the landscape of *Disgrace*. In Salem itself there are times when the yellow of mimosa blossom or the scarlet of aloes noticed by other writers relieve the historical village's somewhat dreary setting.

JOHN MAXWELL COETZEE has been awarded more major local and international literary prizes that any other South African, and the postmodernist nature of much of his writing puts his works in a different category from the predominantly realist responses to the South African scene that we have encountered. Cape Town has been the hub of Coetzee's life and work, but both have ranged far and wide and *Disgrace* is the first of his major novels to have an Eastern Cape flavour, albeit a bitter one. He is a distinguished academic who, until his recent relocation to Australia, was Arderne Professor of English at the University of Cape Town, where he had been on the staff for more than 30 years. Apart from nine major novels and two semifictional autobiographies, Coetzee has published influential works of literary criticism, among them *White Writing: On the Culture of Letters in South Africa.* In it several chapters are devoted to examining how writers have endeavoured to find new ways of reading the South African landscape that are not prescribed, as they sometimes have been, by some of the conventional ways of interpreting the landscape imported from Europe, where the topography is very different. As we have noticed on our tours so far, writers have many ways of seeing, describing and interpreting the places that speak to them – it is part of the fascination of exploring the literature of place.

BATHURST

Dan Wylie
William Selwyn

Just under two years after the founding of Bathurst, Thomas Philipps, who had been allocated a farm near the town and a site for a town house in it, states in a letter to his sister, 'Bathurst is done away with by proclamation.' The administrative centre had been moved to Grahamstown by the governor, Lord Charles Somerset, back from leave and ready to overturn many of the decisions of his temporary replacement, Sir Rufane Donkin. But Bathurst was not entirely 'done away with'. Attractively set among farmlands and bush-covered hills, it is a place where town and country blend harmoniously.

The Bathurst of today seems as far from 'the turmoil and cares that surround busy men' as the 'Sweet Bathurst' celebrated by William Selwyn in 1847. Few take time to sample its leisurely atmosphere and explore the town's many interesting features. It is simply on the road between Grahamstown and Port Alfred and, like the persona in Dan Wylie's poem who passes through the district in a minibus, the traveller catches mere glimpses of aloes, the big pineapple, a craft centre, erythrinas, windmills and irrigation sprays.

DAN WYLIE
Travelling

1. Minilux

Craft Centre. Metal Magic. Aloes
hum in their market of henna, a pineapple
bursts from the hill. Toposcope, a windmill
exclaiming *Climax*. Irrigation sprays
stitching new seams across lean fields,
erythrinas' unruly flamenco. And the sea.

This eye will leave no blade of light,
no guts of flattened rabbit
unblessed. Memory accumulates miles
without friction; curiosity leaps the Kowie,
contented and absolute as a cat stretching.

Out of the scorched ether of Radio An-
Dante guitars, atoning for their sins, shriek.
But for now, Hell is of no consequence.
Companionably clasped is my Virgil's jaw;
the sun curls up on our ruby necks.

Ahead, the moon rises, plump as a down pillow.

from The Road Out

To those who are or have been closely acquainted with Bathurst, as was
William Selwyn, a phrase from Wylie or a couplet from Selwyn may conjure
up more detailed pictures. Wylie's 'erythrinas' unruly flamenco' brings to
mind Bathurst in the spring, when the huge erythrinas that line its streets are
covered in scarlet-orange flowers. The toposcope he mentions marks the spot
on a hill near the town from which 1820 Settler locations were surveyed. It
affords excellent views of the surrounding countryside and
coastline, and identifies areas where various parties settled.
The pineapple bursting from a hill is on the farm
Summerhill Park just outside Bathurst, where visitors can
observe pineapple fields so characteristic of this part of the
Eastern Cape from a platform on the largest (artificial) pineapple in the

world. 'Craft Centre. Metal Magic' suggests that Bathurst is no mere relic of a settler past; it includes the population of Nolukhanyo – originally established for Mfengu people – eager to display their wares at the entrance to the town.

WILLIAM SELWYN
From Farewell to Bathurst

Dear beauteous spot, while I bid thee farewell
A train of sad thoughts like a mountain stream's swell
Pour into my soul, and the effort is vain
To repress its o'erflowings; why need I refrain?
Why long for his sordid insensible heart,
Who with spots so enchanting regretless can part,
Or his grovelling soul that ne'er glowed with delight
While gazing on scenes thus with loveliness bright.
    Sweet Bathurst, I leave thee to mingle again
In the turmoil and cares that surround busy men;
But thy vivid remembrance, congenial spot
Shall fondly be cherished whate'er be my lot.
Thy evergreen forests, thy verdure clad hills,
Thy kloofs and thy valleys, their torrents and rills,
Thy pastures luxuriant o'er studded with herds,
'Mong fragrant mimosa all vocal with birds,
Yon chaste lowly temple whose Sabbath day toll
Melodiously echoes from each grassy knoll,
Old ocean whose billows loud dashing on shore
The listening ear soothe with their far distant roar,
Each neat cheerful cottage where healthful delight
Where plenty and peace and contentment unite;
These gardens and fields whose munificent soil
Rewards with exub'rance the labourer's toil;
The friends who with kindness none e'er can transcend
First welcomed the stranger nor ceased to befriend; –
These all on mind's tablet a picture will form
In colours as fair as the bow 'mid the storm.
   . . . .

BATHURST 1847

from Cape Carols and Miscellaneous Verses

More than 150 years after Selwyn's departure from Bathurst, many of the features he imagines forming a picture on 'mind's tablet' are little changed. The 'chaste lowly temple' – St John's church – is the oldest unaltered Anglican church in South Africa. Many 'neat cheerful' cottages are scattered around Bathurst. It is still characterised by 'gardens and fields with munificent soil'.

Selwyn's Victorian sentimentality contrasts with the matter-of-fact tones which disguise the deeper musings of Wylie, the present-day poet. For both of them, however, Bathurst represents a stage on a journey: for Selwyn simply a place where he has lived and been happy, and of which he has fond memories; for Wylie a fleeting but vivid part of 'The Road Out', which is his journey of inner discovery.

In 1834 Captain Charles Jasper Selwyn came to the Cape as Commanding Royal Engineer on the eastern frontier. He and his wife Sophia, who were childless, brought with them nine-year-old William Godsell, the orphaned natural son of a cousin of Jasper. Young William Godsell attended the Grahamstown School and was profoundly influenced by its principal, Francis Tudhope. Pupil became teacher in 1841 when he was seventeen years old, and when Major and Mrs Selwyn left Grahamstown in 1842, William opted to remain in the colony. In 1846 he took up a teaching post at the Bathurst School, and while there changed his surname from his mother's Godsell to his father's Selwyn; as WILLIAM SELWYN he married a teacher from the Bathurst Girls' School. Selwyn chose a new career – banking – and in 1848 moved to Port Elizabeth, where he remained until his death in 1892.

For many years Selwyn had been writing verse in his spare time and, in 1891, 70 of his poems were published as *Cape Carols and Miscellaneous Verses*, all the profits going to the Ladies' Benevolent Society. 'Benevolent' would aptly have described Selwyn himself. He adhered to an essentially practical, caring Christianity and many of his verses are religious reflections on events of the day or texts from the Bible. As we have seen in Port Elizabeth with 'An Algoa Bay South-Easter', he also writes amusing ditties. Selwyn was not a great poet but, in his own way, he provides views of his time and place that are worth considering.

FAMILY LETTERS AND A CHRONICLE

Jeremiah
Goldswain

Thomas Philipps

A number of the British settlers who occupied this part of the Eastern Cape kept diaries or journals or wrote letters home, some of which were published more than a century after they were written. They present a kaleidoscope of views of the land of their authors' adoption and, like the historical novels mentioned earlier, often move from initial dismay through hardship to adjustment and affection. Two of the most interesting of these works come from men at the opposite ends of the social scale: the lowly Jeremiah Goldswain and the lofty Thomas Philipps.

The diary kept by Jeremiah Goldswain from 1819 to 1858, and published by the Van Riebeeck Society in 1946 as *The Chronicle of Jeremiah Goldswain*, offers a lively picture of the life of an ordinary settler. Goldswain's idiosyncratic spelling and breathless style, without punctuation or paragraphing, provide entertainment in themselves, and the piling of incident on incident in the earlier sections of the *Chronicle* keeps the reader riveted.

JEREMIAH GOLDSWAIN was born in 1802 in Great Marlow, Buckinghamshire, the only child of poor parents. He decided at the age of seventeen to go to the Cape, where he hoped to do well and then return rich. His parents did all in their power to dissuade him, but the stubborn streak which characterised many of his actions, and often got him and others out of tight corners in the land of his adoption, made the young lad deaf to all their pleas. In February 1820 he sailed for the Cape in the *Zoroaster* as a member of John Wait's party. He, and others who had signed indentures, were to serve their master for six years in exchange for rations, wages and half an acre of land.

The land allocated to Wait's party was east of the Bushmans River on the site of what had once been the place of a Dutch farmer. Goldswain records that they 'named this place Ravin hill as we saw sum Ravens [probably crows] aflien about the place'. Later it was called Belton – the farm on which the poet Robert Bruce was born 30 years later.

JEREMIAH GOLDSWAIN

When we came to the Bushmans River the Field Cornet was forst to git a farmer to show him the way: we ware a bout twelve days on our jorney: we came to our jurneys end a bout noon. This had been a Duch farmers place: thear ware meney of the postes of the Cattle Kraal still standing and the postes of the dweling House: they ware more or less burnt but we did not know the meaning of them been burnt at that time but we found out afterwards that the Kaffers had merdred they farmer and all his famley and had taken a way all his Cattle. We named this place Ravin [Raven] hill as we saw sum Ravens aflien about the place so we thought that was the best name for it ... The place ware we was Located [was] just in a line with jargers Drift [Jager's Drift] and about 3 Mites [miles] from the Drift on the Bushmans River and wen the Tide was down we could cross the River by polling off our Shues and Stokings and waiding thrue at needepe: they Rivers in this part of Afreck are not so wide or so deap as they are in England and meney other Cuntreys. The morning after we arived on the Land we commenced sarching fo aplace to build an House for our Master and also a place to plow and soe his seeds and we soone found the pleas ware the Duch farmer had had ploud and sowed his weat and barley as the stuble was still standing and quit fresh. I should have mentioned that wen Mr. Wait went to Cape Town wile we laid in Simon's Bay he ingaged a Mr. Roades [Rhodes] a schochman averey respectable man who had seen beter days and who had ben a chustum to farming in Scothland and he atended to the turning up of the soil for the Orenge Grove and Orcherd wile they remainde off us ware inploid som in faling Timber: one pear of sawyers ware set to work in sawing timber for making of plowes and harrowes and Quartring for doores and window frames and also bord for doores and windowe sheters: and they remainder of the men sum digen post holes and uting postes and sticks for wateling to make a watling and dorbd House and for theathing the House we cut long Grass out of the flaes (ponds) and it was not Long before we had the house finished and plowes and harrowes mad and they Land plowed and sowed and the cropes all in the Grown: and when we saw Mr. and Mrs. Wait comfutley situvatied in thear new Howes and everey thing ware planted we now thought it Quit time to ask for sumthing for our selves as we ware giting nothing nothing more then the 3/4 of pound of meal (corn ground but not sifted) and two pounds of verey poor meat that had not fat on it to frie so that if it was beef we ware forst always to stue it and if we wanted if it ware but a half peneysworth of salt we had to pay for it to our Master.

from The Chronicle of Jeremiah Goldswain

A dispute over wages and rations in which Goldswain played a major role forced Wait to release him and his fellow workers from their contracts. They obtained their discharges but were compelled to make their own way in the colony without fixed employment or abode.

Thus began a period of wandering for Goldswain, during much of which Bathurst was home base. He worked as a sawyer on building projects such as Bradshaw's Mill, just outside Bathurst, a water-driven woollen mill built during 1821 and 1822 and restored in 1976. He had to be 'soornin' [sworn in] as a soldier to help defend the colony and was often called out on patrol either to retrieve stolen cattle or to search for Xhosa people who had crossed the Fish River without passes. At one time Goldswain obtained a government contract for supplying lime to all the posts in the area; at another he worked for the Commissary Department, carrying supplies to the front. He tried his hand at trading and shopkeeping, and eventually bought a farm near Grahamstown. In the *Chronicle*, calamities minor and major are recounted with gusto: his pockets are picked and all his money lost just after leaving Belton; he loses his way or his oxen; thunderstorms or pelting rain impede his progress at inopportune times; he is gored by a cow or falls off his horse, eats a poisonous bean or is struck by lightning; his house is burnt down and all his possessions lost; he and his family suffer from illness, shortage of money and of food. Calamities are, however, balanced by successes and eventually this man of humble origins becomes prosperous and the bumpy ride on which his chronicle takes us is smoothed out. It ends in 1858, although Goldswain died only in 1871.

Jeremiah Goldswain came to South Africa as an indentured servant; Thomas Philipps came as the leader of a party from Wales, where his family had been well-to-do landowners with aristocratic connections. Letters written mainly to his sister Catherine during the first ten years of his residence here were preserved by the family and, in 1960, published as *Philipps, 1820 Settler*.

THOMAS PHILIPPS, born in 1776, was in his early forties when he arrived at the Cape with his wife, Charlotte, and their seven children – a mature man of good education who had trained for the Bar, although he had become a banker. Philipps decided to emigrate when hope of a political career was dashed and, almost from the day of his arrival, he played a prominent part in the affairs of the colony, often opposing the authorities both locally and in Britain and pleading for better conditions for the settlers and for the eastern part of the Cape in general.

Philipps and his party were allocated land about 8 km north of Bathurst, where he established a farm he called Lampeter after his home village. In 1825 he moved to a better site on the coast between the Kasouga and the Kowie rivers and Glendour, as he named his farm, became a thriving concern. After the death of his wife in 1834 he moved to Grahamstown, where he died in 1859. By then he had become a champion of the Cape, as the book he wrote in 1834 – *Advantages of Emigration to Algoa Bay and Albany* – proclaims.

Philipps's writings differ from those of Goldswain in their more erudite style and in the broader pictures he offers of society and his surroundings than the narrow, personal, albeit entertaining views of his fellow settler. As he writes on one occasion to Catherine: 'I shall be again talkative for half my pleasure in the enjoyment of every scene is from the idea that I shall *attempt* a description of them to my distant Friends.'

The comments in Philipps's letters about the weather and the ups and downs of farming provide little pictures of life for a 19th-century newcomer in the Eastern Cape. He complains about the authorities and describes, with pride, the building of his house. He admires new species of flora and fauna – some of which are sketched by his wife – but is sentimentally attached to the garden flowers of his former home.

> Strelitzias, several kinds of vines and aloes, Orange and Lemon Trees, Cucumbers, Melons, Pumpkins etc, all in the open air, appeared very singular. But nothing gave us so much pleasure as the first English flower blossoming, such is the force of habit! The Cowslip, Primrose or Snow drops, all these neglected flowers of the hedges which we used to pass by with such indifference, would here have the first place in the garden.

Philipps visited many parts of Albany and one of his most charming descriptions is of a week-long picnic on the banks of the Great Fish River – a very genteel affair in a clearing in the bush roofed with canvas where 'a long Table and a rustic sofa on each side accommodated as happy a party as ever sojourned together, and at night the illuminated roof and the gentle rustling of the Leaves around gave the appearance when viewed from the outside of a Vauxhall in Miniature'. British to the core as Philipps was, and bigoted in many of his opinions, his letters, nevertheless, offer some interesting views of the 'Settler Country' of his day and of some of the further reaches of the country he toured in 1825.

GUY BUTLER'S *PILGRIMAGE TO DIAS CROSS*

A major literary work set in this part of the Eastern Cape is Guy Butler's long narrative poem, *Pilgrimage to Dias Cross*. It was published in 1987, a year before the 500th anniversary of the visit to the southern African coast of the Portuguese explorer Bartolomeu Dias, who was seeking a sea route to India. It is out of the situation of racial injustice that was coming to a head in the 1980s, and out of his love for South Africa and concern for its peoples, that Butler's poem emerges. His evocation of the part of the Eastern Cape in which the poem is set also manifests the poet's love of this terrain and his sensitivity to the resonances place may offer. In the prologue to his poem, Butler explains:

> Angered by the political exploitation of differences between the peoples of his country, the ageing speaker makes an imaginary pilgrimage to a favourite spot: Kwaai Hoek, or False Island, the headland off the southern African coast where Dias raised a cross five centuries ago. On his way he is joined by historical ghosts who haunt the immediate hinterland. Between sunset and midnight the pilgrims cross the no-man's-land of sand dunes which connects the headland to Africa. They make a fire from flotsam, and keep vigil there, until the spirit of Dias appears. His presence enables them to affirm their common humanity and to share their songs, which transcend their divisive histories.

Within a radius of 20 km of Dias Cross, which is situated between the mouths of the Bushmans and Boknes rivers, are five other sites: the Theopolis mission station (now on private farmland) and the farms Belton, Melkhoutboom, Glenshaw and Richmond, at each of which another pilgrim joins the protagonist on his way to Kwaaihoek. (All are now private property and may be visited only with their owners' permission.) The pilgrims who join the poem's 'ageing speaker' at each place in turn represent the Khoe, Xhosa, Boer and British peoples who have inhabited the territory which is the poem's setting. We shall observe each site through the eyes of Butler and some of them through the eyes of other writers as we join his 'historical ghosts' on their pilgrimage. It is not only what the poet helps us to see but what sounds we hear and whom we meet that make this journey a memorable experience. It is also because place, in *Pilgrimage*, becomes a vehicle for ushering the reader into an appreciation of the aspirations of each group and for demonstrating the damaging effects of separation.

Theopolis mission station

At Theopolis we listen to the Khoe convert Cobus Boesak singing nostalgically of his people's history, and hear other imagined sounds from the past.

> Between the dark scrub and the moonwhite stones –
> deserted site proposed for the City of God –
> I hear a murmur of birds, a scraping of twigs
> washed by rippling voices quickened by clicks.

Designed to minister to the Khoekhoe, Theopolis – City of God – was located on land granted to the London Missionary Society on the banks of the Kasouga River. It was established in 1814 when the first missionary, together with a band of people from the older station of Bethelsdorp, was sent there to carve a settlement out of beautiful but isolated terrain. Under the Rev. George Barker, who was its 'Ruling Missionary' from 1821 to 1839, Theopolis became a large, thriving village with a lively Christian community. It was abandoned and all its buildings burnt down during a rebellion in 1851, and today the only remains of old Theopolis are a few dry-stone walls hidden in dense bush, and a solitary grave in a small grove on the banks of the river. It is the grave of Sarah, George Barker's wife, who died in 1836 giving birth to her fourteenth child. Cobus Boesak, a well-known Khoe member of the Theopolis community, played a prominent part in Egazini – the Battle of Grahamstown – when, with his band of buffalo hunters, he opened fire on the attacking Xhosa warriors and turned the tide of the battle. It is an action he seems, in the poem, to regret.

Belton Farm

Next along the pilgrims' way is the farm Belton, initially called Raven Hill:

> Near raw ploughed earth on 'Raven Hill'
> are angry voices; silences; we hear
> in English dialect loud argument
> surge and subside in the heat of desert wind.

Here Jeremiah Goldswain, member of John Wait's settler party, joins the other pilgrims. As recorded in the passage from his *Chronicle* that is quoted above, immediately upon arrival at the site allocated to them, the men in Wait's party set to work to build a house for their master, plant an orchard and make farm implements from local material. Then, after a lengthy dispute – hence the 'angry voices' and 'loud argument' – Wait had to agree to free them from their contracts. At Belton a group of scattered stones in a grove of erythrina is all that remains of Wait's house – probably a later one than that Goldswain helped to build. Nearby grows a lemon tree, surrounded by bush – a lonely reminder of the orchard to which he refers.

Melkhoutboom Farm

> At Melkhoutboom near Boknes River mouth
> Karel Landman shouts, 'Trek! Trr-ek!'
> A cry to curdle the sky. Above ten waiting wagons
> a bamboo whipstock waves, the whiplash flickers,
> licks air like a snake's tongue, cracks above the backs
> of the first of sixteen pairs of bullocks to the span.
> Long chains lift from the grass, wheel spokes turn,
> wince under weight, their iron tyres cut
> deep ruts into wet turf.

Representing the Afrikaner people in *Pilgrimage to Dias Cross* is Karel Landman from the farm Melkhoutboom near Alexandria. After the frontier war of 1834–1835 many Dutch farmers left the district to seek a new life in the interior. Some departed under the leadership of Jacobus Uys and others under Landman, who left only towards the end of 1837 with a party of about 40 families. They journeyed to Natal, where Landman played a prominent part in Trekker affairs. He settled near Glencoe, where he died in 1875, the longest-surviving Trek leader. Landman's soliloquy in Butler's *Pilgrimage* expresses poignantly the central problem of the history of the Eastern Cape, indeed of Africa: land.

> *Always this dream of possessing land,*
> *of being possessed by it. Land can grip*
> *the spine of a people, like my people, or the Jews.*
> *But where different peoples dream about*
> *the same piece of earth, the dreams clash*
> *and the frontiers darken and bleed.*

A memorial to Karel Landman and to Trekkers from these parts was erected in 1939. On a giant globe, Africa is straddled by an ox-wagon making its way – in Butler's words – to that illusive 'pastoral people's paradise'. It stands on a hill about 30 km north of Alexandria, surrounded by panoramic views of the region Landman left in search of the promised land. It is a good vantage point from which to observe the typical hilly terrain of this part of the province, and to ponder questions of land occupation and use that so often underlie the ways in which landscape is perceived in literature.

Glenshaw Farm

After the sounds of cracking whips and creaking wagons, Butler introduces the sounds of mourning as we approach the grave of Nongqawuse.

> Like rolbos blown to a halt in a fence we stop
> beside a copse of old, dark trees. A hole
> in the ground, a mound of damp clods. Some Xhosa men
> come stumbling into the streams of the wind
> to a weird, slow dirge. They place in the pit
> a shrivelled corpse in a worn kaross.
> Women squat on the grave's edge; they keen and weep.

Nongqawuse, the Xhosa representative among Butler's pilgrims, was the prophet of the cattle killing tragedy of 1856–1858. Her story, and its effects on our history and literature, is told in a later chapter when we visit her home on the banks of the Gxarha River, just east of the Kei. Local tradition maintains that after the cattle killing and a temporary exile to Cape Town, Nongqawuse settled in the Alexandria district and died there in 1898. On the farm Glenshaw, between Boknes and Alexandria, lies her grave, protected by a grove of indigenous trees in the middle of open pasturage, where some of the most beautiful dairy herds in the district graze: an ironic reminder of the thousands of cattle lost through Nongqawuse's prophecies.

Richmond Farm

The last of the pilgrims is James Butler, whom we observe through the window of the farm Richmond on the banks of the Boknes River, the closest site to the cross.

> Drawn by a candle-lit window at 'Richmond'
> we all stare into a room. The light picks up
> 'James Butler' in black on a leather bag.
> A very young man unpacks his letter book,
> moves to the table, trims the candle.
> Shoulders shaken by spasms of coughing,
> he waits with patience, goose-quill poised.

James Butler was the grandfather of Guy Butler, and today's attractive farmhouse incorporates that part in which he stayed in 1877 as the guest of the owners, the Rev. Barnabas and Mrs Barbara Shaw. This is where Guy Butler pictures him writing the diary to be published in 1996 as '*Jim's Journal*', a contribution in its own right to our literature.

JAMES BUTLER was born in London in 1854 and, in 1876, probably suffering from tuberculosis, he was sent to the Cape in the hope of recovering his health. He lodged first in Grahamstown and then with kindly people in various parts of the Eastern Cape before moving to Cradock, where he became strong enough to return to England in 1879. Within a year he was back and, in 1881, he married Annie Laetitia Collett. They had five daughters and two sons, one of whom – Ernest – was the father of Guy Butler. In Cradock, James Butler became well known for his kindness, staunch principles and active participation in municipal affairs and church ministry and for establishing the *Midland News and Karroo Farmer*, which he edited from 1897 until his death in 1923.

'*Jim's Journal*', based on letters home, reveals a lively mind, interested in everything around him. In this passage, written at Richmond, one can see that his description of a common sight in this part of the world – Cape weavers and their nests – shows an observant eye and a delighting heart. James Butler's recognition that bird-nesting might be considered 'unjustifiably cruel' – as it certainly is from today's perspective – shows a certain respect for the environment. His qualms are overcome by his desire to share the joys of nature with others.

> 16.XI.77 Friday. Fine
> This morning went bird-nesting; I hope we shant be considered as unjustifiably cruel as such a judgement on us would be incorrect. *We* having the opportunity of observing many of the wonders of nature are delighted with them and wishing that many of our friends may have something of the same pleasure, and hoping possibly in some small way to cultivate a love of Nature which has done so much to make our banishment tolerable we do as we do, not for 'sport' or for the fun of the thing but for the sake of gaining knowledge for ourselves and imparting some of it to others. After this long explanation let me proceed to describe our mornings search. Having observed a large number of nests on the reeds in the river

about half a mile from the house we repaired thither and considered how we could best get at them. Wading to them was not inviting as we did not know the depth of the water, the bed of the river was of soft mud and we were ignorant of the character of the inhabitants of the water besides fish, crab and iguanas. One of the latter we surprised on our path. The best way seemed to be by running a pier out into the river, so breaking off branches of trees and collecting logs of wood we constructed a pier of twelve or fifteen feet long and by this means were able to get some of the nests and eggs belonging to 'yellow finks'. These nests are neatly made of long flat grasses and are about the size of an ostrich egg but have the entrance from underneath; they are attached to one, two or three reeds about three feet above the water and sometimes there are two nests on the same reeds one above another. The eggs from one nest were of a light green and from another of a very pale drab but spotted alike. Two were found in one nest and three in another.

Dias Cross

On the quest for a sea route to India, Dias and his crew probably reached the mouth of the Keiskamma, which they named Rio de Infante, and after turning back they planted a padrão (a stone pillar surmounted by an inscribed cross) on the first suitable promontory where the weather allowed a landing. Its site was in dispute for many years, but the recovery of the original cross in 1938 by Eric Axelson proved that Kwaaihoek was the false island chosen by Dias to imprint on this part of Africa the sign of the cross. The discovery on the promontory and in the sea below it of crystalline fragments that differed from any of the local rock is an exciting story. Around 5 000 of them were pieced together to re-form Dias's cross, now housed in the library of the University of the Witwatersrand. A replica, presented by the Portuguese government during a 1988 re-enactment of Dias's voyage, and constructed, like the original, of white Portuguese limestone, now stands on the site. It may be reached by a beach walk from either Bushmans River Mouth or Boknes, or across dunes from an inland parking area.

Of the sixteen sections of *Pilgrimage*, ten are set at or near the cross. Butler's recreations of the locale where there is no sound but 'the interminable pounding of the sea' are superb.

From Pilgrimage to Dias Cross
2

On the highest coastal hill
in a gap in the shaken trees, I pause;
shadow-blotched, still as a stone-age man, I stare.

A dazzle of sands
staggers into the far white froth of the sea;
sea receding south into the arctic ice,
sweeping east to India,
west to the Americas,
but here to the north it beats
this blunt butt-end of Africa:
beaches, cliffs, dunes and coastal scrub,
this mini-desert of sand.

Far, on its seaward fringe
the focus of my eye:
a lonely wreckage of rocks
half-in, half-out of the endless thud
and sliding hiss of the tides;
a bonewhite cranium crowned with scrub
dark and evergreen.

Sea encountering sand, rock encountering sea,
and sea and land all round encountering the sky;
unbroken its encirclement, it rises
doming round and over those far rocks and me.

No sound except
the interminable
pounding of the sea.

Butler gives Dias a prophetic role, and the ghostly sailor leaves the scene
with this advice to the pilgrims and their descendants:

You!
You are nowhere near your farthest east,
still have to double your Cape of Storms.
Speak! Hope for hearers!
Act! And pray for friends.

Guy Butler's role as creator of *Pilgrimage to Dias Cross* is also prophetic. Rooted in place and in history, his poem looks to a future of peace and reconciliation in which people's common humanity is acknowledged, just as the pilgrims share their songs – the last sounds we hear in the poem. It is an ideal now enshrined in South Africa's Constitution.

COASTAL RESORTS

The coastline between the Sundays and Great Fish rivers consists of sandy beaches interspersed with rocky outcrops and backed by thick, dark-green coastal bush and dunes – some of great size. Many rivers flow into the Indian Ocean along these shores and, at the mouths of some, holiday resorts, villages and towns have grown up. The largest of them, Port Alfred, never developed into the harbour it seemed to promise and it, like its neighbours, has to depend largely on recreation and retirement for its development. On the whole, then, this is a region for leisure, enjoyment and contemplation. Released from what one of them calls 'the hurly-burly' of daily life, poets visiting one or other of the sites along this part of what is known as the Sunshine Coast have been inspired by scenes that catch the eye and calm the spirit or set the mind pondering some question of existence. This is a journey to be undertaken in a holiday spirit.

Woody Cape

First we look at Chris Mann's poem 'The Dunes at Woody Cape' from his collection *Heartlands* (2002). 'Our heartlands', he explains, 'are felt encounters with places that resonate in our memories.' For Mann, Woody Cape, along with many other sites in the Eastern Cape and beyond, is such a place.

Chris Mann

A 60 km stretch of coastline from the mouth of the Sundays River, past Cape Padrone to Cannon Rocks, is one of the most spectacular locales in the Eastern Cape. Huge shifting sand dunes separate the sea from inland bushveld and forest. Seashore, dunes and forest together form the 25 000 ha Alexandria Forest Reserve, destined one day to become part of Greater Addo. At the eastern end of the reserve is Woody Cape, where high sandstone cliffs, topped by dense vegetation, afford a view of the dune fields that makes one conscious of an immensity of space and of an unspoilt world rarely experienced in everyday life. As Mann says, 'Calm rinses steadily through you' in a renewing encounter with the landscape.

CHRIS MANN
The Dunes of Woody Cape

The dunes spread out their hills before you as you look at them.
Slope after scalloped slope of sand, further than the eye can see.

From where you climb, the view takes in the sea and its horizon.
Slowly, the molten wrinkling of the swells crumples on the shore.

You scoop up a handful of the hot sand, and run it into a palm.
The granules are the brown, the white and orange of sea-shells.

Faint memories of geological time-spans drift in, but do not fix.
You lift your head. The furthest dunes are white as cuttle-fish.

The nearest are fawn, bleached fawn. They shoulder above you.
Sprouts of sea-grass and light green, spiky reeds adorn their base.

You could be on an outing, in a garden of meditation writ large.
Its boulders are clumps of milkwood, its raked floor is the sand.

Calm rinses steadily through you. What follows could be grace.
And then you're ready, to turn and go back into the hurly-burly.

from Heartlands

Bushmans River Mouth and Kenton-on-Sea

Robert Bruce
Harold Sampson

Many people – writers included – have happy memories of holidays at
Bushmans River Mouth and Kenton-on-Sea, or Bushmans and Kenton, as
they are familiarly known. Bushmans lies on the western bank of the river
after which it is named, and Kenton between the Bushmans and Kariega
rivers, whose mouths are a mere 2 km apart.

Strandloper middens in the vicinity of Bushmans River Mouth confirm –
as its name implies – that this was once an abode of the San. Its modern history begins only in the latter part of the 19th century, when farmers from the
hinterland began using the site for picnics by the sea and then for holidays. In
'Boat Song', written in the early 1870s, Robert Bruce describes a boat trip
down the Bushmans River from Belton to its mouth. The poem begins with
three song-like stanzas:

Where the dancing sunbeams quiver
  On the rippling waves we glide,
Swiftly down the Bushman's River
  Floating with the falling tide.

Merry song and ringing laughter
  Sound our dancing boat above,
Echo's voice floats faintly after
  Mingling with the cooing dove.

Flow'rets yet with dew-drops sparkling,
  Morning's mists still in the sky,
Mirror'd hills in shadows darkling;
  As our bending oars we ply.

After this merry introduction the poem changes in style to something more
narrative as the friends row towards the sea through 'grassy vale and bush-clad
steep', noticing such details as the fragrance of mimosa, drops of light like diamonds dripping from their oars and the flash of a loerie in the bush. Near the
end of the journey other sights and sounds greet them.

Now wide, and wider, spreads the stream,
And many a loud, discordant scream
Of heron, stork, and ocean bird,
From hill to hill is echoing heard.
In yonder reach the boat-house stands,
And those short poles mark covered sands.
Row on – no breath to waste in speech,
We pause not till we gain the beach.

And now the waves, uneasy motion
Proclaims our near approach to ocean.
See there, the mighty billows glancing,
As on the swell our boat is dancing.
But now is gained the destined strand,
And light young feet leap on the land,
And some in loving converse walk,
Seeking the dripping sea-weed's stalk,
And some select the tiny shell,
Or bathe where seething billows swell.
And while they lunch in some cool cave,
The lonely boat rocks on the wave.[1]

Only the language of the poem tells us that this is not a present-day picnic. Almost every detail that Bruce notices characterises this tranquil milieu to this day – even the posts marking the height of the tide. The 'cool cave' where the friends lunch is on the east bank of the river, where Kenton developed as a holiday resort some years after its companion settlement, although now it is the larger of the two.

A less carefree note is struck by Harold Sampson's 'Bushman's River Mouth', written more than half a century after Bruce's 'Boat Song'. It is like a delicate watercolour painting of the place, but at the same time a reminder of life's transience, and also a reminder that stories about Bushmans encompass more than pleasant holiday memories. One story is of the wreck of the Norwegian barque *Volo* in 1897. Wooden relics of the ship have been incorporated into some of the 'peeping toy houses' of Sampson's poem which are situated near the sea among coastal milkwoods. For many years other parts of the *Volo* were visible, half buried in the sand between Kwaaihoek and the mouth of the Bushmans River and, as recently as 1998, the ship's anchor re-emerged.

HAROLD FEHRSEN SAMPSON
Bushman's River Mouth

There are boats green and white boats
wet ropes draggled with weed
and houses peeping toy houses
where no roads lead.

I see a seabird white and curving
its hour away from the waves
a cameo cut from floating foam
to put over sailors' graves.

A wreck came fifty years ago
with wild sails bursting over the sweep
of the surf – its broken back
and bolts now drift in the sands' sleep.

Is there no wreck still, on the shore
that life is to eternity,
no other proud masts and broken sails
that bravely went to sea?

No other broken back of dreams maybe
to last in wind and sands
beside the print of children's feet
in a world God understands?

By then the seabird white and curving
down the blade of the river
past the toy houses over the green boats
will have gone forever.

from Selected Poems of Harold Fehrsen Sampson

Kasouga

Harold Sampson
Dan Wylie

In *Kasouga Sands: The Story of the Eastern Cape's First Seaside Resort* (1991), Doris Stirk writes of the special magic of Kasouga – a small holiday resort between Kenton and Port Alfred. Whether for those returning year after year with families who have been holidaying at this spot for decades, or for occasional visitors falling under its spell for a weekend or a few hours, Kasouga certainly has a magic to which several poets attest.

These stanzas from Harold Sampson's 'Kasouga' depict this unsophisticated seaside resort as the perfect retreat from his workaday desk.

A hammock in the twisted trees
within the spell of whispering seas.
Against a moon-pale sky
a woodcut of black leaves
twigs and crooked branches
rooted in darkness.

Somewhere in life
a man at a troubled desk
staring at words –

But here afar
a spirit at ease
in the listening trees
beneath a tangled star.

As at Bushmans, Strandloper middens and Stone Age implements are found among Kasouga's dunes, and its name is derived from a Khoe-San word that probably means 'place of leopards'. There are still signs of game tracks leading to a spring where herds of game once came to drink. From late in the 18th century the land was farmed by trekboers. Under the British, it became a quitrent farm, later to be purchased by settler families, and in the 1880s its owner pioneered Kasouga as a private holiday resort. In season oxwagons trundled through the bush, bringing everything necessary for a sojourn at the beach. In time plots were laid out and sold while the so-called Green became public ground, where shack owners could erect their shelters each year.

Now, on the Green – a level grassy tract of land – stands an assortment of permanent, home-built holiday cottages. They lie close to a tranquil lagoon beyond which the beach stretches towards a distant fringe of breakers. The dramatic Ship Rock appears to be anchored just offshore, and remnants of several actual wrecks lie half-buried in the sand or lodged among Kasouga's rocks.

The background scene in Dan Wylie's 'Kasouga' is a collage of Kasouga images, to each of which the poet gives a life of its own. Perhaps it is not only the dog who is in 'pursuit of a dream / where no one's ever been'. Kasouga has the power to speak to the recesses of mind and soul as well as to the senses.

DAN WYLIE
Kasouga

The torn hem
of a cold front advances
out of a darkening sea,
the rusted wreck
burrowing into the sand
like a mussel:
why is it I
keep trying to hide myself,
keep longing
to bury myself in a woman,
keep breathing out and,
on reaching the pit
of breath's undertow,
wishing never to come up?

And why does the poem,
despite all that, insist
on chiselling its figure
on the pitted poop of Ship Rock,
and accommodate the sun
that laps the lagoon
and the crazy dog that dances
across the mercurial dunes
in pursuit of a dream
where no one's ever been?

from The Road Out

Port Alfred

Local people and personal friends of Port Alfred call it Kowie or eCawa, the name of the river on whose estuary the town is situated, probably derived from the pleasant-sounding Khoe word *Qoyi* – rushing. Leisure rather than rushing is, however, characteristic of the town's atmosphere.

Visiting poets Michael King and Peter Wilhelm see Kowie through the eyes of holiday-makers. King's 'Walking Along West Beach, Kowie' is a poignant evocation of one of the resort's beaches, and of the stone pier that guards the entrance to the Kowie River. People familiar with Port Alfred will recognise the scene that King paints so finely and some may well, like the poet, associate it with memories of past friendships. For newcomers it is a scene to be stored in the memory and a poem to help bring it back.

*Michael King
Peter Wilhelm*

MICHAEL KING
Walking Along West Beach, Kowie

The horizon is obscured by mist. The waves
Probe and withdraw, loosening the shore line.
The water-laden sand fills and empties
In time with the suck and surge of the tide.

The pier stretches into the mist. Its initial
Massive stones merge into conformity
And then fade to a blurred shapelessness –
An impression of being, without certainty.

Memories hover around the West Beach
Of friends, their youthfulness now passed, no longer
Walking in time, who slip away in benign retreat
Before they surrender into the mist.

The early morning light strengthens. Here
The day breaks the dawn's mystery.
We touch the wet rocks that make up the pier
And return to the car, to go home.

in Carapace 8 (1996)

For the most part, Port Alfred is imbued with the kind of tranquillity that permeates King's poem, for it is a popular holiday and recreational resort as well as a favoured place for retirement. The town is dominated by its river, arched bridge and the marina that now fills the once unkempt swamp of the Kowie's estuary. On either side of the Kowie, hilly suburbs, hewn out of the bush, are dotted with holiday and residential houses that vary from seaside cottages to mansions. There is, however, another side to Port Alfred: shanties clinging to the steep banks above the old road into the town from the north are reminders of the poverty that dogs many eCawa families. And, as Peter Wilhelm's poem hints, Port Alfred – a border town – has at times felt the effects of conflict: attacks during the frontier wars; a military establishment on the town's doorstep during the Second World War; even, as Wilhelm imagines, repercussions from the conflict on the Angolan border during the apartheid era, when conscripts might have holidayed here; and, during the same era, suffering and protests in Nemato township – out of sight of holiday-makers.

PETER WILHELM
Port Alfred – for Chris Mann

New borders have come but this Border stays:
stays like the lodger who's queer in his ways
but pays in a currency of fishlore, foamsuck, sun
spreadeagled like a kite over this estuary. Gun
boys on vac have their 'min dae' in this outpost
of the Fifties and the over-Sixties can boast
of Retirement in a perpetual post-prandial paradise
which, though not inflation-free, offers the lowest price
for the enormous, perhaps sentient, vegetables
which we should all, like blacks, head-carry to tables.

We're feastlings here, berrying in the sun,
tossed by the surf that sucks in our nose;
cast the line deftly, it sinks as it flows.
From the huge dunes you can kite windily. Run.

from Falling into the Sun

MICHAEL KING and PETER WILHELM are writers of a very different ilk. King is a school teacher with only one collection of poetry to his name: *The Fool and other Poems*, privately published in 1987. Wilhelm is a full-time journalist who has published novels, novellas, short stories, poems, plays, journalistic articles and criticism, and has won several prestigious literary awards. Both write of Port Alfred as visitors, but as visitors seeing the town through different eyes.

King was born in 1950 in the Transkei and grew up and was educated in the Eastern Cape, before going to Oxford where, like Chris Mann, he won the Newdigate Prize for Poetry. Now he lives and teaches in Cape Town but is well acquainted with Port Alfred, where he has often visited his parents. Wilhelm was born in Cape Town where he, too, now lives. He spent some of his early years in the Transkei living with grandparents, but for most of his life Johannesburg has been home-base.

Kleinemonde

Spring in the coastal region of the Eastern Cape is highlighted by the scarlet glory of large coast coral trees – *Erythrina caffra*. In 1898 a collection of poems by M E Barber, who grew up on the farm Tharfield, adjacent to what has become the settlement of Kleinemonde, was published for private circulation. It is called *The Erythrina Tree and Other Verses*. The title poem in this collection expresses Barber's delight in the 'Bright, glorious Erythrina tree / Queen of the forests near the sea'. She longs to escape from 'life's stern battle' to the shelter of this beautiful tree, which is associated with her early home on the coast, and to hear only the 'song of birds and bees'.

M E Barber
Thomas Philipps

MARY ELIZABETH BARBER (born Bowker) was a lover of everything natural in the country to which she had been brought in 1820 at the age of two. Her work as a student of plants, birds, animals and butterflies was recognised by many of the scientists of her day, including Charles Darwin, and she was also a remarkable artist. Barber's verses were written for the amusement of herself and her friends; although they reveal no great talent as a poet, they paint pleasing, sometimes amusing, pictures of her surroundings that add a gentle note to the literature of the Eastern Cape.

M E BARBER
From The Erythrina Tree

A Carol of the Woods

Bright, glorious Erythrina tree,
Queen of the forests near the sea,
Herald of springtide, wild and free.
Thy scarlet blossoms reared on high,
Above the woods in beauty lie,
Tinted in russet-purple dye;
While morning beams in laughing glances
Are quivering amongst thy branches,
And glowing flowers as day advances.

Bright, glorious Erythrina tree,
Queen of the woodlands near the sea,
Haunt of the sunbird and the bee.
'Neath sunny skies they feast for hours,
Quaffing the nectar of thy flowers
Whose scarlet petals fall in showers.
On dark and amethystine wing,
Flitting from flow'r to flow'r they sing
Their joyous songs to thee in spring.
A shower of ringing notes on high,
Apparently from out the sky,
Descend to earth all merrily;
While the cicada's ceaseless strain
From day to day – again, again –
Is heard through forest dell and lane
Thrilling the woods, a wild refrain.
...
Bright, glorious Erythrina tree,
Remote from cities – near the sea
My winged thoughts have flown to thee.

Queen of the woods, I love thee well,
Oh! for a home with thee to dwell
For ever in the forest dell.
From life's stern battle would I hide
By some bright sparkling fountain side,
Regardless of all time or tide.
Forgotten be the world's wild roar,
The turmoil of her careworn shore.
Oblivion shield me evermore,
My canopy the sheltering trees,
My dream the song of birds and bees,
Good-bye to all things saving these.

from The Erythrina Tree and Other Verses

Kleinemonde can be a place of delight – somewhere to escape from the pressures of life, as Mary Elizabeth Barber longs to do, and indulge in a fondness for natural beauty and outdoor pursuits. The scene is little changed from that described in 1823 by Thomas Philipps, except that a medley of holiday houses have been built on the sloping banks of the resort's twin rivers. The 'Magnificent Park' to which he alludes was probably Tharfield, the home of the Bowker family to whom M E Barber belonged, and still one of the most beautiful farms of the region.

> Instead of the romantic, we were reposing in a Magnificent Park, below us on the left Kleine Monden (now called the Lyndock and the other the Wellington) made an elegant curve as if formed or assisted by art, its waters clear and unruffled and beginning to increase from the tide coming in thro' its subterraneous passages, the Banks gradually sloping, quite unusual in any other River in this country, and the whole view terminating with the Southern Ocean billowing with its never ending surf.[2]

6 TIME, SPACE AND

LITERARY LANDSCAPES

THE KAROO

The Karoo, once you have been given the hint, is the eroded ruins of a world, the great lake and its giant reptiles gone but for a few bones and ripple marks, gone like Sodom and Gomorrah in earthquake and fire, epochs of reptilian life abolished, stone scorched and purged, and then sculpted clean and bare into noble shapes, the tactics of the elemental artist spelt out in the fine sand of the watercourses, his signature clear in the cirrus clouds. You can see all this because the air is dry, distances clear, and scarcely a shrub grows higher than your knees. In that vast semi-desert it is difficult to forget your smallness; the colour and size of the shrubs is shy; growth slow and stubborn; the dinosaurs seem to be saying, through the small swift lizard, the camouflaged snake, the armour-plated tortoise: we've learned our lesson, we'll stay small. The extremities of the seasons, from snow to blinding sun, drive the lesson home: no luxury here; every year frost and fire will search you and find you out.

Guy Butler's succinct description of the Karoo from his autobiographical *Karoo Morning* (1977) suggests an immense time-scale as well as an immensity of space that is contrasted with the diminutive shrubs that cover the earth and the sense of smallness that is often induced in those who are confronted by the landscapes of this part of the Eastern Cape. The Karoo is a place of extremes: the vast and the tiny; heat and cold; drought and flood; colours that range from drab to brilliant. In the minor Karoo classic *The Diary of Iris Vaughan*, the young diarist's father, in one of his 'savige' moods, terms it 'the godforsaken karoo', but to many it has conveyed a sense of the divine, variously interpreted; to some it has offered simply a sense of something beyond the material or touching the inner recesses of the mind. Given these large dimensions it is not surprising that the Karoo has bred or inspired some of South Africa's most notable writers and artists.

Our present literary journey takes us on a circular route through the heart of that part of the Great Karoo which lies in the Eastern Cape. It passes through the small towns of Cookhouse, Somerset East and Pearston, crosses the plains of Camdeboo to Graaff-Reinet and, with a brief sidetrack to visit the Valley of Desolation, moves on to Nieu-Bethesda. Finally, it encompasses Cradock and its neighbouring farms and mountains, a district particularly rich in literary connections. Just as there is an interaction of greater or lesser significance between writer and landscape, so there may be an interaction between reader and landscape. As we travel through this part of the Karoo, whether on the page or in reality, what we read of its poetry, autobiography, novel, short story or drama affects the way we see these places. What we experience of these places affects the way we read Karoo literature.

COOKHOUSE

Chris Mann

In Chris Mann's poem 'Cookhouse Station' the call to acknowledge the presence of the shades gives place a new dimension. The concept of the shades or spirits of the ancestors comes from African spirituality. To Mann they are not only the spirits of the ancestors but also all whose lives have gone to the making of our own – family members, friends, teachers, writers, even adversaries – and they may be acknowledged wherever we are in time or place.

CHRIS MANN
Cookhouse Station

For my sister Jackie

If you ever pass through Cookhouse Station
make certain you see what is there.
Not just the long neat platform beneath the escarpment
and the red buckets
and the red and white booms
but the Christmas beetle as well
which zings like a tireless lover
high in the gum-tree all the hot day.

And whether your stay is short
and whether your companions
beg you to turn away from the compartment window
does not matter, only make certain you see
the rags of the beggarman's coat
before you choose to sit again.

And even if there might be no passengers
waiting in little heaps of luggage when you look
make certain you see
the migrant worker with his blankets
as well as the smiling policeman,
the veiled widow as well as the girl
the trainee soldiers whistle at,
otherwise
you have not passed that way at all.

And if it is a midday in December
with a light so fierce
all the shapes of things tremble and quiver
make certain you see
the shades of those who once lived there,
squatting in the cool of the blue-gum tree
at ease in the fellowship of the after-death.

And if you ever pass through Cookhouse Station
make certain you greet those shades well
otherwise
you have not passed that way at all.

from Mann Alive!

The little town of Cookhouse on the edge of the Karoo evokes diverse associations – the Slagtersnek tragedy, for instance, and a mention (as Roodewal) in Thomas Pringle's journal; but it is the often anthologised poem 'Cookhouse Station' that gives it a particular literary association. The poem describes the station in the heyday of rail communication, when many passengers travelled through Cookhouse. Today that station is a sad relic of its past, all but deserted during the day. Buildings once well kept look neglected and depressed. There is no movement in the shunting yards. The branches of pepper trees on the platform hang so low that they obscure the 'Cookhouse' signs. The gum trees to the side of it stand in a forlorn row, gathering dust. Are the shades of all who have passed this way still there? Mann tells us that if we do not 'greet those shades well' we 'have not passed that way at all'. Chris Mann's poetry is rooted in local culture and his experiences of landscapes and people but, as in 'Cookhouse Station', it often encompasses something beyond the here and now and suggests that all time and space are interconnected.

SOMERSET EAST

Walter Battiss

'The loveliest mountain in Africa – the Boschberg – Mountain of Trees – flowing with waterfalls and garlanded with wild flowers' is Eve Palmer's description, in *The Plains of Camdeboo*, of the mountain that provides such a splendid backdrop to the town of Somerset East. Thomas Pringle, who visited in 1820, found the front of this wooded mountain 'superbly beautiful' and it is described with equal enthusiasm in the journals of earlier travellers.

The Xhosa chief Rharhabe is said to have had his great place on the Bosberg during part of the 18th century, and the area took the name of his wife, Nojoli. Later, the foot of the Bosberg was chosen by the British colonial government for a farm set up in 1815 to produce supplies for border garrisons. The farm was named Somerset for Lord Charles Somerset, governor of the Cape, and after it closed in 1825, a town grew up on the site. Today it is an attractive place, renowned for its gardens and many early 19th-century buildings, among them the elegant parsonage, now a museum, and the Battiss Gallery, once an officers' mess.

The creativity of Walter Battiss, who is best known as an artist, also found expression in the written word, including poetry:

> His life was a poem. His acts were poems. He painted poems. And he also wrote poems. A few. Some were interspersed among the drawings, paintings and photographs in *Limpopo* (1965), surely the most beautiful book ever made in this country. Some were printed in *Ophir* poetry magazine (1967–1976). Some were printed in his handmade book, *Nesos* (1968). And some were left where, like Walt Whitman, he negligently tossed them aside.[1]

WALTER WAHL BATTISS was born in his grandfather's house in Somerset East in 1906. Later his parents rented the old officers' mess and established a private hotel where the family stayed until moving, in 1917, to the Orange Free State. In the opening chapter of *Limpopo* – 'Rain in the Karoo' – Battiss gives a brief, typically humorous outline of his life. The cryptic assertion 'My father was a waterfall, my mother a butterfly' is explained later:

> My father spent his time taking the guests on picnics to an astonishing waterfall on Glen Avon farm in the Boschberg. At the age of six I found it easy for my father and the waterfall to be one and the same manifestation of paternal energy. My mother was small and flitted around, delicate yet supermobile, the abstraction of a butterfly.

Battiss skims through the story of the family's life in the Orange Free State, his jobs in the civil service, and training and jobs as a teacher in the Transvaal. In 1936 he was posted to the Pretoria Boys' High School, where he taught for nearly 30 years. 'Now in 1965', he writes, 'I am a professor at the University of South Africa, Pretoria. This seems enough of banal biography and I would rather return to the Karoo.' Then follows the poem below in which he meditates on a favourite theme – negative and positive time and space.

WALTER BATTISS
Untitled

Flat veld sandpapered to smoothness
Distant antheaps like pimples on a boy's face
Deep dongas offering the therapy of shade
Shadows as pale as hotel soup
Birds interfering with the sky
Fish, making the water drunk
The approaching storm coughing out its red dust
The Karoo says: –
The infinity of space
is negative and positive space
cancelling out each other
The infinity of time
is negative and positive time
cancelling out each other
Life is sculptured time
By living we make shapes in time
Karoo mountains –
a fierce beauty for the initiated only
Karoo hour –
An hour without an omen

from Limpopo

Walter Battiss's life was far from banal. He became one of South Africa's best known artists, renowned for his sense of fun yet with an underlying seriousness in his ideas and works. His artistic output was prodigious and varied and his writings extensive. Unconventional in dress and opinions, he opposed blind conformity and encouraged the celebration of life and art, often in the face of bitter opposition. He brought the art of the San people to the notice of the public, copied many of their rock engravings and paintings, and wrote important books and articles on this subject and others connected with South African art. More personal in tone, *Limpopo* and *Nesos* are treasures of creative travel literature.

For Battiss, reality and fantasy were two sides of the same coin and he invented, in collaboration with others, the world of Fook Island, of which – as Ferd the Third – he was king. He maintained that this happy, imaginary world was the reality within ourselves and, therefore, present wherever we are. Some of the island's artefacts – stamps, banknotes, passports, coins, flags and banners – are displayed in the Battiss Gallery. His Fook books are an idiosyncratic form of literature. There is even a Fook alphabet and – if one can understand Fook language – Fook poems.

Battiss's art, although the human figure dominates much of it, is embedded in a love of landscape awakened during his childhood in Somerset East. Battiss was an exuberant teacher who loved to share his creative gifts and enthusiasm for art with others and, during the 1970s, he conceived the idea of establishing an art gallery in Somerset East. Less than a year before his death in 1982, he attended the opening of the Walter Battiss Art Museum in the very building where his family had run their hotel and he had first become, in his own words, 'art-crazy'. Although not fully representative, the selection of paintings (oil and watercolour), drawings and graphics that Battiss bequeathed to the gallery constitutes a fair sample of his works. They convey the same delight in the perceived world, the same gift for transforming what he saw into startling images, and the same depth of thought that characterises his poems.

PEARSTON AND THE PLAINS OF CAMDEBOO

Ernst van Heerden

Eve Palmer

Isobel Dixon

About 15 km from Somerset East, as the road passes over Bruintjieshoogte, the view expands in every direction. An undulating floor dotted with koppies stretches to a distant horizon of mountains. It is a part of the Karoo that has achieved literary fame through Eve Palmer's book *The Plains of Camdeboo*. About halfway along the road that crosses these plains lies Pearston, a little town overwhelmed by a vast landscape. Pearston has evoked from passersby a number of literary responses and has its own literary figure of note – the poet Ernst van Heerden.

In a side room of Pearston's Dutch Reformed church – one of the most beautiful in the Eastern Cape – is a display of pictures and writings relating to Ernst van Heerden. The display includes copies of four poems directly inspired by Pearston. All refer to the poet's father, who ran a general dealer's store in the town; all show an affection for Pearston and the Karoo landscape in which it is set; all are in Afrikaans. One of these poems, 'Karoonag' ('Karoo Night'), has been translated into English for this book by Malcolm Hacksley.

ERNST VAN HEERDEN
Karoonnag: Pearston

Kan sterre helderder
en onpeilbare swart swarter?

Planete brand en gloei,
swaeldamp tussen stelsels stuif ...

Die engele dans ontelbaar
op elke naald se punt ...
Met alle spikkels ewewigtig
en apart:
on-trapees-gebonde sweef-arties.

Nou lê die slange stil,
en merinolammers, en springbokke,
en graatjies, en vinke,
net otters and spoke loop,
en ek ...

Rus in vrede:
Voortrekkers en padbouers,
transportryers en veeboere,
dorpsmense, en my pa en ma,
van doer by Bruintjieshoogte
tot doer by Tandjiesberg.

from Teenstrydige Liedere

Karoo Night: Pearston

Could ever stars be brighter?
Plumbless darkness blacker?

Planets burn and glow,
brimstone vapour sifts through galaxies ...

Innumerable angels dance
on every needle point ...
Every poised pinprick shines distinct,
an acrobat flying free of sky's trapeze.

Now the serpents all lie still,
like the merino lambs, the springbuck,
the meercats, the finches;
only otters and phantoms walk the night,
like me ...

Rest in peace:
pioneers and roadbuilders,
waggoners and stockmen,
townsfolk, and my mum and dad,
from way up there on Bruintjieshoogte
all the way to distant Tandjiesberg.

translated by Malcolm Hacksley

The Karoo is renowned for the clarity of its night skies and Van Heerden transforms the skies over Pearston into poetic images with a clarity of their own: we see those skies and the stars that adorn them and sense the silence of the night. The poem reminds us of some of the people who have inhabited or crossed the plains of Camdeboo between the distant mountains of Bruintjies-hoogte to the east and Tandjiesberg to the west. Ernst van Heerden's parents, as well as various historical groups of people, are presences in the poem – echoes from the past, rather like the shades of Chris Mann's 'Cookhouse Station'. The poet remembers the itinerant cattle farmers, or trekboers, who first settled officially in the area in the 1770s. He remembers Voortrekkers from this region who joined others from Graaff-Reinet to trek north in the 1840s, and transport riders who used the old highway across the plains, as had many 18th- and early 19th-century travellers from Europe. The townsfolk the poet remembers trace their history back to the middle of the 19th century when Pearston – named after the Rev. J Pears from Somerset East – was established as a centre for worship and church administration.

ERNST VAN HEERDEN was born in Pearston in 1916 and during his school-days there he was – at the age of twelve – appointed *Eastern Province Herald* correspondent for Pearston, being enjoined by the editor 'not to burden the paper with florid descriptions of nature, but to stick to the facts'. Thus began his writing career. Writing was coupled with a love of English literature instilled by his mother, but it was in the realm of Afrikaans literature that Van Heerden made his mark on the cultural history of South Africa.

Schooling was completed in Port Elizabeth at the English-medium Grey High School. After studies in literature at Stellenbosch and in Europe, and a travel bursary in the United States, Van Heerden took up a lecturing post in 1959 at the University of the Witwatersrand in Johannesburg, where later he became head of the department of Afrikaans and Nederlands. Between 1942 and 1996, fifteen collections of his Afrikaans poems were published, and a selection of those poems, in English translation, appeared in 1986 as *The Runner and the Shadow*.

In 1948 Van Heerden won an Olympic silver medal for a group of poems about sport placed second at the arts festival run concurrently with the games in London. Many other awards and honours came Van Heerden's way during his academic career and after his retirement in 1981. Pearston honoured him in 1989 with the freedom of the town. Eve Palmer was honoured in the same way and, at a ceremony to mark that occasion, a message was read from Ernst van Heerden, in which he wrote: 'When reading Eve's works – whether dealing with a herd of Springbok scampering across the veld or the inimitable scent of rosemary and thyme – I am struck by her poetical way of looking at things and by the way so many of her paragraphs read like the purest poetry.' Clearly these two very different writers shared a love of this part of the Karoo. They were born in the same year –1916 – and they died within a year of each other – Van Heerden in 1997 and Palmer in 1998.

EVE PALMER was born on the farm Cranemere, about 12 km west of Pearston. Farming is almost synonymous with Camdeboo, but no farm in the district is better known than Cranemere. The reason is partly literary: Eve Palmer's *The Plains of Camdeboo*. The product of dedicated research, enlivened with anecdote and the passion of personal experience, the book tells the story not only of Eve's family, the Palmers, who have been on Cranemere since 1880, but of the whole region. In the opening chapter she writes:

> It is a country flooded by sun; lonely, sparse, wind-swept, treeless on the flats for many miles. In very good years thirteen inches of rain may fall in a year; in bad years three; and mostly it is somewhere between the two. After rain the Plains wave with grass and smell of honey and flowers; in drought they are desert. In between such times they are karoo – moorland, the early travellers called them – covered with low karoo bushes, little perennial daisy bushes with long, thin, wandering roots and tiny tough leaves that survive where grass cannot, and succulents of many kinds, breeding sheep with good bone and meat, and finest wool.

Palmer's response to place is not only to recreate for her readers its present character, but to find in its present evidence of its past. Like Van Heerden, she evokes the presences of trekboers and travellers, farmers and townsfolk. Palmer also makes us aware of the prehistory of the plains, which goes back millions of years, of the abundant game that once enjoyed the freedom of this space, and of precolonial peoples – the San and the Khoekhoe – for whom it was home, as well as of the Xhosa of neighbouring Bruintjieshoogte and later of the plains. All these associations are set against the background of the region's geology and, most importantly, for she was a botanist, of its flora. *The Plains of Camdeboo* is an all-encompassing and sensitive portrayal of this area. It helps to shape a reader's perceptions of the Karoo.

Pearston lies on the edge of one of the richest fossil-bearing districts in the world, and the Palmers, encouraged by the renowned palaeontologist Dr Robert Broom, who lived for some years in Pearston, discovered many a fossil on Cranemere. As Eve Palmer says:

> Travelling through the quivering air of the Plains of Camdeboo, it is almost impossible to believe that there was ever a time when the climate of this land was different, when the Karoo was mainly swamps and lakes. Yet the Karoo was once a vast lake fed by a huge river, possibly larger than the Nile, which meandered across the country from the north, spreading a great sea of mud over the land. Here lived and died the millions of reptiles big and small which lived in this remote muddy world, here they left their bones, and here in course of time the climate changed and the mud became shale, holding within it these bones, themselves become like rock in hardness. These are Dr Rubidge's fossils of today.

Dr Rubidge, like Dr Broom, collected many fossils from this area and they may be seen at his museum at Wellwood near Nieu-Bethesda. Stone Age implements going back thousands of years have also been found in abundance on the plains and in the adjoining mountains, while paintings by San artists adorn many rock shelters. Fossils as well as San artefacts and copies of their paintings – all found on Cranemere – are housed in the farm's interesting little museum.

Once the San hunter-gatherers regarded the plains as theirs, but as others moved in and occupied the land they retreated to the mountains and eventually succumbed to the gun. Their demise is one of the tragedies of Africa. As Eve Palmer says, 'they belonged to the wind, the veld and the mountains, and it is here we think of them for they were part of these things as no one else in Africa has ever been.' Most of the Xhosa people of the district are descended from forebears who came only after the cattle killing episode of the 1850s. All inhabit the world of Eve Palmer's Camdeboo books.

Eve Palmer trained in London as a journalist and could write with a novelist's gift for narrative and a poet's gift for lyricism. As a botanist, she could also write with a scientist's gift for accuracy. As well as such personal works as *The Plains of Camdeboo* (1966), *Return to Camdeboo* (1992) and *Under the Olive: A Book of Garden Pleasures* (1989), Palmer produced, with Norah Pitman, the first major book for general readers on the trees of South Africa, followed by a three-volume work on the trees of southern Africa. With her husband, the adventure novelist Geoffrey Jenkins, Eve Palmer also wrote *The Companion Guide to South Africa*. It reveals the interest in history and the landscape of this literary couple who lived in Pretoria but frequently visited Cranemere. Jenkins draws on the Eastern Cape (but not this region) for only one of his sixteen best-selling novels: *Scend of the Sea* is set off the Transkei coast. His wife's re-creations of the landscapes of her early home are among the finest in Karoo literature.

> Most people who travel our Karoo remember the drought, the sand, the stunted karoo bush, the empty river-beds, a muted landscape of black and grey and dun bushes, red and cinnamon earth, and a white hot sky above ... But after rain the *whole* veld blooms. The common karoo bushes flower in yellow, strawberry pink and blue, the thorn vygies in purple, and the other vygies in every shade. Many grow in communities together so that there are not pinheads of colour but great bright stretches

merging into one another, not the flaring oranges and yellows of the desert flowers of Namaqualand but richer and softer. Airmen flying over the Karoo compare it then with a giant Persian carpet, and from the air the Plains of Camdeboo must indeed have an Eastern richness.

❦

We leave Pearston with Isobel Dixon on her way across the plains to her home town, Graaff-Reinet, and we may identify with her poem 'Pearston' if we regard the town as merely a place on the way to somewhere else and the farms of the plains as little more than flashing pictures seen from a car window. If one wants to make closer acquaintance with the presences of the plains and with its literary heritage it is, however, worth stopping in Pearston and looking beyond its 'one drab street', or arranging to visit Cranemere and its private museum, which houses many artefacts that readers of *The Plains of Camdeboo* will recognise.

ISOBEL DIXON
Pearston

I'm never glad of Pearston
in the day,

a hot, flat town, that's barely more
than one drab street and one superfluous stop,
pause for a closer look at dust and heat.

A glimpse of man's strange clumsiness,
the stubborn will to build things
squat and dull.

Even the pines, in one dejected row
are shabby-edged and filmed with dust.
Perhaps the open plain was better left
untouched.

Yet after dusk
there's comfort in the distant view
of one small clustering of lights
beneath the darkening overflow of sky
and passing through, I'm glad of light
that's warm behind the window's lace,
and one late watcher on the stoep.

Just one last stretch ahead,
the town's a breath, a step to home
with something mutely brave, despite itself,
in every plain facade.

from Weather Eye

GRAAFF-REINET AND THE VALLEY OF DESOLATION

Poems about Graaff-Reinet highlight some of its most memorable features: the curve of the Sundays River in which the town lies; its encompassing wilderness and mountains; Spandau Kop; its predominantly white buildings, set off by the foliage of trees along a regular grid of streets and by its verdant gardens. Beautiful in itself and held within a river's embrace and the setting of the 14 500 ha Karoo National Park, Graaff-Reinet has earned the titles of 'gem', 'jewel' or 'oasis' of the Karoo.

F C Slater
E du Pisani
Isobel Dixon
C J Driver

FRANCIS CAREY SLATER
Graaff-Reinet

And now beset with bleak regret
The trekkers trek from Graaff-Reinet:
From Graaff-Reinet, that dappled gem
On the desert's dusty hem;
Graaff-Reinet – green oasis –
Round which Sunday's waters hiss
In a yellow coil, when rain
Rouses them from stagnant pain.

Spandau's Peak – that sunsets burn
And the dove-clouds dally on –
Fashioned like the haughty stern
Of a Spanish galleon,
Rock-browed Spandau gazes down
On a chess-board featured town,
Where in clean-cut squares are seen
Houses white and gardens green.

Hard by, Desolation's Vale
Yawns to greet the screaming gale:
There gigantic pillars rise
Shoring-up the sagging skies,
Rude, fantastic, piled-up stones,
Like monstrous dragons' mouldering bones,
Ruins, where some eye might see
Relics of lost Nineveh.

– So, beset with bleak regret,
The trekkers trek from Graaff-Reinet:
They look their last on Spandau's Peak;
Tandjesberg their sad eyes seek;
Vineyards, gardens, houses white
Fade before their failing sight,
As with sore hearts and eyelids wet
The trekkers trek from Graaff-Reinet.

from The Collected Poems of Francis Carey Slater

ETIENNE DU PISANI
Graaff-Reinet

Guarded by a dark hill
handcuffed by a dry river
inequalities and history

A cluster of trees
lights and buildings

A sun-bleached
windswept village
glamorized as
the Gem of the Karoo.

from One

ISOBEL DIXON
Fruit of the Land

In Sunday school we heard of Caleb's men –
the branch laid long between broad shoulders
and the wealth of grapes hung heavy ripe and sweet.
I never found a crayon purple-black enough
to colour in that promised land's first fruit.

Our yard possessed its own abundance then.
We left the small tart apricots to worms
but raced the birds to get the pickings
off the vines. Inched up the poles and crept along
the trellises, clipping the wiry twigs

with blunt-beaked secateurs, a hand to couch
the bunch's weight, so easily bruised.
We cut and ate and filled the baskets
past their plaited brims. Our shoulders ached
with carrying such freight of sweetness to the house.

You buy them almost year round now –
pay solid pounds for every stem.
But worth it even if the price were sphere for sphere,
each small explosion in the mouth
the precious milk and honey of nostalgia.

from Weather Eye

Slater's 'Graaff-Reinet' verses, written in the 1930s, paint a historical picture of the town as he imagines it to have appeared a century earlier – the time of the Great Trek. Isobel Dixon's 'Fruit of the Land' presents a more personal response to Graaff-Reinet as she looks back on her late-20th-century childhood, and her more focused picture invites the reader to imagine feeling and tasting as well as seeing the fruit of the town's renowned vines. Slater's glowing descriptions of Graaff-Reinet and Dixon's nostalgia are deflated by Du Pisani's minimalist modern poem, which implies that it is not as glamorous as its 'gem' epithets suggest, and his image of Graaff-Reinet 'handcuffed by a dry river / inequalities and history' is a reminder of the town's troubled past.

Named for one of the Cape's governors, Cornelis van der Graaff, and his wife, Reinet, Graaff-Reinet was established in 1786 by the Dutch East India Company at the request of frontier farmers. Soon, farmers and officials were at loggerheads with one another and with the indigenous people within and without the colony. The British occupation of the Cape a decade later was not favourably received by the burghers of Graaff-Reinet, who attempted to set up an independent republic. Relative calm prevailed during the rule of the Batavian Republic, but the unpopularity of British rule (re-established in 1806) led many Graaff-Reinetters to seek freedom from the shackles of a government they distrusted – hence their participation in the Great Trek of the 1830s. Contentiousness has not been confined to the town's colonial elements. Cape rebels from Graaff-Reinet were involved in the South African War of 1899 to 1902 and anti-apartheid campaigner Robert Mangaliso Sobukwe, founding leader of the Pan Africanist Congress, was born and is buried in Graaff-Reinet, where political disputes have often raged.

When leaving Graaff-Reinet today's visitors or residents may, however, like Slater's trekkers, be 'beset with wild regret' or, like Isobel Dixon, carry with them 'the precious milk and honey of nostalgia'. Graaff-Reinet, the Eastern Cape's oldest town, is one of her most beautiful. Its range of museums and proclaimed architectural heritage sites makes it also one of her most interesting.

ISOBEL DIXON, who won the 1990 Sanlam Literary Award for an unpublished collection of poems – *Weather Eye* – lives in Cambridge in the United Kingdom and works in London as a literary agent, very often helping to encourage South African writers and introduce them to the world. One can be glad that her own work has been introduced to the world through the publication of *Weather Eye*, in which she explores various kinds of landscape both literal and metaphorical. Many of them are the landscapes of the Eastern Cape, where she was born – in Umtata – and grew up – in Graaff-Reinet. We have already met Isobel Dixon in Grahamstown and in Pearston on her way home to Graaff-Reinet. Here, in her home town, she writes with meticulous attention to detail of such delights as the picking of grapes, linking it to the biblical story of Caleb reaping the fruits of the promised land. 'Fruit of the Land' is a sensual poem; it is also a poem of nostalgia without being self-indulgent. There is a joyousness in Dixon's writing that invites one to share her pleasure in the observed world, which is, often, the world of her homeland.

Situated 14 km outside Graaff-Reinet is the Valley of Desolation, referred to in the third stanza of Slater's 'Graaff-Reinet'. The images he uses are no exaggerations. This valley is one of the region's, indeed one of South Africa's, most spectacular natural wonders and a site that has inspired a number of poets to think in equally expansive terms. From the head of this valley the views are awe-inspiring: in the foreground huge, precariously piled columns of rock, tumbled lichen-covered cliffs, and a jumble of fallen rock debris; in the distance, the extensive plains of Camdeboo, far-off mountain ranges and landmarks such as Spandau Kop, Tandjiesberg and the Kompasberg.

Slater, in 'Graaff-Reinet' as well as in his poem 'The Valley of Desolation', which focuses exclusively on the site – and C J Driver, in the poem 'Once' – recognise in the scene images of fallen civilisations, but beyond that their responses differ. Slater finds it a place of exultation rather than of the desolation he associates more with 'life's highways' than with this secluded place where he experiences a sense of God's presence:

Down amid life's highways – *there*, is Desolation, –
  There baneful doubt bites deep into the soul, –
There prayer is stifled and budding hopes are blighted, –
  There obscured the path is and eclipsed the goal.

– Ye who are weary of life's unceasing tumult, –
  Who would find peace, feel God exceeding near, –
Come to this fane among the hills this Valley –
  Not of Desolation – this Vale of Prayer!

For Driver, recently returned from exile, the valley is a reminder of events in his own life and of the impossibility of going back to 'Once'. It is also a reflection of the apartheid era's attempts to build impossible edifices. There is neither consolation nor desolation in his response, only a sense of inevitability. As with these poets, readers will find their own connections and meanings in the Valley of Desolation, but no one will forget the sense of time and space the site evokes.

C J DRIVER
The Valley of Desolation
Once

Notice: Do not even think of throwing stones.

I thought I might have found the perfect place:
It went awry, or had been all along.
It seems as if a builder started here
To make a desert temple out of stone
And then got bored. Great rocks are piled
On lesser rocks, and upward stacked like years
In crazy thoughts of history.
                              I thought
I'd learn at least to live with what I found
Intolerable, but could not keep my peace.
I tried to get away with thinking things
Illegal. I was wrong. The state demands
One's heart and head ... So next I raised my hands
In supplication or despair, but found
Surrender meant one's soul. One goes away.
One's not afraid to say. One needs to keep
One's private counsel. And one doesn't judge.

It has its own magnificence, to fail
In such a large-scale way. The view from here
Goes all the way to where the desert ends
In light refracted through the very edge
Of sun obscured by mountains.
                              One forgets
The scale of things.
                         It's strange to lose one's past
And then to get it back again.
                              There's little new
In exile: we've done it all the time, you see;
Emperors are the same, whichever view
They take of history. They build these cities
Which then fall down. And Nature does the same,
Just a bit more slowly. It's no surprise
To find oneself now gazing down a gorge
And keeping well away.
                         One's learned to cope.
It's turned out well. The sell-by date is passed,
But once again one is the man one was,
Or so they say who know me best of all.
I'm far too old to go around again.
The point of 'Once' is once.
                         And then one's dead.

from In the Water-Margins

NIEU-BETHESDA

The Karoo village of Nieu-Bethesda in the Sneeuberg some 60 km north of Graaff-Reinet has provided the impetus for an array of plays, novels, poems and short stories. It has also attracted a number of writers to take up residence in or around the village or to attend workshops in its Ibis Centre, which promotes both the visual and the literary arts.

Much of the inspiration for all this creativity stems from the Owl House, now a museum but formerly the Nieu-Bethesda home of Helen Martins, who was born there in 1897. After a period away training and practising as a teacher, she returned late in the 1920s to nurse her ailing parents and remained in Nieu-Bethesda until 1976, when she ended her own life by drinking caustic soda. In 1945, after both her parents had died, 'Miss Helen', as she

Athol Fugard
Sheila Fugard
Don Maclennan
Robert Berold
C J Driver
Brian Walter

was known locally, began transforming their ordinary little property. This was done with the help, at different times, of three untrained artisans – Koos Malgas being the most notable of them – who worked under her direction, using such available materials as paint, cement, glass and wire. Interior walls of the house were painted in bright patterns and then covered with coloured glass, ground fine in old coffee grinders. Together with the many mirrors Helen set at angles to catch the light from sun and moon as well as from dozens of lighted candles and lamps, this created, for her, a brightly illuminated ambience. Today, even without the candle- and lamp-light, the mirrors and the glitter from the glass-encrusted walls, together with the idiosyncratic furnishings and decorations that fill every room, create an astonishing environment. Helen named this world of fantasy, light and colour The Owl House.

The fantasy extended into the garden behind the house, which Helen called the Camel Yard. There, hundreds of cement, wire and glass creations form an

apparently orderless crowd of animals (many of them camels); human and mythical figures; and birds (predominantly owls); while among them all are crude architectural structures. Cut-out stars are held aloft by pieces of wire and, along the fences, wire is shaped into the words of quotations from *The Rubáiyát of Omar Khayyám* as well as several 'labels', including Miss Helen's bold assertion: 'This is my world'. Almost all the figures face east – or the direction Helen Martins labelled 'east' – but, although two writers have chosen the name 'The Road to Mecca' for her creation and her story, Islam is only one of the religious traditions suggested in the yard. Adam and Eve wrestle with the snake; shepherds, wise men and camels travel to Bethlehem; there is the figure of a buddha and artefacts representing other religions. Helen copied whatever was to hand – postcards, Christmas cards, books, household objects – to feed her intense creative urge and express a yearning for something beyond her drab life and environment. It is hardly surprising that the so-called Outsider Art of Helen Martins has stimulated the creativity of others.

C J DRIVER
Die Nieu Bethesda:
The Owl House

If I had a gun, Koos, I'd shoot myself.
— Helen Martins —

Instead, she waited till he'd gone away
And then she swallowed caustic soda.
In hospital, she took three days to die.

Ground glass in her eyes was the first wounding;
The next was crippled hands. And people talked ...
Perhaps it's best to choose the time oneself.

Someone took the money which she'd put away.
The Persian rug went next, the good table,
The crimson lamps. The glass-eyed owls stare still

From their wire cage, and fragmented glass glints
On every wall and chair: if we could have
Enough of light, if we could have enough

Of time, there'd be no need for hate or haste.
The concrete pilgrims raise their heads and hands:
A sign says *East*, but never where it was.

Mermaids call the geese to come, but no one
Fills the pools for them these days. I have seen
The future, and I fear it's mainly dust.

from In the Water-Margins

Before the Owl House and the enigma of Helen Martins became widely known, Don Maclennan, who had visited the house and had conversed and corresponded with her, wrote the short story 'The Road to Mecca'. Published in *Contrast* in July 1978, it preceded Athol Fugard's play of the same name, which was first staged in 1984. Maclennan paints, through the eyes of a supposed neighbour living in Soetbron, the lonely, misunderstood life of Zelda Thomas and the puzzling products of her imagination. Soetbron and Zelda closely resemble Nieu-Bethesda and Helen Martins respectively, and the narrator describes the village, the house and the yard very much as they appear today.

> In winter, when you look down onto Soetbron from Olson's Nek, you see a patchwork of red and gold trees, emerald green lucerne fields, white house walls and green and red roofs. Then you notice that the cold wind from the Renosterberg seems to have swept the coloured folk into the south-east corner of the valley like a whiskbroom sweeping rubbish, because their houses, built of mud brick, sinkplaat and yellow-grey stone are hardly distinguishable from the hillside against which they huddle, unlike ours which seem to have nothing to be ashamed of ...

> Everyone knows children are afraid of owls, and Zelda's were very frightening birds. They were big, some of them two feet high, with large glinting eyes of green and red and brown. The frightening thing was that at night their eyes caught every little stray thread of light and made them look as though they were staring into your soul, like real owls do. They were set like watchdogs everywhere, even on the stoep next to her front door, where they were arranged as though sitting quite naturally on the stones and branches Zelda had put there for them ...

> By now the yard was crowded. There were thirty camels and double that number of people of all kinds, and Collingwood said it reminded him of a church bazaar ... Where she had not made ponds and bird baths, she had put up huge suns, stars and flowers on flexible wire stalks. They stood high over everything else, also in the east. And strange buildings began to grow in the spaces between everything else, a small city of mosques, minarets and towers with people leaning out of them looking at the great mass of things below in amazement ...

Maclennan's story emphasises the suspicion of conservative villagers towards the artist and her creations. It is a theme Fugard explores more deeply in his play. *The Road to Mecca* has been performed many times in South Africa and abroad, and in 1991 was filmed on location with Yvonne Bryceland, Kathy Bates and Athol Fugard himself in the roles respectively of Miss Helen, her friend Elsa Barlow, and Dominee Marius Byleveld. Elsa represents the young friends Helen had in her later years, and Marius the conservative people of the Nieu-Bethesda of her day. Helen seeks freedom through the self-created world to which she clings: Marius 'for her own good' wants her to move into an old-age home.

ATHOL FUGARD
From The Road to Mecca

(Light has now faded. MISS HELEN fetches a box of matches and lights the candles on the table. The room floats up gently out of the gloom, the mirrors and glitter on the walls reflecting the candle light. ELSA picks up one of the candles and walks around the room with it, and we see something of the magic to come.)

ELSA: Still works, Miss Helen. In the car driving up I was wondering if the novelty would have worn off a little. But here it is again. You're a little wizard, you know. You make magic with your mirrors and glitter. 'Never light a candle carelessly, and be sure you know what you're doing when you blow one out!' Remember saying that?

HELEN: To myself, yes, Many times.

ELSA: And to me ... after you had stopped laughing at the expression on my face when you lit them for the first time. 'Light is a miracle, Miss Barlow, which even the most ordinary human being can make happen.' We had just had our first pot of tea together. Maybe I do take it all just a little for granted now. But that first time ... I wish I could make you realize what it's like to be walking down a dusty, deserted little street in a God-forsaken village in the middle of the Karoo, bored to death by the heat and flies and silence, and then to be stopped in your tracks – and I mean stopped! – by all of that out there. And then, having barely recovered from that, to come inside and find *this!* Believe me, Helen, when I saw your 'Mecca' for the first time, I just stood there and gaped. 'What in God's name am I looking at? Camels and pyramids? Not three, but dozens of Wise Men? Owls with old motorcar headlights for eyes? Peacocks with more colour and glitter than the real birds? Heat stroke? Am I hallucinating?' And then you! Standing next to a mosque made out of beer bottles and staring back at me like one of your owls!

The Owl House may have brought Nieu-Bethesda to the public's notice but the village has, in its own right, stimulated the imaginations of the many visitors who venture onto the untarred roads leading to this unlikely mecca, while writers have explored aspects of its colonial, precolonial and even postcolonial history.

Situated in an isolated valley among the foothills of the Sneeuberg, Nieu-Bethesda is guarded by the highest peak in the Karoo, the Kompasberg. In the village the highest point is the Dutch Reformed church spire, a reminder that the settlement was established as a church centre in the 1870s when it was given the biblical name, Bethesda. In sparsely populated Nieu-Bethesda time moves slowly and a mixture of agricultural plots and large gardens, together with wide furrow-lined, untarred streets, provides a spaciousness reminiscent of a bygone age.

ROBERT BEROLD
Nieu Bethesda

Windmills,
old retainers,
rake the wind.

The clouds
well fed
airbrushed with aluminium.

In ancient times
(Gondwanaland)
this place was swamp

inhabited by dinosaurs.
Now it's encroaching desert
dusted over with sheep.

The children blow in
from the township
drunk with poverty.

The Buddhists
quiet on their
rafts of breath

toboggan down
the unimaginable
Tibetan snows.

The sky around them
a deep
and thirsty blue.

from The Fires of the Dead

ATHOL FUGARD's play *Valley Song* focuses on the life of this village. A deep attachment to the soil, as represented by the grandfather, Buks, who has lived his life in the valley growing vegetables, is set against the opportunities offered by the city, where his granddaughter longs for fame as a singer. 'You plant seeds and I sing songs,' she says. *Valley Song* is a play of grace and earthiness, full of affection for Nieu-Bethesda. In an opening soliloquy about the most mundane of objects – pumpkin seeds – Fugard captures the Eastern Cape inflection of the village people and conveys a sense of the valley in which Nieu-Bethesda lies – of its seasons, its setting, its scents and sounds, its people and its products.

Athol Fugard
From Valley Song

Author [*producing a handful of pumpkin seeds from his pocket*]:
Genuine Karoo pumpkin seeds. Ja. 'Ware Karoo Pampoen saad!' This is
the so-called 'Flat White Boer' variety – that's the actual name! – Flat
White Boer pumpkin. You know them – those big, round, white beauties – you sometimes still see them on the roofs of little farm cottages
when you drive through the Karoo – well, this is how they start out. One
of these, together with a little prayer for rain, in a hole in the ground.
And in a good year, when you get that rain, this little handful could give
you up to a hundred of those beauties! Now is not the time to plant
them. In my village, in the Sneeuberg Mountains, the soil is still bone
dry and rock hard with frost – our winters are a long and serious affair!
So you put them away in a little tin – with a lid – the mice get very hungry in winter! – and you put the tin on a shelf in the kitchen or the
garage or wherever you keep your other seeds – cabbage, carrot, beet-
root, beans, onion, peas, mealies ... they all do well in the Valley – and
you wait for spring. Because when that comes ... ! [*a little laugh*] ... when
old Spitskop has got his head in the clouds again, when the Valley has
had its first rain and the danger of a late frost is passed, and that won-
derful smell of damp earth is mingled with the fragrance of roses and
pine trees, when the world is rowdy again with birdsong and bleating
lambs and noisy children, that's when you take those little tins down
from the shelf and go out to your vegetable akkers and start planting.

Sheila Fugard has also created an important literary work out of the material
of Nieu-Bethesda – her novel *A Revolutionary Woman*. The Fugards have a
home in Nieu-Bethesda, where from time to time they visit, enjoying the life
of the village and a bond with the earth of the Karoo they both love and in
which Athol, who was born in nearby Middelburg, has his roots.

All the characters in *A Revolutionary Woman* (1983) are imprisoned by
their own backgrounds and by their relation to the isolated, drought-ridden
Karoo village where they live. Fugard's novel reads like poetry, with a subtle
interweaving of the mythical and the actual, of an interior and an exterior dialogue, and of the landscape as symbol, as influential presence and as realist setting. Drought is both part of the story and symbolic of the rural society of the
1920s, with its ingrained racism and rootedness in a lifeless past that allows no

nourishing vision of the future. Like the Kompasberg, which presides over Nieu-Bethesda, the Lootsberg of the novel provides a backdrop to the story of the village Fugard renames New Kimberley, but remains largely symbolic.

The vision for the future of Christina – the revolutionary woman – is imbued with Hindu myths and beliefs, while the presiding Lootsberg represents a distant and beautiful goal which has to be achieved by climbing to the summit and ringing the 'crystal gong', a phrase which recurs like a refrain throughout the novel. The vision is, however, hers alone and she fails to entice her pupil Ebrahim to leave the droughtlands and follow the path to the crystal summit of the Lootsberg. He is caught up in the Karoo: 'He cannot escape this land. The Karoo is inside him, and the images are already branded across his eyeballs.'

In the quoted extract, the references to minor Hindu gods explain themselves. *Maya* is the illusory nature of the world according to Hindu philosophy. An *ashram* is a settlement or home. Ahmedabad and the Sabarmati River are in Gujurat, Gandhi's home state in India. Shiva is one of the chief gods in the Hindu system, and Kasturbai Gandhi's wife.

SHEILA FUGARD

The Lootsberg mountains, with the dense clumps of bush, and weatherbeaten rock, tower. Forms cavort in stone: Hanuman, the monkey god, who is adept at scholarship, and makes sense out of confusion. Then, the wise *naga* serpents uncoil their subtle wisdom. They see through *maya*, and recognise the world as a clever illusion. Past and present are almost interchangeable, and there's only a flow of persistent images. The mind creates its own pain and happiness. The Indian Ocean flows. Gandhi's *ashram* appears. The Sabarmati river is close. Ahmedabad is on the horizon, and the city glowers. The sacred cows file past. There's a grove of pipal trees, and they give their shade. Gandhi approaches. He's spruce and wears a white *dhoti* and his eyes are smiling. He carries a staff, the trident of Shiva, and holds a child's hand. She's the Untouchable girl, and he's going to educate her. She's become his adopted daughter. Kasturbai follows him, and wisdom informs her eyes. The small procession moves on. The Untouchable girl dances, and Kasturbai claps her hands, while Gandhi leads the way. They climb the Lootsberg. The *naga* serpents throw down a ladder, and Hanuman the monkey god provides a map. Then, they reach the summit, that crystal heart of mountain. Gandhi rings the anvil there. The mountain sings and the sound is awe-inspiring. Suddenly, the dark continent is purged. The land behind me is like a sea, and the light across the foothills is white. We talk on the verandah. The afternoon allows a respite of warmth. My host, Abraham de Loor, speaks.

'How do you like "Bergzicht"?'

He's an enthusiastic amateur farmer. His lined face and stooping body of a former judge from the Transvaal settle uneasily here, like a tree, withstanding the drought.

'It's a beautiful place.'

'We are close to the mountain.'

The Lootsberg towers, and attempts a seduction of the sky. They cut us down to size, and we are like flies on the face of the earth. Abraham de Loor speaks again.

'Hard soil ... poor crops ... and always drought. This is our heritage, so we survive because of the silence and the sight of the mountains. Do you understand that it's enough for me?'

from A Revolutionary Woman

SHEILA FUGARD was born Sheila Meiring in England in 1932, and came to South Africa with her Irish mother and South African father when she was eight. She studied drama at the University of Cape Town before she met and married Athol Fugard in 1956. In Cape Town the Fugards set up the theatre workshop known as the Circle Players. During the early years of their marriage they worked together on a number of theatrical enterprises in Cape Town, Johannesburg and Port Elizabeth. Later, Sheila Fugard developed her own creative talents as poet and novelist, and a voice of her own – unusual and resonant – in the domain of South African English literature.

A Revolutionary Woman was the third of Fugard's novels. Her first, *The Castaways* (1972), also has an Eastern Cape setting – the Pondoland coast – but she is not primarily a regional writer. Her three volumes of poetry – *Threshold* (1975), *Mythic Things* (1981), and *Reclaiming Desert Places* (1992) – include poems in which the landscape of the Eastern Cape has clearly been the springboard for her ideas but her poems tend to image universal rather than regional aspects of the landscape. The meditative quality of Fugard's writings, and the close identification with nature which they reveal, have sprung largely out of the Buddhist way of life (derived from Hinduism) that she has espoused.

In 1998 the Ibis Arts Centre in Nieu-Bethesda spearheaded an unusual creative effort – the !Xoe site-specific art project. It was concerned mainly with the response to place of visual artists, but one of the twelve installations set up in and around Nieu-Bethesda included poems by the literary artist Brian Walter. Just as the visual artworks were presented not in the usual milieu of a gallery but in the landscapes that had inspired them and were their subject matter, so Walter's poems were presented not in a book but as visual objects related – both in shape and content – to the landscape in which they were set.

BRIAN WALTER

Absence

His heart
'seemed full of little
bits of glass, that hurt.'

This dawn broke with a great
vacancy, ground into hurtful bits:
an emptiness of quagga and trekbokke,
of a hunter's small foot-trail so telling
that you could feel the absent bodiness
that had pressed each print into each careful form:
an emptiness of hearts once plucked like the string
of the gorah bow that drew this place, its hills
and all its dawn-dimmed stars, to one.
The tendon-spirit that curved that bow is broken,
and who of us can now ever really know that fat star
Canopus, pronking in the grey hollow dawn, who gave
the hunter his cunning arm and flick-sharp eye, and took
from him a fasted emptiness. The beauty of this broken place
can never be the same.

In all the heart of this place small sharp chips, as of glass
crunched into grains, of dreams that humanly dreamt
themselves, lie broken, in this place, dreams
that could feel the dark of springbok flanks
ripple upon kindred ribs: sacred hunter
of the dawn, story-teller, singer
of the rising day: dead, ground
down, hunted away by men
whose own hearts would break
up and draw apart, men who
never understood
the game.

from Tracks

A booklet published in association with the project explains that 'the word !Xoe denotes "home-land" or "home-place" in the language of the !Xam, a nomadic San hunter-gatherer people that once inhabited the Great Karoo'. Land or place is, therefore, the common denominator of the !Xoe presentations. Explaining the installation on which she and Brian Walter collaborated and which was called 'Quest: A Journey into Sacred Space', artist Elaine Matthews writes: 'the installation was conceived of as facilitating a quest or journey into landscape so as to create an awareness of the sacred in nature'. It was also a literary journey with a difference – one which cannot be repeated, for the installation was temporary, but it can be imagined through the poems that are published in the Ibis Centre's booklet and Walter's collection *Tracks*. The poems, painted on the glass that formed part of the installation, could be read against the background of the landscape with which their words engage. They deal, Matthews explains, 'with colonial intrusions into the landscape and the destruction of the San vision of a connected relationship between humanity, the earth, animals and the universe'. Each of the four poems contains a quotation from Olive Schreiner's *Story of an African Farm* and each refers to one of the cardinal points of the compass. They are shaped or 'concrete' poems, their forms suggesting natural objects such as pods, eggs, skulls and fossils. This amplifies the idea of interconnectedness and underlines the installation's theme of birth, death and renewal.

'Absence' provides a multidimensional view of the Nieu-Bethesda milieu through allusions to what is *not* there: the San hunters; the migratory herds of springbok that once traversed the region; the quagga hunted to extinction. Allusions to Schreiner and to Helen Martins emphasise feminine creativity but also fill out a picture of place that penetrates beyond its physical aspects to its spirit and to its disrupted past. 'The beauty of this broken place can never be the same.'

CRADOCK

At the heart of the eastern Karoo lies the town of Cradock, established in 1813 on the banks of the Great Fish River in what was, at the time, a particularly barren region. Today Cradock is the centre of a rich farming district; it is also the centre of a district rich in literary associations. Such treasures of South African literature as Olive Schreiner's *The Story of an African Farm*, Guy Butler's *Karoo Morning* and his early poetry, as well as some of the works of contemporary novelist Etienne van Heerden, are set in and around Cradock – a town which in turn profoundly affected the lives of these authors. Visitors or brief sojourners too have found inspiration in this district, while that delightful little work, *The Diary of Iris Vaughan*, paints a child's picture of the town.

Cradock and Olive Schreiner

In a poem entitled 'A Visit to Olive Schreiner Country', Cherry Clayton proclaims that the vicinity of Cradock and, indeed, 'the whole Karoo' is 'Schreiner country'.

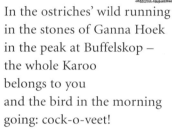

> The thing about this place
> is that you're everywhere
> and everywhere I see
> your face
> dissolved in this clear time
> and clearer space.
>
> In the ostriches' wild running
> in the stones of Ganna Hoek
> in the peak at Buffelskop –
> the whole Karoo
> belongs to you
> and the bird in the morning
> going: cock-o-veet!

Olive Schreiner lived in the town from 1868 to 1870 and on farms in the district from 1875 to 1881 with an additional five-month period in 1894. This was a small portion of the 65 years of her life, but the most creative in terms of imaginative writing. Olive Schreiner is a dominant and haunting presence in this part of the Eastern Cape and many writers have been inspired by her. That 'the whole Karoo / belongs to you' is, however, a dubious claim.

OLIVE EMILIE ALBERTINA SCHREINER was born in 1855 at the Wesleyan mission station of Wittebergen in the northern mountains of the Eastern Cape. Six years were spent there before the family moved further south to Healdtown, where they stayed until 1866 when Olive's father, Gottlob Schreiner, was forced to resign as a missionary. The influence of these years and places on Schreiner's writings is discussed in the next chapter. The concern here is with Cradock.

By 1868 Gottlob was bankrupt. Because her parents were unable to support their younger children Olive was sent, at the age of thirteen, to live in Cradock with her brother Theo and sister Ettie, who were fervent practitioners of a puritanical faith. Olive, who refused to go to church and turned her back on many of the beliefs that they held dear, was in constant conflict with them, which made this an unhappy time for her. Later, when she lived on farms in the district of Cradock, she came to love the Karoo landscape and to celebrate it in her fiction but, at this stage, the town and its restrictive society held little appeal.

In Schreiner's novel *From Man to Man* there is a lengthy description of an unnamed town. It has 'red karroo to the right of it, red karroo to the left', is surrounded by 'flat topped mountains' and below it there is a river with 'dried mud banks' in winter and filled with 'dark sand-laden water' in summer. She describes what is clearly the Cradock she remembers, sketching in a few redeeming features such as the vibrant market square and the dawn view from a nearby koppie: 'the whole plain was golden and the roofs of the little flat houses glinted – then the town was beautiful'. The overriding impression is, however, unflattering.

> During nine months of the year, while the winds blow, clouds of dust whirled along the streets before thunderstorms; when the gusts came, great clouds of sand rose from the market square and met the still mightier clouds raised from the wide sandy plain; and the town was shrouded in sand.

Schreiner portrays the society of the town in equally derogatory terms.

> It was a dull narrow little life enough, lived there among the flat-roofed houses, far removed from the currents of life and thought of the great world beyond.

One of those 'flat-roofed houses' is that in which Schreiner lived with her siblings. Now a heritage site known as Schreiner House, it is situated in Cross Street. In 1986 it became a satellite museum of NELM and was opened to the public. This simple, carefully restored dwelling conveys a good sense of the period; in the house an exhibition tells the extraordinary story of Olive and her remarkable family, and the backyard with its herb garden, water pump and lemon tree enhances the sense of a lived-in home.

Near Schreiner House is the Cradock Library, which provided the author with many of the books she read so avidly during later years when she lived in the district. After she died, her own books were donated to the library. Most of the original collection has been transferred to NELM in Grahamstown.

Nearly 27 km outside Cradock is the Mountain Zebra National Park where, although it has no direct link with the author's life, visitors may experience typical Schreiner scenery. One of the park's guesthouses – the restored 1836 farmhouse, Doornhoek – was used in the television film of *The Story of an African Farm*, and one may sit on its stoep or on the steps leading to its loft and gaze at the view while listening with the ear of the mind to the voices of the novel's characters. Mimosas, kiepersols and a stony koppie behind the house add to the impression of finding oneself inside one of Schreiner's books.

Eastern Cape farms in Olive Schreiner's life and her fiction

In 1870 Theo and Ettie Schreiner left Cradock and Olive began a semi-nomadic existence, visiting relations and friends and earning a living as best she could in various parts of South Africa. In 1875 she returned to the Cradock district. From then until 1881 the young woman worked as a governess on several farms, where she had the space and time to devote to writing and revising her three Eastern Cape novels – *The Story of an African Farm* (1883), *From Man to Man* (1926) and *Undine* (1929) – as well as a few shorter fictional pieces.

At the first of these farms, Klein Gannahoek, about 40 km from Cradock, Schreiner worked for the Cape Dutch family of the Fouchés. She frequently visited her friends, the Cawoods, at Gannahoek, which was within walking distance. The second was Ratelhoek, a further 30 km from Cradock, where she worked for nearly three years for another Cape Dutch family, the Martins. A short spell with the Cawoods at Gannahoek then preceded an eighteen-month stint further off on the farm Leliekloof in the Winterberg, to which the Fouchés had moved.

The farm setting in each of Schreiner's three Eastern Cape novels is a distinct imaginative recreation of elements drawn from these farms, as well as of elements from her birthplace, Wittebergen, and her childhood home in Healdtown.

It is probable that an early draft of the best known of Olive Schreiner's novels, *The Story of an African Farm*, was written at Klein Gannahoek where the author had a room of her own, attached to the house and in which she taught the Fouché children and did her writing. Photographs taken in 1893 by her husband, Cron, give some idea of the appearance of the farmhouse, now a ruin. In 1988 an archaeological investigation of the site revealed the ground plan and probable structure of this house. Other structures identified in its vicinity included a tack or wagon shed, a pig or goat enclosure, a gravesite, a large stone-walled kraal, a huge boulder and a hut. These features, as well as the red, locally made bricks of the house and the stone walls of the enclosures, tie in with the descriptions of the farmhouse in *The Story of an African Farm*. Klein Gannahoek's surrounding landscape of open plain skirted by low hills with stony koppies is also reflected in the novel.

Descriptions of the fictional farm in the opening chapter of *The Story of an African Farm* are among the most memorable depictions of place in South African literature. Part of the clarity of Schreiner's descriptions, throughout her writings, comes from careful lighting. Here, within a few pages, she juxtaposes pictures of the farm by moonlight and by daylight. References to the farm's physical features are consistent through to the end of the novel, when we are shown Waldo sitting in the sunshine with his back against the red-brick wall of the farmhouse. The 'kopje' that has played its part in the story is there; even the sunflowers have not been over-looked. Schreiner has absorbed the very being of the place into herself and everything about her African farm is precise in her visual imagination.

> The full African moon poured down its light from the blue sky into the wide, lonely plain. The dry, sandy earth, with its coating of stunted 'kar-roo' bushes a few inches high, the low hills that skirted the plain, the milk-bushes with their long, finger-like leaves, all were touched by a weird and an almost oppressive beauty as they lay in the white light.
>
> In one spot only was the solemn monotony of the plain broken. Near the centre a small, solitary 'kopje' rose. Alone it lay there, a heap of round iron-stones piled one upon another, as over some giant's grave. Here and there a few tufts of grass or small succulent plants had sprung up among its stones, and on the very summit a clump of prickly-pears lifted their thorny arms, and reflected, as from mirrors, the moonlight on their broad, fleshy leaves. At the foot of the 'kopje' lay the homestead. First, the stone-walled 'sheep-kraals' and Kaffir huts; beyond them the dwelling-house – a square red-brick building with thatched roof. Even on its bare red walls, and the wooden ladder that led up to the loft, the moonlight cast a kind of dreamy beauty, and quite etherealized the low brick wall that ran before the house, and which enclosed a bare patch of sand and two straggling sunflowers. On the zinc roof of the great open wagon-house, on the roofs of the outbuildings that jutted from its side, the moonlight glinted with a quite peculiar brightness, till it seemed that every rib in the metal was of burnished silver.
>
> Sleep ruled everywhere, and the homestead was not less quiet than the solitary plain.
>
> ...
>
> The farm by daylight was not as the farm by moonlight. The plain was a weary flat of loose red sand sparsely covered by dry karroo bushes, that cracked beneath the tread like tinder, and showed the red earth every-where. Here and there a milk-bush lifted its pale-coloured rods, and in every direction the ants and beetles ran about in the blazing sand. The red walls of the farmhouse, the zinc roofs of the outbuildings, the stone walls of the 'kraals', all reflected the fierce sunlight, till the eye ached and blenched. No tree or shrub was to be seen far or near. The two sunflow-

ers that stood before the door, out-stared by the sun, drooped their brazen faces to the sand; and the little cicada-like insects cried aloud among the stones of the 'kopje'.

Schreiner described her time at Ratelhoek with the Martins as 'the quietest and best' of her life. There she had a 'quiet parlour' to use as a study where most of *The Story of an African Farm* – drafted at Klein Gannahoek – was written and much of the work done on *From Man to Man* and *Undine*. She writes from Ratelhoek, 'we have had splendid rains and the country is looking beautiful. It was too dry for the orange trees to blossom at the right time but they are all in blossom now. As I sit writing the sweet scent comes in at my window.' This is echoed in the opening paragraph of *From Man to Man*: 'The scent of the orange trees and of the flowers from the garden beyond, came in through the partly-opened window, with the rich dry odour of a warm, African, summer morning.' The farm in this novel cannot, however, be too closely correlated with the actual farm Ratelhoek, where work on it seems to have begun. Its setting owes as much to other remembered locales as to this one, as much to mountainous terrains as to the wide expanses of the Karoo.

> Tucked away among the ribs of a mountain in the Eastern Province of the Cape of Good Hope is a quiet, tree-covered farm ... In the bush that covered the mountain sides were leopards, who came down at night and carried off lambs from the kraals; in the tall trees in the bush were little grey, long-tailed monkeys, and wood-doves, and cock-o-veets, who cried and called all day; in the rocks that crowned the mountain troops of baboons climbed and fought; and down in the valley among the thorn-trees were mier-kats and great tortoises, and hares who paid visits to the lands. Almost all day from the open windows of the house you might see at intervals the sheep among the long grass on the mountain side or down in the flat; or catch sight of, far off, moving specks, which were the goats moving in and out among the thorn trees. All day long the great glass doors and windows stood open; through them came the scent of orange blossoms from the orangery before the door, and from the garden beyond where the hollyhocks and dahlias and marigolds and four-o'clocks made a bed of colour. In spring time there was the sweet scent of the blossoms from the long orchard beyond the flower garden; and in the summer, at Christmas time, the flat was a sea of gold with the yellow flowers of the thorn trees, and the honey scent came up to the house; and in autumn there was the faint, acid smell from the falling figs and peaches which lay on the ground in the brown trampled grass.

Schreiner claimed to love *From Man to Man* more than any other of her novels, yet it was never completed and was published only after her death. It is now out of print. Although flawed, it is a moving work with a strong feminist message, and a novel that deserves to be better known, not least for its marvellous evocations of place.

A harsher picture of a Karoo farm is painted in *Undine*. There are echoes, at times, of the farm Schreiner depicts in *The Story of an African Farm*, and she uses the same technique of picturing by day and by night.

> Karoo, red sand, great mounds of round iron-stones, and bushes never very beautiful to look at and now almost burned into the ground by the blazing summer's sun. An old Dutch farmhouse built of the brightest red brick to match the ground and stones; an old stone wall broken down here and there at irregular intervals, as if to allow for the ready ingress and egress of the hundred enterprising goats, whose delight it is daily to regale themselves on the deformed peach-trees and leafless cabbage stalks which the enclosure contains; an old tent-wagon, whose tent and floor have long gone the way of all flesh – wood flesh – into the fire; an ancient willow-tree, which stands vainly trying to reflect itself in a small pond of thick red fluid, and under which may at all times be seen a couple of dirty and benighted ducks, who there disport themselves under the happy delusion of its being water.
>
> All these parts compose a picture in which, when looked at by daylight, it were hard work to find the slightest trace of beauty; but to-night, penetrated in every nook and corner by the cold white light of an almost full moon, there is a strange, weird beauty, a beauty which the veriest sheep-souled Boer that ever smoked pipe or wore vel-skoen might feel if he had but one ray of light left in him.

Most of *Undine* is set away from the Karoo, but memories of the farmhouse of Undine's childhood flash out at various points in the story, and the end of the novel looks back to its beginning as the dying Undine, in far-away Kimberley, looks at the stars and remembers her early home.

> She looked up at the old stars that she had looked up to and loved from her childhood as other men love their friends of flesh and blood – the dear old stars that had shed their light on the thatched roofs and stone walls of the old farm on the Karoo; that had looked in at the window of the little white-washed room, and on the leaves of the small brown Testament, and the little child who cried and prayed there; the same and

yet, to-night, looking so strange and new to her. Over the tumult and agony that reigned within, they spoke a great peace, and she lay still and watched them.

    'Twas one of the gorgeous nights when the sky, shooting light from a million points, overwhelms and silences us; and the little circle of our life, that has seemed to fill all creation, sinks to its proper size – a shadow, a breath of wind that, being or not being, matters not.

At Leliekloof, the cold air of the Winterberg suited Schreiner despite her proneness to asthma attacks. She writes to her sister Catherine: 'We are having bitterly cold weather here among the mountains. Already we have had two heavy falls of snow about the house. But the cold suits me well and I am much better than I was all the summer.' Although the short story 'Dream Life and Real Life' – next to *African Farm*, the most popular of the author's fictional works – has, like the novel, a Karoo setting, it was written in this cold mountainous region.

    Little Jannita sat alone beside a milk-bush. Before her and behind her stretched the plain, covered with red sand and thorny 'Karroo' bushes; and here and there a milk-bush, looking like a bundle of pale green rods tied together. Not a tree was to be seen anywhere, except on the banks of the river, and that was far away, and the sun beat on her head. Round her fed the Angora goats she was herding; pretty things, especially the little ones, with white silky curls that touched the ground. But Jannita sat crying. If an angel should gather up in his cup all the tears that have been shed, I think the bitterest would be those of children.

The overriding sense of an Eastern Cape farm that Schreiner's work conveys is of human solitude – even insignificance – in a vast, sometimes arid, sometimes beautiful, but largely unsympathetic terrain, where profound thoughts about the meaning and purpose of life mirror the immensity of the landscape.

Schreiner and Buffelskop

In 1881 Schreiner travelled to England, where she remained through most of the decade. There, in 1883, *The Story of an African Farm* was published, and almost at once the author became famous. 1889 saw her back in South Africa, settled for a while at Matjiesfontein in the western Karoo. In 1892, on a visit to her friends the Cawoods at Gannahoek, Olive met their neighbour, Samuel Cron Cronwright. After another brief visit to England she returned and, in February 1894, she and Cron were married at the Karoo town of Middelburg.

Olive and Cron Cronwright-Schreiner, as they chose to be called, settled on the farm Krantz Plaats close to Olive's old haunts. One day, during the five months of their time there, they climbed a neighbouring mountain, Buffels-kop. In his biography of her Cron said that he had never seen Olive so rapt as she drank in both the distant view and the immediate sight of 'the beautiful spike of red flowers full of butterflies'. Before they descended she said, 'We must be buried here, you and I, Cron. I shall buy one morgen of this mountain top and we must be buried here.' The plot was purchased and the resolution never forgotten. 'The thought of that quiet resting place' often brought comfort to Olive during the vicissitudes of her later life; apart from occasional brief visits, it was a life spent far from the Eastern Cape.

After her death in Cape Town in December 1920, Olive was buried in the Schreiner family plot in Maitland cemetery. When Cron returned from Europe some months later, he obtained permission to have her body exhumed and made arrangements with an undertaker and mason to prepare a tomb on top of the mountain. Buffelskop's ironstone cap was too hard to penetrate, so a rounded sarcophagus was built on top of it. How well it suits its environment.

Cron travelled on the same train as Olive's body from Cape Town to Cradock, picking up the little coffins of 'Baby' and Nita at De Aar on the way. In 1895 Olive had given birth to a baby girl who lived less than a day. For the next eighteen years the coffin containing the baby's body accompanied Olive wherever she went but, while she was abroad, it was kept at De Aar in a temporary grave. Nita was the last in a line of pet dogs of that name – her coffined body had also been kept at De Aar.

The three coffins, accompanied by a small group of friends, including a baby, were carried up the steep inclines leading to the mountain's summit. All was unceremonious, in keeping with Olive and Cron's freethinking philosophy, but there was an impromptu salute when a large white bird soared above the scene. It was a reminder of the allegory in *The Story of an African Farm* of the hunter who spends a lifetime searching for the 'vast white bird, with silver wings outstretched, sailing in the everlasting blue' he once glimpsed in reflection in a lake. The hunter dies holding just one feather which has fluttered slowly down from a white sky onto his breast. In the novel, the bird represents Truth. Olive Schreiner had spent her lifetime on the same quest.

The story of the re-interment of Olive Schreiner is one of the strangest in the saga of South African English literature. It is recounted in Guy Butler's edited facsimile of Cron Cronwright-Schreiner's diary, *The Re-interment on Buffelskop*. Like Butler himself, many South African writers, as well as others interested in Olive's writings or her story, have climbed to the site of her grave on Buffelskop – a not inconsiderable mountain.[2] A number of them have captured, through poetry, something of this astonishing place and the associations it brings to mind.

Roy Campbell's 'Buffel's Kop' describes an imagined visit – there is no evidence that he ever climbed Buffelskop – and resonates with allusions to the place and to Schreiner's life and writings.

ROY CAMPBELL (1926)
Buffel's Kop
(Olive Schreiner's Grave)

In after times when strength or courage fail,
May I recall this lonely hour: the gloom
Moving one way: all heaven in the pale
Roaring: and high above the insulted tomb
An eagle anchored on full spread of sail
That from its wings let fall a silver plume.

Anna Purcell, a close friend of Olive and Cron, was unable to be present at the re-interment but visited Buffelskop soon afterwards. Her seven stanza poem 'Olive Schreiner's Grave in the Karroo' sings the praises of Schreiner's 'genius-soul'; here only the first stanza is given. As in Campbell's poem, the bird of the hunter allegory haunts Purcell's verse.

ANNA PURCELL (1921)
From Olive Schreiner's Grave in the Karroo

Within the great Karroo she loved so well
She lies at rest upon a lonely peak
Whose summit seems to meet the radiant skies –
Clear-cut against the dome of azure hue.

The dark-plumed Bird of whom in youth she told,
Which plaintively did utter its low cry,
Now hovers o'er her tomb with outspread wings,
As if to guard some sacred cenotaph.

Even in Stephen Gray's unsentimental poem, of which only the first part is
reproduced here, the bird makes an appearance – it is probably the Cape
Vulture, popularly known as the lammervanger – bringing something eerie to
his experience of climbing Buffelskop.

STEPHEN GRAY
From In Memoriam: Olive Schreiner

You chose to outdo the living
buried on a koppie a mile high
with the world's view over blue shimmering horizons
it took twelve porters three days to haul
your coffin up these greasy slopes
to pack you away in a dome of rock
taking Buffelskop as your natural cathedral
and you the lightning conductor

we worked at it all morning to reach you
with a survey map cameras and packs
and in your honour braaied lunch in clouds
of herb-smelling fire alongside your sarcophagus
there's not much to say to the close dead
one functions normally
a trifle embarrassed

and although not one of us was superstitious
we had to admit it was eerie
in the vast gathering of thermals
that the shade of a lammervanger
should crisscross us up there
symbolizing your kind of freedom
probably watching from its height for prey.

in New Coin (1997)

Margo Wallace recalls a visit to the gravesite in a long poem in which distant views and close-up details of the terrain blend with imagined sounds from the past. She achieves a marvellous recreation of the experience and of the place. These few lines are from the heart of the poem:

MARGO WALLACE
From Buffelskop: Olive Schreiner's Gravesite

Now,
I sit where the red rocks have split
And hurtled – pitched a spontaneous cairn
On the Buffelskop outcrop
Like a twisted forehead
Frowning out over the goat-strewn plain,
Seeing dry rifts of riverbeds
Like collapsed arteries,
Hearing the scuff of heavy black cloth
And unsteady, burdened feet:
The camera cannot take
These tricks of the mind and air,
Cannot hold the shifting breath
Of timeless, repeated anxiousness;

There are, indeed, aspects of the experience of climbing Buffelskop and seeing the grave and the view, that neither a camera nor a poem can capture.

Schreiner, the person

There was – perhaps still is – something mesmerising about Olive Schreiner's personality. She was small in stature with abundant dark hair and large expressive eyes. Her conversation was animated and intense and, in company or on her own, she often paced up and down talking to herself. Her remarkable intellect developed without the assistance of formal schooling: Olive learned to read and write at home, and she absorbed ideas and information from books as well as from her own observations. She oscillated between a need for solitude and a need for company; between a desire to be selfless and a tendency to self-absorption. Her strong views and unconventional behaviour sometimes alienated her from others, but she made a number of deep and lasting friendships with both women and men. Family was important to Olive and, despite fundamental differences in outlook and personality from some of them, she maintained contact with the members of her large, dispersed family through visits and letters.

Were Schreiner's asthma attacks psychosomatic or purely physical? Was there a connection with her smoking habits? Were there allergies which made one place more conducive to attacks than another, and what was the true nature of the angina suffered in her later years? What is certain is that her chest problems caused great distress to her and those who cared about her, and that they played a role in her inability to settle anywhere or to sustain her creative work for long periods.

Sympathy with victims of oppression, cruelty or injustice made her espouse a number of unpopular causes, the first among these being the liberation of women from oppression. Her novels are strongly feminist and some of her dreams and allegories also plead for the liberation of women from the bonds of a male-dominated society, while her treatise *Woman and Labour* became required reading for serious feminists in the early 1900s.

Schreiner's sympathies during the South African War were with the Boers rather than the British and, during the First World War, with the conscientious objectors. Modern readers are sometimes shocked by her use of the terms 'kaffir' and even 'nigger', but she did not intend them to carry derogatory connotations. Particularly in her later years, she espoused the cause of the 'native' people of South Africa, resigning, for instance, from the Women's Enfranchisement League when there was pressure to work for the enfranchisement of white women only. She also pleaded, in her pamphlet *Closer Union*, for the dropping of all distinctions of race or colour in the new state of South Africa to be formed in 1910.

Olive knew the Bible well and particularly admired the Sermon on the Mount, but found the doctrine of the divinity of Christ unacceptable and rejected the judgementalism of dogmatic forms of Christianity. She refused to participate in any form of religious ceremony and regarded herself as a freethinker. Her belief in the unity of all things – God, humanity, animals and everything in the material world – began at an early age and persisted through her life.

Olive Schreiner's greatest cause for thanksgiving, as she wrote to her friend Mary Brown, was 'to have loved so many things, and enjoyed Nature so much', and it was often to nature that she turned for solace in times of unhappiness. Her novels and stories are filled with many typical Eastern Cape plants: kiepersol, milk bushes, willows, prickly pears, aloes, wild asparagus, ice plants, plumbago, jasmine. The song of birds is often heard in them, particularly that of the cock-o-veet (bokmakierie). Red sand, stone koppies, ironstone outcrops and the sky by day or night feature in many a scene. The mimosa or thorn trees on the farm Thorn Kloof in *From Man to Man* are a leitmotif in the novel, helping to mark the passage of time with their seasonal changes. In other works natural phenomena also have a role to play, but above all they help to create a sense of place: a sense of a place which could be only the Eastern Cape. Olive loved the small things of the veld: ants, spiders, horned beetles, butterflies and the insects in flowers. Some of the smaller animals, like long-tailed monkeys and dassies, also find their way into her writings. It is her sense of the unity of all things that makes her so conscious of her surroundings and so well able to make us conscious of the milieu of her stories. Above all it is love:

> I can't describe to anyone the love I have to this African scenery; it is to all others as the face of the woman he loves best is to a man as compared to all other faces. It is not like at all – it is different.[3]

Schreiner's often solitary contemplation of the extensive landscapes she encountered in the Eastern Cape, and of the details of their flora and fauna, evoked a response that came from the inner depths of her being. Emily Hobhouse, who first met Olive at Hanover in 1902, writes:

> It is hard for my unskilled pen to find words to describe your South African Olive. One gained breadth and grandeur from her. She gave me the illimitable feeling of the veld. She gathered Time and Space into herself and absorbed them.[4]

That very absorption of Time and Space makes it possible for her to present them in imaginative form through the settings of her novels, stories, dreams and allegories, so that we too are given 'the illimitable feeling of the veld'. It is a feeling entirely appropriate to the magnitude of Olive Schreiner's vision and the extent of her themes.

Cradock and Guy Butler

An account of the reburial of Olive Schreiner on Buffelskop appeared in the *Midland News*. It was written by Mary Butler, one of the party that accompanied the three coffins to the site. She was the aunt of Guy Butler, who in his autobiographical *Karoo Morning* recalls being taken up the mountain by Aunt Mary to visit the grave. For the future writer, it was among a number of seminal experiences connected with Cradock and its mountains. Olive Schreiner and her story became one of the passions of Guy Butler's life and he became a writer whose name, like hers, is inseparable from Cradock.

FREDERICK GUY BUTLER was born on 21 January 1918 in Cradock. There he grew from child to boy and boy to young man, learning about life, as most do, from the world around him. Family, teachers, friends, books were all important influences but, in a particular way, Guy Butler learned from the material world: from features of the town itself and from its encompassing mountains. He had a passion for collecting and this helped him to learn directly from nature, which he observed with a mixture of the scientist's analytical mind and the artist's longing to recreate the observed world in terms of the ideas he was absorbing. He left Cradock in 1936 to attend Rhodes University in Grahamstown, promising his father that he would become either a teacher or a journalist, but nurturing in his heart the desire to be a poet. Both his father's wishes and his own dream were fulfilled: Guy Butler became an exceptional teacher and a poet of distinction as well as much else.

Karoo Morning, the first volume of Butler's autobiography, tells the story of his Cradock years. In the third volume, *A Local Habitation*, which focuses on his Grahamstown years, he says, '*Karoo Morning* attempted to evoke what it meant to be me in that place at that time.' Butler's development as a person and as a creative artist was profoundly affected by Cradock in the years between the two World Wars. It was also affected by the people, particularly family – immediate and extended – among whom he grew to maturity.

In 1974 the Butler family home, 'The Poplars', on the corner of Bree and Church streets, was so badly damaged in floods that it had to be demolished, and other features of the Cradock depicted in *Karoo Morning* and in Guy Butler's Cradock poems have disappeared or changed. The wide, tree-lined streets remain where water furrows run alongside them in which Guy, although forbidden, played as a child (as did the naughty brother Charles of

Iris Vaughan's diary). The Anglican and Wesleyan churches in Bree Street are much as Butler describes them. Gilfillan bridge; the railway station; the large Dutch Reformed church that replicates St Martin-in-the-Fields in London, were landmarks then as now.

The neighbouring mountains still watch over the town as they did over Guy Butler's formative years. In 'Cradock Mountains', he celebrates the role they played:

> Your bone-bare silhouettes are etched
> upon my irises; your stance
> takes three dimensions in my skull:
> your base bedrocks memory.
>
> You presided over
> all the formative forces,
> clouds, winds, characters,
> who planted, nourished, pruned to a basic shape
> whatever I shall carry to the grave.

The presiding mountains are a catalyst for providing a lively series of images of the world of Butler's Cradock. They are also the means of meditating on the poet's inner world of memory and of encapsulating the growth of his mind. As we observe that growth, through the poem, we are made aware of the immediate – the sound of a Cape robin, the smell of lucerne, the sensation of heat, the sight of pear blossom – and beyond that, of the universe:

> and wondering, felt the slow whirl of the world
> that pressed against my feet, and the constant sun
> still burning invisible ten million miles
> away, out there, over your edge, on my left.

Descriptions in 'Cradock Mountains' of herdsmen and farmers coming into town give a sense of the whole district and of the town as a farming centre and forum for discussing the issues of the day. And there are other pictures of Cradock, one of the most arresting being the account of market day. Colours and objects tumble all over the page and we are reminded that the visual arts, particularly painting, were among Butler's enthusiasms. He sees as a painter would, yet translates the visual into the images of poetry. Although the market no longer plays such a prominent role in the life of the town, there are other colourful sights in present-day Cradock that contrast with the muted colours of the enclosing landscape:

> diluted ochres and umbers, dim purples,
> and greys and blues bled pale by the heat

The mountains that presided over the formative forces of Butler's early life are so deeply embedded in his memory that he feels instinctively that he will acknowledge them even when about to die:

> it's quite on the cards I shall give you a last eyes-right
> when I am about to die.

Guy Butler died in Grahamstown on 26 April 2001 at the age of 83.

Karoo Morning is, in a way, an expansion of 'Cradock Mountains' and the idea that the material world can, in itself, be a teacher. Three incidents selected from the book highlight ways in which Cradock itself and its Karoo situation among rocky mountains were among the 'formative forces' of Butler's life.

In the first chapter, 'Beginnings', Butler recalls his childhood impressions of Cradock in terms of walks through the town in the company of siblings, nursemaid or mother.

> If you are taken for a walk in the early morning, north-wards, up Bree Street, the sun is on your right and the blue shadows of beefwood tree-trunks across the street look like the rungs of a huge ladder reaching into the pure light at the end of it. And if you are taken for a walk in the afternoon, southwards, down Bree Street, the same thing happens, except that it does not end in the same happy way: for at that end, beyond the fine old houses, is the gaol; and no one likes that place ...

As we follow in the child's tracks we see the Cradock of the 1920s through a child's eyes. Each landmark or incident is a learning experience. Such concepts as death, the awesomeness of school, the difference between weddings and funerals, the forbidding thought of 'gaol' become part of his consciousness.

Chapter 12 of *Karoo Morning*, 'Mainly Among Mountains', corresponds with Butler's teenage years, during which there were many other, more sophisticated learning experiences, including factual lessons about the geology of the district. From Uncle Norman's mason, 'old Barter', he learns that:

> 'Sandstone is like white bread samidges. Comes in layers, you see. Get your chisel on the right spot, and she cleaves open clean and flat. But ironstone is like "doodgooi": solid and same all through. It don't cleave open clean. You've gotta shape it, chip by chip. But it's hard, man, and blue, and it's got iron in it. That's why it rusts red and brown with the rain.'

Later, the young Butler learns from Uncle Charles about another rock, lydian-ite, and a significant symbol is born.

It was a great moment in my mental history. Up to this point much of my thinking tended to categorise experiences as 'sandstone' or 'ironstone': sandstone stood for experience, for tradition, for raw materials that had been through great chastenings of wind and weather, growth and decay, and then been laid down in workable strata, vast laminated books of knowledge; ironstone stood for raw instinct and energy tapped from the molten heart of things, still defiant and resistant to wind and weather, primordial, difficult to work, innocent of secrets and knowledge. There was much sandstone in my parents, and much ironstone in myself. Sometimes it seemed I was a small, untidy dolerite outcrop surrounded by great, level, sandstone mountains of ineluctable authority and poise. Growing up seemed to be an inevitable weathering process – ironstone being broken down, granule by granule into sand, and levelled out into beds.

But here, at the interface, was lydianite, neither sandstone nor ironstone: something comparatively rare, a product of two worlds, partaking of both, belonging to neither; something which lent itself to shaping, neither philosophical nor instinctual, sophisticated nor primitive, traditional nor original, but essentially between, exposed on both sides, a useful, bastard, frontier stone.

The mountains, as much as old Barter and Uncle Charles, are his teachers.

A third learning experience related to place is the young Butler's realisation of the dividedness of South African society. Apartheid is made visible through the outward and visible signs of such places as Cradock's cemeteries.

Across the river from the location was the cemetery for blacks. Tombstones were unknown. Here or there was a cement slab with a name, a date, a text, in a hand not used to writing in capitals in wet cement. But the whole place, from a certain aspect and in a certain light, could glitter like gossamer – from the hundreds of glass bottles, large and small, which had been brought to hold the precious tribute of a bunch of flowers. Flowers! Where did they obtain them? At what cost? A new grave there – with the long, damp mound of earth, and a fading wreath of marigolds on it – was the sight which made a line of Virgil's, which I had seen discussed out of context, become a final formulation of one of my sentiments – *Sunt lacrimae rerum, et mentem mortalia tangunt.* (There are tears for our lot, and mortal fortunes touch the heart.)

At the other extremity of the town, on the other side of the river, beyond the green park and the sports stadium, lay the white dead, by denominations, weighed down, many of them, by tons of Paarl granite with gilt lettering: a fascinating, stony archive. In their efforts to demonstrate piety, affection and family pride, these memorials somehow exorcised poetry and sublimity. Small human vanities and concerns were stamped on the place; whereas among the bottles, Mexican poppies and wild tobacco plants a few miles away, one felt the liberation of death.

There is evidence in Butler's writings, as in his life, of a profound sympathy with the lot of the unfortunate. As these passages also indicate, he recognised human idiosyncrasies and could portray them with sharp irony. Descriptions of the cemeteries highlight an interesting interplay between person and place: the contrasting cemeteries are a visual manifestation of societal structures and also reveal much about differing attitudes to life and death. Humanity may stamp more of character than it intends on its physical structures.

Guy Butler left Cradock in 1936 to study at Rhodes University in Grahamstown and never again lived there permanently, yet the Karoo never left him. After graduating from Rhodes University and teaching for a few months in Johannesburg, Butler enlisted in the South African armed forces. In December 1940 he married Jean Satchwell, and soon afterwards left to serve in Egypt and Syria. His first encounter with Europe came with the Allied invasion of Italy and, after the end of the Second World War, he went to Oxford on a scholarship. The year 1948 found him back in South Africa lecturing at the University of the Witwatersrand in Johannesburg. He moved in 1951 to Grahamstown, where he remained for the rest of his life.

Apart from 'Cradock Mountains', a number of Guy Butler's poems are devoted to the Cradock region. Images of the Karoo haunt many others. One of the most beautiful of these images appears in his long 'Elegy', subtitled 'For a South African Tank Commander Killed in Action in Italy, October 1944':

> I would you slept where grey mimosas churn
> cream-yellow pollen on the tombs, and tall
> red aloes, winter's candelabras, burn
>
> on all the hills: where, once the spring rains fall,
> the silken freesia from its silver stalk
> might swing a censer for your burial.[5]

Butler's first play, *The Dam*, was based on the building of a dam by one of his uncles farming in the Cradock district. In the opening chorus the audience is invited to imagine, to listen and to watch.

MALE VOICE:	Listen a little to us,
	Let the doors of your hearts swing open.
FEMALE VOICE:	Watch for an hour or two,
	Let your restless limbs relax.
MALE VOICE:	Imagine the great escarpment, the Great Karoo –
	Huge sandstone table hollowed into valleys,
	With level cliffs lending its treeless mountains
	A firm and parallel repose.
FEMALE VOICE:	Listen – echoing through Time's broken corridors
	The hiss and rustle of seas that set the sandstone strata.
MALE VOICE:	Watch the first cell split in two, and walk
	Between dim ferns the size of baobab trees;
	And in your opening mind's eye see
	Vast scaly reptiles dwindle down ...
FEMALE VOICE:	To six-inch lizards and the shy, sly snake.

Tales from the Old Karoo, published in 1989, took Butler back to what he calls, in the introduction, 'my part of the world'. Windmills and gates; ostriches and tortoises; goats and jackals; kiepersol and klapperbos are just some of the typical Karoo objects that come into the stories. One of the stories most deeply embedded in the environment – 'The Mountain Tortoise Cure' – illustrates how the ingrained relationship with a person's early environment colours attitudes and actions in spite of separation. A doctor, recently returned after a long absence in Europe, crosses the landscape to attend to a patient on a remote farm.

> The Poisonous *tulp* after which the farm was named was not in bloom, but the *slangkop* was – dozens of yellow racemes on long stalks like cobras' heads, swaying. Sinister? Perhaps. But part of himself. Somewhere, about two hours ago, he'd started noticing such things again. Of course, he'd pointed out this and that to Janet on the journey, affixing names to flora and fauna. But now it was as if the initiative had passed from him to them. The outline of things, their shapes, small and large, were naming him, nailing him with their sudden recognitions of things in his mind. He was riding into himself, a self that he had almost forgotten, which had last been as vivid only in dreams and nightmares in Edinburgh or Utrecht, or daydreaming on a barge drifting down the Rhône.

The doctor's experience of finding identity through recognising features of the landscape sounds autobiographical. The Karoo named Guy Butler as it had Olive Schreiner.

Guy Butler, Cradock and Matthew Goniwe

In Butler's poem 'Ode to Dead Friends', written in the 1980s, one of the stanzas is devoted to Matthew Goniwe, the author of the stark poem 'These Walls', which is a response to a place without landscape, without people, without sound – a prison cell. Who knows what other poems by this gifted young man may have been lost?

> These Walls
>
> Walls, walls, walls.
> Walls all around me.
> Four walls,
> Four cold companions,
> Four deaf and dumb.
>
> Close, too close
> Strong, rigid, firm,
> Close, too close,
> They explode into my consciousness,
> Big, bulking, bold.
>
> Close, too close,
> Closed.
> Silence seals my soundless box.

In 'Ode to Dead Friends', Butler recounts part of Goniwe's story:

> We were born in the same small town.
> You wrote from jail, for help with English verse.
> Bright boy, from grim Lingelihle, you had grown
> to manhood while our tyranny grew worse.
> Were freed; imprisoned; freed;
> again you meet warm gatherings of friends;
> are ambushed; tortured; after days found, dead;
> and there, for Law and Order, your story ends.
> But not for wife, child, brothers, comrades, these
> for whom you are still magical.
> We praise you! I recall
> putting on Handel at news of your release.
> You blew in on the wind. 'Look! I've arrived!'
> And round my room you jived
> To the Hallelujah Chorus, laughing and alive.[6]

MATTHEW GONIWE, born in 1947 in the Cradock township of Lingelihle, became a school teacher who worked for improvements in the education of his people and for a political place for them in their own land. His activities brought him into conflict with the authorities of the day and, in 1978, he was sentenced to three years in prison under the Suppression of Communism Act. From prison he wrote to Guy Butler for help with the writing of poetry, and a singular friendship developed between them. As Butler's poem indicates, his release from prison in 1981 did not mean real freedom. Other detentions followed, interrupting a brilliant teaching career, his family life and his political campaigning. In 1985 Goniwe's burned and mutilated body was found beside the road near Port Elizabeth. The gruesome details of Goniwe's assassination, along with three companions, by security force agents, were disclosed more than a decade later in the hearings of the Truth and Reconciliation Commission.

Cradock and Etienne van Heerden

The funeral of Matthew Goniwe and his associates – the Cradock Four – was a massive display of solidarity with their cause. It was probably this funeral that inspired Etienne van Heerden's short story 'The Bull and the Bishop', set in a 'small town named after an English governor from the colonial era'.

Cradock and the Karoo are as deeply embedded in Etienne van Heerden's consciousness as in those of Olive Schreiner and Guy Butler, and as important in his writings. In an event humorously recorded by Van Heerden in *De Kat*,[7] a helicopter brought together, on the top of Buffelskop, these three Cradock writers from different generations. Olive Schreiner was born in 1855 and buried on the mountain in 1921; Guy Butler was born in Cradock in 1918 and is on his seventh or eighth visit to the grave; Etienne van Heerden was born in 1954 and spent his early years on a farm at the foot of Buffelskop, next to Krantz Plaats, where Olive lived briefly after her marriage. This experience took Etienne back to sights, smells and sounds from his childhood and to how he had imagined Olive Schreiner creeping out of her grave to look over the valley and the farm where he lay in bed scared stiff and suffering, like her, from asthma. She was also to haunt the world of Van Heerden's fiction particularly in the short story 'The Resurrection of Olive', set on that farm. It is a story with a double life, for it is also woven into his novel *Kikuyu*.

In *Kikuyu* Etienne van Heerden writes in a mode typical of postmodernism, reminding the reader from time to time that he is a writer writing about the youth of a writer who is both himself and not himself. He has the power, as a storyteller, of changing the story – selecting events and people from the past, conflating or expanding time, remaking characters, even introducing a mythological beast – Kikuyu. The illusion of a factual story comes largely from the authenticity of its setting. Such features as the town library with its Schreiner room, the railway line, the Great Fish River, the road linking farm and town are real. The smells and sounds of a Karoo night and scores of allusions to trees and plants, birds and animals characteristic of the region, take the reader right into the world of the farm Soebatsfontein.

Occasionally, however, fantasy touches the setting. The father of Kikuyu's protagonist, Fabian, has been prescribed LSD. Ma has to record his dreams. Here, Van Heerden takes us from the reality of the present scene into a hallucinatory state in which landscape and personal consciousness merge:

> Around them stretched the endless Karoo night, and the small constellations of light from towns like Cradock, Graaff-Reinet, Murraysburg or Aberdeen were insignificant interruptions in the massive open landscape, the swirling nothingness that lay stretched out under the stars, under the milky way, exposed to the soft hand of the dew or the cold eye of God, or the night breezes that pushed smells unhindered across the landscape, stirring the lukewarm air that had dammed up in the hollows, pushing it out over the plains, further, further, away to the emptinesses that grew bigger and bigger, the horizon that still beckoned as Pa dripped off the end of it and became landscape and stood spinning on the bedroom floor, explaining hesitantly, 'I melt from the edge of the Camdeboo, I drip, I drip ...'

The kaleidoscopic story of the summer of 1960 on Soebatsfontein dips into past and future, veers between reality and fantasy. The bones of Olive are removed by Fabian and a friend from the sarcophagus on Buffelskop, wired together and erected on a cross. The author has explained this surreal event as a resurrection of the imagination, important to a writer writing about a writer. It also has political implications. Olive, according to Tant Greet, 'could write life back into the country' – much-needed life, as events in both novel and short story reveal.

After the death of ETIENNE VAN HEERDEN's father when the author was fourteen years old, the family moved to Stellenbosch, where the young man completed his schooling and studied law, Afrikaans and Nederlands at Stellenbosch University. Some years later, Van Heerden embarked on an academic career at the University of Zululand and, in 1986, returned to the

Eastern Cape as a member of the department of Afrikaans and Nederlands at Rhodes University in Grahamstown. There his literary and academic reputation became firmly established, a reputation based on novels, short stories, cabarets and academic publications. All were written in Afrikaans and most have subsequently been translated into English. Some of the short stories in *Mad Dog and Other Stories* (1992) have Eastern Cape settings, as do the novels *Ancestral Voices* (1989), *Leap Year* (1997) and *Kikuyu* (1998).

In 1997 Van Heerden moved to the Western Cape and a post at the University of Cape Town but, it seems, the Karoo still has a hold over his imagination, for his most recent novel, *Die Swye van Mario Salviati (The Silence of Mario Salviati)*, is set in an imaginary village in the Karoo.

Cradock and Iris Vaughan

In 1956 *The Diary of Iris Vaughan* was submitted to the South African magazine *The Outspan* by its author, the now-adult Iris Niland, and the editor decided to publish it in instalments. Convinced that it was genuine by the reaction of readers who had known Iris Vaughan as a child and remembered many of the events she described, the publishers hailed it as a major literary find. It came out in book form in 1958 and has been a perennial favourite ever since, ranking in popularity with the child diaries of Daisy Ashford and Marjorie Fleming.

The diary opens:

> Today is my birthday. I am going to write a diry a diray a diery Book. Pop told me I could ... Every one should have a diery. Becos life is too hard with the things one must say to be perlite and the things one must not say to lie.

It is not clear when this frank diary was begun but it covers the years of the South African War (1899 to 1902) and just after, a period during which Iris's magistrate father – his Irish temper often described by Iris as 'savige' – was transferred from town to town in the Eastern Cape. Maraisburg (now known as Hofmeyr), Cradock, Pearston, Grahamstown, Fort Beaufort and Adelaide are described with the freshness of a child's observation. Maraisburg 'has no trees or rivers. Only sand and two hills and some milk bush becos it is the godforsaken Karroo. That is what Pop calls it.' Pearston 'is a very small place. It has a river but no water in. We live in a hotel. It is a bad one. It has earth floors.' Fort Beaufort is 'prettier than Adelaide, but it will never be nice to us. We came over a bridge. The river is Kat. Bridge is called Victoria. Here is a tall fat looking fort like an upside down Malays cap. It is called Martelo tower.' A brief visit to

Grahamstown does not impress: 'There is a cathedral here. It does not look up to much. Not for a cathedral. Not as nice as our dutch church.' That would have been the Dutch Reformed church in Adelaide, where the family had its longest sojourn, and for which Iris seems to have felt the greatest affection. Many adventures happen to them there as in the other towns of the region, all recounted with relish and a disregard for 'suitable' expression and juxtaposition.

> Before we came here we lived in Cradock. It is a big town with a park and a railway train and a criket club. It is also a place where come many sick people called con sumtiffs who have a sickness of the lungs rotting of the lungs. Lots of them never get well. Pop is not a consumtiff. He comes from Wales the consumtiffs come from England ... In Dundas street our house had a big pear tree and we had a foto taken under it. All had to wear the best clothes. Charles had his cross look becos he did not care to wear his best shoes they pinching him so madly. The foto taking man tried to make him laugh and said look at the canery bird coming out of the black foto taking box which stood on three sticks with a black cloth over his head. But charles just mad a worse look come on his face. He gets sulks. His sulks came out in the foto and spoilt it. Once he got bad sulks and walked in the water furrow with his best clothes on just before we went to a party ... In Cradock were nice trees in the streets by the furrows. Here are no trees. In Cradock was a Slippery Rock where we have fun. Every afternoon Katryn takes us to the Rock. We climb to the top. In the middle of the rock, it is a very long great rock, is a lovely slippy footpath. You sit on top and someone pushes you and you sail away fast to the bottom just like a bird sailing in the air the wind blowing your hair and a strange noise in your ears like bees bussing. Mom made us take a bag to sit on becos we wore our drawers out sailing on our tails so much.

The diary ends when IRIS VAUGHAN is thirteen. Thereafter she completed her schooling and attended Rhodes University for a short time. She taught for a year before marrying a farmer, Jehu Niland. Widowed at 32, she settled in King William's Town, where she worked as a journalist. Later the story of her life was taken up in two books of reminiscences: *These Were My Yesterdays* and *Last of the Sunlit Years*, published in the 1960s. They portray the world of a fairly ordinary white family living in the Eastern Cape in the first half of the 20th century. *The Diary* remains Vaughan's masterpiece. It brings to this tour of the Karoo a light note but is not without some penetrating observations of its time and place.

BUSH WORLD'

Olive Schreiner's name and her works are inseparable from the Karoo, but the mountainous midlands of the Eastern Cape also had a profound effect on her and there are important echoes of this region in her writings. In the unfinished short story 'Diamond Fields', Schreiner calls it the 'bush world' and characterises it as an idealised, paradisal place with luxuriant vegetation and inhabited by many birds and small creatures.

> 'Oh yes,' said the woman, 'think of some places in the old Colony, not up-country in the Karoo and grass 'veldt', but down in the bush world. There where the cock-o-veets sing in the still forest all day and the monkey ropes hang from the trees, and jasmine and geranium grow in open spaces, and the mosses and ferns by the water, and the white clematis hangs from the trees!'

This 'bush world' corresponds in some respects with the milieux in which the author spent her early years.

Between her birth in 1855 and leaving her parents' home among the mountains to live with her siblings in Cradock in the Karoo, Schreiner moved from the northern mission station of Wittebergen, to Healdtown near Fort Beaufort in the foothills of the Winterberg, and briefly to Balfour in the Kat River valley. Later she worked for a year in Dordrecht in the Stormberg. She also spent, as we have seen, eighteen months on the farm Leliekloof in the Winterberg. On the page we shall follow a biographical rather than geographical order in viewing these places, but those wishing to see them with their own eyes may like to combine a visit to one or other site with the Stormberg or Winterberg journeys that follow on from here.

THE WITTEBERG

OLIVE SCHREINER was born on 24 March 1855 to Gottlob Schreiner and Rebecca Schreiner (formerly Lyndall) at the Wesleyan mission station of Wittebergen, situated near Herschel just south of the Eastern Cape's borders with the Free State and the kingdom of Lesotho. Her names, Olive Emilie Albertina, commemorated three dead brothers – Oliver, Emile and Albert. Her place of birth was perched on a rocky promontory in one of the more arid sections of the Witteberg, or 'white mountains', a western spur of the Drakensberg range. 'Rocks of every conceivable size and shape, ragged, weatherworn, and lichen covered, lay jumbled together, or scattered in wild confusion, and in silent eloquence told of the ages gone by,'[1] writes Arthur Brigg, a mission-

ary who moved to the Wittebergen station when the Schreiners left it in 1861. He describes the long, low whitewashed house with thatched roof, clay walls and small windows, in which Olive Schreiner was born, and the adjacent chapel, which he says was 'more imposing in appearance'. Brigg also describes a number of features that are recreated in Schreiner's fiction, such as a dam with weeping willows; a garden with fruit-bearing trees and a row of syringas; and, in the spaces between the rocks of the steep crag on which the mission station stood, primeval bush and trees – the haunt of innumerable birds. As the site is today difficult to access, for most of us it is necessary to rely on the account of Brigg and those of Schreiner herself in making connections between the author's real and fictional worlds as they relate to Witteberg, although one may gain a general sense of the milieu by visiting the region.

Schreiner's first home witnessed the dawn of her con-sciousness of self and of the natural world around her. Although there were painful memories, Witteberg (as the family called it) seems, on the whole, to have been associat-ed in Schreiner's mind with a fairly secure childhood, during which there were moments of illumination as well as of creative day-dreaming that were to affect the rest of her life. Nearly half a century after leaving it, she records how a slight breeze evokes her first home:

> Just now [night] I went and stood in the dark at the corner of the house, and the soft sweet damp air that blew round it made me feel all at once that I *was* a little child at Witteberg again – I didn't remember it, I seemed to *be* there.[2]

Witteberg is recreated in various guises in Schreiner's novels. The opening chapter of *From Man to Man*, entitled 'A Child's Day', is, by the author's own admission, largely autobiographical. Images, such as the one below, of the 'old farm' permeate the novel.

> The farmhouse stood on the spur of a mountain, and the thorn trees in the flat below were already shimmering in the sunlight. After a while she put on her kappie and walked slowly down the steps and across the bare space which served for a farmyard. Beyond it she passed into the low bushes. She soon came to a spot just behind the kraal where the ground was flat and bare; the surface soil had been washed off, and a circular floor of smooth, and unbroken stone was exposed, like the smooth floor of a great round room. The bushes about were just high enough to hide her from the farm house, though it was only fifty yards off. She stepped on to

the stone slowly, on tiptoe. She was building a house here. It stood in the centre of the stone floor; it was a foot and a half high and about a foot across, and was built of little flat stones placed very carefully on one another; and it was round like a tower ... She was building it for mice.

When she visited her birthplace in 1893 Olive wrote to her husband:

> Cron, I had a beautiful time up at Witteberg. That little white thatch-roofed house perched among the great rocks and bushes on the edge of the krantz was *just* as I'd pictured it all these years. There was the great flat stone by the house on which I was making a house when I heard that my little brother Cammie was born, and [there] are the bushes with the funny smell under which I sat alone the first time I ever realized my own individuality and the mystery of existence.[3]

In the chapter 'Times and Seasons' in *The Story of an African Farm* some of the memories 'indelibly printed in the mind' Schreiner describes must have been drawn from Witteberg. They reveal a psyche that, even in childhood, bore the marks of a deep thinker who responded with sensitivity to the world around her and with questions about her place in it. Among these memories are:

> Remembrance of delight in the feel and smell of the first orange we ever see; of sorrow which makes us put up our lip, and cry hard, when one morning we run out to try and catch the dewdrops, and they melt and wet our little fingers; of almighty and despairing sorrow when we are lost behind the kraals, and cannot see the house anywhere ... We look at the white earth, and the rainbow, and the blue sky; and oh, we want it, we want – we do not know what ... One day we ... look up at the blue sky, and down at our fat little knees; and suddenly it strikes us, Who are we? This *I*, what is it? We try to look in upon ourself, and ourself beats back upon ourself. Then we get up in great fear and run home as hard as we can. We can't tell anyone what frightened us. We never quite lose that feeling of *self* again.

One of Schreiner's most firmly held beliefs – that all things are part of a living whole – had its genesis during these years. In a letter written in 1892 to the Rev. John T Lloyd, a Presbyterian minister in Port Elizabeth, she writes:

> I have never been able to conceive of God and man and the material universe as distinct from one another. The laws of my mind do not allow it. When I was a little child of five and sat alone among the tall weeds at the back of our house, this perception of the unity of all things, and that they were alive, and that I was part of them, was as clear and overpowering to me as it is to-day. It is the one thing I am never able to doubt.[4]

Schreiner's passion for rocky places also stems from Witteberg. Here she describes her first home to her friend Havelock Ellis:

> The house stands on the very edge of a high cliff or krantz of pure rock, perched, as I have seen no other house in all my wanderings, on the very edge of the rocks like an eagle's nest. I think, from the position, I have acquired that passionate love of rocks and precipices which has followed me all my life and been stronger than any other feeling I have for natural aspects except for the blue sky and stars.[5]

All Schreiner's novels with Eastern Cape settings feature children moving, often through harsh ordeals, from innocence to experience, and often the age of innocence is linked to images from nature just as childhood experiences of nature were vitally important in the author's own nurturing.

In spite of having six siblings the Olive (or Emilie, as she was first called) of Witteberg lived largely in a dream world and was regarded as a 'queer little child', like the protagonist in her novel *Undine*. Yet she was intensely aware of the real world which encompassed her and years later was able to describe it in detail.

> All was very still and brown there also. The little peach trees that stood in rows were shedding their half ripe fruit, which fell into the long yellow grass beneath them, and the fig trees along the wall had curled up the edges of their leaves. Rebekah followed a little winding footpath among the grass to the middle of the orchard, where a large pear tree stood, with a gnarled and knotted stem. There was a bench under the tree, and the grass grew very long all about it. She looked around to find a spot where the tree cast a deeper shade than elsewhere. Here she walked round and round on the grass, like a dog, and then lay down on her back in the place she had made. It was like a nest, with the grass standing several inches high all round.[6]

The nest image here and in Schreiner's description of her first home perched 'on the very edge of the rocks like an eagle's nest' is significant. It is not unusual for both nest and early home to be depicted in literature as places of security and of return. Gaston Bachelard, in his book about the connections between psychology, place and poetry – *The Poetics of Space* – writes, 'If we return to the old home as to a nest, it is because memories are dreams, because the home of other days has become a great image of lost intimacy.

Schreiner paid two return visits to the Witteberg region which we know about: the one in 1893 quoted above, shortly before her marriage to Cron Cronwright, and an earlier visit in 1870, at the age of fifteen, to relations who farmed at the foot of the 2000 m Avoca Peak near Lady Grey. This also took place at a period when she was entering a new phase in her life, marked at the time by an insistence on being called Olive rather than Emilie. Then it was for her a place of freedom where she could take long walks and rides and enjoy the scenery and the wild flowers and plants she loved.

This north-east corner of the Eastern Cape offers some of the province's grandest scenery. Some of the roads and passes that wind steeply through the region, as well as present-day towns such as Elliot, Maclear, Barkly East and Rhodes, would be foreign to Schreiner but, like her, we can contemplate its natural delights and make them our own. This is something the Grahamstown poet Dan Wylie does in 'Malpas Farm, Rhodes'. The lammergeier coasting 'away along the cliffs' *would* be familiar to Schreiner. It is her 'white bird'.

DAN WYLIE
Malpas Farm, Rhodes

A lammergeier
coasts away along the cliffs,
unravelling their ragged sleeves.
For her, care is redundant.
Bulbuls,
down here in the garden's
earthbound wreckage,
bicker among my thoughts.
I sit
against a peeling pillar,
momentarily overwhelmed
by a gossip of white-eyes,
by waterfalls wrestling under ice,
by runnels torn in the hill's flank
like some predator's attempt
at an old tough hide.
So much lingering pain:
the violence we do one another.
A wind plunges among the poplars;
I feel leafless;

I am afraid
of unstable parts of myself,
as I would be of having claws.
If only I could shed all that,
like paint, like a season,
only lighten like these flakes
of snow, tinier than whims,
only dissolve
beyond the cold regrets
of the furthest ridge.

from The Road Out

HEALDTOWN

In 1861, at about the time of Schreiner's sixth birthday, her family moved to Healdtown, a Wesleyan mission station established in 1853 on the site of an earlier London Missionary Society station. There Gottlob Schreiner took charge of the Technical Institute, set up by Governor George Grey in 1855. He found this a difficult task and financial problems led him to break an LMS rule against trading for personal gain. In 1866 he was forced to resign and the remnants of the family moved to Balfour.

In subsequent years Healdtown developed into a major educational centre through which a number of leaders of the black community passed. Nelson Mandela matriculated there and in his autobiography, *Long Walk to Freedom*, he describes the Healdtown of 1937:

> Located at the end of a winding road overlooking a verdant valley, Healdtown was far more beautiful and impressive than Clarkebury [Mandela's previous school in the Transkei]. It was, at the time, the largest African school south of the equator, with more than a thousand students, both male and female. Its graceful ivy-covered colonial buildings and tree-shaded courtyards gave it the feeling of a privileged academic oasis, which is precisely what it was.

Healdtown is situated in the foothills of the Winterberg, about 10 km northeast of Fort Beaufort. In 1956, a year after celebrating its centenary, Healdtown came under Nationalist government control in terms of the Bantu Education Act of 1953. Soon all but the primary school closed down. The 'graceful ivy-covered colonial buildings and tree-shaded courtyards' of the old institution of Mandela's day fell into disrepair. Now a secondary school has been re-established in new buildings and the settlement is once again alive with young voices and colourful uniforms; but derelict buildings – including the mission house in which the Schreiners lived – are sad reminders of the ravages of time and of apartheid.

Of Healdtown Olive Schreiner writes:

> My childhood was so bitter and dark, but I cling to the memories of it and especially the places I lived at. They were so unutterably lovely and it was in nature I found all the joy and help I had in those lonely years.[7]

In Schreiner's writings a particular kind of place is associated with a feeling of consolation and joy. It 'can be linked indisputably with Healdtown',[8] and its genesis was a kloof below the garden of the mission house that is a place of natural beauty and serenity, where plants clothe its precipitous sides in tangled abundance and water trickles over boulders, occasionally collecting in quiet pools. It is connected with a seminal experience in Schreiner's life.

In 'The Dawn of Civilisation', an article said to have been 'her last words, in 1920', Schreiner describes in detail an event that occurred when, she says, she was nine years old – that would have been during the Healdtown years. After a sleepless night she walks out early one morning 'along the mountain tops on which my home stood'.

> I walked till I came to a place where a little stream ran, which further on passed over the precipices into the deep valley below. Here it passed between soft, earthy banks; at one place a large slice of earth had fallen away from the bank on the other side, and it had made a little island a few feet wide with water flowing all round it. It was covered with wild mint and a weed with yellow flowers and long waving grasses. I sat down on the bank at the foot of a dwarfed olive tree, the only tree near. All the plants on the island were dark with the heavy night's dew, and the sun had not yet risen.[9]

Schreiner explains that at the time she was burdened by a sense of the world's suffering apparent to her in all the instances she had witnessed or heard of oppression, conflict and cruelty towards animals and towards humans like the convicts she had seen 'going past to work on the roads'. She recalls a feeling of being weighed down by the whole universe.

And then, as I sat looking at that little, damp, dark island, the sun began to rise. It shot its light across the long, grassy slopes of the mountains and struck the little mound of earth in the water. All the leaves and flowers and grasses on it turned bright gold, and the dewdrops hanging from them were like diamonds; and the water in the stream glinted as it ran. And, as I looked at that almost intolerable beauty, a curious feeling came over me. It was not what I *thought* put into exact words, but I seemed to see a world in which creatures no more hated and crushed, in which the strong helped the weak, and men understood each other, and forgave each other, and did not try to crush others, but to help. I did not think of it as something to be in a distant picture; it was there, about me, and I was in it, and a part of it. And there came to me, as I sat there, a joy such as never besides have I experienced, except perhaps once, a joy without limit.[10]

This, Schreiner tells us, was the most memorable and important day of her life, and this experience is reflected in various ways in her novels and stories.

The experience is transposed onto Waldo in *The Story of an African Farm* and the time altered from morning to evening.

'The evening before last, when it was just sunset, I was a little footsore and thirsty, and went out of the road to look for water. I went down into a deep little "kloof." Some trees ran along the bottom, and I thought I should find water there. The sun had quite set when I got to the bottom of it. It was very still – not a leaf was stirring anywhere. In the bed of the mountain torrent I thought I might find water. I came to the bank, and leaped down into the dry bed. The floor on which I stood was of fine white sand, and the banks rose on every side like the walls of a room. Above, there was a precipice of rocks, and a tiny stream of water oozed from them and fell slowly on to the flat stone below. Each drop you could hear fall like a little silver bell. There was one among the trees on the bank that stood out against the white sky. All the other trees were silent; but this one shook and trembled against the sky. Everything else was still; but those leaves were quivering, quivering. I stood on the sand; I could not go away. When it was quite dark, and the stars had come, I crept out. Does it seem strange to you that it should have made me so happy? It is because I cannot tell you how near I felt to things that we cannot see but we always feel.'

The protagonist in Schreiner's novel *Undine*, experiences an inexplicable feeling of joy and of oneness with all of life as well as with something beyond herself for which she longs. In a passage of similar length, Schreiner describes 'a little kloof', the time is the same – sunset – and Undine, too, descends to 'the bed of a mountain torrent' that is 'lined with smooth white sand'. A tiny stream of water 'had the soft, silver sound of far-away evening bells, and everything else was very silent'. Against the evening sky 'the branches of the oliventrees were visible, with pale, quivering up-pointed leaves', and in that space, 'a great hush came and a great joy, for heaven is not a long way off, nor the beautiful for which we thirst'.

In *From Man to Man* and in the short story 'Dream Life and Real Life' there are similar secluded, enclosed natural spaces that are linked to experiences of consolation. There can be little doubt that the kloof experiences in her fiction echo Olive Schreiner's own. Even as a child she rejected the dogma and some of the practices of Christianity but there is always a sense in her writings that 'heaven is not a long way off', and that all life is one.

Another lifelong passion – the love of nature – was intensified during the Healdtown years. The death of her dearly loved sister Ellie at the age of seventeen months strengthened Olive's growing doubts about the religious teachings with which she was being fed, and helped, she maintained, to make her into a freethinker. It also affected her attitude to nature.

> I used to love the birds and animals and inanimate nature better after she was dead; the whole of existence seemed to me more beautiful because it had brought forth and taken back to itself such a beautiful thing as she was to me.[11]

A simple headstone in a womblike space among natural trees below what would have been the Schreiners' garden in Healdtown marks Ellie's grave. It is not far from the consoling kloof.

BALFOUR, HERTZOG AND DORDRECHT

There is no clear evidence in Schreiner's fiction of connections with Balfour, the Schreiners' next home, although she spent about two years there, or with Hertzog, to which her parents moved after she was sent to Cradock and where she visited them from time to time. That both are situated in the Kat River Valley, which was at the time thickly wooded and surrounded by mountains, does, however, suggest that they may have been part of the author's memory and recreation of what she called the 'bush world'.

Dordrecht, set against Dassiebank, which is part of the Stormberg range, affected Schreiner more deeply although she lived there for only about a year when she was in her mid-teens. Something never fully explained, involving a supposed engagement that was later broken off, happened to the young girl here and she left quite suddenly to return to her parents at Hertzog. The town may not have much to remind us of Schreiner – the house in which she stayed was demolished in 2000 – but a narrow wooded dale on Dordrecht's outskirts does have a sense of her presence. It was, and still is, an area accessible to the public and the kind of secluded, rocky place Schreiner would have enjoyed. Perhaps this place, like those at Witteberg and Healdtown, lived in her imagination and contributed to the kloof experiences in her fiction.

8

THREE

STORMBERG WRITERS

The Penhoek Pass on the main road to the north between Queenstown and Aliwal North crosses the Stormberg, a range of mountains that runs from east to west about 60 km south-west of the more spectacular Drakensberg and Witteberg, where Olive Schreiner was born. In a region renowned for sheep farming, although it once held out the promise of a lucrative coal mining industry, wide stretches of open countryside and scattered hills contrast with moderately high mountains. There, as the name Stormberg implies, extremes of weather characterise the climate. Dordrecht, Molteno and Sterkstroom are the Stormberg's main centres, all towns with interesting personalities but they have diminished in importance with time.

This region has inspired three rather different writers: English author William Plomer; Afrikaans painter and prose writer (in both Afrikaans and English) Johannes Meintjes; and the prose fiction writer Farida Karodia, whose father and mother were classified as Indian and coloured respectively.

William Plomer
Johannes Meintjes
Farida Karodia

MARSH MOOR AND WILLIAM PLOMER

William Plomer, a renowned British writer with South African connections, spent a brief, post-matriculation period on the farm Marsh Moor, among the higher peaks of the Stormberg. For the young Plomer it was an important period during which he began to see the direction his life was to take. Although he enjoyed some aspects of farm life, 'providence', he writes, 'had not really designed me to speculate on the possibilities of commerce and agriculture but on the magic of words'.[1]

At Marsh Moor he absorbed what he saw and experienced, and later transformed much of it into fiction, pre-eminently in the short story 'Down on the Farm'. He also read a good deal, wrote in secret and sent some poems to Harold Monro, a 'poetic impresario' in England with whom he had begun corresponding shortly before going to the Stormberg. Monro responded sympathetically – providing the first formal recognition of Plomer's talent as a writer.

WILLIAM CHARLES FRANKLYN PLOMER was born in 1903 in Pietersburg (now Polokwane) of British parents. In his autobiographical writings Plomer recounts that his 'first memory of any significance' was of 'a brilliant spring morning at Louis Trichardt', to which his parents had moved in 1909. He writes that from then on he took an 'increasing pleasure in the

visible world and was indeed trained to do so by my mother, herself richly endowed with what may be called the visual appetite'.[2] That 'visual appetite' is often expressed in William Plomer's writings through his response to place, including the Stormberg, and in recreations in words of the 'visible world'.

During Plomer's childhood and youth England and South Africa vied for his affections. His father loved Africa, his mother loathed it and the family moved frequently between the two, settling in neither. Part of Plomer's early education was at St John's College in Johannesburg; he then attended schools in England – Beechmont and Rugby – and returned to St John's for his final years. There he developed an interest in art and literature and began experimenting with writings of his own. Uncertainty about what to do after matriculating was resolved by his going to work as a kind of apprentice farmer under a scheme organised by the 1820 Settlers Memorial Foundation. Charles Plomer, with fond memories of his own youth when he travelled around the eastern part of the Cape Colony doing odd jobs, chose, for his son, the farm Marsh Moor near Molteno and, at the age of seventeen, William Plomer arrived in the town.

> Molteno, a one-horse town, had its main street, its railway and police stations, its hotel, a few shops with chickens pecking about on the threshold, a Dutch Reformed church, a Wesleyan Methodist chapel, and much smaller, an Anglican church. The streets were few, wide, dusty and drowsy; an occasional ox-wagon creaked past; everybody knew everybody else's business, and small scandals took on colossal proportions; Europe seemed a conception as remote and unreal as heaven or hell; and the cats, asleep on the window-sills or hearth-rugs, looked as tranquil and detached as so many images of Buddha.[3]

Marsh Moor, about 25 km north-east of Molteno, is still in the hands of the Pope family, whose forebears welcomed William Plomer in 1921 and treated him 'with friendly consideration'. Plomer worked for Fred Pope, grandfather of the present owner, Charles, and son of the first member of the family to buy the farm in 1895. Fred's son Stanley was five years old when Plomer was there and he retained vivid memories of the young man's storytelling and of the caricatures he drew.

Among other tasks, Plomer worked with the sheep on the farm. Seasonal procedures such as lambing, docking and shearing, all so graphically described in 'Down on the Farm', continue at Marsh Moor. The farmhouse Plomer knew has been replaced but a number of stone buildings described in his autobiography and his fiction still exist.

What is even more evocative of Plomer's writings is the landscape. In *Double Lives* he describes the setting of Marsh Moor as 'a great amphitheatre enclosed by mountains'. In 'Down on the Farm' he describes two farms lying 'in a broad valley shaped like an amphitheatre'.

> In the middle of that superb landscape there is a patch of low-lying ground which is thickly covered for a few days in the spring with yellow flowers. They spring from the bulb so quickly that nobody notices them until they are out, when the wind, already warmer, carries their fragrance towards one or other of the two farmhouses. For right through the middle of the flowers runs the fence which divides the two farms, Adventure and Brakfontein, lying in a broad valley shaped like an amphitheatre.[4]

During leisure hours Plomer explored Marsh Moor.

> Not the least of my pleasures was to wander in the mountains, where the solitude was complete and the wild flowers unknown to me – tree-heaths, curious liliaceous plants, and canary-yellow dwarf arums with mottled leaves and a wicked-looking puce finger pointing rigidly upwards in the sheath of each flower – and I discovered some unknown caves adorned with spirited and elegant Bushman paintings, ritual and hunting scenes carried out in black, white and red and yellow ochres. So I lacked neither a garden nor a picture gallery.[5]

The flora of the district, the caves and the mountains feature in Plomer's short story and, occasionally, in other fiction. In the upper reaches of today's farm cave paintings of exceptional interest and beauty survive and the terrain is rich in floral treasures. In the background are ramparts of rock and mountain peaks, which include the highest point in the Stormberg.

In 'Down on the Farm' Plomer also describes the region's occasional climatic extremes from which the Stormberg derives its name: dust storms when crimson dust 'crowded on through the sky until at last the mountains withdrew in a blood-coloured fog'; thunderstorms with 'lightning leaping from cliff to crag and sewing sound and fury with giant stitches of livid light'; hailstorms with 'the roar of ice on ironstone audible long before its arrival above the amphitheatre'. A snowstorm and its consequent thaw have an important role in the story.

Less detailed Stormberg settings are found in Plomer's episodic novellas 'Portraits in the Nude' and 'Ula Masondo's Dream'. Both satirise colonial attitudes and display what, in a letter from Marsh Moor to Harold Monro, Plomer called his 'congenital love for any sort of vaudeville'. In the novel *Turbott Wolfe*, published in 1926, there are also echoes of Marsh Moor,

although it is difficult to extricate them from images gleaned at Entumeni in the then Natal. Plomer had moved there in January 1923 to help his parents run a trading store. Soper's farm in *Turbott Wolfe* is reminiscent of Marsh Moor, and the character of Soper himself was probably suggested by that of Fred Pope. Other characters in Plomer's fiction also have their genesis in his Stormberg days, as do some of his views of race relations, about which he argued at times with his employer. *Turbott Wolfe* tells the story of love across what was then known as the colour bar.

William Plomer found inspiration in the district's literary associations. 'The Eastern Province is not without its literary associations, and the knowledge that two distinguished writers had grappled successfully among such rocky peaks as those of the Stormberg with the solitude of intellectual exile gave me comfort.'[6] One of these was Olive Schreiner, the other Thomas Pringle. 'Africa,' writes Plomer, 'as a place to abide in, defeated him [Pringle] as it later defeated Olive Schreiner, but both were spiritually and artistically victorious.'[7]

Africa as a place to abide in also defeated William Plomer. His year and a half at Marsh Moor was succeeded by less than four years in Natal. There he met Roy Campbell and Laurens van der Post, with whom he collaborated on the magazine *Voorslag*, an endeavour significant to the history of South African literature. Plomer lived in Japan and in Greece from 1926 to 1929, after which he settled permanently in England, where his working life, apart from a spell in Naval Intelligence during the Second World War, was bound up in the literary world. He worked as a publisher's literary adviser, edited and introduced the works of others – including several South African writers – and published works of his own in the genres of poetry, novel and short story. In addition he wrote one biography, collaborated with Benjamin Britten as librettist for several operas and produced four autobiographical works. Plomer was awarded the Queen's Gold Medal for Literature in 1963 and a CBE in 1965.

Between 1929 and his death in 1973 William Plomer visited South Africa only once – in 1956 – but he never forgot his South African days. He encouraged South African writers and often gave talks on South African themes. Letters preserved in the NELM archives reveal that, as he writes to Guy Butler on 13 January 1958, 'Africa doesn't leave me alone'. In a correspondence begun in 1956 with Johannes Meintjes, Plomer frequently refers to the way in which Meintjes's letters and writings bring back his Molteno days: 'a strange bittersweet recollection of my far-off days in the Stormberg'. A year before his death, referring to a work by Afrikaans writer Hennie Aucamp, *Op die Stormberge –*

a compilation of writings about the region which includes an Afrikaans translation of 'Down on the Farm' – Plomer writes to Meintjes:

> I like to think of myself being, in a miniature way, a 'regional' writer of
> the Stormberg. I can't pretend I was blissfully happy at Marsh Moor ...
> but, do you know, this book gives me a pang of heimwee both for the
> Stormberg & for my lost youth.[8]

MOLTENO AND JOHANNES MEINTJES

In the introduction to *Complex Canvas: A South African Approach* (1960) – a
book about the Cape Province written and illustrated by Johannes Meintjes –
the author writes:

> This book attempts to reveal the Cape Province in a new and possibly
> novel way. It is neither a history nor a guide-book, neither a factual docu-
> ment nor a cultural survey. It attempts to convey something of the intrin-
> sic wonder of the country, the moods, atmosphere and other qualities
> underlying the obvious. Being essentially a painter of mood, memory
> and the imagination, the drawings are mostly a mergence of several
> aspects, manipulated to intensify what was found most arresting and, in
> conjunction with the text, attempt to convey the very feel of the country.

In many of his writings and in his paintings Meintjes succeeds in conveying
'the very feel of the country', particularly of the Stormberg region and of the
family farm, Grootzeekoegat, which lies in a smaller neighbouring range, the
Bamboesberg, 25 km north of the district's principal town, Molteno.

JOHANNES MEINTJES was born in 1923. He spent the first five years of his
life at Grootzeekoegat and, after the death of his father, moved to Riversdale
in the Western Cape. Ten years later, when he was fifteen, the family moved to
Cape Town, where he completed his schooling and attended the University of
Cape Town. After further studies in Europe Meintjes returned to South Africa
and established a name as one of the country's most talented young artists. In
1949 he began visiting Grootzeekoegat, exploring the farm and restoring the
homestead. He was drawn back time after time but settled there permanently
only in 1969. From then until his death in 1980, Meintjes focused much of his
attention on the farm, the town of Molteno and the Stormberg region.

Best known as a painter, Meintjes was also a prolific writer, writing with
equal facility in Afrikaans and English. Novels, short stories, plays, autobiography, biography, history and other forms of non-fiction flowed from his pen.
The real and the imagined, the lyrical and the substantial merge in both his

paintings and his writings; both are filled with colour and both indicate a sensitivity to scenery as well as to people. Meintjes writes with the eye of a painter.

Frontier Farm (1955) is Meintjes's autobiographical account of Grootzeekoegat. 'Over the Bamboesberg', he writes, 'sprawls an old farm called Grootzeekoegat – "the great pool of the hippopotamus." There the early trek farmers outspanned and beheld a vast and majestic landscape.' The farm was in the Meintjes family from 1854 but the house was built much earlier and, when Johannes Meintjes knew it, may have been the oldest surviving homestead in the Cape.

Perhaps there was something prophetic in what Meintjes wrote about it:

> The veld is ruthless in reclaiming its own; human beings have an innate inclination to destroy, to uproot; the African is very much like the ant – they carry away bit by bit until nothing remains; the storms of the fierce African sky crumble walls back to their original soil ... But in that lonely landscape, isolated from the rest of mankind as it used to be, on a hill exposed to all the elements, the old house has stood massive and firm as the rock it is built on.

After his death Grootzeekoegat passed out of the family, and not many years ago the homestead which had given Johannes Meintjes assurance and stability, and which he had restored with love and patience, was razed to the ground. The veld and mountains remain as Meintjes describes them and the homestead lives on because he has recreated it in paint and word with what Plomer calls his 'visual exactitude'. In *Frontier Farm* his pleasure in the property is manifest.

> Grootzeekoegat after the rain was breathtakingly beautiful. Gorgeous colours flickered through the spiralling mist and low clouds, and the glitter of streams of water, the colourful flitting of ecstatic birds was part of the glorious pattern. The colours of the fields varied from bright green to black, from blue to red, and suddenly one noticed the emerald green moss on black tree trunks, the yellow and blue ironstone, flaming yellow on the *kriedorings* (lycium arenicolum) – no wonder that one felt like racing through the veld like a mad thing.

Along with the farm's physical features and the countryside's extremes of weather, Meintjes records the same sense of isolation and loneliness Plomer felt at Marsh Moor and which both writers associate with the experiences of Olive Schreiner.

> I have been fortunate in having an intimate knowledge of nearly all the places in which Olive Schreiner lived ... This intimate knowledge of her South African background, in some cases unchanged to this day, has helped in more ways than can be assessed in understanding the woman. The strangeness, the beauty and the loneliness of the area from Dordrecht to De Aar, Kimberley to Grahamstown, has been part of my life as it was of hers.[9]

Meintjes felt an affinity with her, and in his biography of Schreiner traces, with sympathy, the influences of place on her personality.

Meintjes's biographies of other notable South Africans include those of several Boer leaders as well as the Xhosa chief Sandile. Stories of the Great Trek and of the South African War intrigued Meintjes and he wrote histories of both. He also produced *Stormberg, a Lost Opportunity*, a well-researched account of hostilities in the north-western Cape between British forces and the Boers of the republics to the north along with their allies, the Cape rebels. The book captures the scene, the atmosphere, the feelings of the participants; it conveys a sense of the whole Stormberg region and of each of the places that come into the story; it portrays, with clarity, the people and events of the time. An imagined post-war scene at the end of the history reads like something from a novel.

> The war was over, and for weeks the Stormberg lay white with snow. Then came the thaw, and rivers roared. Then everything froze in one of the biggest freeze-ups in living memory. But it was a beautiful spring, and Molteno foamed with trees in full blossom, red and pink and white. At Stormberg Junction the children of railway-workers played with spent bullets, British water-bottles (some punctured with bullet holes), bully beef tins and with the scores of odds and ends left in the wake of two armies. The wind sighed through the empty stone forts, and through the Molteno cemetery. Carts and carriages again rolled freely through the streets and on farm roads, and the clip-clop of the hooves of horses was as usual, without urgency, without haste. Soon the last vestiges of war vanished. The outward signs were gone or inspected on sight-seeing trips. For the rest the war lived on in the eyes of men and women, either in companionship, distrust or hatred – until the course of South African history brought a different language to the eyes.

Molteno, close to the scene of a major British-Boer encounter, is at the heart of Meintjes's history of conflict in the Stormberg. The town was established in 1874 by George Vice on his farm Onverwacht and named for the Cape's prime minister. Coal had been discovered at nearby Cyphergat in 1860 and its mining and transport became the economic basis of a thriving town and railway network. The coal mined in the dis- trict was, however, of a low grade and many of the seams petered out. Sad-look- ing dumps can be seen in places along the road. When better-quality coal was then found in Natal as well as the Transvaal, Molteno, along with a number of the smaller towns along the line of rail, fell into decline. From about 1905 only the farming of merino sheep in the district kept them alive.

Of special interest to admirers of Meintjes's work is the collection of his paintings in Molteno's High School. Donated by his widow, it has been preserved by the school with care and pride. Along with some of his artist's tools and the desk at which many of Meintjes's writings must have taken shape, the paintings form a heritage of note. Another reminder of his association with Molteno is the library where the artist-writer worked part-time. It is housed in a large stone corner building once run as a shop by George Vice, and above it is a museum which Meintjes, with his interest in the past of the town and district, helped to build up. In honour of Molteno's centenary in 1976, Meintjes wrote *Dorp van Drome* (town of dreams), and in his 1960 *Portrait of a South African Village* he tells the story of the discovery of over a thousand photographic plates in the storeroom of Mr A Lomax, who had been Molteno's pharmacist and photographer between 1894 and 1909 – an outstanding pictorial record of the times.

Novels by Johannes Meintjes in both English and Afrikaans show 'the strong and unusual feeling of South Africa' which Plomer believes his fellow writer 'can convey in a way that nobody else does – I mean the particular places & atmospheres that have affected you most'.[10]

Even Meintjes's biographical and historical writings convey what he calls in the introduction to *Complex Canvas* 'something of the intrinsic wonder of the country, the moods, atmosphere and other qualities underlying the obvious'. His life and works form a complex canvas on which the Stormberg stands out in bold colours.

STERKSTROOM AND FARIDA KARODIA

A third writer associated with the Stormberg region is FARIDA KARODIA, born in 1942 in Sterkstroom, where she grew up and went to school. After training in Johannesburg as a teacher, Karodia left South Africa. She worked for a while in Zambia and in 1969 emigrated to Canada, where she is now based, although she spends time in both South Africa and India.

Exile drove Karodia to writing as a way of connecting with her home country from which she was excluded because her passport had been withdrawn. She has written novels, short stories, radio plays and film scripts. Short stories in *Coming Home* (1988) and *Against an African Sky* (1995) have various South African backgrounds, and her first novel – *Daughters of the Twilight* (1986) – is set in Sterkstroom and its environs. *Other Secrets* (2000) is a reworking of this early novel, with the addition of two further parts, and in it Sterkstroom is renamed Soetstroom.

The opening of *Daughters of the Twilight* sets the scene and the mood.

> Sterkstroom is a small dorp in South Africa. It is the type of town that you drive through en route to some other place, happily forgetting that you've ever been there. For us, however, it was home, the only one that my sister, Yasmin, and I had ever known.
>
> There was nothing remarkable about this little town of approximately twenty-five hundred people, not counting the blacks because there were no census figures available for them.

And a sense of this place pervades the rest of Karodia's story, created by means of short descriptive paragraphs linked to the narrative and unobtrusive comments on season, weather or time of day.

> All the streets were unpaved. When traffic was heavy, windows and doors had to be shut to keep out the dust. Wind too was an aggravation, blowing the fine, black coal-dust off the abandoned mounds to cover everything with a grey sheen. It was worse when there was a hot berg wind, like today. Whenever we complained about these conditions, Nana reminded us that it was the mine which kept Sterkstroom alive.

Similarly economical brushstrokes sketch the town's environs as the Mohammed family visits neighbouring farms, or travels to Aliwal North or East London.

The story focuses on Meena and Yasmin Mohammed, on their Indian father and coloured mother and grandmother and, particularly in the later novel, on Yasmin's daughter, Soraya. The family runs a general store in Sterkstroom. Forced by the Group Areas Board out of their home and business, they move to the isolated village of McBain, which becomes the focal point of the narrative.

Sadness, bitterness and tragedy are the keynotes of both novels, yet attachment to family shines through, together with a peculiar attachment to place despite unhappy associations.

I should have been glad to put McBain behind me, to bury it with some of my more unhappy childhood memories, but when I gazed out over the desolate landscape and realised that this might be my last visit, I was seized by pangs of nostalgia.[11]

The outer world images the fortunes and emotions of Karodia's characters. Searing berg winds, barren landscapes, black coal-dust, dry dongas and gullies, and black crows which 'carked and bobbed in the skeletal trees' are relieved occasionally by gentler images such as the view from Penhoek Pass, where 'down below the valley opened in a patchwork of brown and ecru while the hovering mist thinned and disintegrated'; or the experience of new life after rain: 'the veld was a festival of insect industry ... I took huge gulps of air while, above the pale green stubble, thousands of white butterflies hovered and lurched. The air was alive with the flutter of wings.'[12]

Many of the features to which the novels refer – wide, unpaved roads, dust and wind, cold winters, the park which forms the town square, 'undulating veld, broken here and there by kopjes' – characterise Sterkstroom and its surroundings in fact as in fiction. Situated among the foothills of the Stormberg, Sterkstroom was established in 1875 as the site for a Dutch Reformed church. As with Molteno, coal was the reason for its growth during the last decades of the 19th century, and the petering out of coal seams was the reason for Sterkstroom's later decline. Abandoned mounds of coal such as those to which the novelist refers are still visible alongside roads in the vicinity. Railway tracks, as in Karodia's evocation of the countryside, 'snake away' into the distance. Shops catering for the townspeople and the farming community that surrounds it have always been a feature of Sterkstroom. One of them was that of the Karodias, which probably suggested this description:

Mohammed's General Store specialised in dry goods and catered specifically to the African trade. The interior was filled with stacks of blankets reaching to the ceiling; billy-cans hung from the doorway in tight bunches and the

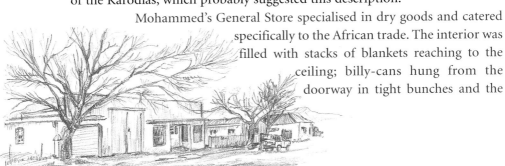

three-legged cast-iron pots popular with Africans for outside cooking were propped up against the door; beads and colourful bangles festooned shelves stacked with rows of plastic shoes.[13]

Another, more imposing shop has been converted into Sterkstroom's museum, whose well-ordered displays chart the fluctuating fortunes of the district. It now includes a feature on Farida Karodia herself. On one side of the River Hek – the *sterk* (strong) *stroom* (stream) – a few attractive Edwardian homes are interspersed with Sterkstroom's plain suburban houses. On the other, new housing is replacing some of the derelict dwellings in the old 'location'. The park in which Meena sat defiantly on a 'whites only' bench is dreary and overgrown but a number of brightly painted shops from which life spills out into the street proclaim a new vibrancy.

Parts of *Daughters of the Twilight* and *Other Secrets* are fictionalised versions of Farida Karodia's own experiences, and the Sterkstroom/Soetstroom and McBain settings reflect her early memories. The novels reveal a response to the Eastern Cape that is profoundly influenced by a loathing of the racial attitudes and the mechanisms of apartheid which victimised people classified other than white. They also reveal how deeply 'home' may be etched on the memory.

9

FOUR LITERARY FIRSTS

THE WINTERBERG

The effort of travelling in the Winterberg region, where roads are untarred and often winding and precipitous, is well rewarded by its scenery and by the literary and historical associations that are gathered here. Mountains rise to over 2 000 m and rivers winding down to join the Great Fish have created fertile valleys in which the peoples of the region have, at various times, farmed or hunted. The Winterberg has engendered several South African literary firsts. Thomas Pringle was the first writer to publish English poetry that drew its material from the South African landscape, and Ntsikana was the first traditional Xhosa poet to have a composition translated into English and printed. Harriet Ward was the first novelist to set a work entirely in South Africa while Marguerite Poland sets her first adult novel here. We visit three valleys – the Baviaans, the Kat and the Mancazana – as we view the Winterberg landscape through the literary creations of these writers.

THE BAVIAANS RIVER VALLEY AND THOMAS PRINGLE

Thomas Pringle's Scottish party was granted land in the Baviaans River valley, far from the locations of their fellow settlers of 1820 which were situated in *Thomas Pringle*

the Albany district south of Grahamstown. A wide gravel road threads its way up the valley, criss-crossing the rockstrewn bed of the Baviaans River. Along this route the first reminder of Pringle is the stone church that commemorates the settlers of the area and contains the remains of the poet. It stands in an open space to the left of the road and close by is the Eildon farmstead, which has been in Pringle hands since Thomas's time. Further up the road, against a broken rock face, is the San cave he mentions in his poetry and on a ridge beyond it stands a cairn commemorating the spot where the Dutch field-cornet who escorted Pringle's party to their location proclaimed *'daar leg uwe veld* – there lies your country'. Further, on the right, is the site of the settlers' first camp and first religious service, also marked by a cairn. We are clearly in Pringle country.

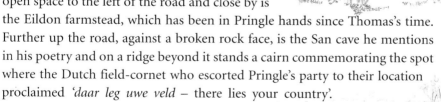

THOMAS PRINGLE was born in 1789 near Kelso, in the border region of Scotland. A fall as a baby rendered him physically disabled for life, and he relied on a crutch to get around – a fact that is hard to grasp when one reads about his exploits in some of the wilder parts of the Eastern Cape. His disjointed hip hindered him from engaging in the more active aspects of the family pursuit of farming, which meant that he enjoyed educational advantages over his siblings. He progressed from school to university and then to various clerical jobs in Edinburgh, where a love of literature had the chance to develop and some literary efforts of his own were published. Family fortunes had by this time declined and the Pringles had become tenant farmers. Thomas Pringle felt that it would be beneficial to his father and other members of the family to make a new start in a foreign country where they could all settle together and regain something of their former status as landowners. It fell to his lot, as the one with clerical skills, to enter into negotiations for emigration to the Cape. They left the valley of the Teviot in Scotland with a mixture of sadness and keen anticipation:

> Sweet Teviot, fare thee well! Less gentle themes
> Far distant call me from thy pastoral dale,
> To climes where Amakosa's woods and streams
> Invite, in the fair South, my venturous sail.

It was the 'venturous sail' of the *Brilliant* that carried Thomas and his family to Algoa Bay, where they landed on 15 May 1820. After about a month in Port Elizabeth the Pringle party began its arduous journey by ox-wagon to their location at the foot of the Winterberg.

> At length, after extraordinary exertions and hair-breadth escapes – the breaking down of two wagons, and the partial damage of others – we got through the last *poort* of the glen, and found ourselves on the summit of an elevated ridge, commanding a view of the extremity of the valley. 'And now, *mynheer*,' said the Dutch-African field-cornet who commanded our escort, '*daar leg uwe veld* – there lies your country.' Looking in the direction where he pointed, we beheld, extending to the northward, a beautiful vale, about six or seven miles in length, and varying from one or two in breadth. It appeared like a verdant basin, or *cul de sac*, surrounded on all sides by an amphitheatre of steep and sterile mountains, rising in the back-ground into sharp cuneiform ridges of very considerable elevation; their summits being at this season covered with snow, and estimated to be from 4,000 to 5,000 feet above the level of the sea. The lower declivities were sprinkled over, though somewhat

scantily, with grass and bushes. But the bottom of the valley, through which the infant river meandered, presented a warm, pleasant and secluded aspect; spreading itself into verdant meadows, sheltered and embellished, without being encumbered, with groves of mimosa trees, among which we observed in the distance herds of wild animals – antelopes and quaggas – pasturing in undisturbed quietude.[1]

Pringle was deeply attached to Scotland and 'fond recollections of former years' surface from time to time; yet in the six years of his residence in South Africa, less than four of which were spent in the Eastern Cape, he made its landscapes, its peoples and many of its problems his own and etched them distinctly and memorably in prose and poetry.

Pringle's major South African work, *African Sketches*, was published in 1834 and comprised two parts: *Poems Illustrative of South Africa* and *Narrative of a Residence in South Africa*. References and quotations here are taken from Robert Wahl's edited versions, published separately in 1970 as *Poems Illustrative of South Africa* and *Thomas Pringle in South Africa*. The *Narrative* – on which *Thomas Pringle in South Africa* is based – is a classic of frontier literature and of the journal–diary genre, a work to which one is drawn again and again for the interest of its content and the beauty of its prose. Poems, too, present vivid pictures of the surroundings encountered by British settlers in the Cape, filtered through the mind of a sensitive, well-informed man of courage and faith who used the poetic techniques of his time to felicitous effect.

Among poems about the Baviaans Valley settlement – soon known as Glen Lynden – 'Evening Rambles' is particularly successful in stimulating the imagination to see the place as Pringle experienced it. This long poem may also function as an unusual guide to today's scenery. To wander through the valley (with, of course, the farmer's permission), recognising features of the landscape, trees and flowers, birds and other creatures encountered by Pringle in the 1820s, creates links with the past and with his poetry that are not easily forgotten.

The poet imagines himself setting out on a meditative ramble in the late afternoon, passing at first through a grove of mimosa trees whose perfume and yellow blossoms remind him of 'primrose-tufts in Scottish dell', but he forgets his homeland as he notices a different kind of scenery.

Soon we raise the eye to range
O'er prospects wild, grotesque, and strange;
Sterile mountains, rough and steep,
That bound abrupt the valley deep,
Heaving to the clear blue sky
Their ribs of granite, bare and dry
And ridges, by the torrents worn,
Thinly streaked with scraggy thorn,
Which fringes Nature's savage dress,
Yet scarce relieves her nakedness.

As he lowers his eyes he observes gentler views than these 'prospects wild, grotesque and strange'. One may enjoy the colours of spekboom, aloe and erythrina (bean trees) in yesterday's poem and in today's place.

But where the Vale winds deep below,
The landscape hath a warmer glow:
There the spekboom spreads its bowers
Of light-green leaves and lilac flowers;
And the aloe rears her crimson crest,
Like stately queen for gala drest;
And the bright-blossomed bean-tree shakes
Its coral tufts above the brakes,
Brilliant as the glancing plumes
Of sugar-birds among its blooms,
With the deep-green verdure blending
In the stream of light descending.

As he wanders on, the poet notices the sounds of nature and observes some of the area's smaller game, such as the duiker. Then he reaches his 'wonted seat' above a 'Bushman cave', a splendid vantage point from which to contemplate the topography of his adopted home. Paintings on the rock face have faded or

been defaced over the centuries: Pringle himself wrote his name on the wall above them, but the date he inscribed – 1825 – and some of the San artwork remain visible.

My wonted seat receives me now –
This cliff with myrtle-tufted brow,
Towering high o'er grove and stream,
As if to greet the parting gleam.
With shattered rocks besprinkled o'er,
Behind ascends the mountain hoar,
Whose crest o'erhangs the Bushman's Cave,

(His fortress once, and now his grave,)
Where the grim satyr-faced baboon
Sits gibbering to the rising moon,
Or chides with hoarse and angry cry
The herdsman as he wanders by.

Spread out below in sun and shade,
The shaggy Glen lies full displayed –
Its sheltered nooks, its sylvan bowers,
Its meadows flushed with purple flowers;
And through it like a dragon spread,
I trace the river's tortuous bed.

The poem goes on to describe in detail the river and its banks, including the 'cradle-nests with porch below' of the weaver birds. Then gradually the sun begins to set, twilight waves 'his shadowy rod', nocturnal animals emerge and, finally, the call of an owl reminds the wanderer that it is time to return home.

But lo! the night-bird's boding scream
Breaks abrupt my twilight dream;
And warns me it is time to haste
My homeward walk across the waste,
Lest my rash tread provoke the wrath
Of adder coiled upon the path,
Or tempt the lion from the wood,
That soon will prowl athirst for blood.
– Thus, murmuring my thoughtful strain,
I seek our wattled cot again.

The 'wattled cot' refers to the 'beehive hut' that Thomas built for himself and his wife during 1821. It was sited near the spot where the principal Pringle homestead, Eildon, was later built and where descendants of the Pringle family – not directly of Thomas, for he and his wife were childless – still reside. The site is now occupied by a modern hunting lodge but beside it grows the very witgat tree beneath which Thomas Pringle composed some of his verses, and it was probably here that he composed 'Evening Rambles' and poems such as 'The Emigrant's Cabin'. The latter describes his home and new way of life in the form of a dialogue between himself and his friend John Fairbairn. The opening lines set the scene.

Where the young river, from its wild ravine,
Winds pleasantly through Eildon's pastures green, –
With fair acacias waving on its banks,
And willows bending o'er in graceful ranks,
And the steep mountain rising close behind,
To shield us from the Snowberg's wintry wind, –
Appears my rustic cabin, thatched with reeds,
Upon a knoll amid the grassy meads;
And, close beside it, looking o'er the lea,
Our summer-seat beneath an umbra-tree.

From Glen Lynden, Thomas Pringle made a number of excursions to other parts of the colony and recorded his responses in prose and verse. He travelled at different times to Cradock and Somerset East; across the Zuurberg to the Enon mission; twice to the Albany district; and across the Karoo to Cape Town.

The poem 'Afar in the Desert', on which Pringle was complimented by Samuel Taylor Coleridge, epitomises his appetite for journeying and observing every detail of the natural world. Nearer home he also roamed the valleys and mountains of the Winterberg, even crossing the newly declared frontier on 'various exploratory excursions into the waste country' – the so-called Ceded Territory, which was supposed to be unoccupied by either indigenous inhabitants or European settlers. Pringle, in spite of the disability he hardly ever mentions, ascended the highest of the Winterberg mountains on horseback and foot and explored the Mancazana, the Koonap and the Kat River valleys. In his accounts of these excursions and in poetic meditations on them the beauty of the region is highlighted, but also the sadness of its deserted character because of the eviction of its indigenous residents and the departure of the missionaries who had lived among them. This part of the Winterberg is to this day a strange mixture of scenic beauty and devastation, bearing the scars of successive settlements, evictions, battles and neglect, in the midst of what should be a fertile and productive region. The purpose of one of Pringle's expeditions was to explore the Mancazana Valley.

The scenery both of this and of the other chief branches of the Koonap River was of a very impressive character. The aspect of the country, though wild, was rich and beautiful. It was watered by numerous rivulets, and finely diversified with lofty mountains and winding vales, with picturesque rocks and shaggy jungles, open upland pastures, and fertile meadows along the river margins, sprinkled as usual with willows and acacias, and occasionally with groves of stately geelhout. Many of the mountain sides and kloofs were clothed with forests of large timber. At the time I refer to, the whole of this tract had been for some years abandoned to the undisputed occupation of the wild animals, which had consequently flocked to it in great numbers from the surrounding districts. In no other part of South Africa have I ever seen so many of the larger sorts of antelopes; and the elephant, the rhinoceros, and the buffalo were also to be found in the forests, though we *saw* none of these animals on this occasion. But the remains of Kafir hamlets, scattered through every grassy nook and dell, and now fast crumbling to decay, excited reflections of a very melancholy character, and occasionally increased, even to a most painful degree, the feeling of dreary *lonesomeness* which the wild grandeur of the scenery tended to excite.[2]

The wider valley of the Kat River is evoked in 'The Desolate Valley', in the first four stanzas of which Pringle sets the scene with all the mastery of visual composition displayed by Thomas Baines, who explored the same region about twenty years later and recorded similar scenes on canvas.

THOMAS PRINGLE
From The Desolate Valley

Far up among the forest-belted mountains,
Where Winterberg, stern giant old and grey,
Looks down the subject dells, whose gleaming fountains
To wizard Kat their virgin tribute pay,
A valley opens to the noontide ray,
With green savannahs shelving to the brim
Of the swift River, sweeping on his way
To where Umtóka hies to meet with him,
    Like a blue serpent gliding through the acacias dim.

Round this secluded region circling rise
A billowy waste of mountains, wild and wide;
Upon whose grassy slopes the pilgrim spies
The gnu and quagga, by the greenwood side,
Tossing their shaggy manes in tameless pride;
Or troop of elands near some sedgy fount;
Or kùdù fawns, that from the thicket glide
To seek their dam upon the misty mount;
    With harts, gazelles, and roes, more than the eye may count.

And as we journeyed up the pathless glen,
Flanked by romantic hills on either hand,
The boschbok oft would bound away – and then
Beside the willows, backward gazing, stand.
And where old forests darken all the land
From rocky Katberg to the river's brink,
The buffalo would start upon the strand,
Where, 'mid palmetto flags, he stooped to drink,
  And, crashing through the brakes, to the deep jungle shrink.

Then, couched at night in hunter's wattled shieling,
How wildly beautiful it was to hear
The elephant his shrill *reveille* pealing,
Like some far signal-trumpet on the ear!
While the broad midnight moon was shining clear,
How fearful to look forth upon the woods,
And see those stately forest-kings appear,
Emerging from their shadowy solitudes –
  As if that trump had woke Earth's old gigantic broods!

from Poems Illustrative

Although he delights in what he sees, Pringle's recreation of the natural world is seldom mere picturing but usually, as here, has metaphorical implications. In the last four stanzas of the poem he reflects on the crumbling Xhosa huts and the 'roofless ruin' of a mission chapel in a valley where the gospel had once been preached and where Ntsikana had lived. It may seem, the poet argues, that evil has triumphed, but a day will come when the dry bones not only of this place but also of the world's vale of desolation will be brought to life.

But the Appointed Day shall dawn at last,
  When, breathed on by a Spirit from on High,
    The dry bones shall awake, and shout – 'Our God is nigh!'

Pringle's residence in the Eastern Cape from May 1820 to August 1821 was the most fruitful of his literary career. Other achievements lay ahead. When his brother William arrived from Scotland in 1822, Thomas handed over the leadership of the settlement to him and left the eastern frontier to take up employment in Cape Town. Experiences there left him despondent and in dire financial difficulties. It was, however, a period of benefit to his adopted land, for, largely through Pringle's efforts, freedom of the press in the colony was attained and events set in motion that led to the departure of the autocratic British governor, Lord Charles Somerset.

On 16 April 1826, after a year back in the Eastern Cape, Pringle left South Africa. He and his wife intended to return but ill health prevented their embarkation and, in 1834, a month short of his 46th birthday, Thomas Pringle died in London. In 1970 his body was re-interred in the memorial church at Eildon in the valley where his family party had made their home 150 years previously.

THE BAVIAANS RIVER VALLEY AND MARGUERITE POLAND

Like Thomas Pringle, Marguerite Poland is fascinated by the landscape, flora and fauna of the Winterberg and sympathetic towards the indigenous people of the region. The setting of her first adult novel, *Train to Doringbult* (1987), embraces many typical features of the landscape of the Baviaans River valley.

Marguerite Poland

The Doringbult of the title is a mythical railway siding used as a threat against naughty children. Other places in the novel are true-to-life – Grahamstown, Cradock, Cookhouse, or the site of what has become the Gariep Dam on the Orange River, but the farms of the Baviaans valley on which the story centres are given fictional names. The novel opens with a description of Blackheath, the home of Jan and Elsa de Villiers.

> The light, just rising cobra-coloured up above the *bult*, was fading out to green, to white. Still the ridge was dark, shadowed with euphorbias, with *gwarri* and *karee* and a cold wind was washing in across the lands and down towards the Rooikloof where thickets, clustered at the *krantz*'s lip, loomed like huddled cattle, branches white as horn.
>
> Near the house a pair of *dikkops* ran back and forth across the lawn and Elsa, standing alone in the darkness of the kitchen window (she had not lit the lamp) watched them circle in towards their nest beneath the hedge.

This passage is typical of the canvas of *Doringbult* – finely covered with local details of setting. Euphorbias and small shrubs and trees such as gwarri and karee are common in the area. The bult or ridge of hills, the kloof, the krantz or ravine and even figures such as 'cobra-coloured' light and thickets looming like 'huddled cattle' are appropriate to the milieu. Birds are ubiquitous. Here, dikkops – large plover-like birds – nesting in the hedge suggest comfort. Later, a more ominous note is sounded with the sighting of another bird.

A *hamerkop* lumbered up. Jan watched its wing shadow jigsaw on fragments of stone, steady small and swift across a *krantz*. It turned ponder-
ously, sank down among the trees. He felt a slight unease as he followed
the pattern of its flight. He knew *Thekwane*, the gaunt-winged
hamerkop, relic of a pterodactyl, an ancient bird that wades in *vleis*
and sees the destinies of men reflected from the sky. There – a star
streams: someone's heart has fallen over. *Thekwane*, seeing it, dedi-
cates another of its feathers to the dead. Jan looked away irritated. He
was absorbing Elsa's own strange cosmology, full of birds and stars, creatures and beliefs taken from her father Norman Southey and from old
Nontinti.

According to Xhosa tradition it is unlucky to kill a hamerkop, or to have one
of these birds fly over one's hut. In the novel their appearance always precedes
disaster, and Poland introduces other local myths which add to the novel's
Eastern Cape context.

In *Train to Doringbult*, greed, revenge, racial intolerance and attitudes of
male superiority, as well as drought and rain and the land itself, contribute to
a tragic conclusion. Poland's bold handling of such issues enlivens the literary
associations of the Winterberg and gives Pringle country a modern dimension.

THE KAT RIVER VALLEY

Ntsikana

There is a link between South Africa's first important English poet – Thomas
Pringle – and Ntsikana, the first Xhosa poet to have his works written down
in the vernacular and translated into English. Thomas Pringle heard the
haunting African music and words of 'Sicana's Hymn' when it was sung by
Xhosa people visiting Glen Lynden in 1825 and, in the notes to his poems, he
provides a translation of this hymn side by side with a Xhosa version. There
are also several references to Sicana – Ntsikana – in Pringle's works. Both men
are associated with the Winterberg, their residence in that part of the Eastern
Cape overlapping by only one year: Pringle arrived in the Baviaans River valley in 1820; Ntsikana died in the Kat River valley in 1821.

Ntsikana's poetry, in the form of the four hymns he composed after adopting the Christian faith in about 1815, links traditional African forms of composition and those of the West as well as Xhosa imagery and the language of
Christianity. The so-called Great Hymn was written down in 1822, just one
year after Ntsikana's death and, in 1827, printed and published with an
English translation – the first South African oral composition to be treated in
this way. It has survived in various written and oral versions as a living piece

of literature that is widely known, and used. Ntsikana's other hymns survived through constant use but were written down only in the early 1900s.

NTSIKANA was born in about 1780 at Quakeni, situated in that extension of the Winterberg known as the Amatola. He stayed there with his mother's family until his early teens, when his father, at that time living among the Ndlambe, sent for him, and Ntsikana moved to the Gqora in the Kat River district. Ntsikana's father, Gaba, was of noble descent and hereditary councillor to Ngqika. After Gaba's death, Ntsikana inherited his role as councillor and developed into a talented orator, singer and dancer. The story of his conversion to Christianity is best told in the words of the Rev. John Knox Bokwe, who in the 1870s collected information from old people who either had known Ntsikana or were acquainted with his family. He then combined this material with various written versions of Ntsikana's life. Bokwe's lively retelling of the stories assumes the immediacy of an eyewitness account. Of Ntsikana's life-changing vision he writes:

> Ntsikana one morning went, as usual, to the kraal. The sun's rays were just peeping over the eastern horizon, and, as he was standing at the kraal gate, his eyes fixed with satisfied admiration on his favourite ox, he thought he observed a ray, brighter than ordinary, striking the side of his beast. As he watched the animal, Ntsikana's face betrayed excited feelings. He enquired of a lad standing near by: 'Do you observe the thing that I now see?' The lad, turning his eyes in the direction indicated, replied: 'No, I see nothing there.' Ntsikana, recovering from the trance, uplifted himself from the ground, on which he had meantime stretched himself, and said to the puzzled boy: 'You are right; the sight was not one to be seen by your eyes.'

Later that day, during a local celebration, a strong whirlwind arose each time Ntsikana stood up to join in the customary dancing. Bokwe continues:

> All at once, the vision of the bright rays which he saw in the morning shining gloriously on the side of his favourite ox, Hulushe, is recalled to his remembrance, and without a single word of explanation, or apology to any one, he orders his people to get ready to return home! ... As they

neared home, they came to a small river. Here Ntsikana threw aside his blanket, plunged himself into the water and washed off all the red ochre that painted his body.[3]

Ntsikana called this 'the day of my renewal' and from then on he held services morning and evening in his hut or under a tree, singing, praying, speaking about the new religion of Christianity. Some believed that Ntsikana's sudden conversion came about without previous contact with Christian teachers, for in 1815 there were no mission stations beyond the Great Fish River. It is more probable that Ntsikana had, as a youth, heard Dr Johannes Theodorus van der Kemp speaking and had had contact with the itinerant preacher James Read, both of the London Missionary Society (LMS).

Ntsikana probably visited the Rev. Joseph Williams, also of the LMS, during the brief existence (1816 to 1817) of a mission station in the Kat River valley, where he would have learned more about the Christian faith. Refused a hearing by Ndlambe, Ntsikana moved to Ngqika's place at Mancazana, where he advised the chief against fighting Ndlambe – but to no avail, for in 1818 followers of the rival chiefs fought in the battle of Amalinde. Ntsikana was also opposed to the militancy of Ndlambe's prophet, Makana, who incited his people to attack Grahamstown in 1819.

Through all this time of conflict Ntsikana preached peace and continued drawing people to his daily services, despite harassment and persecution. After his death in 1821 his followers – obedient to Ntsikana's final request – moved to Chumie, the Glasgow Missionary Society's station, where some of them were among the first of the Xhosa to be baptised.

Ntsikana's hymns were integral to the daily services which he conducted. The first, Ntsikana's Bell, was a call to worship; the second, Life Creator, was sung as his congregation settled down. Then, after talking to his people for a while, Ntsikana would introduce the Round Hymn and lastly, after preaching and prayers, the Great Hymn: 'He is the Great God, who is in heaven.'

The two best known are the Bell Hymn and the Great Hymn. The Bell Hymn summoned people to listen to the word of the Lord. The third verse goes:

> It has fenced in, it has surrounded,
> This land of your fathers,
> He who obeys it by responding will be blessed.
> Ahom, ahom, ahom, ahom, ahom!

In this hymn the spread of the word of God is imaged as fencing in the ancestral lands.

In his poem 'Ntsikana's Bell' Guy Butler tells of a visit to the prophet's grave at Thwatwa in the Winterberg, which lies on the Gqora, a tributary of the Kat. The district at the end of the 20th century is even bleaker than the 'Desolate Valley' of Pringle's day.

> A desolate stretch of over-farmed smallholdings,
> ill-kept shacks, dead motor cars, pigs, goats
> and ragged people, many weaving their way
> to a week-end of oblivion.

At Thwatwa, Butler witnesses an old woman striking the *intsimbi*, the bell rock, with a stone, producing the three notes which suggest the chant with which Ntsikana's bell hymn begins: *Sele! Sele! Ahom, ahom, ahom!* Despite the day's disappointments and embarrassments he leaves satisfied: 'I've paid my respects to Ntsikana's grave / I've heard his bell ring clear from the hand-struck stone.' Butler also refers to Ntsikana's Bell Hymn at the end of *Pilgrimage to Dias Cross* and uses the bell sound, *Sele! Sele! Ahom, ahom, ahom!*, as its concluding line. It is a sound he had first heard in a church in Cradock and, as he says in the poem, it 'got into my bones and still rings there'.

Pringle had found the singing of Ntsikana's Great Hymn equally haunting. Composed in the form of a praise-song or *isibongo*, it comprises a series of praise names for God. Several of the images are of a military nature: God is shield, stronghold and 'thicket' of truth. One is reminded of the warriors of Ntsikana's time and place and the fact that his milieu was a forested region where safety was often sought among its dense vegetation, and where groves of trees were sometimes sacred places. Hunting and pasturing being two major Xhosa activities, the words 'he hunteth for souls' and he 'amalgamated flocks' take on special local meanings. The reference to the Pleiades also has local implications: the seasonal appearance of this constellation was the sign for the Xhosa to begin cultivating their lands. As Janet Hodgson shows, Ntsikana 'interpreted Christianity within a familiar framework by drawing on the images, concepts, symbols, literary forms, myths, folklore, music and ritual of the Xhosa tradition to give authority to that which was new'.[4]

Part of that 'familiar framework' was the landscape: the mountains and valleys of the Eastern Cape midlands and the clear skies overhead, bright with stars.

NTSIKANA
Ntsikana's Great Hymn

Ulo Thixo omkhulu, ngosezulwini;
Ungu Wena-wena Khaka lenyaniso.
Ungu Wena-wena Nqaba yenyaniso.
Ungu Wena-wena Hlati lenyaniso.
Ungu Wena-wen' uhlel' enyangwaneni.
Ulo dal' ubom, wadala phezulu.

Lo Mdal' owadala wadala izulu.
Lo Menzi weenkwenkwezi noZilimela;
Yabinza inkwenkwezi, isixelela.
Lo Menzi wemfaman' uzenza ngabom?

Lathetha ixilongo lisibizile.
Ulongqin' izingela imiphefumlo.
Ulohlanganis' imihlamb' eyalanayo.

Ulomkhokeli wasikhokela thina.
Ulengub' inkhul' esiyambatha thina.
Ozandla Zakho zinamanxeba Wena.
Onyawo Zakho zinamanxeba Wena.
Ugazi Lakho limrholo yini na?
Ugazi Lakho liphalalele thina.
Le mali emkulu-na siyibizile?
Lo mzi Wakhona-na siwubizile?

He is the Great God, who is in heaven;
Thou art Thou, Shield of truth.
Thou art Thou, Stronghold of truth.
Thou art Thou, Thicket of truth.
Thou art Thou Who dwellest in the highest.

He, Who created life (below), created (life) above.
That Creator who created, created heaven.
This maker of the stars, and the Pleiades.
A star flashed forth, it was telling us.

The Maker of the blind, does He not make them of purpose?
The trumpet sounded, it has called us.
As for his chase, He hunteth for souls.

He, Who amalgamates flocks rejecting each other.
He, the Leader, Who has led us.
He, Whose great mantle, we do put it on.
Those hands of Thine, they are wounded.
Those feet of Thine, they are wounded.
Thy blood, why is it streaming?

Thy blood, it was shed for us.
This great price, have we called for it?
This home of thine, have we called for it?

J K Bokwe's translation, with revised orthography

THE MANCAZANA RIVER VALLEY

In November 1847 a woman in her late thirties rode on horseback through the *Harriet Ward*
Winterberg with a small party of friends and, although the War of the Axe was
in its closing stages, they were escorted by only a handful of dragoons. Her
husband was on military duty elsewhere and her young daughter left behind
as Mrs Harriet Ward set off from Grahamstown on a 250-mile round trip. It
was not the kind of freedom usually enjoyed by a Victorian woman, but was
typical of Ward's independent spirit and enthusiasm for sightseeing.

> Start not, reader, at the notion of ladies riding for pleasure with armed
> escorts in a heathen land. Many a time and oft have I traversed these
> enamelled plains, too much exhilarated with the grandeur of the scene
> to think of danger.[5]

That 'exhilaration with the grandeur of the scene' is reflected in all Ward's
writings. She is anxious for readers back in Britain to *see* the exotic world of
Africa that she is experiencing and to be as excited by it as she is. 'It is a beautiful land, with its open savannahs, its wooded glens, its heathy mountains, its
green and undulating parks – nature's plantations!'[6] Ward's prose is sometimes florid but at her best she offers readers informative and attractive
images of everything from the grandeur of the highest peak in the Winterberg,
which 'presented the appearance of a huge elephant with a howdah on its
back',[7] to the 'innumerable lovely and curious insects which flutter about in
the sunshine, and give life to the scene'.[8] In Ward's major novel, *Jasper Lyle*,

passages depicting the countryside in every season and at different times of the day are interspersed with the narrative, and she follows the contemporary fashion for 'picturing' a scene in accordance with the specifications of landscape painting, often looking for the 'sublime' or the 'picturesque' in what she sees. More often the reader seems to move through the countryside with the writer – an excellent horsewoman – gathering impressions and relishing the atmosphere.

Ward's works, extensively read in her own day, are now little known. Sensitive readers are today shocked by titles such as *Five Years in Kaffirland* or *Jasper Lyle: A Tale of Kafirland*. We wish that the offensive word could be expunged but that is not possible – it was the parlance of the day – and Ward's responses to the Eastern Cape of the 1840s, political and topographical, deserve attention.

HARRIET WARD – Mrs Ward to her reading public – was born in Norfolk in 1808 into a military family, the Tidys. Her father encouraged her from an early age to write, and her first published piece came out in serial form in a military magazine in 1840. It was a biography of her late father: 'Recollections of an Old Soldier, Written by His Daughter'. In 1831 she had married another military person – John Ward – and thereafter she accompanied her husband wherever the army posted him, including to the island of St Helena and to the Cape of Good Hope. The latter provided the most fertile ground for Ward's literary talents, and from 1848 to 1860 her factual and fictional writings relating to the Cape were widely acclaimed. Very little is known about her after that period, although she died only in 1873.

Ward spent only five years at the Cape. Her husband, Captain John Ward of the 91st Regiment, served on the Eastern Frontier from 1842 to 1847. She accompanied him to the military post at Peddie in the Neutral Territory and, when the War of the Axe broke out in 1846, moved to Grahamstown. This enterprising officer's wife made it her business to learn about the colony's peoples either through personal contact or from local sources and to explore the countryside or gather information about it from those who had. During the war she sent reports to newspapers in Britain, earning the distinction of being South Africa's first woman journalist, and in 1848 she published, in two volumes, *Five Years in Kaffirland, with Sketches of the Late War in That Country, to the Conclusion of Peace. Written on the Spot*. This work was so popular that it ran into four editions, and much of the material Ward had gathered for it was imaginatively reworked into fiction. *Jasper Lyle*, the first novel in our literature to have an entirely South African setting, was published in 1851 and, between that date and 1879, reissued five times. A youth novel, *Hardy and Hunter: A Boy's Own Story*, which promoted the Cape as an exciting and profitable place for young people to settle, came out in 1858 with a second edition in 1859. There were other minor novels and books advocating emigration and, as Valerie Letcher has shown,[9] Ward was also responsible for some 40 articles in periodicals, about a third of them concerning South Africa.

Harriet Ward's accounts of what she called 'Kaffirland' – very much the area we now call the Eastern Cape – encompass many places between Algoa Bay and the Stormberg, between Grahamstown and the Winterberg, between Peddie (where the Wards were stationed) and the Orange River (which she never saw with her own eyes). Tracing her graphic and interesting responses to all these places is impossible here but Ward's visit to the Winterberg in 1847 provides a good example of how her experiences of the Eastern Cape were turned into factual accounts and also used as settings in fiction.

A highlight of the Winterberg journey for the author was a two-day visit to Glenthorn, the home of John Pringle and his family in the Mancazana Valley – the same valley described some twenty years earlier by Thomas Pringle. On the way there, Harriet and her party rested at a farm (presumably in the Baviaans Valley) 'with a pretty, peaceful-looking garden, backed by such cliffs! and interesting from its being associated with the poet, Pringle, and his works, many of them having been written on this romantic spot'.[10]

The Mancazana site that Ward visited in 1847 was part of an additional grant of land to the Pringle settler party made in 1824. Thomas's brother John settled there in 1828 and became one of the most successful farmers in the district; Harriet Ward regarded him as a shining example of the merits of emigration. The house she describes was built in 1841 and destroyed ten years later during the Eighth Frontier War, but the chapel remains. The second oldest Presbyterian church building in the country, it was erected in 1840 with the help of the 91st, John Ward's regiment, but before his arrival in the Cape. It is still in use and is, as Thomas Baines remarks, 'a neat edifice remarkable for its tasteful simplicity'.[11]

Set on a hill among trees and surrounded by graves, the chapel commands a view of the heavily bushed valley that Ward so much admired and which is still a pleasurable sight.

> I could write many pages on the subject of Mr. Pringle's charming and admirably-planned location. I shall long think of the Bushman's haunt, the little chapel in the fertile valley, and, above all, the kindly welcome I met with at Glenthorn, but such agreeable reminiscences must be reserved for another time; these pages are dedicated to a history of war and turmoil, and I must not pause to dwell on pleasant memories connected with my journey through those mountain-ranges.[12]

The writer made extensive use of those 'pleasant memories'. Ward expanded on already detailed descriptions of the Mancazana in *Five Years* for a periodical article, 'The Happy Valley', and for *Past and Future Emigration or The Book of the Cape* (1849), which she edited. She also fictionalised aspects of Glenthorn, the Pringles and the Mancazana Valley in both *Jasper Lyle* and *Hardy and Hunter*.

A deep impression was made on Ward by a San cave near the settlement. In more than one of her accounts the author invites readers to accompany her to 'the beautiful district of the Mancazana'. One does indeed feel as though one is accompanying Harriet Ward and her party as they scramble up a path leading to the cave through a 'labyrinth' of 'intermingling boughs' with thunder rumbling in the distance and a shiver of apprehension because a 'tiger' (leopard) has recently been observed in the vicinity. She describes in detail the overhanging rock and the hunting scene depicted on it – a reminder of Thomas Pringle's fascination with the San cave at Glen Lynden. Two years later Thomas Baines was told that the Mancazana cave paintings were so defaced by smoke 'that they would hardly repay the trouble of inspecting them'.

The cave reappears in other guises in both Ward's novels, while the homestead and its outbuildings, the chapel, the school that so impressed the author, the family and the fertile valley itself are recognisable on many pages. In *Jasper Lyle* the farm Annerley and the Daveney family have their genesis in Glenthorn; in *Hardy and Hunter* the settlement becomes Glen Lion, the farm becomes Llanina, an adjoining cottage becomes the Lindens, and the Pringles are thinly disguised as the Halls. From *Hardy and Hunter* comes this recreation (one of many) of the glen:

Northward, it opened out in vast and wooded plains, bounded by tremendous mountains; but just below the ridge on which we stood, it narrowed to a couple of miles. Here, on either side, rose sharp and serried cliffs, the natural fortifications of the settlement, some of these being sprinkled over with grass and bushes. A little farther on, the valley spread itself into verdant meads, adorned and sheltered by groves of acacias intermingled with the curious euphorbia and tall *geelhout* (fir) trees; the everlasting mimosa was here too, and the prickly pear, besides many superb forest trees. Through the centre of this sweet vale wandered a clear stream, with green banks for its margin, on either side of which fields and homesteads, gardens and cattle-folds gave life and character to a picture rendered more complete by a miniature chapel, lately erected on a turfy slope on the right of the location.

Ward wrote of African farms in the Eastern Cape 30 years before Schreiner. The few known facts of her life make fascinating reading, as Sally Sampson has shown.[13] Were Ward's writings more readily available, an appreciation of the Winterberg as well as of many other sites in the Eastern Cape would be enhanced by the literary use she makes of them. She was a feminist before feminism became a force to be reckoned with, a woman war correspondent 'before the female of the species emerged', the first South African writer to introduce an interracial marriage into fiction and to include in her novels characters drawn from the five major groupings at the Cape of her time – British, Boer, Khoe, San and Xhosa. Her attitudes to frontier issues at the Cape are ambivalent, but Ward's record of events in mid-19th-century South Africa, as well as her fictional versions of them and the physical world in which they were set, enliven both our history and our literature.

10 A WELLSPRIN

OF BLACK WRITING

THE AMATOLA REGION

The Keiskamma River and its tributary the Tyume (also known as the Tyhume) have their sources in the Amatola mountains. The name derives from the Xhosa *amathole*, meaning calves – these mountains are the calves or offspring of the Winterberg. The town of Alice in the Tyume basin has generated an important branch of South African literature; part of the range, Hogsback, has inspired a number of writers; another significant branch of writing comes from Middledrift, near the confluence of the Tyume and the Keiskamma; and two significant novels are set further up the Keiskamma Valley. It is a region in which many battles over claims to the land have occurred, from minor and more serious confrontations among the Xhosa themselves to the major clashes of the frontier wars. Its literature, however, manifests a mingling of cultures and a common attachment to the landscape.

LOVEDALE AND THE UNIVERSITY OF FORT HARE

Printed black South African literature has its roots in the Tyume valley, a wide basin overlooked by the Amatola mountains. The focal point of this valley is the small town of Alice, home of two institutions that have nurtured literature in the wider context of educational growth: Lovedale and Fort Hare University.

J K Bokwe
J J R Jolobe
The Tyume Poets
Basil Somhlahlo

In his poem 'At Stewart's Grave', Francis Carey Slater, who was born near Alice and received some of his schooling at Lovedale, records a 1906 visit to the grave of his father-in-law, Dr James Stewart – second principal of Lovedale – who had died the previous year. Stewart's grave and a 24-metre-tall stone monument to him are situated on Sandile's Kop, adjacent to Fort Hare University. From this hilltop there are excellent views of the Amatola range and the Tyume valley, once the preserve of the paramount chief Ngqika, and an arena in which his son, Sandile, fought in three wars against colonial settlers.

Below the hill in the other direction, a dark cluster of trees on the further bank of the Tyume River marks the site of Lovedale, while on the nearer side of this winding tributary of the Keiskamma lies the campus of Fort Hare University. Alice huddles between the two educational centres.

FRANCIS CAREY SLATER
From At Stewart's Grave

– Mourn Africa! How many come to thee
Who trample on thy sons unheedingly;
With force or with ignoble stealth,
They prey upon thy hidden wealth;
To them the suppliant voices of the land are dumb,
Only for self they come.
But ah, for other wealth he prayed and sought
As through the stubborn years he wrought:
To him the life was more than gold,
To him men's souls were gems of worth untold.

See, down below there in the wooded vale
Through which bright Tyumie flows, there lies Lovedale,
There, dark and light, he toiled and prayed;
There, unafraid,
From earth and earthly shadows took his way
Into the Realms of Day.
And even as Tyumie's clear calm waters run
Steadfastly on, whether in shade or sun,
So in that quiet vale
His work shall still continue and prevail.

See, Hogsback rears aloft that rugged crest,
Where weary cloudlets love to cling and rest:
So shall *his* memory
To us who loved him be a sanctuary,
So shall his steadfast grace
To us remain a resting-place
As we go softly all our years
In joy or tears;
So shall we ever feel his presence near
To guide us on our way, to raise, sustain and cheer.

from Collected Poems of Francis Carey Slater

The story of Lovedale begins with missionary activity. In 1820 John Brownlee of the Glasgow Missionary Society (GMS) set up a mission – the Chumie station – about 13 km from present-day Alice. This was the mission to which the followers of Ntsikana attached themselves after their leader's death. In 1823 the Rev. John Ross joined the missionaries at Chumie, bringing with him from Scotland a small printing press. A year later he, his wife and another missionary, John Bennie, set off with the printing press to establish an outstation which was named Lovedale after Dr John Love of the GMS. During the 1834–35 frontier war this station ('Old' Lovedale) was destroyed, but was re-established soon afterwards in its present location on the west bank of the Tyume.

A seminary primarily for black pupils but also enrolling white boys and girls was opened at Lovedale in 1841. During the War of the Axe (1842–46) the mission had to be abandoned, but thereafter the missionaries returned and continued their work. At the same time the village that had grown up near Lovedale was given the name of one of Queen Victoria's daughters – Alice. The name Fort Hare also originated at this time, but in a very different context from the educational one it was to assume 70 years later. It was a large military installation on the east bank of the Tyume and named for Major-General John Hare, acting governor of the eastern section of the Cape Colony.

The missionaries' evangelistic work included transcribing languages as well as translating and printing portions of the scriptures and other reading matter considered suitable for newly converted Christians. This work of printing and, later, that of book-binding matured into the Lovedale Press, established in 1861. In time vernacular writers began to create their own works, and some of these writings were translated into English and published at the time or later. Lovedale Press was thus highly influential in developing vernacular – chiefly Xhosa – literature, and in making some black writings available to English-speaking readers. Being a mission enterprise, Lovedale Press naturally favoured writings with a Christian flavour, and later this became a contentious matter. Since a fire in 1984 at Lovedale, the press has been situated in Alice itself, with its archives at the Cory Library at Rhodes University in Grahamstown. Recently it has been purchased by its own workers, who have as part of their mission statement 'to empower and develop themselves as shareholders contributing towards the economic, academic and spiritual growth of the region'.

At the side of the road between Lovedale and Alice is a reminder of a well-loved Tyume figure who came out of the Lovedale milieu – JOHN KNOX BOKWE. He was born near Lovedale in 1855. His father was one of the Lovedale Seminary's first pupils and Knox, as he was called, was educated at the same institution from 1869 to 1872 and then worked for Lovedale as telegraphist, bookkeeper and cashier for a further twenty years. During that time he began composing, and in 1885 Lovedale Press published a collection of his songs as *Amaculo ase Lovedale* (Lovedale Music), which was so popular that it ran into many editions. Bokwe also worked with John Tengu Jabavu on *Imvo Zabantsundu*, the first Xhosa newspaper, and in 1914 he published (in English) his carefully researched biography of Ntsikana. Bokwe was ordained as a minister and for most of the last twenty years of his life he worked at Ugie in the northern part of the province, but kept an interest in his old home and was active in pressing for the establishment of Fort Hare University. Bokwe died in 1922. His funeral, Z K Matthews tells us, 'was attended by a vast crowd of people who came great distances to pay their final respects to *Mdengentonga* – the man short in height but tall in accomplishment who had merited so well of his fellow men in his lifetime of work'.[1]

Another writer with Lovedale connections is JAMES JAMES RANISI JOLOBE, who was born in 1902 at Indwe in the Stormberg. J J R Jolobe's achievements were threefold: religious, educational and literary. He served energetically in a number of Eastern Cape churches, including one in New Brighton, and became the first black moderator of the Presbyterian Church in South Africa. He obtained a BA degree from Fort Hare and taught for twenty years at Lovedale, all the while ministering part-time in neighbouring churches. He won three important literary prizes in recognition of his contribution to Xhosa literature, and two years before his death in 1976 the University of Fort Hare conferred on him an honorary doctorate. Jolobe – sometimes called *Imbongi Yomnqamlezo* (the poet of the cross) – published poetry, essays, children's stories, a novella and a novel, translated a number of works from English (and sometimes Afrikaans) into Xhosa and vice versa, worked on the authoritative Xhosa dictionary being produced at Fort Hare, and encouraged Xhosa writing at every opportunity.

In 1946 Jolobe's own translation of his poetry collection, *Umyezo*, appeared in English as *Poems of an African*. He chose to express himself through Western poetic forms, and his subject matter and imagery are also, at times, derivative, but in 'Thuthula', a long narrative in blank verse, his use of Xhosa history and local topography and his descriptions of traditional social practices place the poem firmly in Africa. In 'Thuthula' imagery from the local environment intertwines with language from a very different milieu and literary tradition. Echoes of Keats's 'Eve of St Agnes', for instance, are given an African setting as Thuthula, like Madeleine, prepares to flee with her lover.

> Then she disrobed herself of royal beads,
> A loving gift from *Ndlambe*, regent chief.
> She rolled them with the mat on which she lay,
> And faced the darkness of that winter night.
> And as she crossed the court of royal kraal
> The cock did crow. A certain dog, mark you,
> On haunches sat and faced the heavens dark,
> And wailed a doleful howl as sad as death.

The main setting of 'Thuthula' is the Tyume valley. Here Ngqika (his court name is *Lwanganda*) is pictured roaming around his domain considering the Christian message that has come to him through Ntsikana:

> At *Ncera* by the *Tyume* stream he had
> A cattle post to which he went to nurse
> The call from God, and the surrounding hills
> Increased the flame in meditation lone,
> When roaming among the solitary hills
> Whose beauty brings warm rapture to the soul,
> *I-Ntab'eGqira* and the Hogsback mount,
> With rocky foreheads raised to view the plains
> And forests like a man with bushy face,
> Relieved by streamlets making tiny falls
> Like milk for ever pouring from a gourd,
> The sight of these child falls when seen afar.
> Among these stately mountains he did roam,
> The chief *Lwanganda* at this time of change.

'Thuthula' is a Christian gloss on the rivalry between Ngqika and his uncle Ndlambe, which led to the Battle of Amalinde in 1818. The battle took place at Debe among the Amatola mountains, and saw the defeat of Ngqika. Jolobe tells, in suitably romantic language, of the meeting and falling in love of Ngqika and Thuthula and of her abduction from the kraal of Ndlambe, who had later taken her as one of his wives. He recounts the story of Ntsikana's conversion and influence, and blames the abduction on a plot by Ngqika's councillors to prevent the chief from adopting Christianity. He also blames Ngqika for encouraging Thuthula to break her marriage vows – sacred in whatever tradition they may have been made. At the end of the poem Jolobe proclaims that, although Ngqika is now dead and Ntsikana gone, Christianity still lives and 'will ascend the sky of Africa'. Historians may not entirely agree with Jolobe's version of this period of Cape history and some critics may feel that Jolobe is not quite true to the literary traditions of his own language, but as an artist's view 'Thuthula' brings together in a novel way two major cultures of the Eastern Cape and is, in terms of the Romantic tradition, a fine poem.

The literary fruit produced by Alice was distributed beyond the town's confines and several writers with roots in the Tyume Valley will be encountered on other stages of our tour: Tiyo Soga, the first black ordained minister, at Mgwali, near Stutterheim; S E K Mqhayi in the Buffalo Valley, where this greatest of Xhosa literary figures ('the poet of the nation') spent his last years; A C Jordan in the Transkei; Francis Carey Slater at Hogsback; and R L Peteni in the Keiskamma Valley.

Most of the writers mentioned above are connected with the University of Fort Hare as well as with Lovedale. We return to Sandile's Kop and the view of the university as it is today. Its campus is contained yet spacious, with wide bricked courtyards interspersed, in the older part, with gardens and shady trees and surrounded by handsome buildings in the classical style. There are other, more modern buildings as well as remnants of the fort on whose site the university was built. To one side the lands of Fort Hare's farm – part of its agricultural faculty – and to the other the gardens of a community project sponsored by the university, give the campus a pleasant rural setting.

Stewart of Lovedale – affectionately known as *Somgxaba* – had first mooted the idea of a tertiary institution for black students, but it came to fruition only ten years after his death as the result of a campaign by a group of dedicated people, white and black, supported by churches and the Cape government. The institution grew and flourished and students came from all over Africa to study at Fort Hare, which rejected tribal and ethnic divisions and, from the start, accepted women on an equal basis with men. Nelson Mandela, who enrolled as a student at Fort Hare in 1940, says 'it was a beacon for African scholars from all over Southern, Central and Eastern Africa. For young black South Africans like myself, it was Oxford and Cambridge, Harvard and Yale, all rolled into one.'[2]

In 1959 Fort Hare University was taken over by the National Party government, which attempted to turn it into a tribal college open only to local Xhosa-speaking students. Black academics and students no longer had a stake in the running of their own university; its status declined; and the next three decades witnessed many protests and boycotts. A poem from this era that pictures the setting of Fort Hare with particular clarity and reflects some of the pain of the apartheid years is G C Millard's 'Fort Hare University, Alice, 1960'.

G C MILLARD
Fort Hare University, Alice, 1960

A quiet breathing of sunset
among thornbushes and headless aloes;
this valley townlet is of another century
but takes in the air of this
below blue Amatola Mountains not caring
in their dream what we in our heads
believe we have achieved.

The Tjumie River, warm, dark green,
tough and compact as a Xhosa warrior
flows dutifully below these Roman rectangles
of a university; late sunlight
lingers in ancient Greece
watched by cows, a derelict car,
two donkeys, someone's fence
with barbs all rusted
as black children take a short cut
where a hundred years ago
the redcoats of Britain
walled themselves and watched
for impi and the flow of spears.

These white walls and studious windows
have fallen to us;
armed with decree and Law from our Capitol,
our Forum in Pretoria, we are in charge,
all resistance tidied up with armoured cars;
we have come to educate and have learned
in their numbed, dead-duty acquiescence
like mindless aloes in stiff rows,
that we too have surrendered.

in 25/25: Twenty Five Years of English South African Poetry

The literary traditions of the locale live on. In 1999, to celebrate 175 years of the Lovedale Press, six short literary collections were published – among them *Tracks* by Brian Walter, *Sandbird* by Cathal Lagan, *Seasons* by Norman Morrissey and *A Whistle from the South* by Basil Somhlahlo. All these poets have been on the staff of Fort Hare University and the group has promoted the writing and the reading of poetry in this area and beyond, while *Tyume*, the Fort Hare creative writing journal in which they and others have been involved, 'seeks to encourage writing locally, in the Alice and Tyume basin regions of the Eastern Cape' and to attract contributions from further afield. The publication's subject matter is not confined to the Tyume basin, although each of these poets has touched on Alice and its university in his work. Somhlahlo's 'The Fort' is one of the group's more unusual creative responses to Fort Hare.

BASIL SOMHLAHLO
The Fort
(University of Fort Hare, S.A.)

'Uneasy lies the head
That wears the crown'
They say
Beside clean waters
Of South Africa's Black pool
Where bathed heady sons
Of mother Africa
Pollution unknown
Haunting sounds
Of distant drums
They bathed sir
They drank sir
They stretched
With no fear

Strong limbs carried those brains
To feed hungry children with fodder of the greats

They fear you now
Mother Africa's child

They shiver at your sight
Winged dove of wisdom
Have you fallen from grace
From the flight of an eagle
To the role of a mole

Take heart for the future
Your power can still rise
Just one close look
On the ways of the wise
And a guide to the young
In the rise to the skies

from A Whistle from the South

BASIL LINDILE SIMILO SOMHLAHLO was born in 1933 at St Cuthbert's
Mission in the Transkei. After school he attended the Jan Hofmeyr School of
Social Work in Johannesburg and returned to the Transkei as a social worker,
always more interested in field than in desk work. His sympathy with the poor
he worked among is expressed in the poem 'Not like Humans' and many of his
poems plead for a respect for the humanity of the downtrodden and, as in
'The Fort', call for them to abandon the spirit of subservience. Somhlahlo was
regarded by those who knew him as a person who was poetic and philosophical by nature and who expressed these gifts in drama and poetry. He travelled
abroad in the 1960s with a drama group, and a number of his poems were
published in journals.

   In 1972 Somhlahlo joined the staff of the University of Fort Hare and from
1974 to 1976 attended the University of Denver, Colorado, on a Fulbright
scholarship. Distance from home seems to have made him see its problems
and the sufferings of its people with a new intensity, and this period produced
nearly half the poems published in *A Whistle from the South*. Among the
heroes he celebrates are Ntsikana, Sontonga (composer of 'Nkosi Sikilel'
iAfrika'), and the great praise-singer, S E K Mqhayi, who are all, like himself,
Christian, and intent in their verses on praising the Lord (whom Somhlahlo
calls Menzi) and invoking his blessings on Africa.

   Bring out the sounds of those forgotten heroes
   Tune up their music to the marching of the times
   Blow those Kudu horns to the rising sun
   AND LET MENZI BLESS AFRICA!!!

This is the last stanza of 'Forgotten Heroes'. In another poem, 'U-Ntsikana', Somhlahlo recalls how Ntsikana – 'red blanketed jewel of the South East land' accepted 'the book' but rejected the 'hopeless button that bought our souls'. Many of his own poems decry in strong terms the effects of greed and discrimination, but affirm Christian teachings. 'Song for My Enemies – 1988' concludes:

> There's a world without favours
> A wall without holes
> There's a river without bridges
> Only truth makes us free.
>
> There's a sound without fury
> There's a valley without shadows
> Every mountain has a waterfall
> Where the water is for all.
>
> There's a blanket big and beautiful
> A robe all can wear
> Big enough we can share
> 'Tis a robe of all humanity.

Somhlahlo died in 1994, too soon to see some of his dreams realised of an inclusive society inhabiting a landscape to which all belong. In a poem about his fellow poet, Brian Walter characterises him as a thorn tree, someone rooted in his environment and also someone who loved argument.

> But now, in my memory,
> you are yourself
> a rooted thorn tree,
> a wag-'n-bietjie boom
> of wryness, stopping all
> who hurry to meetings,
> agendas in their heads.

MIDDLEDRIFT

Noni Jabavu   Fort Hare, Alice, Lovedale and the name Jabavu are inextricably linked. John Tengo Jabavu (1884–1921) was the owner and editor of the first Xhosa newspaper, *Imvo Zabantsundu* (Native Opinion), founded in Alice in 1884, and one of the prime movers in the establishment of Fort Hare University. It was even known to some as *iKoliji kaJabavu* (Jabavu's college). His son, D D T

Jabavu (1885–1959), became professor of Latin and African languages at Fort Hare – the first black professor in the country, and a formidable intellectual and political figure who helped to put the university on its feet. Two books by Professor Jabavu's daughter, Noni Jabavu, have become classics of South African literature: *Drawn in Colour* and *The Ochre People*.

The Jabavu family home was a few kilometres from Alice in the village of Middledrift, near the confluence of the Tyume and Keiskamma rivers.

> And from the front of the house was that perpetual, superb horizon on which we daily feasted our eyes as we say, the princely Amatola Mountains.

The quotation is from Noni Jabavu's autobiographical book *Drawn in Colour: African Contrasts*, published in 1960. Noni, the eldest daughter of the family, has come home from England (where she has lived for some twenty years) to attend the funeral of her only brother. The year is 1955. As Jabavu drives to Middledrift from the airport in East London, she looks out at the countryside thinking 'how unchanging it was while people lived and died'.

> The tarred road that I knew so well between East London and King William's Town across 'the land of the Ama-Ndlambe and the Ama-Ntinde' as we call it in our language, disintegrates into its old dusty corrugations after passing King William's Town and goes on through stunted bush, country that was once 'park' kind of African landscape but is now dotted only with scanty thorn trees; a land of droughts, overpopulated, overstocked. But across the wide, open land and on the distant horizon sharply drawn in the crisp sunlight, I saw the typical, wonderful Cape Province frieze of grandiose mountains.

Nearly half a century later the effects of droughts, overpopulation and overstocking are even more marked, but what Jabavu often calls the 'frieze' of the Amatola mountains on the horizon is as impressive and reassuring as ever. They are, for her, the mountains of home, the home from which she was separated for most of her life.

In the Jabavu garden are three typical Eastern Cape plants that are associated in her memory with the brother she has come to mourn: 'I had last seen him in the flesh here by these euphorbias and plumbagos and Birds of Paradise shrubs leading to this very verandah.' Later, as the young woman walks through the surrounding veld, she remembers 'how as children on our way to school at Lovedale we used to pick gazania petals and put them to our lips one at a time and make kazoos of them, then eat the stalks full of creamy milk'. She remembers that 'the exquisite pale blue plumbago shrub' is called *umthi ka-Maqoma*, the tree of Chief Maqoma'. Plants are links with the past – with home – and are part of the author's response to its landscape.

Jabavu was based for many years in England, living also for periods in Uganda, Kenya and Zimbabwe, yet her writings make it clear that South Africa – specifically, the Alice district among the Amatolas – is home. On her return from Uganda – one of the 'African contrasts' in her book – she writes:

> What mattered at that moment as we stood in the cold dry wintry air was the intense joy of being home again; being where I knew what was what, whether in its crudest white-versus-black forms, or its subtlest and most heartwarming manifestation of family and friends, language, familiar scenes, inspiring landscapes proclaiming our history; where one was no longer an exile among people with whom one had no common ground.
>
> Heaven on earth that day, to tread the soil of my lovely, lovely home-land.

HELEN NONTANDO (NONI) JABAVU was born in 1919 and, like many of her family, she attended Lovedale College, but in 1933 at the age of thirteen she was sent to school in England. Music studies at the Royal Academy were interrupted by the outbreak of the Second World War, during which she married Michael Cadbury Crosfield, the offspring of family friends. *Drawn in Colour* was published in 1960, and in 1962 Jabavu, whose working life was devoted to journalism, radio and television, became both first woman and first black editor of the *Strand Magazine*. Her second book of African reminiscences – *The Ochre People: Scenes from a South African Life* – came out in 1963. On a visit to South Africa in 1976 and 1977 she wrote a series of articles for the *Daily Dispatch* and did a little lecturing at Rhodes University. She claimed at the time to be working on a biography of her father, D D T Jabavu, and an autobiography. Thereafter Jabavu moved, for some years, among various African countries and the United Kingdom. She now lives in retirement in East London.

Noni Jabavu writes as a woman of two cultures – Western, and what she calls Southern Bantu – which puts her in a unique position to explain to outsiders something of the intricacies of African family relationships and protocols, as well as the nuances of the Xhosa language. In *Drawn in Colour* and *The Ochre People*, both reissued in 1983, she accomplishes this with verve and clarity, drawing readers into the lives of her family and friends in the Eastern Cape and into the outlook and customs of their day, just as she draws them into the landscape that has produced her and her family. She is, as the people of the locality would say, 'of-this-place'. Each of these books is a journey of discovery dealing with three places, the common denominator being Middledrift – home. The other Eastern Cape site included in them is her maternal uncle's farm near Tsolo in the Transkei, and we shall meet Jabavu again when journeying through that region.

THE HOGSBACK

On the slopes of the Amatola mountains above the Tyume Valley is the village of Hogsback. Africa and the West mingle in the history of this place; in its stories and its vegetation; in the way of life of its peoples; and in the art and literature to which the Hogsback area has given birth.

F C Slater
Mzi Mahola
Carolyn Parker

Hogsback is a place that enkindles nostalgia. It is also a place that evokes a sense of enchantment: an awareness of the mythical and the sacred. Of the diversity of writers who have responded to Hogsback and its surrounds three are chosen to highlight these themes. All of them record something of the reality of the landscape along with a sense of the 'other' and of their own relationship with the locale.

The English name 'Hogsback' derives from the shape of the three ridged peaks to the east of the settlement. The Xhosa see a woman with a child on her back in these same peaks and call the place Bhukazana. A peak to the north is named Gaika's Kop for the Xhosa warrior-chief. 'Bloodstain'd are these quiet, sloping valleys / Where the red-brown grasses proudly wave,' wrote F C Slater, and there are many reminders in the surrounding terrain that during the frontier wars of the 19th century violence and loss characterised the region.

Now peaceful, the Hogsback remains a place of contrasts: its ancient forests a reminder of a pre-human past; its plantations a reminder of colonial intrusions. Waterfalls and streams glistening in the shadows of trees create a sense of tranquillity and mystery, but the exposed grasslands of the valley below Hogsback offer little respite from a harsh climate. Rhododendrons, oak trees and hazel hedges, berries and deciduous fruits – planted by late-19th-century newcomers from Britain – contrast with a prodigality of natural vegetation. A mixture of holiday resort and smallholdings, Hogsback conveys a sense of ease, while in the overpopulated and eroded plains that it overlooks people struggle to sustain themselves. Sometimes the mist that typifies this part of the Amatola region unifies this diversity under one flimsy blanket, while intensifying the pervasive sense of mystery. As the poets Slater and Mahola indicate, nostalgia for the Hogsback is as real for those who have grown up in its rural villages as for those who have known it as a place of recreation.

MZI MAHOLA
Return to My Birthplace
— *Poetry Workshop, Hogsback, November 1991*

From far away
We came to the mountain
To seek the blessing of its spirits.
For three days and nights
It hid under fog
Befitting
Sacred ground.
In the night
And even through the day
We listened to birds and frogs
Praising the Lord
In the fog.
My nostalgia for years
Brought forth my childhood
Forcing me to woo the spirits
Impatient and demanding
To listen to resonant voices
Of Zizi, Gugu and Mdleleni.
Something was amiss here,
Nor did I hear voices of
Hlongwane, Blom or Koba.
Alone I wandered in the fog
Like a log at sea.
At night I had a dream
Clear as a new-laid egg
The spirits had recognised me.
'Nothing has changed,'
A voice said.
When we left the mountain
Some were intimatised
Some poeticised
Unable to deliver
Except to confirm that
Spirits dwell here.

from Strange Things

FRANCIS CAREY SLATER
In the Mist: Hogsback

A traveller for seven days,
In dust and heat on stony ways,
I won last night these green-rayed islands
Above the brown surge of the veld,
These fluted forest-vales that belt
The sky-clipped Amatola Highlands:
Scenes where my youthful footsteps sped,
Long loved but long unvisited.

Rising at dawn in eager haste
I stared around, but all was waste:
Gaika and Hogsback triple-crowned
In stone-mute seas of mist were drowned;
Streams were submerged and woods also;
The waterfalls, that swiftly cast
Curved nets of iridescent light
From hill-barques to leafed-lakes below,
Were muffled in mist-billows vast
And lost as in a moonless night.

Some say that breath is but a mist,
Which hides from us what's loveliest:
That when we mortals cease to breathe
And melted is the cloudy veil,
Not time nor distance shall avail,
Nor swaddling mist, nor scabbard-night,
To dim our radiance or sheathe
Ultimate beauty from our sight.
– But, oh, I would this mist might rise
Revealing to my earth-born eyes
The heaven that *here* around me lies.

from Collected Poems of Francis Carey Slater

Francis Carey Slater – born in 1876 – and Mzi Mahola – born in 1949 – spent
their early years in the shadow of the Amatola mountains close to Hogsback.
Both attended Lovedale College and both express in their poetry nostalgia for

the landscape of their first homes. In each author Hogsback inspired a number of poems, of which Slater's 'In the Mist: Hogsback' and Mahola's 'Return to My Birthplace' make an interesting comparison. Written almost 100 years apart, these poems record very similar experiences: a return to scenes of youth and the disappointment of finding the anticipated beauty obscured by mist. Both poets are aware of a spiritual dimension behind their experiences of the physical world, although they are viewed from different cultural perspectives. Slater thinks of 'ultimate beauty' beyond this life, yet longs to see 'the heaven that here around me lies'; Mahola longs for recognition from the spirits of his ancestors and the friends of his youth. Through a dream he is assured that spirits indeed 'dwell here'.

FRANCIS CAREY SLATER, grandson of 1820 Settlers on both sides, was born on the farm Umjilo, about 4 km from Alice. At the age of four he moved with his family to the farm Brakfontein about 27 km from the town and situated on the banks of the Keiskamma. Slater's only formal schooling was a two-year spell at Lovedale College. For the most part his teachers were his family and other adult mentors, as well as the standard literary classics of the day and the environment itself. Lessons were also learned from the Xhosa people with whom he played as a child and worked on the farm as a youth. From infancy he was fluent in their language and he often visited his Xhosa friends in their homes, where he listened to their stories and learned about their customs. A volume of poems published in 1935 and entitled *Dark Folk and Other Poems* is a return to the experiences of his youth in the Amatola region, and many of the poems refer to rural activities in the Xhosa context – milking, wood gathering, herding – and to customs such as initiation ceremonies (about which Mahola also composes a verse) or to traditional stories.

In his autobiography, *Settlers' Heritage*, Slater recalls his first visit to Hogsback some time during the 1890s. 'I had long worshipped from afar the Amatola Hills, of which the peaks Gaika and Hogsback form a part. But now, as I approached these magnetic mountains my worship deepened into adoration.' Afterwards he was haunted by the beauty of what he called 'that earthly paradise'. Francis Slater left Alice in 1899 and joined the Standard Bank in Port Elizabeth. During his 30-year career in banking he lived in thirteen different towns in the Eastern Cape, many of which feature in his writings, but the Amatola mountains drew him back again and again. In 1910 he married Leonora Nyassa Stewart. He and his wife honeymooned at Hogsback and, until their deaths in 1958, often revisited the Amatola region. Images from this area abound in Slater's poetry and his only novel, *The Shining River*, is set on the banks of the Keiskamma.

Slater called himself 'Romantic by nature and a Victorian by upbringing'. These two strands affected his outlook on life as well as the style of his writing, much of which was antiquated even in his own time and has little appeal today. There are, however, poetic gems that transcend their time, among them the lyric 'Lament for a Dead Cow' and parts of his long poems 'The Karroo', 'Drought' and 'The Trek', all of them rooted in the Eastern Cape landscape and sympathetic towards its people – English, Afrikaans and Xhosa. As well as the novel, the autobiography and a volume of short stories, Slater produced ten collections of poems, the best of them gathered together in *Selected Poems* (1947) and *Collected Poems* (1957). His literary legacy goes beyond his own works, for this energetic banker and poet helped to put South African literature on the map through the anthologies *The Centenary Book of South African Verse* (1925) and *The New Centenary Book of South African Verse* (1945), which he selected and edited.

Mzi Mahola, born about ten years before Slater died, lived from infancy to the age of twelve with his grandparents at Lushington in the Amatola basin before, in 1962, joining his parents in Port Elizabeth. Schooling at Lovedale College and at Healdtown (where he began to write poetry), followed by an interrupted period of study at Fort Hare University, kept him in touch with this region and with his rural family and friends. Mahola now lives in the urban environment of New Brighton in the Nelson Mandela Metropole. His literary achievement in that milieu is recorded in Chapter Two, but much of his poetry reflects his rural upbringing and reveals a longing for the place itself and its personal associations, as well as for traditions that have largely been lost to modern African society. In another poem about Hogsback – 'Intaba Zebukhazana' – from his first volume, *Strange Things*, Mahola writes nostalgically:

> I long for the berries
> Wild fruit and game
> I miss cliffs and waterfalls
> Spewing fury in white rage
> That petrified me as a child
> Mysteries of nature
> Springs and streams
> No drought could tame,
> Their water is nostalgic.
> I yearn for stock and crops
> Produce of the peasants
> The generous soil
> A pleasure to the tiller.

As a child Mahola listened to the stories of his grandmother and other women of the village, and there is a strong narrative thread in his poems, several of which recount incidents from his rural past. He, like many others of his generation, is a person of two worlds, their contrasting ways expressed in his poetry through a blend of the simple and the philosophic, the past of Hogsback and the present of New Brighton.

A notion persists that J R R Tolkien, author of *Lord of the Rings*, visited Hogsback and was inspired by its scenery when creating the literary landscapes of his fantasy. Tolkien was born in South Africa – at Bloemfontein – but left at the age of three never to return. A children's camp at the resort is called Hobbiton, but Tolkien's hobbits did not originate here.

There is, however, something magical about this place and Carolyn Parker, in her youth novel *Witch Woman on the Hogsback*, interweaves African myths with elements of Western traditions of magic in an exciting story based on the time-honoured theme of a battle between good and evil. The protagonists are two young people of about twelve years from different racial backgrounds but equally in tune with the 'other' world.

In the novel the real and the magical blend. Here, for instance, Parker describes Oak Avenue and a nearby waterfall, known as the Thirty-Nine Steps – real features of the Hogsback settlement:

They left the avenue and walked under the towering pine and blue gum trees, their footsteps silent on the pine needles. Little painted hogs on the trunks of trees marked the way to the waterfall. The path began to descend quite steeply towards a stream bordered by indigenous bush, and the sound of the waterfall became louder as they followed the path among the shrubs and ferns. Kate could just see the white and silver of falling water through the branches ahead of her, when Luvuyo stopped.

Then the mythical Hili, the *tokoloshe*, appears beside this waterfall. In the realistically drawn Hogsback environment the children meet other creatures, such as *uBantu bamlambo* (the river people) and *Mpundulu* (the lightning bird), who, although they originate in Xhosa mythology, speak and act, as the author says, according to her own imagination.

Elsewhere in *Witch Woman* Parker writes in a different mode in which she invests the natural with the magical and the magical with the natural, as in her description of the Spirit of the Tree.

Although formed from the grey-green mist that the tree had seemed to exhale, the Spirit that stood before Luvuyo and Kate was not vague or insubstantial. It appeared as a tall old man, with skin the colour and texture of bark. His beard and hair were long and rough, silvery-green, and his garments seemed to be a compound of lichen, moss and tattered leaves. Meeting his eyes, Kate felt as if she were gazing into a pool of still, translucent green water: beneath the reflecting surface, there was a sense of unfathomable depth. The joints of his hands and the features of his face were gnarled and stiff with age, and when he spoke – as he now did – his voice contained something of the creaking of old boughs in a storm wind.

CAROLYN PARKER was born in 1956 in Johannesburg, where the first sensation she recalls was a swinging motion as she was carried on the back of the Zulu woman who cared for her. Her first experience of language and song was in the woman's voice and of story in the tales she told. These influences and later contacts with Xhosa people make the author sensitive to the African mythology on which *Witch Woman on the Hogsback* is based. Her own Western upbringing in various parts of Africa and in Switzerland also plays its part. Parker's acquaintance with Hogsback was brief but intense. Between 1982 and 1986, while residing in Grahamstown, she frequently visited a property she and her husband had bought at Hogsback and it was there that she wrote the novel. In a note filed at NELM, she writes: 'I was entranced by the place. The mountains, forests, deep-running streams and waterfalls seemed to me to hold an ancient magic that was just beyond my reach.' Parker now lives in Australia but admits to a longing for Africa.

Tolkien may not have visited Hogsback, but there is an intriguing link between it and English literature's most famous writer: William Shakespeare. John Dover Wilson, one of the best-known Shakespearian scholars of the 20th century, worked on his edition of Shakespeare's sonnets while staying with his daughter-in-law, anthropologist Monica Wilson, during 1962. In the preface to *The Sonnets* in the *New Cambridge Shakespeare* (1966) which he edited, Dover Wilson describes her home – Hunterstoun, in the Hogsback – and its setting.

> I began this edition of the finest love poetry in the world in what I think must be the loveliest garden on earth. It lies in a level upland glade shut in by dark forests stretching up to jagged mountain tops, but itself containing a luxuriant orchard and stately trees dotted about it here and

there, while it fearlessly exposes its grassy slopes to the midsummer heat of the southern hemisphere, being watered and cooled by running streams and deep dark pools that give teeming life to birds and flowers of many kinds and colours, while to crown all extend the sweeping curves of a stately house, dwelling-place of a great lady. Shakespeare, I fancy, had imagined just such a home of peace and delight as his Belmont. Or he may even have seen one not unlike it at Wilton. Certainly it was a happy fortune that placed me amid such surroundings when I had to set hand to my last volume in the *New Cambridge Shakespeare*, begun forty years ago. For all the plays in the canon being now published, the *Poems* and the *Sonnets* remained, the former for Professor Maxwell, the latter for myself, and I was here in South Africa sitting one morning early in 1962 under the shade of a deodar tree, with a copy of the *Sonnets* in my hand to begin what after four years would become the volume the reader has before him. In the soil I have described the work took root at once and went on steadily growing ...

KEISKAMMAHOEK

R L Peteni

Marguerite Poland

Two notable Eastern Cape novels are set near the small town of Keiskammahoek, which lies in a large natural basin ringed by mountains of the Amatola range. They are R L Peteni's *Hills of Fools* (1976), set in a rural village in the district, and Marguerite Poland's *Shades* (1993), set at St Matthew's Mission, about 6 km from the town.

Hills of Fools is a Romeo and Juliet story about the tragic consequences of love between Bhuqa, a young man from the Thembu village on one side of the Xesi (Keiskamma) River, and Zuziwe, a beautiful maiden from Kwazidenge, the Hlubi village on the other. Ancient rivalries, their origin forgotten, have left a legacy of irrational hatred which is exacerbated when one of Zuziwe's relatives is killed in a stick fight between the young warriors of the two villages. Central to the story is the Xesi River, not 'important as rivers go' but 'to the villagers of Kwazidenge it is as important as the Nile to Egyptians, the Thames to Englishmen, the Vaal to South Africans'. It is both a life-giving place and one of destruction.

When the heavy rains come, the Xesi river becomes an agent of death, with its waters the colour of blood, the blood of overpopulated, impoverished, dismal villages. The life-giving soil is washed from the grain lands by rushing torrents which follow in the wake of severe droughts and furious hailstorms, giving the river the dark colour of blood. The river swells into a raging torrent and becomes a monster which destroys people, animals and crops along the river valley. But the normal function of the river is to give life to both the Thembu village and the Hlubi village impartially. The frowning, unscaleable cliffs on its banks are shared by both sides equally, or almost equally. On the Hlubi side there are tall trees under which herds of cattle lie after they have drunk their fill of water in the river. Lower down, on the Thembu side, the river spreads out into a natural swimming pool, with a shallow end for younger children, and a deep end with a large flat stone at the water's edge, from which good swimmers jump into the water.

This is the meeting place of the lovers and the site where some of the violent events recounted in *Hill of Fools* originate, but the river is more than a setting for the story. It flows through the novel as a symbol of separation, functioning at times as metaphor: 'something warned her that their love was likely to be deep and dangerous, and her passion as irresistible as the current of the Xesi river when in flood; Zuziwe is 'a girl as bright and beautiful as the clear waters of the Xesi river'; the waters of the Xesi river 'were at this time as clear and full of laughter as her eyes'.

Sometimes the Xesi takes on an allegorical function. Here Zuziwe sits on the bank of the river:

> After a time she noticed that two distinct currents came from the two sides of the island higher up the river and met at a point opposite the spot where she sat. The course of each current was smooth and even, but when they met, their flow was arrested and their progress disturbed. Then they reorganized themselves and formed a bigger, stronger current which flowed down smoothly again. The current moved on in one single sheet of water. Then it curved smoothly and noiselessly over an uneven shelf of rock, and when it landed at the bottom of the shelf, it broke up into a chaos of foam and noise, and into minute splashes of water which were tossed high up into the air ...

The cadences of its language and the story's rural characters and background of tradition give *Hill of Fools* a local flavour, as does the use of Xhosa place names: Bhukazana for Hogsback; Mthwaku for St Matthew's; Qoboqobo for Keiskammahoek.

RANDALL LANGA PETENI was born at Zingcuka near Keiskammahoek in 1915. He attended Lovedale College and the University of Fort Hare, graduating in 1939 with a BA degree. During the next 30 years Peteni became prominent in education as a teacher, headmaster and dedicated member (later president) of local and national teachers' unions. From 1969 to 1981 he lectured in the English department of Fort Hare. Among a host of other activities, including the acquisition of Honours and master's degrees, this energetic man wrote two books. *Towards Tomorrow* is a history of the African Teachers' Association of South Africa, *Hill of Fools* a novel written in English and published in 1976. Later it was translated by the author into Xhosa and adapted for radio. Peteni died in 2000 at the age of 84.

One of the seeds of MARGUERITE POLAND's novel *Shades* was planted under the shadow of the Amatola mountains nearly 30 years before the 1993 publication of the book. It was a visit to St Matthew's Anglican mission, 6 km from Keiskammahoek, where the author's great-great-grandfather, the Rev. Charles Taberer, had been a missionary from 1870 to 1914. Another seed had germinated during an earlier visit by Charles Taberer to Johannesburg to meet his daughter, the author's great-grandmother, Daisy Taberer Brereton. She, with her husband William Brereton, had also lived at St Matthew's. A number of other links with the past contributed to the concept and execution of *Shades.* It is not, however, a biographical work, nor a history of the mission. St Matthias is a reflection of St Matthew's; four of the novel's characters are inspired by Poland's forebears; some events in the story are true to the period in which it is set; but the novelist gives place, character and story lives and truths of their own.

In the world Marguerite Poland creates from the Keiskammahoek region, the imported culture of England and the church are sometimes in conflict, sometimes in harmony with the customs and spirituality of the local Xhosa. The world of *Shades* is a world in which there is tragedy and gladness, rivalry and accord, darkness and light. The novel is set at the close of the 19th century and just after – the time of the rinderpest and the beginnings of labour recruitment for the gold mines. A wider time-context is also suggested: the frontier wars have taken their toll in the past; the destructive consequences to rural society of migrant labour loom ahead. The spatial setting, centring on St Matthias, is also seen in a wider context and its fine texture makes *Shades* one of the best imaginative recreations of place in the literature of the Eastern Cape.

Mission outstations; Grahamstown; the Pirie bush; the faraway gold mines are distinctly pictured, but St Matthias is the pivotal locale in *Shades,* and its features are etched on the reader's visual imagination as it is viewed by different characters. This is how Walter Brownley first encounters the mission and its environs:

Instead of passing by cultivated farmlands, hamlets and orchards as he'd expected, they'd turned east and journeyed on towards a low, dark ridge of bush-clad hills. He should have taken warning when Klaus Otto told him that along those distant valleys the Frontier Wars had once been fought and that the bones of warriors remained unclaimed in the more isolated reaches of the countryside. Scanning the silent slopes ahead, it seemed to Walter as though the land had been abandoned, not from choice but from compulsion, and that something of the brooding of a battlefield remained: a frontier such as this – so much dark monotony – seemed to be a place for soldiers, not for priests.

Nor should he have been lulled into complacence by the sudden and unexpected sight of the abundant mission gardens, the large grey church, the houses of the catechist and carpenter and the Reverend Charles Farborough's bungalow with its fragrant garden – a small enclave of order and repose – when the wagon breasted the last hill and started the dusty descent towards the little settlement of St Matthias. He should have fled the wide, hot madness of those plains.

Everything in *Shades* is underpinned by a consciousness of locality and by a linking of events through allusions to place and its associations. The bush-clad hills; the pastures, cattle kraals and huts around the mission; the Kaboosie (a spur of the Amatola range) and the dense forests on neighbouring slopes; the mission house and its English garden; the curate's lodge, the workshops and print-room; the Mtwaku River; dust and wind and sun; drought and rain; birds and stars; and the church with its 'deeply shadowed arches' are among the novel's recurring, often haunting images.

The catalyst for some of the tragic events in *Shades* is the rinderpest, a contagious and fatal cattle disease that swept through Africa during the 1890s. The loss of cattle both from the disease and from the slaughter of beasts to prevent its spread led to impoverishment and despair, making men susceptible to the lure of work on the mines. Poland encourages us to *see* the effects of this historic episode.

No more red cattle were driven out to pasture. No sleds were drawn along the dusty track by oxen, led by boys. The wind sent dust spectres back and forth across the plains and the roads were empty. Women hoed the fields. Men and children, bowed beneath another yoke. There were no oxen to inspan for ploughing. The earth was broken into small uneven patches ready for planting.

The shades, or spirits of the ancestors, link the novel's present with the past. They are also a link with its future, for Poland is writing a hundred years after

their time about her own shades. In a 1993 interview, the author explains the importance to her of the concept of the shades:[3]

> This whole theology of shades is important to me. That sense of continuity of belonging, of bringing your immortalities with you. I feel one is an inheritor, not just genetically, but of a whole family thing.

There are over twenty references to the shades in the novel and, as in Chris Mann's poem 'Cookhouse Station', acknowledging their presence imparts a sense of place that goes beyond the physical.

The novel also presents a fine imaginative portrayal of a specific place. St Matthew's, established in 1855, became prosperous and productive but it has become, to some extent, a ruined settlement. Much of the good work of the missionaries was lost when the apartheid government took over their mission school in the 1950s and hospital in the 1970s.

What Walter Brownley fears for it in the fiction of *Shades* can now be observed in fact.

> He could feel the silence of the Amatolas pressing in around him: aloof, distant, covered with black-green bush. There was no poetry in any of his books to describe such a landscape – no poetry, no words. He had decided, long ago, that his God – his most dependable, predictable Creator – had retreated in defeat before the God who had invented this. One day those same dark-sapped bushes would march in and reclaim the mission and its cultivated lands. He was sure of it. There was nothing like the ruins of settlements to underscore the impotence of man against a place like this. The great church, buttressed in stone, would one day be the haunt of owls.

What is now a government school is in fairly good condition, but the hospital buildings are mere ruins, its services having been moved to Keiskammahoek after the government takeover. The workshops and printing press set up by the missionaries have disappeared; the water furrows designed by the first missionary are overgrown; the mission buildings featured in *Shades* are dilapidated and their gardens a wilderness. Poverty is rife. But decay is not absolute. The imposing stone church, built during the time of Poland's great-great-grandfather, Charles Taberer, has been restored largely through the efforts of Tony Taberer, another of the missionary's descendants. It has thus been rescued from being merely 'the haunt of owls'.

On a visit to St Matthew's in 1991, in one of the coincidences that accompanied the writing of *Shades*, Marguerite Poland met a returning exile whose
forebears had also lived at the mission:

> This man had come home. And that home was the same place that my
> family had always considered to be theirs.
>
> In his heart he carried remembrances that were tied to the same sky,
> the same earth, the same far hills, the same veld and plain and pasture.
> While in exile these were the things that had sustained him. He recalled
> them as lovingly as did those I knew. Then we spoke of the mission with
> a sense of common discovery despite the different journeys that had
> brought us there that day.
>
> 'This is our history and our place,' the doctor said. 'It must be built
> again.'[4]

Much of the literature of the Amatola region suggests the same idea: 'This is
our history and our place.'

A PATCHWORK

OF WRITINGS

EAST OF THE WINTERBERG

Our tour of the region east and south of the Winterberg and Amatola ranges passes through mountains and hills, across river valleys and along coastal stretches. It takes us to small and medium-sized towns such as Cathcart and King William's Town, to a San cave and the remote mission station of Mgwali, a farm and the large port city of East London, the lonely grave of the poet Mqhayi on a hillside and the legendary Cove Rock on the coast. There are reminders everywhere of conflicts over the occupation of land and of those who have defended or fought for it – the San, the Khoekhoe, the Xhosa, British soldiers, German settlers, Afrikaans farmers, missionaries who sought to win people to the Christian faith, Nationalist rulers who tried to parcel out the land on their own terms, and anti-apartheid activists struggling for freedom from oppression. Writers' responses to this landscape of dispute are as varied as the terrain itself and the people who have claimed it as home. Their writings form a patchwork of different genres and different attitudes.

CATHCART

Cathcart was established in the 1850s as a military post and named for the colonial governor, Sir George Cathcart, who brought the Eighth Frontier War – the War of Mlanjeni – to a close. Today it is a quiet rural centre in the mountains surrounded by sheep and cattle farms and offering extensive views across the valleys of several rivers that feed into the Great Kei. The town is situated on the slopes of the Windvogel mountain. The name means 'bird of the wind', a reminder perhaps of the San, who once lived with the freedom of birds in this district. There are many caves decorated with the paintings of these hunter-gatherer people so ruthlessly hunted by human rivals who wanted to occupy the territory they had roamed for centuries.

Mark Swift
André Brink

From a rocky perch above a San cave on the Windvogel, the poet Mark Swift looks out over a view of the countryside which includes Cathcart – 'a half-baked town on the rim of the world' – and a tiny train winding through distant hills. He contemplates the fate of the artists of the caves and the advance of peoples who have used violent means to attain their ends. To him this is 'the landscape of the brutal mind'.

MARK SWIFT
Windvogel Mountain
(*Cathcart, Eastern Cape*)

From this fastness, this haphazard
   castle of stone and air, we straddle
      the galleries daubed by San.
Below us, on painted rock, the long-dreamed,
   long-dead kudu are brought to their knees
        by pin-pricks.

Hills away, a slow-coach train draws
   a thin, black line
      across ochre impasto. The centipede
of iron and its distant halt, a half-baked
   town on the rim of the world, betray
      the advance of history, of hair-trigger men
        on the make.

This is the landscape of the brutal mind,
   beyond the reach of compass
      or intention. It is cradle
and deathbed, slung between poles of dawn
   and darkness, of fire and ice.

Below us, in their warrens, the hunters cowered
   as quarry, driven to earth by shod
      and blinkered centaurs. Men of the sky,
at home on the wind, they were brought to their knees
      with their painted prey.

from Testing the Edge

MARK SWIFT was born in 1946 in Queenstown, about 50 km north of Cathcart, where he spent most of his youth. Three collections of poetry – *Treading Water* (1974), *Seconds Out* (1983) and *Testing the Edge* (1996) – have confirmed him as a poet of substance. As Jack Cope says in his introduction to Swift's first collection, 'True poetry is rife with messages and portents which transcend its historical and geographical moment.' This is true of much of Swift's intense, searching poetry, in which his encounters with objects in the outer world often involve reflections about self, home (including this region), travel and exile.

Swift studied graphic art in East London and worked for publishers and on newspapers in Cape Town for some years. He now lives and works in the south of England, but although he has found material for his poems in Britain and on the continent of Europe, the thoughts expressed in them often return to Africa.

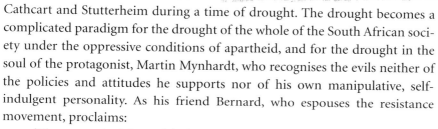

The most important setting in André Brink's 1978 novel, *Rumours of Rain*, is a farm somewhere between Cathcart and Stutterheim during a time of drought. The drought becomes a complicated paradigm for the drought of the whole of the South African society under the oppressive conditions of apartheid, and for the drought in the soul of the protagonist, Martin Mynhardt, who recognises the evils neither of the policies and attitudes he supports nor of his own manipulative, self-indulgent personality. As his friend Bernard, who espouses the resistance movement, proclaims:

> 'Those wonderful, terrible droughts that stripped the veld so you could see the very bones of the earth. Like a sheep's skeleton. Until you arrived at a point beyond despair and cursing and fear, in a stillness you'd never known before. I remember there was something so utterly clear and pure about the feeling. And only then, usually, the rains would come.'

The plot of *Rumours of Rain* moves from place to place and ranges back and forth over the life of Martin, who is an Afrikaans businessman living in Johannesburg, but at the story's heart is a period of 'four critical days' spent on the family farm in the Eastern Cape – a scene to which the author constantly returns. Brink has said that he finds it important to visualise the places in which the events of his stories occur. In *Rumours of Rain* the farm in the Cathcart district, although it is never named, has obviously been so clearly visualised in the author's mind that he is able to imprint it on the visual imagination of the reader both in outline and in detail. Through the many twists of the plot, descriptions of the farm appear that are like a series of carefully composed oil paintings.

> Where the road made a sharp bend to the right, the lights shot out into the void beyond. There was a very sudden drop there, invisible from as close by as fifty yards: a rift torn into the guts of the earth, probably long before the advent of man. Presumably it had either exposed deeper, fertile layers, or else in the course of time the sides of the valley had caved

in, bringing down the humus of rotten plants and opening up courses for streams. For the valley was luxuriant, perennially green, and in the daytime one could follow the fingers of virgin forest along the beds of fountains and a hidden stream; there were even ferntrees and palms, apart from a jungle of cycads and plumbago, euphorbias and brushwood and enormous wild-figs, and an incredible variety of aloes.

Also woven into the text are incidental little brushstrokes that evoke some of the typical features of an Eastern Cape farm and of this farm in particular: features such as jackal-proof fencing; a rutted farm road; broken farm implements lying around; the coalstove in the kitchen; the pail of dough waiting to be made into bread; a paraffin tin in the backyard; the cement steps of the stoep; the gentle closing of a gauze door.

The vegetation on the farm is typical of the area and especially well drawn is the virgin forest in which an important encounter between the hardheaded businessman and a mysterious old tribal figure takes place.

As I progressed slowly into the narrow kloof, the bush grew steadily more dense. The trees were taller, with lithe vines suspended from the high branches. Bracken and wild fern. Even palms. It was the beginning of the virgin forest, with the musty smell of rotting vegetation, a resilient mass of decayed leaves and branches so thick I couldn't hear the sound of my own feet; only from time to time the sharp crackling of a breaking twig. There was an awareness of life all around me: rustlings in the grass, a whispering in the foliage, branches swaying suddenly without wind, small hooves pattering off. Bushbuck, monkeys, lizards, louries. These were the very entrails of the farm. I could feel it and smell it and hear it, taste it on my tongue, while overhead the trees broke like a great green wave, a silence hissing in my ears.

And we are never allowed to forget the drought.

They were digging the grave, beyond the huts where the slope of the hill was levelling, near the spot where the water diviner had stopped the day before. There was a small enclosure of aloes, tenaciously clinging to the hard earth and aflame with flowers even in that drought. The picks and spades made little impression on the baked red soil, ringing with a loud metallic twang as they struck what appeared to be solid rock. In spite of the early-morning cold the men were working with bodies bared to the waist and shining with sweat, hiccuping at every blow. Here and there within the aloe enclosure lay the small stony humps of older graves.

ANDRÉ BRINK is one of South Africa's most prestigious writers: a critic, playwright and non-fiction writer, but most famously a novelist whose works have been translated into many languages and read all over the world. Brink writes in both English and Afrikaans, often writing the same novel in each language. He is a great storyteller and a consummate artist with words; he is a popular novelist who deals with serious themes; and divers accolades and honours, literary awards and honorary degrees have been bestowed on him locally and internationally.

Brink was born in 1935 in Vrede in the Free State. He studied local and world literature at Potchefstroom University and the Sorbonne in Paris. He was one of the 'Sestigers', a group of 1960s Afrikaans writers dedicated to fighting apartheid through their works. Before moving to the University of Cape Town in 1991 Brink was professor and head of the department of Afrikaans at Rhodes University but, despite living and working in Grahamstown for 30 years and doing much of his writing during that period, Brink has given a substantial Eastern Cape setting to only one of the fifteen of his novels that have been published to date: *Rumours of Rain*.

MGWALI VILLAGE

Tiyo Soga

Mgwali village, which is associated with Tiyo Soga, one of the Cape Colony's most remarkable 19th-century missionaries and writers, is situated about 25 km off the road between Cathcart and Stutterheim. It lies in pleasant hilly surroundings on the Mgwali River, a tributary of the Kabusi which, in turn, flows into the Great Kei.

TIYO SOGA was born in 1829 in the ancestral lands of his forefathers, the Ngqika people, and started his schooling at the old Chumie mission, which was the forerunner of Lovedale. During the 1846 War of the Axe, the Rev. William Govan – first principal of Lovedale – took Soga with him to Scotland. Educated and ordained as a minister in Scotland, where he married a Scottish woman, Janet Burnside, Soga returned to South Africa in 1857 to become a missionary among his own Xhosa people. First he was in charge at Mgwali and then he moved across the Kei River to Tutura near present-day Butterworth, where he died and was buried in 1871.

Soga's literary work in the vernacular includes a translation into Xhosa of the first part of John Bunyan's *Pilgrim's Progress* as *Uhambo lo Mhambi*, a work that has had an important influence on Xhosa language and literature. Soga also wrote hymns, participated in the revision of the Xhosa Bible, and was a major contributor to the periodical *Indaba*.

Soga's journal and letters written in English, and translations by J J R Jolobe of some of the *Indaba* articles, were published in 1993 as *The Journal and Selected Writings of the Reverend Tiyo Soga*. His writings provide unique insights into mission life and into black consciousness in the Cape Colony of the 1850s and 1860s. His journal as well as his letters to the missionary branch of the United Presbyterian Church records Soga's conscientious, often difficult work as a missionary. Joy over new converts, sadness over backsliders, compassion for the sick and bereaved fill most of the pages but they also include a few descriptions of the mission station and its surrounds. He describes the church at Mgwali, positioned on a 'low gradually sloping hill with the Emgwali washing its base towards the North'.

> On this rise or elevation stands our white washed Emgwali church, a conspicuous object – announcing its glorious design to all who come within sight of the Emgwali station – & who have the curiosity to ask what & whose house it is – Should we ever erect on this our Mount Zion, a more pretending edifice, it will not be easy in this part of the country at least, to find another place of worship, that will rival its claims to picturesqueness of aspect.

To Soga the church building itself has an evangelical role: to attract inquirers. Both church and school have recently been restored to their former state, so one may observe the station much as Soga would have known it 150 years ago and admire the 'picturesqueness of aspect' and clean-cut lines of the conspicuous little whitewashed church. In it a plaque recalls the achievements of Tiyo Soga as Christian, scholar, family man and 'ardent patriot'. William Charles Scully, who visited the Soga family at Tutura in 1869 and accompanied them on a holiday at the coast, describes him thus:

> Tiyo Soga was a tall man of slender build and with a stooping figure. Even at the time I tell of a short, hacking cough gave evidence of the consumption which some years later caused his death. He was not alone a deeply cultivated scholar, but a Christian gentleman in the fullest sense of the term.[1]

KING WILLIAM'S TOWN

Brian Walter
A Prayer on the Road to King

Each week as I bus down to teach poems
of death and life, sorrow and song,
I see, just before King William's Town,
a piece of placid river water shine
in the westering sun.

And I love, from the hill-top road,
to watch the river wend in the valley,
and to see the railway, just below,
tucking into our contour,
and the Grahamstown road on the next crest,
closing in.

And it's strange how all things
come to one:
for where we join the Grahamstown road
we bridge, so near the railway track,
the river which gleamed in twilight
and eased on down, past Biko's
still, still grave, into the town.

It's strange how all things
come to one:
and as all eases to an end,
let my mind be like still water;
let our land lie placid, at peace; and
Azania, and Thy Kingdom, come.

in Echo Poets

Brian Walter's poem 'A Prayer on the Road to King' provides us with our first glimpse ('a piece of placid river water') of the Buffalo River, which flows past King William's Town and on down to East London. As Walter enters King William's Town on the road from Alice and sees the river, the road to Grahamstown and the railway line ahead of him, he thinks of Steve Biko, who is buried between the road bridge and the river in a cemetery now called the Steve Biko Garden of Remembrance. Everything in the poem suggests stillness and ease, and there is a sense of arriving at a place and a time of peace that has been steadily approaching. Today, King gives the impression of hustle and bustle rather than stillness, and it offers many reminders of times of strife and of the conflicting elements that have gone into its making.

The name Bantu Stephen Biko brings to mind a horrifying act of violence: his death in custody in 1977 after being assaulted by members of the South African Security Police. Born in 1947 in King William's Town, Biko was a student activist and an initiator of the Black Consciousness Movement of the sixties and seventies. His grave in King and a statue in East London are reminders of a man who helped to give his oppressed compatriots a pride in being who they were – black South Africans.

Brian Walter
Wendy
Woodward

'Thy Kingdom come' is the prayer of Walter's poem 'A Prayer on the Road to King'. King William's Town's situation on the banks of the Buffalo River is in part due to the establishment in 1826 of a mission station whose aim was to bring the kingdom of God to the people – the Ntinde – who lived in the vicinity. A missionary museum in King is devoted to the story of John Brownlee, who led this mission, and many like him who brought Christianity to this part of Africa. Thomas Pringle greatly admired John Brownlee and made him the subject of his sonnet 'The Good Missionary'. Shortly before his departure from the Cape, Pringle was on his way from Glen Lynden to visit Brownlee, but had to abandon his intention on hearing that the eastern frontier had been crossed the previous day by a military sortie from the colony.

King William's Town and things military are almost synonymous. It is a town of fine buildings, many of them with military connections. Its history is the history largely of the 19th-century conflicts between British military forces and Xhosa warriors. After the clashes of the 1830s a military headquarters was established in the newly proclaimed Province of Queen Adelaide and was given the name King William's Town in honour of the reigning British monarch (Adelaide was his queen). The province was short-lived, but after another frontier war in the 1840s the area was once again annexed by Britain and named British Kaffraria; King William's Town at its heart increased in military importance. Another change came in the 1850s when German legionnaires, initially recruited by Britain to fight in the Crimea, were brought out to settle on land from which the Xhosa had been driven; civilian German settlers later came to join them. Many towns in the vicinity have German names, such as Berlin, Hamburg, Hanover, Potsdam and Frankfort.

Part of the impressive memorial to German settlers in King William's Town is a giant glacial 'erratic' rock symbolising the translocation of people across great distances. Wendy Woodward's poem 'On the Diary of a German Woman', inspired by the diary of the wife of one of the legionnaires, conveys something of the torment it must have been, especially for women, to be translocated from Europe to the alien environment suggested in Woodward's poem.

WENDY WOODWARD
On the Diary of a German Woman in the Eastern Cape

Through the weft of her words,
we see a face in the candlelight
under a roof thatched too lightly
to stave off the rain, or the fear
of the dark and the aloes –
burning with their red lights
under the quiet moon.

She lives in the wilderness,
when all she wanted was a cedarwood kist
and a constant stove,
but what she found
was rain through the roof
onto her birthing bed,
umbrellas over her flickering body
to keep the baby from the rain.

And then delirium –
with spectres who smiled her into Hades,
which had the same greyness and drought
as the frontier her husband guarded
between the baboons and the leopards,
and the long-horned cattle pricking the air
far from the fat cows of green and daisied fields.

from Séance for the Body

WENDY WOODWARD was born in 1950 in Stutterheim, one of the principal German settlements of 1858. She went to school in East London and university in Grahamstown and, although she has not lived here since, she says that she still regards the Eastern Cape, in many ways, as home. After travelling to various parts of the world Woodward returned to South Africa in 1983 and settled in Cape Town, where she teaches in the English department at the University of the Western Cape. The personal writings of 19th-century colonial women and matters ecological are among her interests. Woodward's poetry, collected in *Séance for the Body* (1994), is also concerned largely with women's experiences and, as in the case of the poem 'On the Diary', with the environments in which they find themselves. With fine perception, the poet uses these environments to reflect their emotional states.

NTAMBOZUKO – MOUNT OF GLORY

*Samuel Edward
Krune Mqhayi*

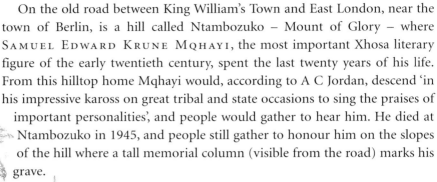

On the old road between King William's Town and East London, near the town of Berlin, is a hill called Ntambozuko – Mount of Glory – where SAMUEL EDWARD KRUNE MQHAYI, the most important Xhosa literary figure of the early twentieth century, spent the last twenty years of his life. From this hilltop home Mqhayi would, according to A C Jordan, descend 'in his impressive kaross on great tribal and state occasions to sing the praises of important personalities', and people would gather to hear him. He died at Ntambozuko in 1945, and people still gather to honour him on the slopes of the hill where a tall memorial column (visible from the road) marks his grave.

Mqhayi was a poet, novelist, historian and translator. He also wrote essays and journalistic articles, biographies and autobiography. His works form a link between oral and literary forms, his outlook a link between traditional Xhosa customs and beliefs and those of Christianity. Many have extolled his knowledge and creative use of the Xhosa language, and his poetry, in particular, earned him great renown in his own day. At first he was called *Imbongi yakwe Gompo* – the Poet of Gompo (a name for part of East London). When it became clear that he was more than a regional writer, he became known as *Imbongi yesiZwe Jikelele* – the Poet of the Race as a Whole – or simply *Imbongi yesiZwe*: the poet of the people.

English translations of Mqhayi's works are few and, of those that exist, not all are easily obtainable; but many of his writings have been described by scholars, making them accessible to non-Xhosa readers, albeit indirectly. *Ityala lamaWele – The Law-suit of the Twins –* was translated and serialised in 1966 in a periodical that has now ceased publication, and sundry translated praise poems appear in anthologies, as do a few pieces of biographical and historical writing. There is also an abbreviated English version of Mqhayi's autobiography – *UMqhayi waseNtambozuko –* 'Mqhayi of the Mount of Glory'.

Mqhayi's autobiography tells of his birth, in 1875, at the village of Gqumushashe in the Tyume Valley and recounts some entertaining incidents from his childhood and early school days in that region. When he was nine years old he moved with his family to Kentani in the Transkei, where he spent six years at the home of his great-uncle. It was an important time for the young Mqhayi, who took an interest in everything around him, learning about Xhosa life and customs and, at the same time, being nurtured in Christian customs and beliefs (for he was a third-generation Christian). He tells us that what interested him most at that time was 'listening to the chief's counsellor, hearing and debating a law-suit'. Out of this experience, combined with two incidents from the Bible, came *Ityala lamaWele (The Law-suit of the Twins)*, published in 1914. Prose, in this work, is punctuated by poetry, and fiction develops into fact in a story that takes on epic proportions and provides an attractive picture of traditional legal procedures.

In 1891 Mqhayi left Kentani to attend Lovedale and, after a few years, moved to a teaching post in East London's West Bank. For the next 30 years teaching, writing and editing were intertwined. He became a subeditor of *Izwi Labantu*, in which his first writings were published, and later editor for two years of *Imvo Zabantsundu*. He taught off and on in East London, Macleantown and Lovedale, contributing much to education and to church life. Throughout, he worked on and published his literary creations and deepened his knowledge of the Xhosa language. Eventually, in about 1925, Mqhayi opted for the independent life of a bard and went to live at Ntambozuko. Never reclusive, he was involved in family, church and community affairs locally and elsewhere, travelling widely and keeping himself informed about the affairs of the day.

The praise poem, or *isibongo*, was Mqhayi's greatest accomplishment. In the traditional form of this declamatory verse, the poet recounts the achievements of a person of importance or celebrates a significant occasion, using eulogistic epithets or 'nicknames' and a good deal of metaphor and repetition. It is not a form in which one normally looks for evidence of a response to place, because the focus is on people or events, but there are suggestions in Mqhayi's verse of an attachment to his surroundings.

In one of the poet's most beautiful praise poems, 'Silimela son of Makinana', the stars play an important role. Jeff Opland explains: 'In this poem Mqhayi praises the Ndlambe chief whom he served as councillor, Silimela, whose name in Xhosa means the Pleiades, a constellation by whose appearance the Xhosa measure the years of manhood following circumcision. Mqhayi glorifies the chief by associating him with this significant constellation, playing on his name, and also by referring to the heroic exploits of Silimela's father Makinana during the last of the frontier wars in 1877.'[2] In his autobiography, *Long Walk to Freedom*, Nelson Mandela recalls a visit Mqhayi made to Healdtown, where he was studying, during which the poet recited 'Silimela'. It was an event, he writes, 'that for me was like a comet streaking across the night sky' and it filled Mandela with pride in his people.

S E K Mqhayi
From Silimela Son of Makinana

Summon the nations, let's apportion the stars:
Let the stars be apportioned.
You Sotho,
Take Canopus,
To share with the Tswana and Chopi,
And all of those nations in loin cloths.
You of KwaZulu,
Take Orion's Belt,
To share with the Swazi, the Chopi and Shangaan,
As well as uncircumcised nations.
You Britons, take Venus,
To divide with the Germans and Boers,
Though you are folk who don't know how to share.
We'll divide up the Pleiades, we peoples of Phalo,
That great group of stars,
For they're stars for counting off years,
For counting the years of manhood,
For counting the years of manhood,
The years of manhood.
I disappear!

in Words That Circle Words

Praise poems may be critical as well as eulogistic and some of Mqhayi's poems
take on a satirical edge, as with that performed for Edward Prince of Wales on
his visit to South Africa in 1925. 'You gave us light; we live in darkness' and
similar phrases express Mqhayi's disappointment in Britain, which had, he
felt, betrayed the interests of its black subjects.

In 'The Sinking of the Mendi' – addressed to the 600 black servicemen who
lost their lives when the ship carrying them to duty in Europe during the First
World War sank in the English Channel – Mqhayi's association of place with
the life of his people is expressed with some poignancy in the third stanza.

S E K Mqhayi
From The Sinking of THE MENDI

You came from your homes and we talked with you;
When you left your children we reached out to you;
Our eyes were wet as we held your hands in ours,
Your fathers groaned, mothers shed bitter tears;
And when you left these mountains and our earth
Your backs turned to the rivers of your birth
Black men of our blood, we said this thing –
'On that far-off shore you are our offering.'

translated by Jack Cope

The poem 'InTaba kaNdoda', written in praise of a small mountain peak near
King William's Town, confirms the importance of nature in Mqhayi's religious
experiences, not for its own sake but for its association in his mind with the
Creator.

S E K Mqhayi
From InTaba kaNdoda

Would that I had tongues, O Mount of my home
O footstool of the God of my fathers,
Thou, whose brow, facing the setting-sun,
Is smitten by the rays of the closing day.
So would I, protected, sing thy praise;
So would I, forsaken, fly to thee,
And kneel in humble prayer by thee,
Who art the stepping-stone between me and my God.
Still shall the aliens stare not understanding,
While, praying, on this slope, I build a ladder,
And scale the vast fatiguing heights, to kiss
The Feet of God the Father – Creator, Most High.

quoted by A C Jordan in an obituary for Mqhayi
published in the South African Outlook,
Sept. 1945

Mqhayi has an interesting link with the South African national anthem, 'Nkosi Sikelel' iAfrika', composed by another person from the Eastern Cape, Enoch Sontonga (1873–1905). Sontonga was born in Uitenhage and educated at Lovedale before moving to Johannesburg. In the 1920s Mqhayi became interested in this hymn, which had gained widespread popularity, and he added seven stanzas to Sontonga's two. The full version was published in 1927.

A star, the sun and the moon are engraved on Mqhayi's memorial on Ntambozuko and it looks out over a view of hills and villages that is typical of the land he loved.

EAST LONDON

The Buffalo River, which we first glimpsed as we entered King William's Town, flows into the sea at East London, where its wide mouth forms South Africa's only river port of economic significance. Together with King William's Town, Bisho (which is the capital of the Eastern Cape) and several smaller towns in the area, East London now constitutes the Buffalo City Municipality. On one hand, East London has an attractive coastal setting characterised by good beaches, lush semitropical vegetation and a series of river-mouth resorts of exceptional beauty either side of the main urban area. There are pleasant suburbs, an excellent museum and many handsome buildings of historical interest. On the other hand, East London's development as a harbour and commercial and industrial centre has imprinted a very different image on its hilly landscape: a conglomerate of factories and businesses, crowded thoroughfares, heavy traffic, and all the other accoutrements of a modern South African city. Mdantsane, where many of the black citizens of Buffalo City live, sprawls over the undulating countryside to the west of East London.

Our tour takes us to Cove Rock, 16 km south-west of central East London, where we shall meet a youth novelist and a writer of children's stories who have used the myths of the locale to bring a literary dimension to this outstanding feature of the coastline. We shall then glimpse early East London as Thomas Baines on his 'solitary journey' in 1849 experienced it, and view the Nahoon and Gonubie area east of the city as seen by William Charles Scully some twenty years later. Parts of a poem and an autobiographical sketch written by a woman from Duncan Village take us into a different world, and our exploration of the East London locale ends with a short poem about Mdantsane and scenes from one of South Africa's best-known books of the second half of the 20th century – Elsa Joubert's *Poppie*.

Cove Rock (Gompo)

The huge bulk of Cove Rock, which the Xhosa call Gompo, looks as though it has risen out of the sea to lie like a beached monster on the very edge of a long sandy stretch of coastline about 16 km from the city centre. It is in two sections, one smooth and domed and covered with stubbly vegetation, the other a tumble of split rocks that appear to have fallen away from the main structure. Between them is a channel of dark swirling water, and on the seaward cliffs of the main rock are two partially submerged caverns into which the sea breaks in a churning froth of waves.

Beryl Bowie
Nola Turkington

Aubrey Elliott, who grew up in the area and gathered information from local people about their customs and legends, explains some of the folklore attached to Cove Rock in *The Magic World of the Xhosa*. Beneath those churning waves the caves are thought to be dry and there the Sea People (or simply the People) live as those on earth, marrying, having children, keeping livestock, growing crops. Their cattle are said to graze on the rock at night; their servant is the monitor lizard who brings balls of dung from the land to smear the walls and floors of the caves just as people's traditional huts are treated. The People are kind and give gifts to earth people – the kind of treasures often gathered along the intertidal zones of a beach – and they, too, like to receive gifts and can become angry when they are not respected. When someone is drowned and the body is not recovered, it is thought that the People have called him or her to be trained as an *ugqirha* who will someday return to practise as a healer. In Xhosa folklore Cove Rock is the dwelling place of the chiefs of the Sea People; in contemporary literature it is the setting of a youth novel and of a children's story, both inspired by the Gompo legends.

Beryl Bowie's 1991 youth novel, *Mystery at Cove Rock*, is set in this neighbourhood:

> In the distance, misty with winter sunshine, loomed the mighty Gompo. The white people called it Cove Rock but that wasn't its proper name. It looked proud and gentle in the afternoon light but Siphiwo knew it was a magic place where, at night, even grown men were afraid to go. His mother had never been near it. As a woman she was even more cautious not to offend the People. Siphiwo slowed down.
>
> The other two caught up with him and it was then that they saw the footprints. They were the prints of a man, deep and dragging as if he had been carrying something heavy. The three boys stared at the footprints in silence.

Rob, newly arrived from England, and Siphiwo, a Xhosa boy, become friends and enjoy fishing together on the rock, until they are caught up in a mystery which nearly costs one of them his life. It is the kind of situation and cross-cultural friendship that are rather common in South African youth novels, but it is well handled by Bowie, and the story is memorable as much for its impressive location and its allusions to Xhosa legend as for its plot.

Legends about the People play their part in *Mystery at Cove Rock*, but it is firmly set in the real rather than the mythological world, and a visit to 'the mighty Gompo' confirms for us the authenticity of every detail of the setting. By contrast, 'Nduku and the Magic Seed', the title story in a collection by NOLA TURKINGTON, takes the children's audience at which it is aimed into the underwater caverns of the Chiefs of the Sea, beautifully imagined by the author.

> Inside the cave was cool and quiet, the air sharp and salty. On the walls, clinging to the smooth dung surface, soft black sea slugs crawled, trailing their eggs like coiled yellow ribbon. Sea anemones, imitating open flowers, clung to the ceiling creating gentle coloured patterns, while great sea ferns, their eight red branches waving slowly, sheltered spiny ghost crabs.

There, Nduku is able to put the healing seeds of the sea, *imbhewu yolwandle*, which she has collected near the rock, to use and win release from the Chiefs of the Sea and the Monitor Lizard.

In 'Nduku and the Magic Seed' Turkington creates a new fictional world from various strands of Xhosa folklore and practice – the collecting of healing plants in the sacred forest of Gulandoda, stories of the Sea People and of Cove Rock (although it is not mentioned by name), the magic power of the seeds of the sea, the training of an *ugqirha*. It is the kind of thing she does with fine sensitivity in a number of her children's books, particularly those based on San stories. Although most of her life has been spent in KwaZulu-Natal, Turkington is captivated by the Eastern Cape, where she has lived since the late 1970s and where most of her writing has been done. The settings and the characters in her stories are drawn from city and country and from different cultural groups. Over 50 books from her pen have delighted children in South Africa and abroad and made a valuable contribution to our literature.

Mystery at Cove Rock was the first of BERYL BOWIE's four youth novels, published in the 1990s. Two of them – *Mystery at Cove Rock* and *Phumlani's Pouch* – are set in the East London area, where the author says that she feels privileged to live. Bowie is a professional writer who specialises in travel articles and short stories for magazines and radio, and she has done much to promote reading and encourage creative writing, especially among disadvantaged children in East London.

The Harbour

East London was set up in 1847 as a landing place for military personnel and supplies. The small town that grew up at this spot was confined at first to the west bank of the Buffalo River. Thomas Baines made his way there in August 1849.

Thomas Baines

> After riding about nine miles more over a beautiful succession of grassy plains and valleys sprinkled with mimosa, I reached the Buffalo; and passing the handsome stone Barrack [Fort Glamorgan], now building, to my left, and the town of East London to my right, offsaddled on the bank of the river, where, having refreshed myself with a bath and made my toilette as well as my means allowed, I sat down under the shade of a thick bush of euphorbia to sketch the river and as much of the town as I could see before entering it.

Later, he views the town through the natural arch of a cave on a sandstone cliff some three miles east of the Buffalo.

> The town of East London was visible in the distance, its little red and white houses contrasting strongly with the green hill beyond, and blue sea below them. The Workington, a brig lying off the mouth of the river, was just beginning to spread her sails to the breeze and in a short time was under weigh, leaving the blue surface of the ocean without a speck to denote that man had traffic upon it.[3]

Today, from Signal Hill high above the sea and river on its east bank, or from the lofty double-storey bridge that spans the Buffalo, the harbour offers one of the Eastern Cape's most dramatic urban scenes. The kind of ship one is likely to observe lying off the river mouth or anchored in this large river port is very different from the *Workington* of Baines's day: perhaps a gigantic carrier loading vehicles from one of the major car manufacturing firms situated on the river's steep west bank, or a tug helping to manoeuvre a graceless container ship through the narrow entrance to the harbour.

Gonubie and Nahoon

In his *Reminiscences of a South African Pioneer*, William Charles Scully – of whom we shall learn more in the next chapter – remembers the Nahoon and Gonubie locale of the late 1860s, when farming families from the hinterland would trek with their stock to the coast for the winter months. Scully writes

W C Scully
Jon Burmeister

in a romantic style that is no longer fashionable, but his description does convey something of the natural beauty of the area. Parts have been set aside as nature reserves, and many of the features Scully recollects have survived urbanisation.

> I often picture the rounded sandhills stretching from the Gonubie Mouth to the Nahoon, with the dark, olive-green boskage that clothed their curves with beauty, and the veil of orange-tinted mystery that at dawn hung like a curtain across that region where sea and sky awaited, breathless, the advent of day. I suppose the placid lagoons still mirror the drifting pageants of cloudland, while the purple kingfishers flit from rock to rock, or poise, fluttering in the air, before they plunge into the crystal water.
>
> I imagine that at windless nightfall the rich, throbbing organ-tones of the Indian Ocean surf fill all the darkling glades. I wonder do the green, flame-winged loories to-day call hoarsely through the aisles of greenery, and the bushbucks bark their angry challenges from the deep and tangled hollows. I wonder do the monkeys, when the forenoon waxes sultry, swing chattering from bough to bough down the hillside, seeking their daily drink in the coolest depths of the kloof, and do the great Nymphalis butterflies, with wings of ochre and pearl, flit among the treetops!

East London's most famous writer of fiction, JON BURMEISTER, who published fifteen bestselling thrillers between 1968 and his death in 2001, lived at Gonubie, but not one of his novels has a local setting because, he maintained, 'a modern thriller must be international to sustain interest.' Yet the Eastern Cape was very close to his heart and one of Burmeister's memories recorded in 1989 in the *Weekend Post* is spending, during his children's formative years, 'every walking moment on Nahoon Beach'. It is, he writes, 'still the best in the world.'[4]

Duncan Village and Mdantsane

In 1998 a creative writing course was held at the Institute for the Study of English in Africa, Rhodes University. Among the work produced during this course and published as *Aerial* are a poem titled 'Born in Gomora' and an autobiographical sketch headed 'Twelve Years: Abuse is All I Know', both written by Buyiswa Mnyamana. They present moving insights into the hardships of life for a black child growing up in and around East London in the 1960s. Mnyamana tells us that she was born in Gomora, a shantytown in Duncan Village in East London.

> It [Duncan Village] was a big location that consisted of a number of shanty towns. Gomora was one of them. Some of the houses looked nice but most were made from old rusted iron sheets. These shanty towns were overcrowded, with very poor environmental conditions. Some streets were tarred, but mostly the streets were untarred and irregular. Few privileged folks owned shops in various areas of the shanty towns. Mostly the population worked in factories in East London: pineapple factories, sweet and fabric factories.

Buyiswa
Mnyamana

Elsa Joubert

Howard Cain

Life in Duncan village was tough, but worse was to come. Buyiswa and a brother and sister are sent to relatives in a rural village, where they are abused and neglected. Eventually their mother takes them back to Duncan Village where their father, a teacher, is addicted to alcohol and their mother has to work as a 'domestic' or a 'labourer' at the pineapple factories to keep the family going. Enrolment as a Girl Guide eventually gives Buyiswa a focus and some basic training in the skills she is later to develop as 'a community nurse, midwife, community builder and developer'. Mnyamana's poem about the extraordinary circumstances of her birth paints an equally convincing picture of a miserable aspect of East London that she is determined to rise above. It concludes:

> Now I understand the turmoil inside me.
> The urge to write about my struggle.
> The urge to write about injustice.
> The deep spiritual conviction in my nature.
> The strange character that I am.
> My everlasting search for justice.

Mdantsane was established in the 1960s as a labour dormitory on the edge of the so-called homeland of Ciskei at a time when the apartheid government was attempting to confine people to designated ethnic districts unless their labour was required in 'white' areas such as East London. Some of the sufferings consequent upon this programme were exposed in a book by Cape Town novelist Elsa Joubert, published in 1978 in Afrikaans as *Die Swerfjare van Poppie Nongena* and translated into English by the author and published in 1980 as *Poppie*. It became a bestseller and changed the racial attitudes of many readers. It has been translated into thirteen languages and adapted as both an Afrikaans and an English play. Recently *Poppie* was voted one of the hundred best 20th-century books from Africa.

The novel is based on the life of a real person, given the fictional name of Poppie Nongena. The facts of the story were related to the author, she explains, by Poppie and members of her family. Joubert welds them into a story that captures the cadences of their speech as well as the strength of their endurance through all the trials and humiliations of life in various parts of South Africa. At one stage Poppie is sent to Mdantsane because she has married a migrant worker from Ciskei. Poppie recounts, with stark simplicity, her first impressions of the embryonic town when she arrives in 1971.

> At first it seemed very raw, that place, says Poppie, because they were new houses. There were rough pieces of cement lying in our way, and the earth was all dug up, and the grass around the house was overgrown. I felt very heartsore because the place was strange and I knew nobody. I felt, really, I'm now quite thrown away. When you get to a strange place it is nice if someone meets you. There I was just put in a new house with my children, but there was nothing there, no people yet in the houses next door, no doors inside, only a front door at the front and a back door at the back. But the house was clean, there were cement floors and panes in the windows, but no ceilings, you had to put them in yourself. There was a water pipe in the kitchen but you yourself had to buy the tap and fix it. The house stood on the slope, there were three steps inside.
>
> Yes, it felt very hard when I walked round the house and saw there was no other person living near us.
>
> We had been put in a desolate place.
>
> Loneliness was all around us.

ELSA JOUBERT was born in Paarl in the Western Cape in 1922. After the publication of her first book in 1956 she became a full-time writer, and her latest work appeared on the eve of her 80th birthday. Many of Joubert's books are about journeys real or symbolic. Her travelogues are considered the best of their kind in Afrikaans. One – *Gordel van Smarag* – is a literary journey to Indonesia in the footsteps of the poet Louis Leipoldt, in which she gains new insights into his poetry, the history of her country and herself as writer. As with *Poppie,* her novels are often built around a journey and deal with the theme of *medemenslikheid* – common humanity.

A different kind of journey is described by Howard Cain in what seems to be his only published poem – 'Mdantsane Daisies' – which appeared in *Under African Skies* in 1998 without biographical note. The reference is to the empty plastic bags that adorn so many parts of South Africa – although recent environmental legislation aims to curb this problem – and the question at the end of the poem has many overtones.

HOWARD CAIN
Mdantsane Daisies

My humble eyes stay down
avoiding their shoes, my shoes
my socks, my right sock
where, lies hidden, my pay –
two hundred and twenty rand.
The young girl next to me, I wonder,
will she get home safe tonight?
The taxi moves and I dare
to look out the window.
There they are, the Mdantsane daisies,
all colours of the rainbow
like washing on a line –
yesterday full and bulging
with bread and samp and milk –
now empty
like my heart.
Respectfully I ask,
'Is this where the journey ends?'

in Under African Skies

12

LAYERS OF LANDSCAPE

AND LITERATURE

THE TRANSKEI

Harold Fehrsen Sampson's poem 'The Wild Coast' provides a poet's eye view of the topography of the whole Transkei. It encompasses the Wild Coast as the region's long coastline is called; the hilly central plateau; and the mountainous north-west. For those who, as the poet says, 'do not know' the Transkei as more than 'a belt of land' there are many surprises and he depicts some of them in finely observed and memorable images. Sampson's poem offers, too, a sense of time, of a land fading into the 'blur of the past'.

HAROLD FEHRSEN SAMPSON
The Wild Coast

Over the wake of the mounding waves
Shouldering shoreward
A belt of land blurs East and West
Rising and falling –

Just that to those who do not know
The rugged beaches vapoured with sheeting foam,
The yellow-wood valleys misted with sea-sound:
Who have not stood in the wood-roped sanctuaries
Webbed with greenbearded age, lit by torn sky
And the flash of jewelled water:
That bountiful stillness spirited with birds
And the vibrant scrutiny of insects:
Who have not climbed to the sun and grass
Overfilled with their waving sleep,
Arced by the sea's blue wonder –

There is a world of waving grass:
White-faced huts looking down on paths and cattle,
On mealie lands without a fence,
Women at work with hoes, bare-breasted,
And over the hill
The chant of young men swinging their way with kerries lifted –
Beyond and beyond, afloat in mirage
Topple the blue peaks of the Drakensberg.

Over the wake of the sidelong waves,
Over the backs of the travelling years
A belt of land fades
Into the blur of the past.

from Selected Poems

We have begun with a poem, but the literature inspired by the Transkei is, on the whole, concerned more with prose than with poetry. It is also a many-layered literature as regards both time and genre. From a pre-literate past come legends, traditional tales and praise poems, and some of these have been transmuted into written forms that have carried through to the present; there are also short stories, novels and autobiographical writings from the 19th and 20th centuries. It is through the imaginative recreations of the material world in such works that we shall view the landscapes of the Transkei: coast-line, plateau and mountains.

LAYER ONE: THE WILD COAST

No road links the many places of interest along the Wild Coast because of the difficulty of traversing the deep valley gorges that typify its immediate hinter-land. One must return to the N2 from time to time and choose another route to the coast to encounter another lovely part of this world. Hiking trails, how-ever, do lead along parts of the coast between the mouths of the Kei and the Mtamvuna rivers. They cross sandy beaches and rocky outcrops; lead past lagoons, through forests and across rivers; pass holiday resorts and villages, and wander through nature reserves. Bird and insect and animal life is as varied as the terrain, but always in the background is the pounding of the sea.

Qolora Mouth

Guy Butler
H I E Dhlomo
M Matshoba
Credo Mutwa
Margaret Gough
Zakes Mda

The first Wild Coast resort across the Kei River is Qolora Mouth, a few kilo-metres from the Gxarha River. Here our literary journey through the Transkei pauses to consider the story of the Xhosa prophetess Nongqawuse. It is a story that changed the course of history not only in the Eastern Cape but for the whole of South Africa. Plays, poems, short stories and recently a novel have focused on the role of the young prophetess in the cattle killing event.

Nongqawuse was the orphaned niece of one of Chief Sarhili's counsellors, Mhlakaza, in whose homestead she lived. It was situated on a hillside near the banks of the Gxarha, a winding rivulet between the lower reaches of the Kei and the Qolora rivers. One day, when collecting water from a pool among the palms and shrubs that overhang the river, the young girl encountered what she believed to be spirits and had conversations with what she called the 'new people'. The dead, they promised, would rise; the people would be provided with new cattle, new corn and many other necessities of life; the sick would be healed and the old made young. The historian J B Peires, who has made a close study of the so-called cattle killing movement, sums up the promises thus: 'peace, plenty and goodness would reign on earth'.[1] The conditions imposed by the 'new people' in order for this happy state to be achieved were that all witchcraft be put away, all cattle killed, all corn destroyed and no new crops planted.

The prophecies are poignantly reiterated in the poetry of Guy Butler's *Pilgrimage to Dias Cross*:

> O Nongqause, O Nongqause! Girl,
> gleaming wet you rose from the pool of Um Gxara.
> You prophesied such victory for the Xhosa!
>
> *Don't harvest your crops! Kill, kill all your cattle!*
> *Our mighty dead with numberless horns will rise,*
> *chanting and lowing, from this river; Umlungu and Mfengu,*
> *all will drown in the sea; old men and women*
> *shall shed their wrinkles and smooth-skinned as I*
> *shall welcome them all with singing and dancing.*

The slaughter of cattle and destruction of crops consequent upon these prophecies led to the death by starvation and disease of an estimated 40 000 Xhosa people as well as cattle deaths of about 400 000, and the loss of 600 000 acres of tribal land to the Cape Colony. Some 150 000 people entered the colony in search of food and most became permanently dependent on the white colonists for a living. Figures are inadequate to describe the human suffering and social consequences of this event, through which the independence of the proud and powerful Xhosa nation was lost.

Many Xhosa people believed, as some do to this day, that the whole thing was a plot by the Cape governor, Sir George Grey, to break their power; Grey and many of the colonists believed that it was a plot by the chiefs to foment

war. Peires finds no evidence to support either of these theories, although he shows that Grey manipulated the situation. It seems that the cattle killing event was probably the result of a tragic delusion, but there were powerful reasons why people believed and acted on the promises relayed to the chiefs by Nongqawuse's uncle, Mhlakaza. Among the reasons was an outbreak of lungsickness that was decimating the herds of many of the clans and the belief that this plague was a result of the displeasure of the ancestors. There was also a general feeling of despair, as every effort that had been made to win back land lost to the white colonists or to prevent their further expansion had resulted only in further loss of land and power. Although driving whites into the sea was not, Peires maintains, one of the prophecies, in the perfect world predicted for the Xhosa the colonists would probably have had no place.

Complicated reasons made some of the Xhosa into 'believers' (*amathamba*) who believed the prophecies and killed their cattle and destroyed their crops, and some into 'unbelievers' (*amagogotya*) who refused to do so. In Zakes Mda's novel *The Heart of Redness* these two viewpoints persist 150 years after the event, the Believers still blaming the Unbelievers for the failure of the prophecies, for – when the day of promised renewal and resurrection came – nothing happened. Even after a second day was posited as the great day, nothing happened. Disaster was inevitable.

A 1935 play by H I E Dhlomo, *The Girl Who Killed to Save*, which highlights the plight of the human victims of the disaster; a highly coloured reconstruction of the story in Credo Mutwa's *Africa is My Witness* (1966), in which the 'voices' are those of agents planted by the governor: and a 1981 short story by Mtutuzeli Matshoba are among a number of literary attempts to explain how such a disastrous event could have come about. In Matshoba's imaginative reworking of Nongqawuse's story within another story – 'Three Days in the Land of a Dying Illusion' – the prophecies come to her as voices in the mind because of her great concern for the plight of her people and her longing for the return of the prophet Makana to save them. Although Matshoba had not seen the Gxarha when he wrote the story, he conveys a good sense of the kind of place in which a young girl might have dreamed the impossible.

The topography of Nongqawuse's pool on the Gxarha may well have played a part in the cattle killing event. Dappled sunlight playing over large stones that lie on the riverbed and the reflections of the palms and other riverine plants that overhang the water help to create an air of mystery. The wind whispers through the surrounding bush and birdcalls sometimes pierce the air.

Perhaps Nongqawuse thought, like many of her people, that she sensed the presence of *abantu bamlambo* – the river people – a thought which enhances for the visitor the notion that this is a place of spirits. Other features of the landscape may also have had a role in convincing people of Nongqawuse's story. Mhlakaza's homestead, a little distance from the pool, looks across a valley towards a river winding among trees at the foot of a steep incline towards the sea, from which mists often blow inland. Dolphins may have swum into the mouth or cavorted in the waves close to shore, seeming to those unfamiliar with the sea to be people rising from it. Some of those who came to Mhlakaza's homestead to verify what he said his niece had seen may have observed what they expected to see – the 'new people' walking on the hillside or rising from the sea.

Among the mysteries of the cattle killing event is the fate of Nongqawuse. Many in her homestead, including Mhlakaza, died of starvation but she was handed over to the magistrate, Major J C Gawler, and eventually taken to Cape Town with her cousin, Nonkosi, who had supported her in the prophecies. There they were confined in the Paupers' Lodge and one of them was subsequently returned to East London. Tradition has it that Nongqawuse settled on a farm in the Alexandria district, where our literary journey through those parts includes a visit to the grave. Her fantasy world, if that is what it was, had brought appalling suffering to her people, both immediate and long-term, but to many she is a figure to be pitied rather than vilified: a deluded child and the agent of forces greater than herself. Margaret Gough conveys the pathos of her situation in a long poem, 'Nonquase'. The last two stanzas sum it up:

> Far from the huts on the hillside
> where the aloes point hands to the sky
> lonely may I linger
> an outcast may I die
> if the Word I give you
> from these chosen lips should lie.
>
> Heavy upon Nonquase
> lie the voices of the dead
> as the weight of the vessel
> drawn full from the river
> weighs the Word upon my head.[2]

Zakes Mda's novel *The Heart of Redness* (2000), which interweaves Nongqawuse's story with one focusing on contemporary life in the vicinity of her home, is in every way an excellent evocation of this corner of the Transkei, whose landscape, history and traditions – as well as some of its present-day problems – feature in the story. The principal setting is Qolorha-by-Sea, parallel in many of its details to Qolora itself. Artistic freedom, however, allows the author to concertina features of the landscape together or move them to suit the dictates of the story, as in this overall view of the locale.

> Bhonco drags his gumboots up the hillock to the trading store. His brown overalls are almost threadbare at the elbows and at the knees. He wears a green woollen hat that the people call a skullcap. He does not carry a stick as men normally do.
>
> Under his breath he curses the trader for building his store on the hill. But the breathtaking view from the top compensates for the arduous

climb. Down below, on his right, he can see the wild sea smashing gigantic waves against the rocks, creating mountains of snow-white surf. On his left his eyes feast on the green valleys and the patches of villages with beautiful houses painted pink, powder blue, yellow and white.

Most of the houses are rondavels. But over the years a new architectural style, the hexagon, has developed. On the roofs of these voguish hexagons, corrugated iron appears under the thatch, like a petticoat that is longer than the dress. This is both for aesthetic reasons and to stop the termites. But Bhonco does not believe in this newfangled fashion of building hexagons instead of the tried and tested rondavel.

From where he stands he can see the Gxarha River and the Intlambo-ka-Nongqawuse – Nongqawuse's Valley. He can also see Nongqawuse's Pool and the great lagoon that is often covered by a thick blanket of mist.

Bhonco, who has revived the cult of the Unbelievers, has lived in the village most of his life. 'Yet', we are told, 'he is always moved to tears by its wistful beauty.' It is, indeed, a moving place with a spirit of its own.

Elsewhere in the novel we view the place through Camagu, an outsider.

As Camagu drives his Toyota Corolla on the gravel road he concludes that a generous artist painted the village of Qolorha-by-Sea, using splashes of lush colour. It is a canvas where blue and green dominate. It is the blue of the skies and the distant hills, of the ocean and the rivers that flow into it. The green is of the meadows and the valleys, the tall grass and the usundu palms.

Mda, himself an artist with brush as well as pen, pictures the place for the reader as he experienced it during a few weeks in 1998 spent at a local resort while researching the background to his novel.

One of the most memorable scenes in the novel is the picture Mda's paints of the home of Zim, the traditionalist – the Believer.

The wild fig tree knows all his secrets. It is his confessional. Under it he finds solace, for it is directly linked to the ancestors – all of Twin's progeny who planted it more than a hundred years ago. Now the trunk is as big as his main hut. As soon as it leaves the ground its branches twist and turn in all directions, spreading wide like an umbrella over his whole homestead. Some branches reach as far as the top of the umsintsi trees –

the coral tree that used to be called kaffirboom during the Middle Generations – and the aloes that surround his yard.

Everyone in Qolorha knows that if you want Zim you will find him under his wild fig tree. He spends most of the day dozing under it, listening to the song of the birds. Neither season nor weather deters him from indulging in this pleasure. He is there in autumn when the tree sheds its leaves, and he is faithful to it even when it remains naked during the winter. When the urge to commune with the tree is strong enough, not even the cold wind from the sea can drive him into the house.

There are four different kinds of ancestors: the ancestors of the sea, the ancestors of the forest, the ancestors of the veld, and the ancestors of the homestead. They are all regular visitors to this tree.

Today the spring weather is particularly beautiful. Green leaves are shyly beginning to appear on the tree. The green pigeons, with their red legs and red beaks, are flying around. Soon they will be feeding on the wild figs that will be ready even before summer. The amahobohobo weaverbirds are adding more nests to the city that is already dangling and would be weighing the tree down if it had not gathered so much strength over the generations.

Hundreds of birds inhabit this tree. Perhaps thousands. People think it is foolish of the Believer to be so close to so much meat without killing even a single bird for supper.

ZANEMVULA KIZITO GATYENI (ZAKES) MDA was born in 1948 at Sterkspruit in the Herschel district of the Eastern Cape, not far from the birthplace of Olive Schreiner. A passage in *The Heart of Redness* seems to have autobiographical overtones.

Camagu is filled with a searing longing for an imagined blissfulness of his youth. He has vague memories of his home village, up in the mountains in the distant inland parts of the country. He remembers the fruit trees and the graves of long-departed relatives. He can see dimly through the mist of decades all the lush plants that grew in his grandfather's garden, including aloes of different types. There are the beautiful houses too: the four-walled tin-roofed ixande, the rondavels, the cattle kraal, the fowl-run, the tool shed ... So many things in Qolorha bring back long-forgotten images.

The Mda family moved to Johannesburg soon after his birth, and Zakes Mda grew up in Orlando East and Dobsonville. He returned to the district during his teenage years, first to visit grandparents and later to attend school there. His father was, for a while, a lawyer in Sterkspruit but in 1963 went into exile in Lesotho, closely followed by his wife and children.

At school in Lesotho, Mda began to write plays and his interest in theatre led to a bachelor's degree in visual arts and literature from a Swiss university, a master's degree in theatre from Ohio State University in the United States and a doctorate from the University of Cape Town. Between 1979 and 1989 Mda wrote six major plays. He has held teaching posts at universities in Lesotho, the United Kingdom, the United States and South Africa and been involved in several theatre projects, particularly where they encourage developmental skills.

Mda's renown as a playwright extends to poetry and to painting, to film, television, newspaper articles and criticism. In 1995 he published two novels: *She Plays with Darkness* and *Ways of Dying*. *The Heart of Redness* came out in 2000. Among them these novels have won five prestigious literary awards. In *The Heart of Redness* Mda returns to his Xhosa roots and to the landscapes of the Transkei. His extensive knowledge of literature gives the novel its own kind of literary layering. There are overtones not only of Joseph Conrad's *Heart of Darkness*, but also of S E K Mqhayi's *The Law-suit of the Twins*, set at nearby Kentani, and A C Jordan's *The Wrath of the Ancestors*, with its Transkei setting and similar conflict between traditional and 'school' adherents. There are also references to the kind of legends that permeate much Transkei literature.

Hole in the Wall

Known in English as Hole in the Wall and in Xhosa as esiKhaleni – place of sound – a wall of rock topped with an uneven covering of grass and scrub and completely surrounded by sea stands just offshore at the mouth of the Mpako River about 8 km south of Coffee Bay. An archway at the wall's base has been formed over millions of years by the action of waves on some of its softer rocks, and it is not surprising that a legend explaining this astonishing formation should have evolved.

In the remote past – so the story goes – a beautiful young girl from a nearby village fell in love with one of the Sea People, who emerged from the waves near the lagoon on the landward side of what was a solid wall of rock. He wished her to go with him as his bride to the underwater world of his people, but her father forbade her ever to go near the water again. One night, when the tide was high, the Sea People brought to the site a giant fish, which battered a hole through the rock with its powerful head. As the Sea People poured through the gap in the wall, everyone except the lovesick maiden fled the scene and the invaders returned to their watery world, taking her with them. Sometimes, when the seas are rough and the wind blows fiercely, the chanting of the Sea People may be heard, but the maiden has never been seen again.

Abelungu country

W C Scully   Legends of a different kind are associated with the country to the north-west of Hole in the Wall in the Mqanduli district and at the mouth of the Xora where, in association with the Tshomane clan, there are pockets of people who call themselves the Abelungu – a term usually used for white people. They claim descent from a person or persons of European origin cast ashore from a wrecked ship during the 18th century. Details of the story vary, some Abelungu claiming descent from a man who goes by various names including Bhati and Jekwa, others from his sister or daughter known as Gguma. Lambasi on the Pondoland coast, where the Tshomane people had at one time lived, features in some of the traditions. This suggests a connection with the *Grosvenor*, wrecked there in 1782. William Charles Scully weaves the story as he heard it into a short story – 'Gquma: or, the White Waif'.

Scully begins his tale with an actual event in an actual setting. He is fishing with a companion of the Tshomane clan, Nqalate.

> The fish had been biting splendidly since midnight, and when at dawn we ran the boat into a little creek which branched from the main lagoon between steep, shelving, rocky banks overhung with forest, we counted out eleven 'kabeljouws,' the lightest of which must have weighed fifteen pounds, while the heaviest would certainly have turned the scale at fifty.

It is a scene such as any Wild Coast fisherman might enjoy. The morning is cool and bracing. A flock of wild geese flies landwards, ospreys settle on a giant euphorbia, and the sounds of other birds and creatures of the forest are heard. As Scully says, 'Fishing usually affords large opportunities for reflection or conversation' and, as their boat drifts across a lagoon, Nqalate tells the author the story of Gquma, which Scully then visualises in his own mind and recreates in fictional form. It is the story of the 'white waif' cast on shore from the wreck of a ship from which there are, according to his version, no other survivors. Scully pictures for his readers a little white girl with long yellow hair found in a cleft in the black reef against which the ship has struck. She is nurtured by the local people and in due course marries the son of their chief. After the death of her father-in-law she, rather than her husband, is regarded as the leader of the tribe. She dies leaving a daughter she calls Bessie – a name that persists in all the stories – and her body is returned to the sea at the edge of the black reef where she was found.

Scully's story 'Gquma' was originally published in 1897 in *The White Hecatomb*. In 1984 a selection of stories from that collection and two others was published as *Transkei Stories*, a publication that helped to revive some interest in an almost forgotten South African writer.

WILLIAM CHARLES SCULLY was born in Dublin in 1855 and came to South Africa with his parents at the age of twelve. At fourteen he ran away from his home in King William's Town to the diamond fields in Kimberley, moving on to the gold fields in Barberton and to Mozambique before returning to the Eastern Cape. There, in 1876, he joined the Cape administration, retiring as a civil servant only in 1914. During that time he worked in Namaqualand and in towns scattered throughout what is now the Eastern Cape, including the Transkei. Scully was an enlightened administrator who, in posts of increasing responsibility, practised an authoritative but sympathetic kind of paternalism towards the people under his jurisdiction. In the course of his duties he gathered local stories and legends as well as personal experiences, which, in many cases, he transformed into imaginative literature.

Scully had very little formal schooling but he read voraciously – the Bible, the works of Shakespeare, and many other classical works of literature or history. Among his special interests were languages, botany and philosophy, and from travelling around the magisterial districts under his jurisdiction Scully also acquired a knowledge of the people and places he encountered.

From 1894 to 1898 Scully was stationed in the Transkei, first at Mount Frere in the north and then further south at Nqamakwe. He travelled, usually on horseback, to many parts of the territory, often lodging with local people and sharing their way of life and their stories. These stories come to us filtered through Scully's western perceptions and flavoured with a somewhat patronising tone. They provide, nevertheless, some excellent illustrations of the topography of a much wider range of Transkei sites than recorded by any other literary figure, giving glimpses into the way of life and customs of both a civil servant of the time and the people for whom he assumed responsibility. We shall meet him again among the mountains of Mount Frere later in this chapter.

Scully published two volumes of poetry and five of short stories, besides three novels and various non-fictional works. His poetry is undistinguished, but some of his short stories have an enduring quality. His memoirs – published in 1913 as *Reminiscences of a South African Pioneer* and *Further Reminiscences of a South African Pioneer* – chronicle life as experienced by a liberal colonial in the Cape in the last decades of the 19th century and the first of the 20th. His obvious taste for new scenes brings to life many of the places in the Eastern Cape to which he was posted. Scully's last novel, *Daniel Vananda*, focused on some of the suffering caused by the 1913 Native Land Act. No new works were published between that year – the year prior to Scully's retirement as chief magistrate of Port Elizabeth – and his death on the Natal South Coast in 1923.

Coastline and ocean

Geoffrey Jenkins
Sheila Fugard

As with Scully's story 'Gquma', Geoffrey Jenkins's *Scend of the Sea* (1971) has its genesis in the story of a shipwreck off the Wild Coast, but it is a work of a very different kind – a bestselling adventure novel.

The facts Jenkins transmutes into fiction are the disappearance in 1909 of the liner *Waratah* with 211 persons on board somewhere south of the mouth of the Bashee River, the mysterious disappearance of a Viscount aircraft in the same area in 1967 and the less mysterious loss of a Buccaneer plane at about the same time. Despite extensive research and several attempts to locate the *Waratah*, no trace of her has ever been found. In 1999 a ship lying on the seabed was confidently declared to be the *Waratah* but it proved to be another vessel, so the search continues.

Out of these facts Jenkins creates *Scend of the Sea*. As readers follow the events he recounts, they observe the Wild Coast from the sea and, in several powerful storm sequences, they view the sea itself, not from the shore as we have seen it on our journeys along the Eastern Cape coast but from the much more intimate position of a storm-battered ship.

> Through my binoculars I examined the shoreline and investigated every splendid headland. The bland sea smiled back with Oriental impenetrability. At length, off the Bashee Mouth itself where *Waratah* was last sighted, I could find no excitement. It was a calm, uncomplicated, beautiful day. It held no mysteries, no deaths. It was a passageway of ships on their lawful business, and ashore the holidaymakers and fisherman went about their holiday occasions.

Off Port St Johns where *Waratah* exchanged her last signals with the ship *Clan*

Macintyre, it is equally calm, and Ian Fairlie, the novel's protagonist, is distracted by the sight of the 'splendid 1200-foot cliffs topped by forests' that guard the river mouth. On the return voyage southward out of Durban the mood changes and Jenkins interlaces his narrative with seascapes that reinforce the excitement.

> I was taken aback at the wildness of the scene. I was aware that this type of storm developed rapidly, and that its storm centre moved equally quickly, but it was nevertheless startling to see it happening before my very eyes. To the south-west, towards East London, the sky was a curious purple-black over the land, and night-black out to sea. It was like looking from a space-ship at the dividing line between night and day on earth. The dying sun was able to create a lightness over the land, but the sea-black was relentless, ominous. Between *Walvis Bay* and the great blackness was a kind of no-man's-land of wind-torn sky and cloud flying at impossible speeds; these were the outriders of the main army of the storm, the light armour probing with quick thrusts the *Waratah's* battlefield of death. All round *Walvis Bay* the seas leaned to a plume of spindrift; they were not so high as steep, a sure sign that the general engagement with the Agulhas Current still lay ahead; the counter-current was still testing the enemy's defences.

This storm builds up to a climax involving the great downward plunge of a wave – the 'scend' of the novel's title, but the mystery is not solved and the journey has to be repeated. The reader once again views the coast, so faithfully described by Jenkins, who is said to have visited every location in which he sets a story.

> It was perfect fair-weather yachting and some of the tension seemed to ebb from us as we absorbed the soporific magic and she ghosted along. We had breathtaking glimpses of black, iron-bound cliffs topped by great forests, for which the territory is famous; we could pick out, by their lofty whiteness like ships' spars, the straight trunks of the *umzimbeet* trees among their darker companions; fragile lagoons came and went at sunset with the chimerical loveliness of an old Chinese print on silk; tree euphorbias hung out stark candelabra of branches against great cliffs and begged to be photographed; here and there the lush strelitzias would over-arch a river mouth with sensuous, tropical beauty, a frame for secret mangrove swamps behind, trodden not by human foot but by the claws of giant crabs as big as soup plates.

Jenkins clearly has a strong sense of place and knows how to use it to create atmosphere, be it one of calm or one of tension.

GEOFFREY JENKINS was born in Port Elizabeth in 1920 but grew up in Potchefstroom. He became a journalist and worked in London, for a time under James Bond author, Ian Fleming; in Salisbury (Harare), where he met Eve Palmer, whom he was to marry; and in Pretoria, where they settled and both devoted themselves to writing. He died in Durban in 2001.

He produced sixteen novels, all of them bestsellers. Ships and the sea were a lifelong interest and many of his novels are filled with the sounds and sights of the sea and with knowledgeable but never boring details about ships and the technicalities of sailing. Jenkins came from a long line of lighthouse-keepers in Wales and his great-grandfather ran a shipping line between Cornwall and the Cape. Always interested in travel both literarily and on the page – he said that writing a book was like going on a journey – Jenkins co-authored *The Companion Guide to South Africa* with Eve Palmer, in 1978. He and Eve spent a good deal of time at Cranemere, her old home in the Karoo, yet *Scend of the Sea* is Jenkins's only work set in the Eastern Cape. In it he makes every incident and every feature of the setting live on the page.

> I have always known shipwreck. Deep inside, I know the foundering of the self and the voices of the castaways of the East Indiaman, *The Berkley*, foundering off the coast of Pondoland.

These are the opening words of Sheila Fugard's novel *The Castaways*, published in 1972 just a year after Geoffrey Jenkins's *Scend of the Sea*. It also has at its kernel a Wild Coast shipwreck, but is a literary work of a very different order.

The wreck Fugard calls *The Berkley* is clearly suggested by the *Grosvenor*, an English East Indiaman that ran aground in 1782 on the sharp rocks of Lambasi Bay, which is situated between Port St Johns and Port Edward, just south of what is today known as Port Grosvenor. It carried 150 crew and passengers and was rumoured to have on board a valuable cargo of coins and gems and to be transporting one of the great treasures of the east – the Peacock Throne of Persia. There have been many attempts at salvage and, until recently, all that has been recovered is some coins and a few cannons and other rusted artefacts. Work continues with greater hope of success but, like *Waratah*, the *Grosvenor* has its mysteries. Unlike it, the *Grosvenor* had many survivors – the castaways of Fugard's novel. Only eighteen, however, of the 128 souls who set out to walk to the Cape reached their destination and the fates of many of them, in particular the women, have never been established.

Stories real and imagined of the trials of the castaways of the *Grosvenor* have inspired several literary works, of which Fugard's novel is the most profound. It looks at the event and its implications, immediate and long-term, through many eyes, and unobtrusively creates a sense of the rather bleak stretch of the Transkei coast where the *Grosvenor* lies buried under shifting sands.

The principal voice in the novel is that of a patient who escapes for a time from the Port Berkley Mental Hospital to search for connections with the wreck of *The Berkley*, with which he seems obsessed. His is an inner journey although, at times, it seems to be happening in the real setting of the locale where the *Grosvenor* was wrecked – a beach where there are 'gulls, the fiercely agitated sea and the burning sand'. The shells he gathers there and strings around his neck relay the sound of voices from the past: those of the captain of the ship; a runaway slave encountered on the way; a local chief; a missionary; an explorer. All are based on characters associated with *Grosvenor* stories or with other incidents in the past of the Transkei.

Christiaan Jordan (we learn his name only towards the end of the novel) draws a map on which he marks places associated with these people and sets out to meet them, explaining, in his confused state, his motivation.

> Perhaps it was the full moon, a peculiar torpor to the sea, or simply the map growing inside me like a geographical tape worm proliferating paths in all directions, radiating from the one dynamic centre of ship-wreck.

With each imagined encounter the patient identifies with the person he meets; he re-lives the wreck; he even identifies with the rusty artefacts discovered near the site where it occurred ('my joints are rusty too'). An unexpected discovery of a site not on his map is a cave in which hides a present-day 'terrorist' with whom he also comes to identify.

Often present on the journey is the enigmatic Buddhist who is, perhaps, guiding him to some resolution of his identity, which is also the identity of anyone who has come by whatever means at whatever period to the shores of Africa. All are castaways, the author seems to say.

Fugard's style encompasses the use of various kinds of writing in creating the fabric of her novel. Interspersed with the mental patient's narrative are news reports, eyewitness accounts of the wreck and the journey south, excerpts from the ship's log, letters, missionary and traveller impressions of early encounters with Africa, instructions from a revolutionary's military manual. The novel is a kaleidoscope of viewpoints and voices and impressions of the landscape. At times the landscape is interior – 'I am an explorer of the inner space, that part of the mind that throws up images' – at others it is exterior – 'I know only what the eye can see – the grain of rock, the foam of the sea, the single green strand of energy penetrating the sand, a rough thought of grass'. The intimate connections between persons and objects in the environment is beautifully expressed.

> The Buddhist comes out of the mirror again, an oriental blending with the sand. He is the dryness of leaves, the wetness of stones, the touch of petals, the dry smoke of an unspoken spirituality. He turns a minute of eternity upon the prayer wheel of his heart, and I swing keenly into the solar rhythm.

In Zen Buddhism – a form of spirituality Sheila Fugard practises – the search, through meditation, for satori, or enlightenment, can involve a koan, which is a mental stumbling block or riddle that must be solved to the satisfaction of a spiritual guide. *The Castaways* is in itself like a koan. It is puzzling, confusing, sometimes frustrating as the reader tries to disentangle the different voices and viewpoints, distinguish the real from the imagined, and sanity from madness. There is, however, much in it that is beautiful, especially in the imaginative delicacy of some of the author's poetic passages.

> The saffron figure bars the entrance to the cave. The Buddhist has outstripped me. I had forgotten him, and now he bars my way. I walk through his yellow compassion, and he breaks apart into a thousand butterflies that weave in front of me, filling the cave with a strange sound of muted wings and an overpowering scent. I beat my way through the butterflies of light into the darkness of Choma.

Meaning may be elusive, but what is certain in the novel is that everything radiates from 'the one dynamic centre of shipwreck'. It is the known shipwreck of the *Grosvenor*, the fate of the fictional wreck of *The Berkley* and of the castaways.

THE SECOND LAYER: THE PLATEAU

The Umtata District

NELSON ROLIHLAHLA MANDELA was born in 1918 at the village of Mvezo on the banks of one of the Transkei's major rivers, the Mbashe, near its intersection with the N2 about halfway between Butterworth and Umtata. He describes Mvezo in his autobiography, *Long Walk to Freedom*, as 'a tiny precinct removed from the world of great events'. It is still a tiny precinct where one can look out from a contemplation platform over the Transkei landscape and reflect on the life of one of the world's great statesmen. A little nearer to the Transkei capital of Umtata is the village of Qunu, where Mandela now has his home and where he spent the early and, he says, happiest years of his childhood. It was, he writes, 'From these days I date my love of the veld, of open spaces, the simple beauties of nature, the clean line of the horizon.' After the death of his father when he was nine years old, Rolihlahla (he was given the name Nelson only when he went to school) left Qunu to go to Mqhekezweni, the Great Place of Chief Jongintaba Dalindyebo, to be brought up as a prospective counsellor.

> I packed the few things that I possessed and early one morning we set out on a journey westward to my new residence. I mourned less for my father than for the world I was leaving behind. Qunu was all that I knew, and I loved it in the unconditional way that a child loves his first home. Before we disappeared behind the hills, I turned and looked for what I imagined was the last time at my village. I could see the simple huts and the people going about their chores; the stream where I had splashed and played with the other boys; the maize fields and green pastures where the herds and flocks were lazily grazing. I imagined my friends out hunting for small birds, drinking the sweet milk from the cow's udder, cavorting in the pond at the end of the stream. Above all else, my eyes rested on the three simple huts where I had enjoyed my mother's love and protection. It was these three huts that I associated with all my happiness, with life itself, and I rued the fact that I had not kissed each of them before I left. I could not imagine that the future I was walking towards could compare in any way with the past that I was leaving behind.

Mandela's road led through the Regent's court at Mqhekezweni, the Methodist school at Clarkebury in the same district, Healdtown College near Fort Beaufort, and Fort Hare University at Alice before it left the Eastern Cape. Apart from a brief visit in 1955 he was not to return to the scenes of his child-

Nelson Mandela
Dene Coetzee

hood until after his release in 1990 from 27 years in prison. He says that he has 'always believed that a man should have a home within sight of the house where he was born'. It is a privilege not accorded many people in today's scattered societies, but Nelson Mandela has returned home and built a house at Qunu. The village has become a place of pilgrimage for many people who respect Mandela as statesman and philosopher. He also deserves respect as a writer who depicts the life of his people and his times with clarity, often in the context of the physical world which encompasses them and which, as someone confined for so many years to an alien place – Robben Island – he deeply appreciates.

In the Nelson Mandela Museum situated in Umtata, the story of Mandela's life and of the steps leading to South Africa's multicultural democracy is told through word and artefact. It is housed in the Bhunga (council) building, built in the classical style in 1930, which from then on was the seat of government of one kind or another.

The release of Mandela from prison in 1990 brought a flurry of poetry to the Transkei – the kind of poetry that is an important layer of Transkei literature – praise poetry. Praise poetry – *isibongo* – is not only a skill of the past, but also a living art form which is practised in many contemporary situations. We have seen how Ntsikana adapted it to Christian worship and how Mqhayi's praise poems were sometimes written down. It is essentially a kind of performance poetry dependent on gesture, tone of voice, audience response and an appreciation of its context. It is also, in most cases, performed in Xhosa, so it comes to an English readership at two removes: those of translation and transcription. Two scholars in particular, Jeff Opland and Russell Kaschula, have helped to put it on the literary map of those who are unfamiliar with Xhosa. We cannot leave the Eastern Cape without viewing it in some small way through the eyes of an *imbongi* – a praise poet.

Praises are heaped on people of importance; on organisations; on sports teams; in religious terms, on God; but not, it seems, on the landscape as such. The closest one can get to a response to the material world in this kind of poetry is the use it makes – often as hyperbole – of animal and cosmic imagery.

Three short excerpts from praise poems in honour of Mandela give some idea of this aspect of their metaphorical language. The first, from one of the Eastern Cape's most renowned practitioners of the art, David Yali-Manisi, was composed in 1954, nearly ten years before Mandela's imprisonment. Even then he is seen as so powerful that he sets rivers roaring, mountains shaking, the earth trembling. Other images are more local: he is a tall secretary bird, or one who clears a way through thorn bushes, and there is a connection with Xhosa mythology in the reference to a river-snake – probably the powerful *Mamlambo* of folklore:

> The world is shaking, sirs!
> The rivers are roaring,
> The mountains are shaking restlessly,
> Mighty nations are stunned;
> Because small nations are shuffling in agitation,
> They are bursting, they are shaking.
> Indeed the world is trembling.
> Indeed the world is trembling.
>
> Aa! Earth tremor!
> The world-shaker is the black one of Mandela,
> The black vibrant one from Sokhawulela
> From Dlomo, from Ngqolomsila,
> The secretary bird from Hala, so tall it stoops at Hala's home,
> The one with strength, the strong iron rod from Ndaba.
>
> The chopper who chops things in thorny bushes,
> Clearing away the darkness of ignorance;
> The one who helps the world to operate;
> The one who towers above the whole world;
> The one who engulfs it like a river-snake.
> The black river-snake that swims in the Vaal River,
> And only goes to drink in the River;
> The servant of the African nations.[3]

In this excerpt from an *isibongo* by the Rev. Lordwyk Xozwa, Mandela is imaged (as he is in a number of other contexts) as one of the most prized animals in Xhosa society – an ox. It was composed at the time of his release in 1990, an event so important that it 'clears the sky'.

> That ox of Bhalizulu was finally released and the sky cleared!
> Because the son of De Klerk disregarded his nations' laws because they
>   were not from heaven
> He opened the prison doors wide, the heavens opened,
> Africans went home led by the ox of Qunu from Bhalizulu.[4]

In Bongani Sitole's 1991 praise poem, Mandela is both domestic animal (a raging bull) and a wild animal so powerful that it causes the stars to fall down.

Hail Dalibhunga! Words of truth have been exposed.
He's the bull that kicks up dust and stones and breaks antheaps,
He's the wild animal that stares at the night sky,
Until the stars fall down.[5]

—

Winds of Change (1995) by Dene Coetzee is a popular novel set partly in Mandela's Transkei – Qunu, Mqhekezweni and Umtata. Although Nelson Mandela, F W de Klerk, Thabo Mbeki and a few other real characters appear briefly, most of the novel's characters are fictitious. It dashes through South Africa's history from the 1950s to the 1990s, telling the story of two sons of a white farmer from Paarl in the Western Cape, one of whom has a white, the other a black mother. They grow up in ignorance of each other's existence – Themba in Mqhekezweni, the royal kraal of the Thembu people of the Transkei where Mandela himself had grown up; Pierre on a prosperous farm near Paarl – and the action of the novel alternates between their two worlds.

Place is not delineated in any detail – Coetzee says that he doesn't write 'literary prose with flowery descriptions' – but he does make the reader aware, through incidental remarks in the narrative, of exactly where they are as the action moves rapidly from place to place. The author explains that 'once he has written a first draft, he visits the places where he has set his story, gets to grips with the location and then goes home and rewrites'.[6] This process certainly helps to make the multiple settings of *Winds of Change* believable.

Coetzee's recreation of the Transkei is not as convincing as that of Jordan in *The Wrath of the Ancestors*, as we shall see – Coetzee is writing from the outside, Jordan from the inside – but *Winds of Change* does give the modern reader, particularly one not familiar with the terrain, some important insights into the landscape and the way of life of this part of the Eastern Cape.

The variety of huts and houses scattered over the hills of the Transkei is one of the region's most memorable characteristics, and the Transkei sections of Coetzee's novel picture a typical Xhosa village: 'a cluster of identical circular buildings – mud brick walls plastered with a mixture of cow dung and soil and painted with white clay', each hut thatched with grass. Several typical activities, such as building and ploughing, are enacted in the course of the story.

The first spring rains brought welcome relief to the Transkei. The dry, red grass came to life and the rolling hills took on an emerald-green countenance.

Every patch of cultivated land was a hive of activity from dawn to sunset. Led by young boys, teams of long-horned, hump-necked oxen toiled up and down the fields. Yokes strained at the drag of the ploughs, manned by the men, as they guided the sharp ploughshares into the earth, turning over the rich, loamy soil. Older men walked alongside, cracking long whips over the backs of oxen to keep them moving forward.

Once Wilson had ploughed his allotted lands, he levelled them with a multi-tooth drag harrow, breaking up the clods to form a fine tilth in which to plant the mealies. Youths with sharpened sticks made holes in the soft soil. Wilson followed, accurately dropping a seed into each hole, stamping the soil and covering the seed.

There are also descriptions of initiation ceremonies – for both girls and boys – of lobola negotiations and of a wedding, all adding to the Transkei flavour of those parts of *Winds of Change* that focus on Themba. The theme of reconciliation of the apparently irreconcilable, both personal and national, is enhanced by helping the reader to see contrasting settings and ways of life.

DENE COETZEE was born in Port Elizabeth in 1944 and grew up in the Eastern Cape before attending Cedara College of Agriculture in KwaZulu-Natal. He now lives near Paarl where he is a nurseryman and stud sheep breeder who has devoted much of his time to organisations that serve the community. *Winds of Change*, which in 1996 won a Commonwealth Writers' Prize for best first novel in the Africa region, is Coetzee's only published novel to date. The poet Lynne Bryer was his sister.

LAYER THREE: MOUNTAINS

Three mountainous districts of the Transkei – Encgobo, about 80 km west of Umtata; Tsolo, about 40 km north of it; and Mount Frere, another 60 km to the north-east – have found their way into literature either as settings for fiction or as re-creations through personal reminiscences.

Engcobo

Joan Broster, author of *Red Blanket Valley* (1967), sat one day on top of a mountain near the trading store at Qebe run by herself and her husband, and looked over the landscape of that beautiful part of the Transkei that lies in the district of Engcobo ('the place of long grass'). As sometimes happens when one regards an extensive view, it reminds her of the infinite.

To the North, dominating the landscape, is the savage upright face of the Drakensberg range, with its dark peaks black against the blue sky. To the

South across a rolling staircase of hills lies Engcobo with its gentle green countryside of softly rounded hills and wooded valleys. And to the East, immediately beneath us, the Qebe Gorge is cradled in great folds of the mountain, its deep ravines uncompromisingly precipitous and inaccessible.

In this high and lonely place so suggestive of the infinite, I was stirred to a deep happiness and a rapturous recognition of the beauty and splendour of the Transkei. Uplifted, I gazed on the high vaulted sky; on the whole green world beneath and on the round mud huts with their spirals of smoke. In the fresh still air the faint cries and noises of the valley floated up. The wood-pigeons wheeled overhead and went sailing on to the krantzes below.

Elsewhere in *Red Blanket Valley* it is the sacred forest of Gulandoda mountain that seems to have an otherworldly dimension, and Broster is profoundly aware of the spirit of this place. Of the yellowwoods that grow among the dense and beautiful vegetation of the forest she writes:

Their rustling whispers murmur of a forgotten time, a pre-human pre-psychic existence.

The sound permeates the heavy scent, and in the deep remoteness of the forest it quickens the response to that outside force beyond awareness, that cosmic sense of past patterns in the moulds of men. And herein lies the vision of the true witchdoctor or Qaba priest: the strengthening and sustaining knowledge of a very old pre-Christian religion in which a kinship with animals is strong, embodying in them mental qualities and ancestral memories.

The same patterns are in all mankind. That knowledge beyond understanding gives meaning to our being.

JOAN BROSTER was a third-generation Transkeian who had grown up in this part of the world, which, she writes, 'had a deep attraction which, like love, cannot be explained', so that when in later life she and her husband, who were living at the time in Johannesburg, were asked to return to take over the trading store at Qebe, they accepted the challenge. There she developed a deep interest in the folklore of the Qaba people, who lived in the surrounding villages, and in the work of the clinics centred on All Saints Anglican Mission, situated between Engcobo and Qebe. Most of all, she grew to love and to study the beadwork, which plays such an important part in the traditional life of the 'red blanket' people. It is almost a form of literature. As Broster explains:

From birth to old age the beads tell a story and blend subtly into the social structure. No facet or phase of life is omitted and each colour has a symbolic significance. The beads are used not only for adornment but also to portray tribal traditions. Being illiterate, the people use the beads as a means of communication.

Broster's *Red Blanket Valley* together with three other books about the Thembu people, their customs, songs and dances, and especially their beautiful symbolic beadwork, records a way of life that has not entirely gone, but does not always sit happily with modernity.

Some ten years after the period of which Joan Broster writes in *Red Blanket Valley*, the Johannesburg writer Mtutuzeli Matshoba records a rather different view of the same area of the Transkei, through which he (or the persona in his story) travels from Queenstown towards Umtata on a brief visit to a territory that has recently been declared an independent state. The title of his story – 'Three Days in the Land of a Dying Illusion' – proclaims that independence or *uhuru* on the terms of the South African apartheid government of the day is an illusion. Men have left the land in the hands of women and children to work in the mines of the Witwatersrand, and Matshoba sees what many notice as they drive through Transkei: poverty, soil erosion and overgrazing.

> The soil was red, ironically reminding me of Avalon and Doornkop cemeteries back home, the land parched and scarred with erosion. In the first fields that we passed the maize had grown hardly a metre high. The weeds, blackjack outstanding, outgrew it. A woman in dusty traditional attire with a baby strapped to her back and two boys in inherited clothes following her, was searching for stems that might have been overlooked at harvest time.
>
> We passed two cows shaving the roadside of sun-scorched grass.

The mountains, however, have the power, as they have had through many generations, to lift the heart.

> The mountains rose high, solid, silent and motionless until they melted into blue-grey and hazy horizons, the only sight that appealed magnificently to my eyes. Below them there were picturesque villages of perfectly circular, thatched rondavels whitewashed for about a foot just below the edges of the thatch and around the windows and doors. This architecture dotted the elevated parts of the landscape on both sides of the road for endless acres.[7]

These contrasts – the grand, the picturesque and the denuded – speak not only of what the eye can see but of what the mind interprets.

Tsolo

A C Jordan
Noni Jabavu

In A C Jordan's historical novel *The Wrath of the Ancestors*, the very fabric of the language conveys a sense of the landscapes in which a tragic story of misunderstanding and betrayal is played out against a background of change and cultural clashes.

Some of the early scenes of the novel are set in the Alice district – at Lovedale and Fort Hare – but the principal setting of *The Wrath of the Ancestors* is the Great Place of the Chief Supreme of the Mpondomise at Ntshiqo in the Tsolo district, north-west of Umtata. St Cuthbert's Anglican Mission, in the same district, contrasts with Ntshiqo, and the narrative is as liberally adorned as a detailed map with paths, roads, bridges and fords, and with the names of Transkei villages, rivers and mountains, missions and towns. Readers travel with an assortment of characters by rail, by car or on horseback within the Tsolo district and beyond it. Or they accompany them to their homes or meeting places: simple village huts, the courtyards of Great Places, the Bhunga in Umtata, school or university residences, and mission classrooms, churches or hospitals, feeling always that they are with them at that time in that place.

Published in 1940 in Xhosa as *Ingqumbo Yeminyanya*, the novel was translated by the author with the help of his wife, P P Jordan, and published as *The Wrath of the Ancestors* in 1980. In an introduction R L Peteni writes:

> The original story, written in what I regard as perfect Xhosa, is one of the most powerful I have read in any language. The author has a keen eye for detail, a delightful sense of humour and a dramatic style. But a translation, at best, can only be a poor imitation. The power and the soul of the original cannot be recaptured in the English version. Xhosa is rich in proverb, flexible in its turn of phrase and wide in vocabulary. In giving literal translations of Xhosa images, idioms and proverbs, the aim is to transport the reader, as does the Xhosa version, to the Tsolo district, to make him feel he is listening to the memorable speeches of Mpondomise counsellors. This effort has been made so that the English-speaking reader may be given a peep into the treasure-house bequeathed to humanity by Jordan

The literal translation of Xhosa images, idioms and proverbs also makes readers feel that they are experiencing the timespan of the novel, so that they see, through Xhosa eyes, the kind of world in which its events occur. Characters set out at dawn 'when the horns of the cattle were just visible against the pale sky' or return 'when the hares were coming out on their evening prowl'. January is the month 'of the *mqungo* grass', December 'of the blooming of the

mimosa', and September 'of the flowering of the *msintsi* [coral] tree'. Time is also indicated by the cycles of the moon or seasonal activities such as ploughing and harvesting or the period 'when the maize crop was ripening to red'. Proverbial sayings often draw on images from nature: 'news never tarries overnight by the wayside, because it is afraid of the dew'; 'the tikoloshe must come out of the reeds [truth must out]'; 'when the old bird dies its eggs go bad' [things go wrong when a leader dies].

The woes of the land of the Mpondomise without their rightful chief are imaged in terms that suit the terrain.

> It was no longer the land of heroes whose exploits used to fill him with pride and exultation. Today, alas, it was a land whose sun was dark, its light grown dim with the shadow of death. In this land the murmuring of bees he had so often heard with the ears of childhood had become the moaning of affliction, and the abundance of milk had become the bitterness of the *mhlontlo* juice.

When the rightful heir claims the chieftainship, he is greeted as the sun by a praise-singer:

> 'Make way, for the Ngwanya offspring of Majola bestirs himself!
> Arise and behold, most glorious of glorious suns!
> Arise and gaze in admiration,
> Glittering eye of the Prince of Heaven!'

Later, the national bard expresses the dissatisfaction of the chieftain's traditional faction in terms of drought:

> 'Say!
> What manner of rain is this we have this day –
> This rain that moistens only portions of land.
> Alas! We die of drought, we simple fools
> Who thought today we lived in a rainy land!'

The plot of *The Wrath of the Ancestors* is not unlike that of a Greek tragedy or a Shakespearian play but everything about it says, 'This is the Transkei.'

ARCHIBALD CHARLES JORDAN was born in 1906 in one of the villages that feature in the novel – Mbokotwana – where his father was headmaster of the school, as well as choirmaster, poet, music composer and keen cricketer. As his widow Phyllis Ntantala tells us in her autobiography, *A Life's Mosaic* (1992), Jordan followed his father along all these paths and, like him, also developed an interest in the language and history of their people. He also showed, from an early age, an interest in literature. At St Cuthbert's Mission at nearby Ncolosi, the missionaries had a profound influence on Jordan and he was, for all his life, a devoted Anglican. These two threads – Christianity and tradition – are very evident in *The Wrath of the Ancestors*.

Primary schooling at Mbokotwana and St Cuthbert's was followed by teacher training at St John's College, Umtata. This led on to Fort Hare University, where Jordan obtained an education diploma in 1932 and a bachelor of arts degree in 1934. While teaching at a school in Kroonstad in the Orange Free State, Jordan acquired a master's degree through the University of South Africa and then returned to Fort Hare as a lecturer, proceeding soon afterwards to the University of Cape Town, where he lectured in the department of African languages for fourteen years. The refusal of a passport to enable him to take up a Carnegie grant in the United States of America forced him into exile in 1962. He lectured first at the University of California in Los Angeles and then at the University of Wisconsin in Madison, where, in 1964, Jordan became professor of African languages and literature. He died in 1968.

Apart from *The Wrath of the Ancestors*, Jordan wrote *Towards an African Literature*, an important historical analysis of Xhosa literature. He also collected, translated and retold a number of traditional stories, which were published as *Tales from Southern Africa* (1973). Jordan's personal knowledge of the Xhosa way of life and his understanding of the conflicts between Christian and traditional Xhosa morality, combined with academic insights into the literature and history of the people of the Transkei, have given South Africa an outstanding writer whose works are of enduring interest.

In Chapter Ten we looked at the Tyume Valley in the Amatola region as Noni Jabavu pictured it in the account of her 1960 visit to southern Africa – *Drawn in Colour*. Here we view the Tsolo district as she depicts it in her 1963 memoir, *The Ochre People: Scenes from a South African Life*. Jabavu was on a visit to her maternal relatives, the Makiwanes. They were well-to-do farmers whose home, Confluence Farm, at the junction of the Tsitsa and Inxu rivers, overlooked the Tsolo mountain. She is more explicit in her depiction of place than Jordan, perhaps because she is describing it as a part-outsider for outsiders.

> The views from the whole homestead were breath-taking. I had long ago given up trying to take photographs of them. You needed what cameramen call a 'zoom lens' for it was giant country, Brobdingnagian sweeps of mountains, valleys, plains and skies. At the back and far across another of these valleys rose the tall conical hill-mountain on its enormous spreading base. That was Tsolo, whose name meant 'pointed'. It was like a splendid phallic symbol, as if a Cyclops had poised and placed it on the landscape. The district was named after it. The formation of hills and ridges

seemed of a different kind from that at Middledrift. Here the gargantuan terraces of the rise in altitudes from coast-line to South Africa's famous plateaux, table-lands, were seen from a different angle: features which used to give us moments of torture in geography classes at school ...

Certainly it was a 'green and pleasant land', less drought-stricken than ours farther south – a climate affected by the altitudes, the slant of terraced terrain, trade winds, distribution of grass lands and plains and forests. And its inhabitants seemed, like my uncle, inclined to live high on ridges, a typical southern African characteristic, for we say 'we like to see and be seen, not huddle in declivities'.

Mount Frere

In 1894 W C Scully was sent to the district of Mount Frere north of Tsolo *W C Scully* in the land of the Bhaca as magistrate. He travelled extensively through the district under his jurisdiction as well as through parts of neighbouring Pondoland, a region of grassy hillslopes backed by mountains and cut by gorges of considerable depth. Mount Frere is no longer the quiet village where Scully was stationed, but its situation still appeals.

The village of Mount Frere is, as regards scenery, most beautifully situated. Its site is a grassy plateau several thousand feet above sea-level, which commands magnificent views on three sides. To westward arise the densely forested Umgano and Manzinyama Ranges; to northward spring the enormous mass of the Intsiza Mountain and the soaring peaks of the Vinyanè; to eastward lies Pondoland, with the lofty Taba'nkulu dominating its grassy hills and valleys.[8]

Returning from a visit to a village on the northern banks of the Tina River, Scully's horse refuses to cross a drift in the Ghoda bush. Enquiries elicit the story of a young girl, forced to marry against her will, who drowns herself in an adjacent stream when she learns of the ritual murder of her lover. No horse will pass this spot on the night of the new moon. Scully reworks the story, as was his wont, into the fictional 'Ukushwama' and, as was also his wont, the setting of the story is painted with factual accuracy.

The Ghoda bush is a narrow strip of forest running down the side of a steep mountain which forms one side of a valley, the other side being formed of a perpendicular cliff, at the foot of which a stream brawls. The strip of forest does not quite reach the stream, a grassy glade, about twenty-five yards in width, lying between. Over this glade the footpath leads. The Ghoda is about a mile from Numjala's kraal, and just beyond it is the drift over the stream.

'The Imishologu', an equally sad tale of bereavement, this time of a mother, is set in Pondoland.

> Whoever has traversed the valley of the Umzimvubu River below the Tabankulu Mountain, in that vicinity where the Tsitsa, the Tina, and the Umzimhlava streams have carved their several devious courses almost through the vitals of the earth to the main water-way, has seen the roughest part of Pondoland, and seldom feels inclined to repeat the experience.

We may not all have the good fortune to visit the more remote parts of the Transkei and may not, as Scully suggests, wish to repeat the experience if we do, but his stories certainly whet the appetite for exploration.

LANDSCAPE PERSONIFIED

The last layer of Transkei literature to be uncovered is also probably the earliest historically – the traditional tale. Such tales are not usually set in specified places although they often convey a good sense of the kind of milieu in which they are imagined. The village, sometimes the Great Place, the hut, the courtyard, the cattle kraal may play their part in a story. Events may take place in a forest, beside a river or pool, in a cave, on a hillside or out in the fields. Seasons come and go. The passage of time is sometimes marked by the movement of the moon or the stars. Birds and animals, real or mythical, are part of the world of traditional stories – stories that reflect not only the values and traditions of the people who passed them down from generation to generation, but the physical world in which they lived.

A C Jordan translated and retold some of the *iintsomi*, or fictitious, mythological stories of his people, in *Tales from Southern Africa*, published in 1973, and others have done the same. Often such stories were communal efforts, audience as well as storyteller – usually a woman – elaborating a well-known tale. Something is, therefore, lost when they are cast in written form but they do retain much that is entertaining and illuminating, and many of them are among the treasures of our literature.

In one of the tales in Jordan's collection – 'The Story of Nomxakazo' – a wondrous creature called Maphundu (He-of-the-Nodules) appears to the warriors of the chief Dumakudi who are raiding far and wide for cattle to please his beautiful daughter, Nomxakazo.

One day, the warriors came to a great fertile valley where myriads of cattle were grazing. Overlooking this valley was an animal of immeasurable size. Its face was a solid rock, its eyes and ears and nostrils like deep red caves. On its body were tall mountains and low hills, large rivers and small streams, big deep lakes and small shallow puddles, large forests and small thickets, fertile lands and barren deserts. In some regions of its body it was summer, and everything was fresh-green and beautiful: in others it was winter, and everything was covered with snow. But the warriors were so greedy for the loot that they took no notice of this object. For all they cared it was nothing more than a mountain forest of extraordinary size and shape. So, with shouts of joy they rounded up the cattle. But just as they were beginning to drive them away, the animal spoke to them in a very deep but calm voice: 'Those cattle that you are driving away – do you know whose they are?'

STOLEN CATTLE OF MAphundu

The warriors take no notice and drive away all the cattle from the Great Valley. This gives Maphundu the right to carry off the princess. Her father's violent disregard for his people and his neighbours and her greed have brought disaster. The land is barren, the royal household destitute, and disease, hunger and death afflict the people. It is only when Nomxakazo learns – through a series of trials – to be truly human and respectful of others and of the environment that happiness can be restored.

Maphundu's body is a marvellous representation of the topography of the region, and Nomxakazo's story provides a unique way of viewing the land and of recognising the importance of respecting it. As we look back on the world through which we have travelled – a world filtered through the perceptions of a multiplicity of writers, and expanded by our own experiences – we may each construct our own Maphundu. To contemplate, in doing so, this region of South Africa is to recognise a magnetism that has drawn and will continue to draw writers to embrace the Eastern Cape, and to celebrate its strange and varied beauty, or lament the marks of suffering and conflict that it bears, through their art – the art of words.

NOTES

CHAPTER 2

1. *Sunday Times* interview, 14 March 1982
2. *Illustrated Rhodesia*, 24 September 1972
3. 'Apartheid' in Dirk Klopper (ed.), *Anatomy of Dark* (Pretoria, 2000)
4. 'Autopsy' in ibid.
5. 'Windscape' in ibid.
6. R Murphy (ed.), *Contemporary Poets of the English Language* (London, 1970), p. 449
7. William Selwyn, *Cape Carols and Miscellaneous Verses* (Cape Town, 1891)
8. From Dennis Brutus, *Stubborn Hope* (Oxford, 1978)
9. Ibid.
10. From Dennis Brutus, *Still the Sirens* (Santa Fe, 1993)
11. Henry Lichtenstein, *Travels in Southern Africa* (reprint, Cape Town, 1928), vol. 1, p. 294
12. C I Latrobe, *Journal of a Visit to South Africa* (reprint, Cape Town, 1969), pp. 207-8
13. J R Wahl (ed.), *Thomas Pringle in South Africa* (Cape Town, 1970), pp. 12-13
14. Jimmy Matyu, 'Pay-day Murder' in Linda Rode and Jakes Gerwel (comp.), *Crossing Over* (Cape Town, 1995)
15. Mzi Mahola, 'We Shall Reap in Tears' in *When Rains Come* (Cape Town, 2000)
16. *New Coin* (34, 1), June 1998, p. 89
17. *Kotaz* (2, 1), March 1999, p. 2
18. *New Coin* (34, 1), June 1998, p. 90
19. Mxolisi Nyezwa, 'the poet's failure' in *song trials* (Pietermaritzburg, 2000), p. 20
20. Mxolisi Nyezwa, 'song trials' in ibid.
21. Mxolisi Nyezwa, 'love' in ibid.
22. *New Coin* (34, 2), July 1998, p. 74
23. Thomas Baines, *Journal of Residence in Africa*, ed. by R F Kennedy (Cape Town, 1961), vol. 1, pp. 25, 28, 29, 63, 108-9

CHAPTER 3

1. P FitzPatrick to Nugent FitzPatrick, 28 October 1913, NELM archives
2. P FitzPatrick to A J Wright, May 1921, NELM archives
3. J R Wahl (ed.), *Thomas Pringle in South Africa*, p. 216
4. Ibid., p. 74
5. Ibid., p. 76
6. Ibid., p. 71

CHAPTER 4

1. Dan Wylie, 'Winter Solstice' in *The Road Out* (Cape Town, 1996)
2. Thomas Baines, *Journal of Residence in Africa*, p. 10
3. Harriet Ward, *Five Years in Kaffirland* (London, 1848), pp. 240-1
4. T Sheffield, *The Story of the Settlement* (Grahamstown, 1912), p. 193
5. Sipho Sepamla, *Hurry Up to It!* (Johannesburg, 1975)
6. Marion Baxter, *Bitter Aloes* (n.p., 1998), p. 18
7. *Four South African Poets*, interviewed by Susan Gardner (Grahamstown, 1986), p. 10

CHAPTER 5

1. B M R, *Under the Yellowwoods* (Grahamstown, 1878)
2. *Philipps, 1820 Settler*, ed. A Keppel-Jones (Pietermaritzburg, 1960)

CHAPTER 6

1. W Saunders in *Walter Battiss*, ed. by K Skwran and M Macnamara (Johannesburg, 1985), p. 200
2. Arrangements to visit the site may be made through Schreiner House in Cross Street, Cradock, or through NELM in Grahamstown.
3. R Rive (ed.), *Olive Schreiner: Letters 1871–1899* (Cape Town, 1987), p. 169
4. *Emily Hobhouse: Boer War Letters*, ed. by Rykie van Reenen (Cape Town, 1984), p. 188
5. *Guy Butler: Collected Poems*, ed. by L Wright (Cape Town, 1999)
6. Ibid., pp. 247-8
7. *De Kat*, November 1990

CHAPTER 7

1. Arthur Brigg, *'Sunny Fountains' and 'Golden Sand'* (London, 1888), p. 101
2. S C Cronwright, *The Life of Olive Schreiner* (London, 1924), p. 329
3. Ibid., p. 249
4. Ibid., p. 218
5. Ibid., p. 61
6. Olive Schreiner, *From Man to Man* (London, 1926), pp. 43-44
7. Karel Schoeman, *Olive Schreiner: A Woman in South Africa* (Johannesburg, 1991), p. 104
8. Ibid.
9. Ibid., pp. 104-5
10. Ibid., pp. 105-6
11. Rive (ed.), *Olive Schreiner: Letters*, p. 213

CHAPTER 8

1. William Plomer, *Double Lives* (New York, 1945), p. 162
2. Ibid., p. 80
3. Ibid., p. 148
4. 'Down on the Farm' in *William Plomer: Selected Stories*, ed. by Stephen Gray (Cape Town, 1984)
5. William Plomer, *Double Lives*, p. 152
6. Ibid., p. 154
7. Ibid., p. 156.
8. Plomer to Johannes Meintjes, 11 January 1972, NELM archives
9. Johannes Meintjes, *Olive Schreiner* (Johannesburg, 1965), preface
10. Plomer to Meintjes, 26 May 1957, NELM archives
11. Farida Karodia, *Other Secrets* (Johannesburg, 2000), p. 376
12. Farida Karodia, *Daughters of the Twilight* (London, 1986), pp. 134, 140-1
13. Farida Karodia, *Daughters of the Twilight*, p. 35; *Other Secrets*, p. 46

Chapter 9

1. J R Wahl (ed.), *Thomas Pringle in South Africa*, p. 29
2. Ibid., pp. 103-4
3. J K Bokwe, *Ntsikana* (Lovedale, 1914), pp. 8, 11
4. Janet Hodgson, 'The Genius of Ntsikana' in *Literature and Society in South Africa*, ed. by L White and T Couzens (Cape Town, 1984)
5. Harriet Ward, *Jasper Lyle* (London, 1852), p. 174
6. Ibid., p. 1
7. Harriet Ward, *Five Years in Kaffirland*, p. 305
8. Harriet Ward, *Hardy and Hunter* (London, 1859), p. 327
9. V. Letcher, 'Trespassing beyond the Borders: Harriet Ward as Writer and Commentator on the Eastern Cape Frontier' (Ph.D., Rhodes University, 1996)
10. Harriet Ward, *Five Years*, p. 307
11. Thomas Baines, *Journal of Residence in South Africa*, p. 118
12. Harriet Ward, *Five Years*, pp. 306-7
13. Sally Sampson, '"Far Plains and Echoing Valleys": Harriet Ward: An Officer's Wife on the Frontier', *Annals of the Grahamstown Historical Society*, 24 (1994)

Chapter 10

1. Z K Matthews, *Freedom for My People* (Cape Town, 1981), p. 69
2. Nelson Mandela, *Long Walk to Freedom* (London, 1994), p. 51
3. *The Argus*, 1 December 1993
4. *La Femme*, supplement to *Eastern Province Herald*, 10 November 1993

Chapter 11

1. W C Scully, *Reminiscences of a South African Pioneer* (London, 1913), p. 84
2. Jeff Opland, *Words That Circle Words* (Johannesburg, 1992), p. 235
3. Thomas Baines, *Journal of Residence in South Africa*, pp. 133, 134
4. *Weekend Post*, 10 June 1989

Chapter 12

1. J B Peires, *The Dead Will Arise* (Johannesburg, 1989), p. 312
2. Margaret Gough, *Selected Poems* (1999)
3. David Yali-Manisi in R H Kaschula (ed.), *The Bones of the Ancestors are Shaking* (Cape Town, 2002), p. 282
4. Ibid., p. 269
5. Ibid., p. 277
6. *Country Life*, March 1996
7. M Matshoba, *Call Me Not a Man* (Johannesburg, 1979), pp. 158, 159
8. W C Scully, *Transkei Stories*, ed. by Jean Marquard (Cape Town, 1984), p. 254

BIBLIOGRAPHY

Much of the material for this book has come from the extensive collection of press clippings at NELM; from reference and guide books; flower, tree and bird books; and from information provided by authors or their families, and by residents of some of the places that have been visited. Many background books have been consulted. Among those I have found most useful are Neil Mostert's *Frontiers: The Epic of South Africa's Creation and the Tragedy of the Xhosa People*; T R H Davenport's *South Africa: A Modern History*, *The Real Story: Reader's Digest Illustrated History of South Africa*; Gaston Bachelard's *The Poetics of Space*; Malcolm Turner's *Shipwrecks and Salvage in South Africa*; and Harold William's *Southern Lights: Lighthouses of Southern Africa*.

Works cited, and a few background works specific to the area, are listed in bibliographies for each chapter. Out of print books of literary significance are available for consultation at NELM.

CHAPTER 1

Barrow, John. *An Account of Travels into the Interior of Southern Africa in the Years 1797 to 1798*. New York: Hopkins, 1802

Driver, Charles Jonathan. *In the Water-Margins: Poems*. Cape Town: Snailpress in association with Crane River, 1994

Forbes, Vernon S with John Rourke. *Paterson's Cape Travels, 1777 to 1779*. Johannesburg: Brenthurst Press, 1980
  Pioneer Travellers of South Africa: A Geographical Commentary upon Routes, Records, Observations and Opinions of Travellers at the Cape, 1750–1800. Cape Town: Balkema, 1965

Gordon, Robert Jacob. *Robert Jacob Gordon, Cape Travels, 1777 to 1786* (edited by Peter Raper and Maurice Boucher). Houghton: Brenthurst Press, 1988

James, Alan. *Morning near Genadendal: Poems*. Cape Town: Snailpress, 1992
  Producing the Landscape: Poems. Cape Town: Upstream, 1987

Latrobe, C I *Journal of a Visit to South Africa in 1815 and 1816*. London: Seeley, 1818

Miller, Ruth. *Poems, Prose, Plays* (edited and introduced by Lionel Abrahams). Cape Town: Carrefour, 1990

Sparrman, Anders. *A Voyage to the Cape of Good Hope* (edited by V S Forbes; translated from Swedish). Cape Town: Van Riebeeck Society, 1975–1977 (in 2 volumes)

Thunberg, Carl Peter. *Travels at the Cape of Good Hope 1772–1775* (edited by V S Forbes; translated from Swedish). Cape Town: Van Riebeeck Society, 1986

CHAPTER 2

Agherdien, Yusuf, Ambrose C George and Shaheed Hendricks. *South End: As We Knew It* (edited by Roy H du PrÈ). Port Elizabeth: Western Research Group, 1997

Allen, Geoffrey and David Allen. *The Guns of Sacramento*. London: Robin Garton, 1978

Baines, Thomas. *Journal of Residence in Africa, 1842–1853* (edited by R F Kennedy). Cape Town: Van Riebeeck Society, 1961–1964 (in 2 volumes)

Brutus, Dennis. *Still the Sirens*. Santa Fe: Pennywhistle Press, 1993

Stubborn Hope: New Poems and Selections from China Poems and Strains.
London: Heinemann, 1978

Burgess, Yvonne. *Anna and the Colonel: An Alternative Love Story.* Johannesburg:
Ravan, 1997

If You Swallow You're Dead'. In: Gray, Stephen (ed.), *Modern South African
Stories: Revised and Expanded Edition of On the Edge of the World.*
Johannesburg: Ad Donker, 1980, 1983

A Life to Live: A Novel. Johannesburg: Ad Donker, 1973

Measure of the Night Wind. Sandton: Penguin, 2002

Say a Little Mantra for Me. Johannesburg: Ravan, 1979

The Strike: A Novel. Johannesburg: Ad Donker, 1975

Carruthers, Jane and Marion Arnold. *The Life and Work of Thomas Baines.* Vlaeberg:
Fernwood Press, 1995

Clifton, N Roy. *Moments in a Journey.* Toronto: Clarke, Irwin, 1983

Finn, Hugh. *The Sunbathers: And Other Poems.* Salisbury: The Poetry Society of
Rhodesia, 1977

Fugard, Athol with Don Maclennan. *The Coat, by Athol Fugard [and] The Third
Degree, by Don Maclennan: Two Experiments in Play-Making.* Cape Town:
Balkema, 1971

Cousins: A Memoir. Johannesburg: Witwatersrand University Press, 1994

A Lesson from Aloes: A Play. Oxford: Oxford University Press, 1981

with Ross Devenish. *Marigolds in August: A Screenplay.* Johannesburg: Ad
Donker 1982

*Three Port Elizabeth Plays: The Blood Knot, Hello and Goodbye, Boesman
and Lena.* London: Oxford University Press, 1974

with John Kani and Winston Ntshona. *Sizwe Bansi is Dead; and, The Island.*
New York: Viking, 1976

Gough, Margaret. *Selected Poems.* [Canada: s.n.], 1999

Griffiths, Reginald. *Children of Pride.* London: Jarrolds, 1959

Harradine, Margaret. *Port Elizabeth: A Social Chronicle to the End of 1945.* Port
Elizabeth: E H Walton, 1996

Lagan, Cathal. *Sandbird.* Alice: Lovedale Press, 1999

'"The Sacramento Way": Christmas, 1996'. *New Contrast 99* 25(3), 1997

with Basil Somhlahlo and Brian Walter. *Mendi: Poems by Cathal Lagan, Basil
Somhlahlo and Brian Walter on the Sinking of the Mendi.* Alice: Echo Poets,
1994

Latrobe, C I. *Journal of a Visit to South Africa in 1815 and 1816.* London: Seeley, 1818

Lemmer, André. 'Song for South End'. In: Lemmer, André and Viv England (comp.)
Where the Rainbow Ends: A Poetry Anthology. Pretoria: Academica, 1991

Lichtenstein, Henry. *Travels in Southern Africa in the Years 1803, 1804, 1805 and 1806*
(Translated from German by Anne Plumptree). Cape Town: Van Riebeeck
Society, 1928–1930 (in 2 volumes)

Lorimer, Eleanor K. *Panorama of Port Elizabeth.* Cape Town: Balkema, 1971

Mahola, Mzi. *Strange Things.* Cape Town: Snailpress, 1994

When Rains Come. Cape Town: Carapace Poets, 2000

Matyu, Jimmy T. *Shadows from the Past: Memories of Jabavu Road, New Brighton.* Roggebaai: Kwela, 1996
'Pay-day Murder'. In: Rode, Linda and Jakes Gerwel (comp.) *Crossing Over: New Writing for a New South Africa.* Cape Town: Kwela, 1995

Nortje, Arthur. *Anatomy of Dark: Collected Poems of Arthur Nortje* (edited by Dirk Klopper). Pretoria: Unisa Press, 2000
Dead Roots: Poems. London: Heinemann, 1973
Lonely Against the Light: Poems by Arthur Nortje. New Coin Poetry 9(3&4), 1973 (special issue)

Nyezwa, Mxolisi. *song trials* (edited by Robert Berold). Pietermaritzburg: Gecko Poetry, 2000

Poland, Marguerite. *The Bush Shrike.* Johannesburg: Ravan, 1982

Pringle, Thomas. *Narrative of a Residence in South Africa.* London: Moxon, 1835
Thomas Pringle in South Africa 1820–1826 (edited by John Robert Wahl). Cape Town: Longman, 1970

Sam, Agnes. *Jesus is Indian and Other Stories.* London: Women's Press, 1989

Schauder, Colin D. *The Historic Village of Bethelsdorp.* Port Elizabeth: The Historical Society of Port Elizabeth & Walmer, 1970

Selwyn, William. *Cape Carols and Miscellaneous Verses.* Cape Town: Argus Printing and Publishing, 1891

Walter, Brian. *Baakens.* Alice: Lovedale Press, 2000
Tracks. Alice: Lovedale Press, 1999

CHAPTER 3

FitzPatrick, Sir James Percy. *Amanzi: A Private Record of the First Decade.* Uitenhage: The Author, [1924?]

Wallis, J P R. *Fitz: The Story of Sir Percy FitzPatrick.* London: Macmillan, 1955

Latrobe, C I. *Journal of a Visit to South Africa in 1815 and 1816.* London: Seeley, 1818

Kruger, Bernhard. *The Pear Tree Blossoms: A History of the Moravian Mission Stations in South Africa 1737–1869.* Genadendal: Moravian Book Depot, 1966

Hewett, Bruce. *Songs with Silent Music: Selected Poems.* [Cape Town: Salesian Press, 199-]

Meiring, Jane M. *Sundays River Valley: Its History and Settlement.* Cape Town: Balkema, 1959

Pringle, Thomas. *Thomas Pringle in South Africa 1820–1826* (edited by John Robert Wahl). Cape Town: Longman, 1970

CHAPTER 4

Baines, Thomas. *Journal of Residence in Africa, 1842–1853* (edited by R F Kennedy). Cape Town: Van Riebeeck Society, 1961-1964 (in 2 volumes)

Baxter, Marion. *Bitter Aloes: Stories of the Eastern Cape* (Unpublished short stories)
'Extinction'. In: Joubert, Brian S. (ed.) *Under African Skies: An Anthology of African Verse.* Scottburgh: Poetry Institute of Africa at Unique Publications, 1998

Berold, Robert. *The Door to the River.* Cape Town: Bateleur Press, 1984
The Fires of the Dead: Poems. Cape Town: Carrefour, 1989

Bryer, Lynne. *The Cancer Years.* Cape Town: Carapace Poets, 1999
A Time in the Country. Cape Town: Carrefour, 1991

Butler, Guy. *Bursting World: An Autobiography (1936–45)*. Cape Town: David Philip, 1983

    Collected Poems (edited by Laurence Wright). Cape Town: David Philip, 1999

    A Local Habitation: An Autobiography (1945–90). Cape Town: David Philip, 1991

    The Prophetic Nun: Sister Margaret CR, Sister Pauline CR, Sister Dorothy Raphael CSMV. Johannesburg: Random House, 2000

Campbell, John. *Travels in South Africa: Undertaken at the Request of the Missionary Society*. London: Black Parry, 1815

    Travels in South Africa, Undertaken at the Request of the London Missionary Society: Being a Narrative of a Second Journey in the Interior of that Country. London: London Missionary Society, 1822

Chumani Writers Group. *Umgqala* Nos. 1, 1982 – 4, 1987

Dixon, Isobel. *Weather Eye*. Cape Town: Carapace Poets, 2001

Dugmore, Henry Hare. *The Reminiscences of an Albany Settler*. Pietermaritzburg: Grant Christison, 1990

    The Reminiscences of an Albany Settler: Together with his Recollections of the Kaffir War of 1835 (edited by F G van der Riet and L A Hewson). Grahamstown: Grocott & Sherry, 1958

Goodwin, Harold. *Songs from the Settler City*. Grahamstown: [s.n.], 1963

Gough, Margaret. *Selected Poems*. [Canada: s.n.], 1999

Holleman, Helen (ed.). *Graham's Town: The Untold Story: A Social History and Self-Guided Tour*. [Grahamstown]: Black Sash, 1997

Maclennan, Don. *Letters: New Poems*. Cape Town: Carrefour, 1992

    Reckonings. Cape Town: David Philip, 1983

    Solstice: Poems. Cape Town: Snailpress in association with Scottish Cultural Press, 1997

Mann, Chris. *Heartlands*. Pietermaritzburg: University of Natal Press, 2002

Neville, Thelma. *More Lasting than Bronze: A Story of the 1820 Settlers National Monument*. [Pietermaritzburg: n.d.]

North, Marianne. *A Vision of Eden: The Life and Work of Marianne North*. Exeter, England: Published in collaboration with the Royal Botanic Gardens, Kew by Webb and Bower, 1980

O'Meara, Emily. *Grahamstown Reflected* (photography by Duncan Greaves). Grahamstown: Albany Museum, 1995

Poland, Marguerite. *Iron Love*. London: Viking, 1999

Pringle, Thomas. *Poems Illustrative of South Africa: African Sketches: Part One* (edited by John Robert Wahl). Cape Town: Struik, 1970

Sampson, Harold Fehrsen. *Selected Poems of Harold Fehrsen Sampson*. Cape Town: The Author, 1972

Schreiner, Olive. *The Story of an African Farm*. Johannesburg: Ad Donker, 1975

Sepamla, Sipho. *Hurry Up to It!* Johannesburg: Ad Donker, 1975

Sheffield, T. *The Story of the Settlement: Grahamstown as It was and Grahamstown as It is: Compiled from the Most Authentic Authorities and Issued as a Memento of the Completion of the Settler's Memorial Tower at Grahamstown on the 24th Day of May 1882*. Grahamstown: T & G Sheffield, 1882

Slater, Francis Carey. *The Collected Poems of Francis Carey Slater*. Edinburgh: Blackwood; South Africa: Central News Agency, 1957

Slater, Francis Carey. *The Trek: A Poem*. London: Macmillan, 1938

Teachers' English Language Improvement Project (TELIP) *The Way We See It*; 6, 7, 8 and 9. Grahamstown: Inset, 1820 Foundation, 1987–1988 (variously edited)

Van der Riet, Kathleen. *Morning in the Heart: A Memoir*. Port Elizabeth: Tecoma Press, 2000

Ward, Harriet. *Five Years in Kaffirland: With Sketches of the Late War in That Country, to the Conclusion of Peace: Written on the Spot*. London: Colburn, 1848 (in 2 volumes)

Wylie, Dan. *The Road Out*. Cape Town: Snailpress, 1996

CHAPTER 5

Bancroft, Francis, pseud. *The Settler's Eldest Daughter*. London: Hodder and Stoughton, [1920]

Barber, Mary Elizabeth. *The Erythrina Tree and Other Verses*. London: Rowland Ward, 1898

Barnes, P. *Where Duty Leads: The Life of Colonel Jasper Selwyn, R E*. [S.l.: s.n., 1979]

Bruce, Robert Michael. *Under the Yellowwoods: Poems [by B M R] of Belton, Near Grahamstown, South Africa*. Port Elizabeth: [s.n.], 1978

Buchanan-Gould, Vera. *Vast Heritage*. Bellville: Beau Rivage, [1953]

Butler, Guy. *Collected Poems* (edited by Laurence Wright). Cape Town: David Philip, 1999

  Pilgrimage to Dias Cross: A Narrative Poem. Cape Town: David Philip, 1987

  Richard Gush of Salem. Cape Town: Maskew Miller, 1982

  with John Benyon. *The 1820 Settlers: An Illustrated Commentary* (edited by Guy Butler). Cape Town: Human & Rousseau, 1974

Butler, James. '*Jim's Journal': The Diary of James Butler* (edited by Jane Garner). Johannesburg: Witwatersrand University Press for Rhodes University, Grahamstown, 1996

Coetzee, J M. *Disgrace*. London: Secker & Warburg, 1999

  White Writing: On the Culture of Letters in South Africa. New Haven, Conn.: Yale University Press, 1988

Currie, Marion. *The History of the Theopolis Mission, 1814–1851*. (MA thesis, Rhodes University, 1983)

Goldswain, Jeremiah. *The Chronicle of Jeremiah Goldswain, Albany Settler of 1820* (edited by Una Long). Cape Town: The Van Riebeeck Society, 1946

Greig, Robert. *In the Provinces*. Rivonia: Justified Press, 1991

Howarth, Anna. *Sword and Assegai*. London: Smith Elder, 1899

King, Michael. *The Fool and Other Poems*. Cape Town: Poetry Press, 1987

  'Walking along West Beach, Kowie'. *Carapace* (8), 1996

Maclennan, Don. *Rock Paintings at Salem*. [Grahamstown: The Author], 2001

Philipps, Thomas. *Philipps, 1820 Settler: His Letters* (edited by Arthur Keppel-Jones). Pietermaritzburg: Shuter & Shooter, 1960

Sampson, Harold Fehrsen. *Selected Poems of Harold Fehrsen Sampson*. Cape Town: The Author, 1972

Selwyn, William. *Cape Carols and Miscellaneous Verses.* Cape Town: Argus Printing
    and Publishing, 1891
Shaw, William. *The Journal of William Shaw* (edited by W D Hammond-Tooke).
    Cape Town: Balkema for Rhodes University, Grahamstown, 1972
Stirk, Doris. *Kasouga Sands: The Story of the Eastern Cape's First Seaside Resort.*
    [S.l.: s.n., 1991]
Wilhelm, Peter. *Falling into the Sun: Poems.* Cape Town: Snailpress, 1993
Wylie, Dan. *The Road Out.* Cape Town: Snailpress, 1996

CHAPTERS 6 AND 7

Barsby, Tina. *Olive Schreiner: An Introduction.* Grahamstown: National English
    Literary Museum, 1995
Battiss, Walter. *Limpopo.* Pretoria: Van Schaik, 1965
Berold, Robert. *The Fires of the Dead: Poems.* Cape Town: Carrefour, 1989
Brigg, Arthur. *'Sunny Fountains' and 'Golden Sands': Pictures of Missionary Life in the
    South of the 'Dark Continent'.* London: T Woolmer, 1888
Butler, Guy. *Bursting World: An Autobiography (1936–45).* Cape Town: David Philip,
    1983
    Collected Poems (edited by Laurence Wright). Cape Town: David Philip, 1999
    The Dam: A Play in Three Acts. Cape Town: Balkema, 1953
    Karoo Morning: An Autobiography (1918–35). Cape Town: David Philip, 1977
    A Local Habitation: An Autobiography (1945–90). Cape Town: David Philip,
    1991
    Tales from the Old Karoo. Johannesburg: Ad Donker, 1989
Campbell, Roy. *Adamastor.* Cape Town: Paul Koston, 1950
Clayton, Cherry. 'Olive Schreiner's Tomb, Buffelskop'. In: Bunyan, David (ed.) *25/25:
    Twenty Five Years of English South African Poetry: An Anthology Selected from
    New Coin Poetry, 1965–1989.* Grahamstown: Institute for the Study of
    English in Africa, Rhodes University, 1990
Cronwright-Schreiner, S C. *The Re-Interment on Buffelskop: My Diary, 7–15 June
    1921 and 8th to 29th August 1921* (edited by Guy Butler and N W Visser).
    Grahamstown: Institute for the Study of English in Africa, Rhodes University,
    1983
Dixon, Isobel. *Weather Eye.* Cape Town: Carapace Poets, 2001
Driver, Charles Jonathan. *In the Water-Margins: Poems.* Cape Town: Snailpress in
    association with Crane River, 1994
Du Pisani, Etienne. *One.* Graaff-Reinet: The Author, 1998
First, Ruth and Ann Scott. *Olive Schreiner: A Biography.* London: The Women's Press,
    1989
Fugard, Athol. *My Life; and Valley Song.* Johannesburg: Hodder & Stoughton;
    Witwatersrand University Press, 1996
    *The Road to Mecca: A Play in Two Acts Suggested by the Life of Helen Martins
    of New Bethesda.* London: Faber and Faber, 1985
Fugard, Sheila. *A Revolutionary Woman.* Johannesburg: Ad Donker, 1983
Gray, Stephen. 'In Memoriam: Olive Schreiner'. *New Coin Poetry* 13(3&4), 1977
Hobhouse, Emily. *Emily Hobhouse: Boer War Letters* (edited by Rykie van Reenen).
    Cape Town: Human & Rousseau, 1984

Maclennan, Don. 'The Road to Mecca'. *Contrast 45* 12(1), 1978

Mandela, Nelson. *Long Walk to Freedom: The Autobiography of Nelson Mandela.* London: Abacus, 1995

Mann, Chris. *Mann Alive! Poems.* Cape Town: David Philip in association with the Media Resource Centre, University of Natal, Durban, 1992

Palmer, Eve and Geoffrey Jenkins. *The Companion Guide to South Africa.* London and Johannesburg: Collins, 1978
    The Plains of Camdeboo. Johannesburg: Jonathan Ball, 1993
    Return to Camdeboo: A Century's Karoo Foods and Flavours. Cape Town: Tafelberg, 1992

Purcell, Anna. 'Olive Schreiner's Grave in the Karroo'. In: Cronwright-Schreiner, S C. *The Re-Interment on Buffelskop: My Diary, 7–15 June 1921 and 8th to 29th August 1921* (edited by Guy Butler and N W Visser). Grahamstown: Institute for the Study of English in Africa, Rhodes University, 1983

Ross, Sue Imrie. *This Is My World: The Life of Helen Martins, Creator of the Owl House.* Cape Town: Oxford University Press, 1997

Schoeman, Karel. *Olive Schreiner: A Woman in South Africa, 1855–1881* (translated from Afrikaans by Henri Snijders). Johannesburg: Jonathan Ball, 1991

Schreiner, Olive. *Diamond Fields* (edited by Richard Rive). Grahamstown: Institute for the Study of English in Africa, Rhodes University, 1995
    From Man to Man, or, Perhaps Only. London: Fisher Unwin, 1926
    Letters 1871 to 1899 (edited by Richard Rive). Cape Town: David Philip, 1987
    Stories, Dreams and Allegories. London: Fisher Unwin, 1923
    The Story of An African Farm. Johannesburg: Ad Donker, 1975
    Undine. New York: Harper, 1928

Skawran, Karin and Michael Macnamara (eds.). *Walter Battiss.* Johannesburg: Ad Donker, 1985

Slater, Francis Carey. *The Collected Poems of Francis Carey Slater.* Edinburgh: Blackwood; South Africa: Central News Agency, 1957

Van Heerden, Ernst. *The Runner and the Shadow: A Selection* (translated from Afrikaans by Jean Branford and the author). Cape Town: Tafelberg, 1986
    Teenstrydige Liedere. Cape Town: Tafelberg, 1972

Van Heerden, Etienne. *Kikuyu* (translated from Afrikaans by Catherine Knox). Johannesburg: Kwela in association with Random House, 1998
    Mad Dog and Other Stories (translated from Afrikaans by Catherine Knox). Cape Town: David Philip, 1992

Vaughan, Iris. *The Diary of Iris Vaughan.* Cape Town: Timmins, 1958, 1971

Wallace, Margo. 'Buffelskop: Olive Schreiner's Gravesite'. In: Skinner, Douglas Reid (ed.) *Soundings: An Anthology of Poems Selected from the Entries to the 1988 Sanlam Literary Award.* Cape Town: Carrefour, 1989

Walter, Brian. *Tracks.* Alice: Lovedale Press, 1999

CHAPTER 8

Karodia, Farida. *Against an African Sky and Other Stories.* Cape Town: David Philip, 1995
    Coming Home and Other Stories. London: Heinemann, 1988
    Daughters of the Twilight. London: The Women's Press, 1986
    Other Secrets. Johannesburg: Penguin, 2000

Meintjes, Johannes. *Complex Canvas: A South African Approach.* Johannesburg: Afrikaanse Pers-Boekhandel, [1960]
    Dorp van Drome: Die Geskiedenis van Molteno, 1874–1974. Molteno: Molteno Municipality, 1974
    Frontier Family: A Chronicle of a South African Farm, Its Homestead and Its People. [Johannesburg]: Central News Agency, [1955]
    Olive Schreiner: Portrait of a South African Woman. Johannesburg: Hugh Keartland, 1965
    Stormberg, a Lost Opportunity: The Anglo-Boer War in the North-Eastern Cape Colony, 1899–1902. Cape Town: Nasionale Boekhandel, 1969
Plomer, William. *Double Lives: An Autobiography.* New York: The Noonday Press, [1945]
    Selected Stories (edited by Stephen Gray). Cape Town: David Philip, 1984
    Turbott Wolfe (edited by Stephen Gray). Johannesburg: Ad Donker, 1980
    Collected Poems. London: Jonathan Cape, 1973

CHAPTER 9
Baines, Thomas. *Journal of Residence in Africa, 1842–1853* (edited by R F Kennedy). Cape Town: Van Riebeeck Society, 1961–1964 (in 2 volumes)
Bokwe, John Knox. *Ntsikana: The Story of an African Convert.* Lovedale: Mission Press, 1914
Butler, Guy. *Collected Poems* (edited by Laurence Wright). Cape Town: David Philip, 1999
Hodgson, Jane. 'The Genius of Ntsikana'. In: White, Landeg and Tim Couzens (eds.) *Literature and Society in South Africa.* Cape Town: Maskew Miller Longman, 1984
Letcher, Valerie Helen. *Trespassing Beyond the Borders: Harriet Ward as Writer and Commentator on the Eastern Cape Frontier.* (Ph D thesis, Rhodes University, 1996)
Meiring, Jane. *Thomas Pringle: His Life and Times.* Cape Town: Balkema, 1968
Poland, Marguerite. *Train to Doringbult.* London: The Bodley Head, 1987
Pringle, Thomas. *Narrative of a Residence in South Africa.* London: Moxon, 1835
    Poems Illustrative of South Africa: African Sketches: Part One (edited by John Robert Wahl). Cape Town: Struik, 1970
Sampson, Sally. 'Far Plains and Echoing Valleys: Harriet Ward, an Officer's Wife on the Frontier'. *Annals of the Grahamstown Historical Society* (24), 1994 (published in 1998)
Ward, Harriet. *Five Years in Kaffirland: With Sketches of the Late War in That Country, to the Conclusion of Peace: Written on the Spot.* London: Colburn, 1848 (in 2 volumes)
    Hardy and Hunter: A Boy's Own Story. London: Routledge, Warnes, and Routledge, 1859
    Jasper Lyle: A Tale of Kafirland. London: George Routledge, 1852

CHAPTER 10

Holt, Basil. *Greatheart of the Border: A Life of John Brownlee, Pioneer Missionary in South Africa.* King William's Town: The South African Missionary Museum, 1976

Jabavu, Noni. *Drawn in Colour: African Contrasts.* London: John Murray, 1960
    The Ochre People: Scenes from a South African Life. London: John Murray, 1963

Jolobe, James J R. *Poems of an African.* Lovedale: Lovedale Press, 1946

Lagan, Cathal. *Sandbird.* Alice: Lovedale Press, 1999

Mahola, Mzi. *Strange Things.* Cape Town: Snailpress, 1994

Matthews, Z K. *Freedom for My People: The Autobiography of Z K Matthews: Southern Africa, 1901 to 1968* (edited by Monica Wilson). London: Collings; Cape Town: David Philip, 1981

Morrissey, Norman. *Seasons: Haiku.* Alice: Lovedale Press, 1999

Oosthuizen, G C. *Shepherd of Lovedale.* Johannesburg: Hugh Keartland, 1970

Parker, Carolyn. *Witch Woman on the Hogsback.* Pretoria: De Jager-H A U M, 1987

Peteni, Randall Langa. *Hill of Fools: A Novel of the Ciskei.* Cape Town: David Philip, 1976

Poland, Marguerite. *Shades.* London: Viking, 1993

Shepherd, R H W. *Lovedale and Literature for the Bantu: A Brief History and a Forecast.* Lovedale: Lovedale Press, 1945

Slater, Francis Carey. *The Collected Poems of Francis Carey Slater.* Edinburgh: Blackwood; South Africa: Central News Agency, 1957
    Settler's Heritage. Lovedale: Lovedale Press, 1954

Somhlahlo, Basil. *A Whistle from the South: Poems from South Africa.* Alice: Lovedale Press, [1993]

Walter, Brian. *Tracks.* Alice: Lovedale Press, 1999
    (ed.). *Tyume: Fort Hare Journal of Creative Writing* Nos. 1, 1996/1997 – 4, 2000 (No. 4 also edited by Gertrude Davids)

Wilson, John Dover. 'Preface'. In: Shakespeare, William *The Sonnets* (edited by John Dover Wilson). Cambridge: Cambridge University Press, 1966

CHAPTER 11

Bowie, Beryl. *Mystery at Cove Rock.* Cape Town: Tafelberg, 1991
    Phumlani's Pouch. Pretoria: Kagiso, 1997

Brink, AndrÈ. *Rumours of Rain.* London: Howard & Wyndham, 1978
    Rumours of Rain. London: Allen, 1978, 1981

Cain, Howard. 'Mdantsane Daisies'. In: Joubert, Brian S. (ed.) *Under African Skies: An Anthology of African Verse.* Scottburgh: Poetry Institute of Africa at Unique Publications, 1998

Elliot, Aubrey. *The Magic World of the Xhosa.* London and Johannesburg: Collins, 1970, 1975

Joubert, Elsa. *Poppie.* London: Coronet, 1981

Mandela, Nelson. *Long Walk to Freedom: The Autobiography of Nelson Mandela.* London: Abacus, 1995

Mqhayi, S E K. *The Case of the Twins* (translated from Xhosa by Collingwood August). *Inkululeko* Jan., March 1966 (final chapters published in Frontier April 1966)

'InTaba KaNdoda'. In: Jordan, A C. 'Samuel Edward Krune Mqhayi', *South African Outlook* 1 Sept. 1945

'A Short Autobiography of Samuel Krune Mqhayi' (translated from Xhosa by W G Bennie). In: Scott, Patricia E (ed.). *Mqhayi in Translation*. Grahamstown: Department of African Languages, Rhodes University, 1976

'The Sinking of the Mendi' (translated from Xhosa by Jack Cope). *Poet* July–Aug. 1968

Opland, Jeff (ed.). *Words That Circle Words: A Choice of South African Oral Poetry*. Johannesburg: Ad Donker, 1992

Xhosa Poets and Poetry. Cape Town: David Philip, 1998

Scully, William Charles. *Reminiscences of a South African Pioneer*. London: Fisher Unwin, 1913

Soga, Tiyo. *The Journal and Selected Writings of the Reverend Tiyo Soga* (edited by Donovan Williams). Cape Town: Balkema, 1983

Swift, Mark. *Testing the Edge: Poems*. Cape Town: Snailpress, 1996

Treading Water (edited by Jack Cope). Cape Town: David Philip, 1974

Turkington, Nola. *Nduku and the Magic Seed*. Cape Town: Human & Rousseau, 1992

Walter, Brian. 'A Prayer on the Road to King'. In: Morrissey, Norman and Brian Walter, Cathal Lagan and Basil Somhlahlo, *Echo Poets: Standard Bank Festival of the Arts, Grahamstown, 1993*. [Grahamstown: s.n.], 1993

Woodward, Wendy. *Séance for the Body: Poems*. Cape Town: Snailpress, 1994

CHAPTER 12

Broster, Joan A. *Red Blanket Valley*. Johannesburg: Hugh Keartland, 1967

Butler, Guy. *Pilgrimage to Dias Cross: A Narrative Poem*. Cape Town: David Philip, 1987

Coetzee, Dene. *Winds of Change*. London: Hodder & Stoughton, 1995

Coulter, Jean. *Remembering: The Life, the People and the Places*. Port Elizabeth: The Author, 2001

Fugard, Sheila. *The Castaways*. Johannesburg: Macmillan, 1972

Gough, Margaret. *Selected Poems*. [Canada: s.n.], 1999

Holt, Basil. *Where Rainbirds Call: A Record of the Transkei*. Cape Town: Timmins, 1972

Jabavu, Noni. *The Ochre People: Scenes from a South African Life*. London: John Murray, 1963

Jenkins, Geoffrey. *Scend of the Sea*. London: Collins, 1971, 1972

Jordan, A C. *Tales from Southern Africa* (translated from Xhosa). Berkeley, Calif.: University of California Press, 1973

Towards an African Literature: The Emergence of Literary Form in Xhosa. Berkeley, Calif.: University of California Press, 1973

The Wrath of the Ancestors: A Novel (translated from Xhosa by A C Jordan and Priscilla P Jordan). Alice: Lovedale Press, 1980

Kaschula, Russell H. *The Bones of the Ancestors Are Shaking: Xhosa Oral Poetry in Context*. Cape Town: Juta, 2002

Mandela, Nelson. *Long Walk to Freedom: The Autobiography of Nelson Mandela.*
London: Abacus, 1995

Matshoba, Mtutuzeli. *Call Me Not a Man.* Johannesburg: Ravan, 1979

Mda, Zakes. *The Heart of Redness.* Cape Town: Oxford University Press, 2000

Ntantala, Phyllis. *A Life's Mosaic: The Autobiography of Phyllis Ntantala.* Bellville:
Mayibuye Centre; Cape Town: David Philip, 1992

Opland, Jeff (ed.). *Words That Circle Words: A Choice of South African Oral Poetry.*
Johannesburg: Ad Donker, 1992

Peires, J B. *The Dead Will Arise: Nongqawuse and the Great Xhosa Cattle-Killing
Movement of 1856–7.* Johannesburg: Ravan Press, 1989

Sampson, Harold Fehrsen. *Selected Poems of Harold Fehrsen Sampson.* Cape Town:
The Author, 1972

Scully, William Charles. *Further Reminiscences of a South African Pioneer.* London:
Fisher Unwin, 1913

Transkei Stories (edited by Jean Marquard). Cape Town: David Philip, 1984

INDEX

Figures in italics refer to biographies.

ACKNOWLEDGEMENTS

The author and publishers are grateful for permission for the use in this book of copyright material from the following works, in whole or in part:

Lionel Abrahams for 'After the Caves', 'Sardinia Bay', 'The Scribe' and 'Dredger' from *Ruth Miller: Poems, Plays, Prose* (Carrefour Press, 1990); Marion Baxter for 'Extinction' from *Bitter Aloes*; Robert Berold for 'Dark City' and 'Nieu Bethesda' from *The Fires of the Dead* (Carrefour Press, 1989) and for Zim Mnotoza, 'Albany Road' from *Umgqala* (3), 1985; Joan Broster for *Red Blanket Valley* (1967); Dennis Brutus for 'Tomorrow', 'Jameson Road: Gelvandale' and 'Daylight' from *Still the Sirens* (Pennywhistle Press, 1993) and 'For Them Burness Street is a Familiar Entity' and 'It was a Sherded World I Entered' from *Stubborn Hope* (Heinemann, 1978); Yvonne Burgess for 'And Out of the City', 'If You Swallow You're Dead', *A Life to Live* and *Anna and the Colonel*; Georgia Bryer for Lynne Bryer, 'Love of Hills' from *A Time in the Country* (Carrefour Press, 1991) and 'Vindicated' from *The Cancer Years* (Carapace Poets, 1999); Cambridge University Press for J Dover Wilson, preface to *The Sonnets* by William Shakespeare (1966); Michael Cope for Jack Cope, 'The Sinking of the Mendi'; David Philip Publishers for Guy Butler, *Pilgrimage to Dias Cross* (1987), *Karoo Morning* (1977), *A Local Habitation* (1991) and 'Signal Hill', 'Cradock Mountains', 'Elegy', 'Ode to Dead Friends' and 'Ntsikana's Bell' from *Guy Butler: Collected Poems*, ed. L Wright (1999); Don Maclennan, 'Grahamstown II' from *Reckonings* (1983); Chris Mann, 'Cookhouse Station' from *Mann Alive!* (1982); and R L Peteni, *Hill of Fools* (1976); Beth Dickerson for 'Journey through the Langkloof', 'Flying over the Langkloof', 'Black Rhinoceros', 'Kenton Road', 'Sunbird' and 'Dungbeetle'; Isobel Dixon for 'Aliens', 'Pearston' and 'Fruit of the Land' from *Weather Eye* (Carapace Poets, 2001); C J Driver for 'Storms River: Chaos Theory', 'Grahamstown II: Aubade', 'The Valley of Desolation: Once' and 'Die Nieu Bethesda: The Owl House' from *In the Water-Margins* (Snailpress, 1994); Etienne du Pisani for 'Graaff-Reinet' from *One* (1998); Jean Edmunds for 'South End' and 'Shakespeare in the Park'; Faber and Faber Ltd for Athol Fugard, *The Road to Mecca* (1985); Betty Finn for Hugh Finn, 'Wooden Figurehead', 'Fort Frederick' and 'The Sun-bathers' from *The Sunbathers and Other Poems* (Poetry Society of Rhodesia, 1977); Athol Fugard for *The Blood Knot, Boesman and Lena, Hello and Goodbye, A Lesson from Aloes* and *Marigolds in August*; Sheila Fugard for *The Castaways, A Revolutionary Woman* and 'Valley of Desolation'; Margaret Gough for 'For Athol Fugard', 'In the Settlers' Museum' and 'Nonquase' from *Selected Poems* (1996); Grahamstown Foundation (formerly 1820 Foundation), Inset project, for *The Way We See It*, 6 (1987); Stephen Gray for 'In Memoriam: Olive Schreiner'; Robert Greig for 'Revisiting Salem' from *In the Provinces* (Justified Press, 1991); Lyn Harrison for 'Main Street, Port Elizabeth, 1993' and 'Wordspinner'; Bruce Hewett for 'Elephants in the Addo Mist'; Human and Rousseau and Tafelberg Publishers for Ernst van Heerden, 'Karoonag: Pearston' from *Teenstrydige Liedere* (1972), André Brink, *Rumours of Rain* (1978), Beryl Bowie, *Mystery at Cove Rock* (1991), Nola Turkington,

Nduka and the Magic Seed (1992) and Elsa Joubert, *Poppie* (1980); Alan James for 'St Francis Bay' from *Producing the Landscape* (Upstream, 1987) and 'Cape St Francis: At the End of Summer' and 'Cape St Francis: A Visit prior to Emigration' from *Morning near Genadendal* (Snailpress, 1992); Michael King, 'Walking along West Beach, Kowie'; Kwela Books for J T Matyu, 'Shadows from the Past' and 'Pay-day Murder' from *Crossing Over*, comp. Linda Rode and Jakes Gerwel (1995) and Etienne van Heerden, *Kikuyu*; Cathal Lagan for 'The Sacramento Way' and 'The Soul Dances at the Baakens Valley'; André Lemmer for 'Song for South End'; Don Maclennan for 'Prospect' from *Letters* (Carrefour Press, 1992), 'Grahamstown II' from *Reckonings* (David Philip, 1983), *Rock Paintings at Salem* (2001) and 'The Road to Mecca'; Mzi Mahola, 'We Shall Reap in Tears', 'The Same Procession', 'He Came down the Street' and 'Dying in the Sun' from *When Rains Come* (Carapace Poets, 2000) and 'Return to My Birthplace' and 'Intaba zebhukazana' from *Strange Things* (Snailpress, 1994); Mrs P Melunsky for Kathleen van der Riet, *Morning in the Heart* (Tecoma Press, 1977); NELM for R Mdlele, 'Raglan Road' in *Grahamstown is Not Worth Describing* (Grahamstown, 1994); Oxford University Press for Zakes Mda, *The Heart of Redness* (2000); Penguin Books for Marguerite Poland, *Iron Love* (1999), Marguerite Poland, *Shades* (1993) and Farida Karodia, *Other Secrets* (2000); Marguerite Poland for *Train to Doringbult* (The Bodley Head, 1987); Ravan Press for Marguerite Poland, *The Bush Shrike* (1982), Yvonne Burgess, *Anna and the Colonel* (1997) and M Matshoba, *Call Me Not a Man* (1979); Mark Swift for 'Windvogel Mountain' from *Testing the Edge* (Snailpress, 1996); Time Warner Books for Nelson Mandela, *Long Walk to Freedom* (Little, Brown, 1994); Unisa Press for Arthur Nortje, 'Apartheid', 'Transition', 'Windscape' and 'Reflections' from *Anatomy of Dark*, ed. Dirk Klopper (2000); University of Natal Press for M Nyezwa, 'i cannot think of all the pains' from *song trials* (2000) and Chris Mann, 'Grahamstown Sage' and 'The Dunes of Woody Cape' from *Heartlands* (2002); Brian Walter for 'Old Holy Places', 'A Prayer on the Road to King' and 'Direction' in *Baakens* (Lovedale Press, 2000) and 'Swartkops' in *Tracks* (Lovedale Press, 1999); Peter Wilhelm for 'Port Alfred'; Wits University Press for Athol Fugard, *Cousins* (1994) and *'Jim's Journal': The Diary of James Butler* (1996); Wendy Woodward, 'On the Diary of a German Woman in the Eastern Cape' from *Séance for the Body* (Snailpress, 1994); Dan Wylie for 'Winter Solstice', 'Travelling', 'Kasouga' and 'Malpas Farm, Rhodes' from *The Road Out* (Snailpress, 1996)

Every effort has been made to trace and acknowledge the copyright holders. Should any mistake or omission have been made, the publishers and author apologise and will correct it in the next impression.